THE PATH OF ARCHAIC THINKING

SUNY Series in Contemporary Continental Philosophy
Dennis J. Schmidt, editor

THE PATH OF ARCHAIC THINKING

Unfolding the Work of John Sallis

Edited by
Kenneth Maly

STATE UNIVERSITY OF NEW YORK PRESS

Published by
State University of New York Press, Albany

For information, address State University of New York Press,
State University Plaza, Albany, N.Y. 12246

Production by Cathleen Collins
Marketing by Bernadette LaManna

Library of Congress Cataloging in Publication Data

The Path of archaic thinking : unfolding the work of John Sallis /
    edited by Kenneth Maly.
        p.   cm. — (SUNY series in contemporary continental
    philosophy)
    Includes bibliographical references and index.
    ISBN 0-7914-2355-7. — ISBN 0-7914-2356-5 (pbk.)
    1. Sallis, John, 1938–   . 2. Philosophy, Modern—20th century.
    3. Philosophy, European.   I. Maly, Kenneth.   II. Series.
    B945.S15P38   1994
    191—dc20   94-11959
                                                                              CIP

10 9 8 7 6 5 4 3 2 1

For Jerry,
in honor of
her unwavering support

LEBENSLAUF

Größers wolltest auch du, aber die Liebe zwingt
   All uns nieder, das Leid beuget gewaltiger,
      Doch es kehret umsonst nicht
         Unser Bogen, woher er kommt.

Aufwärts oder hinab! herrschet in heil'ger Nacht,
   Wo die stumme Natur werdende Tage sinnt,
      Herrscht im schiefesten Orkus
         Nicht ein Grades, ein Recht noch auch?

Dies erfuhr ich. Denn nie, sterblichen Meistern gleich,
   Habt ihr Himmlischen, ihr Alleserhaltenden,
      Daß ich wüßte, mit Vorsicht
         Mich des ebenen Pfades geführt.

Alles prüfe der Mensch, sagen die Himmlischen,
   Daß er, kräftig genährt, danken für alles lern,
      Und verstehe die Freiheit,
         Aufzubrechen, wohin er will.

                        Friedrich Hölderlin

COURSE OF LIFE

You too yearned for something greater, but all of us
   Are forced down by love and bent more vehemently by pain;
      Yet it is not for naught that our arc
         Turns into the place whence it arises.

Upward or downward! Does there not still prevail
   In holy night, where mute nature senses days in the twilight of their coming.
      Or in skewed Orcus
         Also a straightness, a law?

This I experienced. For never, as mortal masters do,
   Did you heavenly ones, you preservers of all,
      To my knowledge, with foresight
         Lead me on by a level path.

Let humans test everything, say the heavenly ones,
   So that, richly nourished, they shall learn to give thanks for everything
      And shall be capable of the freedom
         To break into the open, whither they would go.

                  Translated by John Sallis and Kenneth Maly

CONTENTS

REFERENCES TO SALLIS'S TEXTS

All references in the body of this text are references to works by John Sallis and are abbreviated as follows:

BL *Being and Logos: The Way of Platonic Dialogue.* Pittsburgh: Duquesne University Press, 1975. Second Edition: Atlantic Highlands, NJ: Humanities Press, 1986.

C   *Crossings: Nietzsche and the Space of Tragedy.* Chicago: The University of Chicago Press, 1991.

D   *Delimitations: Phenomenology and the End of Metaphysics.* Bloomington: Indiana University Press, 1986.

E   *Echoes: After Heidegger.* Bloomington: Indiana University Press, 1990.

GR *The Gathering of Reason.* Athens: Ohio University Press, 1980.

PR *Phenomenology and the Return to Beginnings.* Pittsburgh: Duquesne University Press, 1973.

S   *Spacings—of Reason and Imagination. In Texts of Kant, Fichte, Hegel.* Chicago: The University of Chicago Press, 1987.

READING SALLIS:
AN INTRODUCTION

Kenneth Maly

This gathering of essays, marking its domain with the subtitle "Unfolding the Work of John Sallis," has a very specific intention: to provoke us to rethink the meaning of the word *continental* in "contemporary continental philosophy." Specifically, it raises the question: Can we still today define "continental" geographically? Or is it incumbent upon us "contemporary" thinkers to define the word *continental*, no longer geographically, but now historically (*geschichtlich*)? We need to recognize original continental works in English—and other non-European languages—to understand better and more fully what that movement means today.

Regardless of the stand that one takes on the work of John Sallis—whether it is one of enthusiastic acceptance, critical acceptance, serious questioning, or outright rejection—still Sallis's work is near the center or at the forefront of the movement called "contemporary continental philosophy." This book intends to advance just this claim—advance it, not as fact to be proven, but as an enigma to be thought.

This book of essays has as its intention, therefore, a critical and in-depth reading and appropriation of the texts of John Sallis. Each essay is devoted to a direct encounter with Sallis's writings. As such, the volume is above all a philosophical *Auseinandersetzung*—in the various and deep connotations of that word—with

1

contemporary continental thought as it is practiced today, both in Europe and in the United States.

The collection of essays presented here sets out, each in its own way, to disclose the philosophical writing, reading, and thinking of John Sallis—distinguishing and gathering, commemorating, confronting, questioning. The essays mark a pathway *from* where Sallis's work has come and *to* where it might now go—this "from" and "to" understood, not chronologically and in a linear sense, but rather spiraling and in the sense of doubling-back.

This volume is original, in several senses. First, it is original in that it is the first of its kind—the first book to deal directly and seriously with Sallis's texts and his work. Secondly, this volume is original in that all of the essays were written for this volume. Not a single one has appeared in print elsewhere.

Thirdly, this volume is original in that, in the issues raised and in the manner of presentation, these essays make manifest the relationship between Sallis's thinking and "origins." Sallis's work does this in the following ways:

a. it takes each text seriously, not as a tractatus or scholarly work that lies dead within the history of philosophy, but as a node of resonance for the enlivening questions put perennially to philosophy;

b. it gets underneath the layers of interpretation and commentary (that always find the "solution" and thus cover up the *question*), in order to let the *questionableness* in each node of issues re-emerge for thinking (thus: archaic thinking);

c. it brings the text being read to life in such a way that those very nodes of resonance, nodes of central tension for the original authors (Plato, Kant, Fichte, Nietzsche, Heidegger, Merleau-Ponty), show a renewed possibility; and

d. it continually delves into those nodes with a mathematical clarity and precision, even though the issues at each node are often themselves imprecise by their very "nature," withdrawing from thinking's purview.

Fourthly, this volume is original in that it shows how Sallis's thinking includes an abiding concern for origins. This is imaged in the phrase "archaic thinking" that I have chosen for the title of this book. Whether it is the beginnings to which phenomenology always returns for its sustenance (*Phenomenology and the Return to Beginnings,* 1973); or whether it is the mythos to which Socratic logos inevitably turns in the play of concealment (*Being and Logos: The Way of Platonic Dialogue,* 1975); or whether it is the return to an originary phase of a thinker's thinking, to a beginning phase wherein something decisive happens, an "unsettling openness" (*The Gathering of Reason,* 1980); or whether it is the limit which encloses metaphysics, but also grants, preserves, and sustains it (*Delimitations: Phenomenology and the End of Metaphysics,* 1986); or whether it is the spacing that "opens reason beyond itself"—to what? (*Spacings—of Reason and Imagination. In Texts of Kant,*

Fichte, Hegel, 1987)—in each case Sallis's thinking is embedded in and always turns/returns to origins, beginnings, the limit or boundary of reason and thought, the boundary that enables, the beginnings which already determines all philosophy, the boundary that instigates and allows all root-unfolding in thinking.

In a way the originality of Sallis's work can be envisioned as an unrelenting attentiveness to the irresolvability and inviolability of this beginnings, this limit/boundary, and of thinking's own, necessarily ongoing tension with the beginnings/ boundary that sustains it but cannot be de-fined. Sallis's originality also shows itself in the excitement that is engendered when he reads a text of philosophy. This excitement emerges, in large part, because Sallis holds each text that he reads (interprets, opens up) to the fire of the inviolability and irresolvability of the beginnings/boundary. Sallis's focusing on and staying with the questionableness that is introduced into philosophical thinking when thinking attends to beginnings/boundary is exciting in the way that it—at its best—moves within the unbinding bounding of that beginnings. This dimension of beginnings *and* of thinking's ongoing grappling with it—necessarily ongoing, for it can have no determinable end, no point of rest—is manifested throughout Sallis's texts. For example, early in *Phenomenology and the Return to Beginnings* (1973), he writes:

> What makes Merleau-Ponty's philosophy so germane to the question of the return to beginnings is the fact that he lets this recoil assert itself with all the questionableness which it introduces rather than resorting to some sham attempt to mask it. (PR 42)

And he circles back to the same issue later, in *Spacings—of Reason and Imagination* (1987):

> Imagine, then, a spacing of closure that would exceed closure, that would perforate its covering, rending and riddling its sphere, opening it ever so minutely toward beginnings that would exceed the end, that would pluralize and defer it, endings. (S 132)

In short, a core part of the original dimension in Sallis's work of thinking, in its heeding the claim of beginnings and boundary, is how it calls into question any notion of *an* original as an independent substance, which would stand over against any reproduction or copy (image). Thus, at root the original character of Sallis's work is not in its standing there *as* "original," but rather in its continual and unrelenting attentiveness to beginnings.

*   *   *

Most recently we find, almost everywhere, the thematizing of reading—from "deconstructive reading" to "hermeneutics as reading" to "Derrida's readings"— and we begin to understand ourselves as "readers." It is almost as if today "doing philosophy" is reading.

But what is reading? Or, with Heidegger, *Was heißt Lesen?*[1] I know of at least two places where Sallis himself publishes his translation of this Heidegger text.[2] At least four questions emerge for us at this juncture: What *is* reading? What does reading mean for Sallis? How does Sallis *do* reading? And how are we to read Sallis? Let me embark on a journey through each of these questions.

(1) What *is* reading? I look to Heidegger's brief text *Was heißt Lesen?* The last line of this text reads: "Without proper reading we cannot see what turns its gaze to us [Sallis: what has us in sight]." For Heidegger what turns its gaze to us— or has us in its sight—is variously said as *das Zudenkende, die Sache des Denkens, die Stille, Ereignis, die Sage als Zeige, Anwesen anwesend,* and most importantly: ἀλήθεια. It is always that with which thinking does not so much have to wrestle or come to terms, but rather that to which thinking needs to correspond. Without proper reading we are not open to what emerges or unfolds for thinking.

Do we know at all any more how to read? What do we read toward—and where from? Why do we read at all? What is called forth and evoked in proper reading? *Was heißt Lesen?* These German words can be alternately rendered and thought as: What is called reading? What does reading call for? What calls forth reading? What takes place in the root-unfolding of reading? What *is* reading? According to Heidegger:

> The sustaining and guiding element in reading is (the) gathering. To what does it [the gathering] gather? To what is written, to what is said in the writing. In the manner that is appropriate to it, reading is gathering unto that which has already laid its claim on us in our own deepest way of being [the emergence of what we are in our ownmost] (*unser Wesen*) without our knowing it—regardless of whether we comply with it or renounce it.[3]

Reading is gathering. Gathering is primarily a gathering of "staying within the truth" (*Inständigkeit in der Wahrheit*). This "staying within" in gathering in turn gathers to the said in the writing. To read a text is to be gathered in truth/ἀλήθεια and to be gathered in what is said/shown in the writing.

Reading the text is doing the work of thinking by awakening in us how it is that we stay within truth/ἀλήθεια and by following in thinking how this staying-in is enacted.

In opening up what proper reading is, we find ourselves entangled within the web of ordinary grammar. In our usual comportment we allow grammar to give us the definitive word on how language speaks. Proper reading, on the other hand, cannot be held back by grammar. Proper reading calls for a dismantling (*Abbau*) of grammar and its hold. Sentences in their sentence-structure cannot reach far enough into what turns its gaze to us, because this gaze comes from within our *Inständigkeit*. Though having grammatical shapes, words and sentences always carry an imaging that is not bound to that grammar. Words then become guidewords for imaging beyond grammar; this imaging is evoked by the way in which we stay in truth in what turns its gaze to reading. Thus we are called to be more attentive, more gathered, for what lies deeper in the words, though not deeper *than* the words.[4] If we hear the saying of language within the deeper saying of the word, only then is reading on the mark—and the affordance of what lies "deeper" than grammar evocatively hints and haunts it. The gathering of reading gathers unto the evocative saying of what has already laid its claim on us "in our deepest unfolding (*unser Wesen*)." Evocative saying does not show a ready-made content, but rather carries an appeal which draws and carries the reader to a transformation of thinking.

Reading, then, is a sounding of the text, "striking" the text—as one strikes a bell—to emit a tone. The sounding of words has a power by which what is gathered in the text falls upon us. Thus the imaging of words flows from the text; words do not stand apart from thinking. The reader intones the text and thus brings to light—or sound—the underlying "truth," being, or disclosure that binds thinking. Thus reading is both an invocation and an evocation.[5]

How to read or sound a text? is the same question as How to say in thinking? For both "reading/sounding" and "saying in thinking" are a gathering to what claims us in our deepest way of being in what is written or said. Thus this "manifold of thinking does not require a new language, but a transformed relationship to how the old language unfolds in its core."[6]

(2) What does reading mean for Sallis? It seems appropriate to respond to this question by turning to Sallis's own ruminatings on reading. These remarks directly follow his translation of Heidegger's *Was heißt Lesen?*

Sallis names a number of aspects that belong to reading. I want here to cite Sallis, to take him at his word, and to move into a close hold on his words—so that those certain aspects of reading that he mentions will come forth. According to Sallis, what Heidegger writes, "literally," is: (*a*) gathering is reading's sustaining and guiding element—what belongs to reading centrally, (*b*) reading *as gathering* gathers to what is written or said in the writing, which (*c*) has (always) already laid its claim on us. Interpreting this Heidegger-text, Sallis writes:

> Two points are to be underlined. First, reading essentially involves coming to be *gathered* to what is *said* in writing, in the text. Second, reading, thus understood, is *responsive*—that is, the gatheredness of reading is not something that one simply initiates; rather it is a response to a certain claim, a demand, already made upon the would-be reader.[7]

Gathering from this Sallis-text, we note that (*a*) reading involves coming to be gathered (*b*) to what is said in writing or in the text—and that reading is thus responsive. Reading, Sallis then says, might be "responsive gatheredness." Doubling back to the Heidegger-text, the responding in this "responsive gatheredness" needs to be bedded in the *Sammlung*/gathering.[8]

One might then say that the gatheredness is "akin to hearing" and the re-sponding of "responsive" is the engagement that reading calls for. Such a reading reengages

> those texts with the *Sache* that they would let sound, letting them re-sound, even if in a tongue that cannot but sometimes sound somewhat strange. Reading may take the form of questioning, for instance, a ques-tioning that would reenact or translate the questioning enacted in those texts; or a questioning that would use the very resources of those texts in the effort to locate within them certain blind spots, residues of dog-matic assertion.[9]

Here Sallis lets come forth a dimension of his own way of reading—which we will address shortly—by referring to "certain blind spots" and "residues of dogmatic assertion." This way of reading works in such a way that—as Sallis says earlier in this Introduction—Heidegger's texts "somehow efface themselves."[10] Thus read-ing involves for Sallis a honing in on and keeping a close hold on the text, so that and until these "blind spots" and "residues" emerge into light. With that emer-gence is mirrored the text's self-effacement: The texts undo themselves when reading holds them to this reengagement that makes the effort to locate blind spots and residues of dogmatic assertion.

Sallis is, of course, fully aware of the ongoing discussions on the "privilege of the question in Heidegger." Noting this discussion, he quotes what he calls "Heidegger's explicit denial of that privilege," a sentence from *Unterwegs zur Sprache:* "The proper bearing of thinking is not questioning, but rather listening to the promise of that which is to come into question."[11] Sallis adds: "Not ques-tioning but, first, listening, hearing—akin to reading, responsive gatheredness, commemoration."[12]

After reading Heidegger on reading, Sallis puts forth here—more "the-matically" than anywhere else that I know of, and yet hardly thematically—that reading

> involves coming to be gathered to what is said in writing, is
>> responsive, responding in gatheredness to the said, and *thus,*
>
> is an *engagement* which reengages the texts, letting them resound,
>
> is (perhaps) a questioning which reenacts the question for the sake of locating the text's "certain blind spots,"
>
> is commemoration.

(3) How does Sallis *do* reading? First, let me mention what appears quite manifest to me, that—at least until quite recently—reading for Sallis meant read-ing texts in the history of philosophy or in the circle of those who "count" as philosophers. (Note that his works, in the order of their appearance, deal with: Merleau-Ponty, Plato, Kant, phenomenology and the end of metaphysics—Plato,

Kant, Hegel, Heidegger, Derrida—Heidegger, Nietzsche.) But his reading of these texts is always in a very specific direction, namely toward that place in the texts where things become crucial, where the *Sache* emerges "in tension," where the thinking of the text reaches an unresolvability (e.g., the transcendental imagination in Kant, the "silent cogito" in perceptual consciousness in Merleau-Ponty, the crossing of the tragic and the Socratic in Nietzsche, ἀλήθεια as the limit of presence at the end of metaphysics in Heidegger).

Earlier I referred to these crucial, unresolvable tensions as "nodes of resonance." *Node* (from the Latin *nodus*) is akin to *knot* (from ME *knotte*, AS *cnotta*, Dutch *knot*, German *knoten*, IE *gn-eut:* to press together) and akin to *knit* (ME *knitten*, AS *cnyttan*, German *knütten*). Knots are (*a*) swellings, lumps, emerging protuberances, (*b*) clusters, comings-together, crossings, intertwinings, meeting-points (of lines, of nerves), aggregates (of particles), and (*c*) points of concentration, "centers."

Thus one might call these nodes of resonance that Sallis's reading holds to and opens up "knots"—knotty issues, entanglements. Taking this image one step further—and hearing the non-static, effervescent character of these "nodes"—I might suggest that what Sallis's reading does is to let loose entrenched structures and concepts, letting them become "decisively unsettled" (GR 176). Thus these nodes are not so much knots as knottings. The nodes of resonance that Sallis's reading lets emerge in a renewed questioning, letting their unresolvability be manifest, are really knottings or knotting images. *Knotting* is emerging swelling up, clustering intertwining, tightening centering. These knotting images are converging points. They bring forth the crossings that tighten the grip of the text—tighten the grip on the text—not letting it go, drawing them tight and holding them to their various entanglements (both their entrenchments and their possibilities). Hermann Paul in his *Deutsches Wörterbuch* says that a knotting (*knoten*) is "a riddle hard to solve, a question hard to resolve, a hindrance hard to get around."[13] Knotting images manifest the enmeshment, the *Sache,* the unresolvable. In physics, a node is the point or surface of a vibrating thing where there is no vibration—a stillness. In a curious sort of way, when the knotting image is reached in Sallis's reading, it is as if one "holds one's breath" and does not move, as if a subtle, refined stillness sets in. The question then is: unto what?

Sallis's way of reading is exemplarily mirrored—though never quite schematic and thus never fully exemplary—in the strategy for reading that he outlines and uses in *The Gathering of Reason.* In leading the reader into that text, Sallis distinguishes four "differently structured spaces," four "interpretive strategies." I read these as four levels of reading (GR 11–13):

a. Duplex interpretation or commentary. This reading doubles the text, but in the simplest doubling, staying within the horizon of the text's original—and traditional—conceptuality, staying with the author, so to speak.

b. Projective interpretation. This reading gathers (Sallis: assembles) the horizon in which the text is "restored" to what is in the text, but "submerged"—and presumably hidden from the author himself or herself at the time of writing. Thus this reading is a matter of "freeing a level of discourse submerged in that text and of establishing its unity by reference to a certain subordinate reflection. . . ." (GR 18) It is a matter of assembling, from within the text, a horizon that is not overtly at work in the text.

c. Inversive interpretation. This reading shows "various texts as inversions . . . of the focal text." This reading brings other texts by the same author into conjunction with the focal text, so that, as these various texts "bump into one another"—get knotted—a concealed layer of the focal text gets "unearthed."

d. Subversive interpretation. This reading brings the text being read into its larger context within the history of thought, re-installs the text within the questionings that are perennial to philosophy, questions that in their unresolvability need to be "decisively unsettled" (GR 176), such that the knotting comes forth in full force.

Whereas these four horizons or "aspects" of reading appear schematic, in enactment they break the bonds of their own schematism. And yet there is a certain hierarchy—not as if one is less a reading than the other, but as if one reading is more prevalent (or even more appropriate) as thinking/reading takes place today. (This prevalence might, of course, be itself a knotting and bring to convergence a certain unresolvable, a tension, the *Sache*.) Thus (perhaps) the work of reading as commentary (the first strategy) is ever and always centrally important; and yet, it would seem, Sallis's work focuses more and more on the inversive and subversive ways of reading. Sallis's reading seems to have moved from reading as projective interpretation (in *Being and Logos*) to, more recently, reading as subversive. Thus he speaks of reading that locates "certain blind spots" and "residues of dogmatic assertion" (in his "Introduction" to *Reading Heidegger: Commemorations*) and of the "phantoms that haunt" Heidegger's text and that "reproduce within it precisely what the text would submit to *Destruktion* or commit to overturning" (E 11) and of Nietzsche's text "*as* a theoretical text [that] crosses itself out, places itself under erasure, indeed placing under erasure the very placement with which it commenced" (C 148).

The question, of course, emerges: Is there a way of reading (namely, reading as gathering in *Inständigkeit* in ἀλήθεια) that is not accounted for in these four ways? Or: Which of these four ways names the evocative saying that reading as gathering gathers unto? In his essay "Voices" Peperzak points out how Sallis distinguishes hermeneutical echo from simple mirroring or repetition, in that hermeneutical echo resounds as an original sound—"an original divergence from an original" (E 5). Something is happening in the echo that does not happen in the text itself, "originally." Thus the "responsive gatheredness" in Sallis's reading is a re-engaging with the text, for the sake of ecstasy, i.e., displacing "the responsibility of our listening from the 'human speech' . . . to the 'speaking of language.'"

Gasché alludes to the elusive possibility that the reading that Sallis does of imagination might, in its radicality, lead to the impossibility of any delimitation of it—so radical "as to exceed being regathered into the circle of self-presentation" (S 153). Thinkable, but somehow not graspable? Questionable, but somehow not? A reading of texts of imagination that frees imagination to its excessiveness—and thus "toward a withdrawal from presence," broaching "a wonder that one could never aspire to surpass" (words that bring *Spacings* to its close and the same words that Sallis has put as title to his essay at the end of this volume).

Scott says that Sallis works "in yoked, unreconciled opposites and in breakage of connections." Sallis's logic is one of "monstrosity" . . . "a logic that holds opposites together in aporetic structures that lack a synthesis of higher identity." This logic of monstrosity that "breaks connections" is always "in an historical context," Scott says.

Scott makes another, significant knotting in how Sallis reads: the knotting of forethought, exacting precision, a seemingly non-elusive premeditated abstraction and the disorder, derangement/madness[14] that comes hand-in-hand. Scott opens his essay by saying:

> John Sallis draws the lines of his thought with a fineness that reminds me of the lines in a Japanese painting. There appears to be no excess. Each mark is exacting, exactly meant, placed with a very fine brush, leaving aside clutter and wasted movement. Among us who premeditate everything, he stands out for his precision and clarity of purpose, for his forethought that demands quiet patience and elimination of each word and innuendo that do not count towards a presentation of precise meaning and simple determination.

Towards the end of his paper Scott then offsets this remark with the other side:

> I have followed Sallis in the serenity of his ordered images; and at the apex of his account, like the single note of an oboe into which my hearing enters, comes suddenly an opening so harsh, a playing out of the presence of the previous order so stark, that I hear in it the collapse of the order of Sallis's thought. That he might have planned it this way does not diminish the strangeness of the sounds that emerge, for in *this* mimetic moment the abstractness of Sallis's thought, its descriptive accuracy about imagination's holding opposites together, its synthetic power to join together the opposites of appearing and disappearing,

all collapse in an unhinging movement that is not unlike "dithyrambic madness."

(4) How are we to read *Sallis?* First, there are those words that belong to Sallis's discourse—poignant words: spacings, hoverings, tunnelings, enroutings, tremorings, crossings, delimitations, twisting free, meaning adrift. Then there are the knotting images that emerge in Sallis's reading/thinking. These knotting images are fairly easy to find, if one reads at all carefully. Their names include:

- the dove of metaphysics who, at the end of metaphysics, must learn to hover between heaven and earth, "resisting the lure of the emptiness above and the illusion of fullness below" (D 16)
- beginnings that calls forth thought and sustains it, but itself withdraws
- the interplay of ἔργον (enactment) and μῦθος (withdrawal) with λόγος
- from image-original to imaging
- reading as hermeneutical echo and the history of philosophy
- mimesis and imagination
- doubling and echo, coincidence and doubling
- intelligible and sensible and their collapse
- reason's eccentricity, imagination, madness
- space and spacing(s)
- Apollinian and Dionysian tragedy
- monstrosity
- imagination: freed from the intelligible, the sensible, and the subjective
  > as the play of imaging
  > as the original ecstasy
  > as abysmal imagination
  > as excessive imagination
  > as eikastic imagination
  > as opening us "beyond ourselves and beyond what can ever be, even ideally, present" (D 28).

If there is a single thread that runs through all of Sallis's work of thinking, it is this last thread, this knotting of imagination. In his first book, *Phenomenology and the Return to Beginnings,* the issue pops up, as somewhat of a surprise to the reader, in the last lines of that text:

One of the names that the tradition has given to the power of persisting in that strife [the strife of thought's calling forth the beginnings, while at the same time being repelled by beginnings—thought's awareness of the finitude within its conceptuality] is imagination. The question is whether there can be a philosophy of imagination which is not also a philosophy of the *cogito.* (PR 116)

From there to his recent book, *Crossings: Nietzsche and the Space of Tragedy,* this knotty image of imagination comes up again and again. Imagination is, in a sense, the dragon that Sallis needs to slay in order to claim his prize at the haunt of Dionysos and Apollo. There is a hint in *Crossings* that he has some more work to do before he can claim that prize. A series of questions marks the pathway of where his reading/thinking on imagination might now go:

> What must be the constitution of imagination if it has the capacity to en-
> gage images that are disclosive of a higher truth? Does it suffice to term
> it *phantasy*? How, then, would one need to reformulate the distinction
> between imagination and phantasy, a distinction that in constantly vary-
> ing forms runs throughout the entire history of metaphysics? Further-
> more, if, in its productive engagement with shining images, imagination
> effects a disclosure of truth, then what must be the character of dis-
> closure and of truth that they can be so linked to imagination? How
> extensive is Apollinian imagination? Do all other forms simply produce
> illusion or are there other forms that bear upon truth? Is there a
> Dionysian imagination, a form of imagination that comes into play in
> tragedy? (C 29–30)

Beyond these just-mentioned clues or markings, I do not presume to be able to answer the question of how to read Sallis. It feels more fitting to let the various essays of this volume show how to read Sallis, i.e., tell it by enacting a reading. And because of the peculiar configuration of how contemporary continental philosophy takes place today—in its seemingly endless differentiations—how to read Sallis cannot be defined by this volume and will not stop unfolding.

Whereas I do not presume an answer to the question of how to read Sallis, what does come to me is a series of questions: Does reading Sallis take a special skill, background, training? Is reading Sallis any different from reading Heidegger, reading Derrida, reading Plato, reading Haar, reading Gasché? In any reading, what is the character of the text being read? What does the context of any text bring to bear on the reading? How does the reading of a text take into account the texture of the text? Texture, text, context.

If reading is of *written texts,* then reading a text also has a context, a specific epochal-historical situation within the history of thought in which the text takes place. For example, a text on Plato today has a context different from that of a text on Plato from the fourteenth century. Or a text on Kant written today will differ from a text on Kant written in 1830. Specifically, how we read Kant today has been irreversibly altered—and perhaps advanced—by the thinking of the past two hundred years in general, and by Heidegger's reading of Kant in particular. Or put differently, reading Hegel within the context of metaphysics is different from reading Hegel within the context in which the limit of metaphysics is thought.

If reading a text takes place and is influenced by the context, then reading a text in context also has a texture, the intertwining of the text with the originary *Sache,* or phenomenon. The texture of the text is the weaving of the text, in its saying, with the whole of what is said/shown, namely the *Sache*/phenomenon: what self-shows in showing, what comes forth in coming forth. This is—to use Heidegger's words—what turns its gaze to us in proper reading.

*   *   *

Finally, then, at the end of this introduction, I come back to where I started, to focus on contemporary continental philosophy. At the beginning I suggested that we need to redefine contemporary continental thought historically rather than geographically—so that, whatever contemporary continental philosophy is, it belongs more to a time (epoch) than to a given place. One could argue that the epoch—at the end of metaphysics, where non-philosophy emerges for philosophy—requires the movement of contemporary continental philosophy to be called "contemporary continental thought."

This moves to a deeper issue: the contemporary way of "doing philosophy." In a way this book and the work of John Sallis mirror the contemporary πόλεμος of philosophical thinking itself. Πόλεμος: *Auseinandersetzung;* the place of con-tention, tension; where the issues come to a head; drawing the "battle-line" for thinking—where one does battle. I locate that tension—or nodal point, knotting—in the relation of text to texture. The central question is: How does reading, as it is done in contemporary continental philosophy, deal with and heed the texture, the intertwining of the word/text with the *Sache*/phenomenon, with what turns its gaze to us? This πόλεμος—of the work of the text (and reading it) in its tension with the phenomenon (and heeding it)—comes forth as one unfolds the work of John Sallis; and this πόλεμος is continually held open therein. *The* tension for contemporary continental thought today is mirrored in the work of John Sallis.

How shall we name the con-tension—the line that gets drawn—in contemporary continental philosophy, which is imaged in the knotting of "text" in Sallis? This line is very complex, yet there is a general tone that staying to the "fire" of this reading/thinking allows to emerge.

One might say that there are two roads that run through how contemporary continental philosophy works, reads, or "plays with texts": (*a*) reading the text at the boundary/limit of metaphysics, a boundary within the context of the text and (*b*) reading the text for the texture, staying with the phenomenon at the boundary—letting boundary emerge as opening: boundary as phenomenon which, when tended, carries within itself its own capacity to open out onto the texture, intertwining with the phenomenon in its unfolding. The story of contemporary continental philosophy is in the con-tension of these two.

More precisely: It is the joining or unjoining of these two roads that makes up the story of where thinking today is, at the end of metaphysics, in phenomenology, in contemporary continental thought, and in the move from one to the other.[15]

In *Positions* Derrida describes what happens in his books as a "textual operation . . . which . . . is entirely consumed by the reading of other texts. . . ."[16] He goes on to speak of the double gesture, marked by an "erasure that allows what it obliterates to be read," a kind of reading that makes the "philosophemes and epistememes" on the one hand "slide . . . to the point of their nonpertinence, their exhaustion, their closure."[17] In that sliding another text opens up, on the other hand: that which exceeds, which gives us to think beyond the closure. But this excess, too, is inscribed (as trace) within the text as it "points in the direction of an entirely other text."[18]

To read the text in this sense, then, is to inscribe the text in such a way that every position is confounded.[19] Any opening is made "only according to lines of force and forces of rupture that are localizable in the discourse to be deconstructed."[20]

Deconstructive reading tries to hold out in front the character of otherness (heterogeneity) in philosophical discourse—deferring, differing—not seeing beyond or underneath/over this otherness (the inner difference of philosophy's texts), insisting that there *is* no legitimate "beyond" or "deeper than." Deconstructive reading, then, begins and stays with paradoxes—all aporias in general—that belong to conceptualization and to philosophy's discourse-character: "One is simply dealing with greater or lesser syntactical units at work, and with economic differences in condensation."[21] Reading is a kind of writing, a double gesture, that opens up the text that is present to its excess, which in turn is opened up in the rupture of "writing the fissure"—writing toward "an entirely other text."[22] Reading never leaves the image or context of the text.

Sallis mirrors this way of reading texts that inscribes—or reinscribes—such that every position is confounded, that gestures such that "philosophemes and epistememes" slide to their exhaustion, that opens up, finally, an excess, which in turn is inscribed as it points to "an entirely other text." Sallis writes that "every text is exposed to the possibility of differing with itself" (E 11). Here, too, fits what he says about reading as a questioning "that would use the very resources of those texts in the effort to locate within them certain blind spots, residues of dogmatic assertion."[23] In this context he speaks of "texts that efface themselves." But unto what?

Deconstructing the opposition between the sensible and the linguistic lets in a drift that is not securable, Sallis writes of Heidegger. "It will be a matter, then, of a reading adrift among various sorts of echoes. There will be, of course, as always, textual echoes, that is, echoes of semantic or syntactic elements within a text or between texts" (E 12–13). At this point Sallis makes a turn to what I am calling the "texture": "But there will also be echoes among the things themselves, that is, among *die Sachen,* that are to be thought . . ." (E 13). This turn would show that Sallis's work is sensitive to the two roads that I have outlined and to the πόλεμος involved in coming to terms with the tension.

But can this turn be made, given the character that text has for Sallis? This is the crux, the knotting—now not the knotting that Sallis sets to and thinks, but rather the knotting that comes along with his reading. For he says, a bit later, "My concern will be, then, to reinscribe several of Heidegger's texts so as to draw them toward the limit, to mobilize the figure of echo in order to free those texts to say what they can say, now, after Heidegger" (E 13). Is this "limit" in which the texts are "freed up" to say what they can say "now"—is it a matter of text, context, or of texture? Or: Whereunto (in the interweaving of text, context, and texture) is this "reinscribing of texts"? More specifically: How does deconstructive reading of the text get to the texture?

The dilemma—the πόλεμος, tension—is even more sharply laid out in *Crossings:*

> This reflection serves notice that Nietzsche's text *as* a theoretical text crosses itself out, places itself under erasure, indeed placing under erasure the very placement with which it commenced. And yet, on the other hand, it goes ahead with its series of rigorously ordered analyses, goes ahead with making its contribution to aesthetic science; that is, the erasure, the displacement from the theoretical pole, remains largely unmarked, unreflected in the text, even though what comes to be said only furthers that displacement and renders the erasure more indispensable than ever. In other words, the text remains at variance with itself, remains divided from itself, lacking identity. One could describe it even as a text that exceeds itself by saying what it could not as such (as the theoretical text it purports to be) say; thus thematizing its proximity to the Dionysian, one would begin to sense the complexity of its inscription. (C 148)

What must reading bring to bear on the text, in order that such a text might "exceed itself"—or more precisely, unto what might a text exceed itself? Is this "exceeding" an opening unto the texture, the *Sache?*

Earlier Sallis says that for Nietzsche "what will have been written" interrupts the "contemplative delight" with which it was to have been written—what will have been written "double crosses that delight" (C 13–14). I have elongated Sallis's sentence and turned it from a passive to an active voice, in order to free up what is submerged in it—namely that the text and the writing of it carries a certain agency, if it is to do anything at all!—as if the text had hands. The difficulty is that, by being "merely" textual, reading is closed off to the texture of the text, to the text's "saying" of and within the ambience of the phenomenon; and a certain arbitrariness sets in, because the measure—even of the boundless, i.e., the non-measurable—is/gets unbound (unconnected) from the phenomenon.

The intertwining (Sallis: crossing) of the various texts that emerge in Sallis's reading is bound by the textuality; but is it given over in enactment to the texture? In *Crossings* Sallis crosses Nietzsche's *The Birth of Tragedy* with related texts of Nietzsche—earlier drafts (some of them given as public lectures), smaller, published texts that bear upon *The Birth of Tragedy,* and notebook entries—and crosses this in turn with Heidegger's reading "and all that it has opened up" (C 7). Sallis calls these a double crossing. Then he writes:

> But then writing across it still another text, reinscribing it but also crossing it out, erasing it, adding to its saying the unsaying that what is said requires. Producing, then, a text that is something of a double of *The Birth of Tragedy,* a phantom, a spirit, that has already begun to haunt it. (C 8)

Is that which haunts *The Birth of Tragedy* another text, or the "phenomenologically" unfolding texture?

Sallis in his reading comes very close to opening out onto the texture. It is almost as if the anticipatory gaze that proper reading has is ready for his reading/thinking to break out of the text-enclosedness. (Indeed it seems as if he has broken out when he speaks of the "echoes among the things themselves.") One is tempted to hear him using the word *text* in a broader, deeper way. But this anticipation is thwarted with the realization that "text" seems not to have this deeper connection to texture. Indeed at times the "piece of writing" takes on a "life" of its own—e.g., when Sallis works through the intricacies of the various letters (or letter-drafts) from Nietzsche to Wagner and the unbound character of the volume when Wagner received it, to raise the issue of what it would have been like, *textually,* if the supplemental texts (read: letters and drafts of letters) had been bound in with the unbound book, "sixteen years later." Indeed, the text becomes above all a written text!

The question is: How does one measure what is a proper reading of texts after deconstructive reading has taken hold? If one is thinking at the core—and not simply engaged in a kind of commentary or scholarly treatise—then deconstructive reading comes up against the call for a transformed way of reading. How is this transformation enacted and where does it take place? Wherein lies the basis for this new reading? In deconstructive reading's strategy of disruption, in what direction does it go?

Let me dwell for a moment on a specific textual moment in *Spacings,* where Sallis speaks of an unparalleled "outbreak of metaphor" in Kant's *Critique of Pure Reason:*

Almost openly it betrays that text and through its betrayal offers an
opening upon certain questions that secretly govern that text while remaining systematically suppressed therein. (S 69)

What is this betrayal? One way to say it is that reason cannot become totally
present to itself, even as it tries. Now, where does this betrayal take place? In the
text or in the texture, the phenomenon? Is it a betrayal of the text? Is it the text's
betrayal? Is it a betrayal that takes place textually, even as the text suppresses it?
OR is the betrayal in the *phenomenon* of reason's critical reflection on itself—and
thus open to further unfolding by reading within the texture?

If the betrayal is of the text, then deconstructive reading will hold open the
fissure of the betrayal—will displace in such a way as to keep open the place of
contradictions, paradoxes, differences. If the betrayal is of the phenomenon (textural), then proper reading will stay with the movement of withdrawal inherent in
the betrayal, stay with even as it opens itself up—the shimmering expanding of
boundary.

On the one hand Sallis indicates that this betrayal is indeed textual: "the outbreak opens upon the question of the spacing of the text itself, the question of its
textuality" (S 69). On the other hand Sallis hints that the betrayal exceeds the text:
What holds reason back from total self-presence (which is the movement of the text
of the *Critique of Pure Reason*) is "another articulation, one which, belonging to a
different order, has a certain priority over the text and to that extent governs it—in
short, a prearticulation" (S 70). With that there seems to be a joining of deconstructive reading with the texture, i.e., the *Sache*/phenomenon. What enables the
creative engagement with the text is not intra-textual, but is the *Sache* itself.

To what extent does Sallis in his writings stay within the textual movements
of disruption and displacement? And to what extent does he move out from the
textual play to the play that is *offered* in the text but goes out beyond, to the texture, to the phenomenon, to the phenomenon-showing, to the emergent emerging?

Do texts exceed themselves? If so, under what rubric? The subversion within
the texts—is it an opening one which enables thinking's transforming engagement
with the texture? If so, does the text itself *as* text enable that enabling subversion?

To the extent that Sallis's work deconstructs texts within texts, to the extent
that it is a play of textual forces, an intervening that gets texts to move (head-on
or obliquely) into the fissure, the other text, to the extent that Sallis's texts on texts
bring forth displacement and disruption essentially *within* that text—to that extent
that work cannot touch the deeper movement of the phenomenon. *That* is simply
not textual in the way that deconstructive reading hears "text." What exceeds the
closure of metaphysics and what exceeds the text (e.g., in Sallis's "excess of imagination") is phenomenologically not nothing, but rather withdrawal. The unfolding of the withdrawal from representation and meaning and presence at the end of
metaphysics is not textual, but rather textural, or phenomenological.

Thinking, writing, and text need the withdrawal for their own rooting. But as phenomenon, this withdrawal engages thinking while it may escape writing.

I have worked on this collection of essays out of gratitude for what Sallis's work has enabled and opened up. For I share with him, what I take to be his challenge also, a reading that re-engages the text in an original way, such that thinking is transformed. For we need to move away from our usual understanding of "what is" and of the "true" *to* a transformed way of the "true" and of being "what it is."

Here I am reminded of Scott's "guest" in his paper, the Vietnam veteran Tim O'Brien:

> In a true war story, if there's a moral at all, it's like the thread that makes the cloth. You can't tease it out. You can't extract the meaning without unraveling the deeper meaning. And in the end, really, there's nothing much to say about a true war story, except maybe, "oh."[24]

I am also reminded of a struggle of which I have only heard and in which I have not participated, indeed cannot fully participate: the struggle of Black women, whose literary tradition, in the words of Katie Geneva Cannon, "is the nexus between the real-lived texture of Black life and the oral/aural cultural values implicitly passed on from one generation to the next."[25] That is the texture of their text. She goes on: "In essence, there is no better source for comprehending the 'real-lived' texture of Black experience and the meaning of the moral life in the Black context than the Black women's literary tradition. Black women's literature offers the sharpest available view of the Black community's soul."[26] This offers a rich notion of texture—and clearly opens up the difference between what is textual and what is textural.

What is the texture of philosophy's texts—or non-philosophy's texts—here, now, at the end/limit of metaphysics? How can we read the text within its context and texture?

Sharpening the lines of this knotting, let me juxtapose two Sallis texts on reading. First, from *Being and Logos:*

> The demand is for a restraint against letting the matters of the *Republic* fall into the molds prepared for them by the tradition and for a playfulness sufficiently lawful and evocative to allow these matters the free space in which to reform themselves. (BL 312)

Then a text from *Reading Heidegger:*

> Reading may take the form . . . of a questioning that would use the very resources of those texts in the effort to locate within them certain blind spots, residues of dogmatic assertion.[27]

Are these two descriptions of reading compatible? Is reading that questions texts for the sake of blind spots and residues of dogmatic assertion in any way alien to reading that allows the matters the free space in which to reform themselves? More succinctly, do both ways of reading take into account that which turns its gaze to us: the *Sache*/phenomenon, the self-showing unfolding itself, that is textured within the text?

I believe that there is a difference between a reading that restrains "against letting the matters [of a text] . . . fall into the molds prepared for them by a tradition," a reading that is sufficiently playful and evocative "to allow these matters the free space in which to reform themselves" (BL 312) *and* a reading that "uses the very resources of . . . texts in an effort to locate within them certain blind spots, residues of dogmatic assertion." Both readings may be subversive. But then: Does the one, the other, or do both ways of reading constitute the clarion call of the πόλεμος that meets us today, on the road of contemporary continental philosophy?

What is the texture to which each way of reading calls us? Does each call us to a different texture? Does the texture have a calling power of its own? Can thinking image that dance of text and texture whereby reading the text moves to and is sustained by the texture that is within it (the text), but deeper, as it (the texture) embraces the text?

Certainly the echoes of the text emerge for thinking. Certainly hearkening to the text and staying to the "fire" of the text's various levels reveal doublings and doublings-back, blind spots, and self-effacements. But how is the text *attached?* Where is its texture? One can certainly grasp the complexity of texts and their textuality—the "textual echoes"—but these "echoes of semantic and syntactic elements within a text or between texts" (E 13) may run the risk of becoming "formalizations." These formalizations (in the words of *Being and Time*) "level off the phenomena to the point that their proper vigor as phenomena is lost,"[28] or the point where the texture is lost.

Finally is it possible that "deconstructive reading," which may intend to be within and be shepherded by the texture of the *Sache*/phenomenon, *in its enactment* is actually contrary to that intention? I see contemporary continental philosophy itself at such a crossroads—and Sallis's work as mirroring this dilemma.

This dilemma, enigma, or knotting is imaged and highlighted when Derrida, in his essay in this volume, pinpoints the "Sallisian operation"—and Sallis's contribution—as one of

> broaching a procedure of the deconstruction of metaphysics, which by way of a certain genealogy of the imagination leads us by assured steps toward a radical dislocation of the very identity of metaphysics, an identity that certain types of deconstruction at least provisionally seem to presuppose. From this point on, it is a certain idea of deconstruction that is at stake, perhaps 'deconstruction itself,' as if such a thing existed that could claim for itself the stable identity of a project.[29]

What "dislocates" so radically the project of "deconstruction itself"—or at least "a certain idea of deconstruction"? If Sallis's genealogy of imagination "leads us by assured steps" to such a radical dislocation of the very identity of metaphysics that is prerequisite for certain types of deconstructions, to where does thinking turn? At the heart of deconstruction is this "menace"—as Derrida then calls Sallis's "thoughtful and vigorous vigilance." What becomes possible in this menace? What does such a thinking enable?

What if this dislocation, when seen phenomenologically—for what it is from out of itself—calls for an inevitable shift to the phenomenon/*Sache?* What if deconstruction is called upon to leave its designated—and to itself unquestionable—arena in the loss of the identity of metaphysics? What if herein is an invitation to thinking to move out from the self-enclosure of the text—to the texture, the *Sache?*

Once again the question is: What is this "freeing of texts" that Sallis speaks of in *Echoes* (E 13)? And what is the "exceeding" that texts do, according to Sallis in *Crossings* (C 148)? Who among today's thinkers dares to stay with *that* domain/phenomenon, until it shows itself from out of itself in its self-showing?

PART ONE

IMAGINATION—IMAGES, IMAGINGS

CHAPTER ONE

Imagination and Metaphysics

THE PHENOMENOLOGICAL "DELICACY OF THE IMAGE"

Françoise Dastur

"Imagination and Metaphysics" is the title of the first chapter of *Delimitations,* a book dedicated to the marking of the limit—end and origin—of metaphysics and to the opening of a space beyond it, within a radicalized phenomenology, as indicated in the subtitle: "Phenomenology and the End of Metaphysics." But this title can also be read as indicative of a broader enterprise of destabilization of metaphysics. We find the markings of this enterprise in other books by John Sallis, from *The Gathering of Reason* (which traces a way to the issue of imagination through the reading of the *Critique of Pure Reason*) to *Spacings* (which shows the essential role of imagination in the constitution of German idealism to *Echoes* (in which the attempt to think "after Heidegger" calls into question the identification of imagination and temporality in the period of fundamental ontology as well as its effacement after the *Kehre*).

For a thinker like John Sallis, who is engaged in the movement of returning to the things themselves (which is called phenomenology), the problem of imagination can, paradoxically, no longer be a regional problem of philosophy. Rather it is, as it was for Sartre,[1] a key to entering the philosophical problematic as such. For, as Sallis points out, the opening to the things themselves is a rigorous renewal of the metaphysical "drive to presence," which involves the releasing of an imag-

23

ing **within** the very things themselves (D X); and it is precisely because phenomenology as philosophy of intuition wants to leave the last word to the things themselves and wishes to let them show themselves from themselves that it must recognize that imaging belongs to showing (D 75).

For Husserl, originary intuition is the "principle of all principles" of phenomenology[2] and fiction is the life-element of phenomenology,[3] so that the phenomenological field can never be defined as a field of mere presence, but as a field where presence is essentially interwoven with absence. This intertwining (*Verflechtung*) of presence and absence—or, as Merleau-Ponty said, of visibility and invisibility—constitutes the infinite field of experience of a phenomenology which is no longer condemned to solipsism (as was Cartesian philosophy) but which is really intersubjective. This means, of course, a redefinition and an enlarging of the concept of intuition. In the first place, intuition can no longer be understood as the self-presence of the subject in the evident *cogitatio,* but must have inherent in itself an element of intelligibility and discursivity. Already in the sixth Logical Investigation[4] Husserl refused the Cartesian opposition between the sensible and the intelligible, which is at the origin of the difference between the two Kantian faculties of knowledge, sensibility and understanding, and their two products, intuition and concept. There is for Husserl a "categorial intuition"; this implies that the category is given to a non-empirical sight, to what we could already name an "imaginal look." And besides, the self-presence of the subject is understood in a non-Cartesian way[5] as a non-immediate relation to its own *Erlebnisse,* its own mental processes; this implies a necessary recourse to the *Vergegenwärtigung,* the rendering present of the imagination. Thus the subject regards itself in a similar position as it regards the others: at a distance which can be diminished only by an act of imagination, a making present of what is absent, the past or future *Erlebnis* of its own or the *Erlebnisse* of the other, which are absolutely nonaccessible in themselves, but which can be appresented in an indirect manner in the *Einfühlung.*

Such an enlarging of intuition, which allows Husserl to speak of a perception of the category[6] as well as of a perception of the other,[7] explains in which sense imagination can still be defined by Husserl as an intuition that is able to bring the thing itself, contrary to what he calls (following Brentano) the "inauthentic" thinking, i.e., symbolic thinking with an "empty" or "unfulfilled" intentionality. In this respect, Husserl is following the Kantian definition of imagination as the power of intuiting an object that is not itself present, which (power) "involves *making present* something which is and remains in another regard *absent*" and therefore "inaugurates a certain play of presence and absence, a gathering into presence" (GR 156). But such a definition—which considers imagination not as merely passive, as sense is—leads Kant to attribute to imagination the power of exhibiting the object (as empirical imagination) or making objectivity possible (as transcendental imagination). This means that in both cases there is an **intrinsic** link between

imagination and perception, image and phenomenon. Given the Kantian definition, image can no longer be understood, as it was in empiricism, as a weakened
perception or intuition, but is now understood as an original intuitive form of the
relation that consciousness has to the objects. The Husserlian theory of imagination is, therefore, just a radicalization of the Kantian interpretation of imagination
as an **active** power of exhibition and a **synthetic** faculty.

In *The Gathering of Reason* Sallis very convincingly shows that the subversion of metaphysics, which he wants to undertake in his reading of Kant, "is developed from within rather than being imposed from without" (D 33) and that the
Critique of Pure Reason itself "installs at the heart of gathering an irreducible absence, an essential withdrawal, a self-withholding of that which would be gathered
into presence" (D 35). It has to do with what he calls an "arc of absence" (GR
165–6) into which all gathering into presence remains inscribed, insofar as the
thing-in-itself which affects the subject's mind is always irreducibly absent in the
phenomenal object to which it has given form. The phenomenal experience is
structurally marked by this "negativity"—the negativity of the noumenon as the
concept marking the limits of knowing—which in a sense has the character of an
Aufhebung of the unsuppressible distinction of the sensible and the intelligible
(GR 170, 171). Kant started from the classical distinction between two worlds, the
sensible and the intelligible; but in the transition from the *Dissertation* of 1770 to
the *Critique of Pure Reason* the purely intellectual knowledge is absorbed into the
sensible one and becomes a moment of the phenomenal knowledge itself (GR
169–70). In his analysis of what he calls "critical metaphysics," Sallis shows in
the three Critiques (*a*) how the old metaphysical distinction between the sensible
and the intelligible is reopened in a new form within a new conception of the sensible itself (first Critique), (*b*) how a new conception of the intelligible founded on
the subject's freedom is conquered (second Critique), and (*c*) how the mediation
between the new conception of the sensible and the new conception of the intelligible is found in the free play of imagination (third Critique). This play is an imaging of the intelligible, i.e., of practical freedom, but without the "metaphysical
security" attached to an ultimate and original intelligible **already given before** his
imaging—an intelligible understood as *Vorhandenheit,* as Heidegger would say.
That is why, as Sallis points out, imagination becomes "ecstatic," not only because
it can no longer be considered as a faculty of the human soul (as something subjective), but also because it is opening to something which is irreducibly absent
and which can never be a *positum* outside the play itself: "Nothing escapes the
play; one finds everywhere only the play of imaging, the play of indeterminate
dyads [. . .] for on that play there is an incessant opening and closing of the distance between what the tradition, since its beginning in the Platonic dialogues, has
thematized as intelligible and sensible" (GR 176).

But if what is imaged in the play of imagination is nothing that is given in advance, then the dyadic structure of imagination, its eikastic interpretation, be-

comes problematic. And this happens explicitly in the phenomenological approach of imagination, as Sallis stresses in "Image and Phenomenon," the fifth Chapter of *Delimitations*. The critique of the image-theory which is to be found in the fifth Logical Investigation aims precisely at the classical conception of a **substantial** difference between immanence and transcendence, interiority and exteriority, *res cogitans* and *res extensa*. We do not have **two** things, one outside consciousness (the real object) and another one inside consciousness (the so-called immanent or intentional object). On the contrary, we have only **one** object, because "the intentional object of a representation (*Vorstellung*) is the same as its actual (*wirklicher*) object."[8] This "sameness" of the object is precisely what Husserl has in mind when later, in the *Ideas* of 1913, he emphasizes that "there is an unbridgeable essential difference" between perception and depicting-symbolic or signitive-symbolic representation.[9] We have already stressed that imagination is an intuition and not a symbolic representation, that it is an intentionality of the thing itself, like perception, and not an **indication** of the original thing through its copy. Husserl puts the eikastic imagination on the side of the symbolic, indicative, and inauthentic intentionality and the phantastic imagination on the side of the intuitive, immediate, and authentic intentionality, because in the case of the symbolic eikastic intentionality there are **two** things, the thing itself and its picture or sign, while in the case of the perceptive or phantastic intentionality, there is an immediate intuition of an "it itself," without any interposition of something other. It is therefore clear that the substantial distinction between a sensible object and an intelligible object—i.e., the classical distinction between the sensible and the intelligible worlds—is built on the presupposition that we, as finite beings, have only an indirect access to things, which are never given to us "in person" but only through the mediation of their appearances and that their "in itself" is the correlate of intuition other than ours, the intuition of a subject possessing an absolute and perfect knowledge.[10] For Husserl, on the contrary, God cannot see things better than we. God is, like us, bound to see them only through their profiles, which are not like the pictures or signs of the things themselves, but the oblique way into which things can only show themselves to us, in a distance which is also the condition of possibility of their manifestation.[11] It means consequently that God has, like us, only an *intuitus derivativus,* because, if he had an *intuitus originarius,* it would mean that **the same thing** which is perceived immediately and adequately by him can be perceived only mediately and symbolically by us. But this view is for Husserl an absurdity, because it would mean that what is immanent for God (only immanence is given absolutely and without the mediation of profiles) can only be transcendent for us, so that there would be no **essential difference** between something transcendent and something immanent. Husserl affirms on the one hand the **sameness** of intentional and transcendent object (in the Appendix of the fifth Logical Investigation) and on the other hand the **essential difference** of immanence and transcendence (in the § 43 of *Ideas*); but there is here no contradiction, because immanence or consciousness is not another realm juxtaposed to the realm of transcendence or nature and considered as substantial as it, but only the **domain of the showing** (D 74) of nature and objectivity for which phantasy is perhaps a better name than its traditional appellation of reason. We find here an example of the unfolding of a difference into an "identity" which has a similarity with the Kantian redefinition of the distinction between sensible and intelligible into the sensible. For the sensible constitutes the unique accessible realm for us, finite beings. This should be emphasized, as does Heidegger in his Kant interpretation, by quoting a passage from the *Opus posthumum* which says that "the thing in itself (*ens per se*) is not another object, but another relation (*respectus*) to the **same** object."[12] For Kant also, there is only **one** world and not a sensible world understood as a mere duplicate of the real intelligible world. But the thing-in-itself, that is the thing which is without us and not for us, is still understood as existing **before** us and as affecting us originally, so that the phenomenon is still understood in the (traditional) eikastic interpretation as phenomenon **of** the thing-in-itself.[13]

Is it possible to generalize the *intuitus derivativus,* as does Husserl, without reference to an already present origin? Is it possible to think the derivative itself as originary, in other words to think the passivity of the reception as originally active and imagination as coming not **after** but **at the same time** as perception? This is what constitutes the real challenge of phenomenology,[14] which is, as Sallis says in a very suggestive manner, "the practice of self-effacement in the face of the things themselves" which leads **at the same time** to "that **reticence** by which thinking holds itself aloof from the things themselves in such fashion as to grant them the free space in which to show themselves" and to "that **engagement** of thought with the things themselves by which it entices them into the open, draws them out, invokes their self-presentation, aids in the birth of their truth" (D 63 and 64). We could say, with the assistance of the Merleau-Pontian way of thinking, that phenomenology is the thought of a *présence écartée,* of a presence involving absence,[15] which essentially implies the intervention of phantastic imagination in the constitution of objectivity—the only sense of being that Husserl knows.

As is the case in the *Critique of the Pure Reason,* in which, as Sallis notes, "there remains scarcely a trace of eikastic imagination" (D 10), there is also a privilege given by Husserl to the phantastic imagination, even as he takes the problem of eikastic imagination into account. In fact, Husserl is the first thinker to unite in a single approach two problematics which have been treated separately before, the problem of the representation of an original in a copy (which comes from Plato) and the problem of the *phantasia*, as an intermediary faculty between perception and ideation (which comes from Aristotle's *De Anima*). We have already seen that these two kinds of imagination are linked to the opposition between an authentic intuitive thinking and an inauthentic indicative thinking, an opposition which Husserl inherits from Brentano. But inside the authentic intuitive thinking there is also the possibility of some "inauthenticity," because there are intuitions that are not presentations of the thing itself, as is perception, but "presentations," *Verge-genwärtigungen,* as for example mental images or memories. Between a perception and a mental image, the difference is in the **modality** of the givenness of the object: it is present in the perceptive experience, while absent in the imaginative experience. But at the same time, this absence is understood by Husserl as a modification of the proto-experience of perception, which is experience of a live presence. Once the level of the live presence is modified by reflection, there is a possibility of an infinite reiteration of the presentations which can in essence become presentations of presentations, memories of memories, images of images and so on indefinitely. This "wonderful process of reflection in presentation," which can go on *idealiter in infinitum,* is only possible if an object is first given to consciousness in a live presence or—in a Kantian way of speaking, which is also used by Husserl in his *Lectures on the Phenomenology of Inner Time-Consciousness*—if an object has in the first place "affected" the subject. It does not mean, however, that this proto-experience can be effectively maintained in its purity, as completely separated from the reflection by which it becomes conscious; in this respect we may say that the proto-experience of affection or perception **does not ever take place, but has always already taken place,** so that the "thing itself," like the Kantian "thing-in-itself," which affects the subject in an unknown manner, "always escapes" a **present** grasp, without however being a mere phantom.[16]

This capacity of infinite reflection is the manifestation of the freedom of the subject that can always escape, as Sartre vigorously pointed out,[17] the constraint of live perception, so that the relative "inauthenticity" of presentation is in fact essential to the constitution of subjectivity itself. And it is the same for the other kind of presentation which is not, like memory, a "**reproductive** modification *simpliciter,* which in **its own essence,** remarkably enough, is **given as modification of something else,**" but which "presentiates 'in' a 'picture'."[18] We have here the phenomenological criterium of the difference between εἰκασία and φαντασία: In phantasy, the reproduction gives by itself the reference to the reproduced thing, where in εἰκασία, in what Husserl calls the pictorializing modification (*die verbildlichende Modifikation*), which is "closely related" to another type of presentations, the sign-representations (*die Zeichenvorstellungen*), the reference to the pictured or designated thing is not given **in** or **with** the picture or the sign itself. Sallis refers here to the fifth Logical Investigation, where we find the first analysis of depicting imagination. Reading Husserl, Sallis writes: "Imaginality is no real predicate; it is not given with the image-object in the way that the redness and the spherical shape, for example, are given. The point is indisputable: Imaginality is not a qualitative or quantitative property adherent to the image-object" (D 69). Sallis concludes that for Husserl "no image is capable of **performing** its representative function, or, more generally, its function of revealing the original" (D 69).[19] For Sallis, however, this criterium is too narrow, because, granting that imaginality is not a real predicate of the image, it does not mean that imaginality is **nothing manifest** in the image-object. Here Sallis sides rather with Nietzsche, who was aware of "the delicacy of the image," which cannot be measured solely with objective standards. Nietzsche understood that the image is capable of showing in itself that it is just an appearance, because "its shining is a shimmering, a tremulous gleaming, which fleetingly and delicately betrays that it is a mere image, not original" (D 71). It is therefore possible, apparently against Husserl, to consider imaginality "not as a property belonging to the image, but rather as the way in which the image **is** (actual), as its mode of actuality" (D 70).

But how can we explain, for example, that shadows and reflections are **immediately** apprehended not "as objects which then have the further character of being images, but rather **as** shadows and reflections of things, that is, **as** images" (D 70)? The perception of a picture, like the perception of a sign, is in fact not a "simple" perception, but involves a complex intentionality, which Husserl analyzes in *Ideas I* with the example of Dürer's engraving, *Knight, Death, and Devil*. The perceptive consciousness does not aim at the physical thing constituted by the picture, but immediately at the depicted realities of what is figured in the picture, the flesh and blood knight, etc., so that, Husserl writes, "the **depicturing picture-object** is present to us **neither as existing nor as not existing,** nor in any other **positional modality;** or, rather, there is a consciousness of it as existing, but as quasi-existing in the neutrality modification of being."[20] What Sallis names the "peculiar delicacy" of the image-object comes from its suspension, its hovering,[21] between existence and non-existence, or its neutrality in regard to being. And we can understand this neutrality of the image as the "reticent" way in which the phenomenon has to appear in order to guide the intentionality, not towards itself but towards the depicted thing. As Sallis writes: "One apprehends the image as already linked up with the original of which it is an image, as opening onto the original, as letting the original show itself. And thus, paintings have a revelatory power which surpasses what one could grant them through a constitutive extension back toward an imaginatively projected original. Their revelatory power flows, as it were, in the other direction" (D 71). Thus in the eikastic dimension itself, we are not called **back** to an already and elsewhere existing original through the copy, but rather pushed **forward** into the **becoming** present of the original. It means therefore that, even here, there are not **two** things, the original and the copy, but only **one** which presentiates itself, i.e., which is **made** present, ver*gegenwärtigt,* through the help of a material present base, which is not perceived as existing in itself, but only as a being-for-something else. Even in the case of what Husserl with precision calls *Abbild,* reproductive picture (for example, a picture representing somebody having really existed, like a picture of Napoleon, in contrast to the Knight of Dürer or the Centaur of Böcklin, who do not exist at all and are "imaginary" beings), we are not dealing with two "realities" or "objects" linked together by a relation of resemblance, but with the **same** "object" that presents itself in a **modified** form in the picture.

Husserl is thus able to lead the two kinds of imagination, εἰκασία and φαντασία, back to the same root, which is the capacity of **presentation:** Both in the image-object and in the free image-representation an absence is made present rather than there being two presences juxtaposed on the basis of their resemblance. The phenomenological scene is therefore very similar to the critical scene, in the sense that the difference between the sensible and the intelligible is for Husserl—as it is for Kant, at least in the first Critique—opened within the sensible itself (D 10), the only realm recognized by Husserl. And we could say from the Husserlian phenomenology what Sallis says from the Kantian critique: "The field of metaphysics as reconstituted in the *Critique of Pure Reason* is a field in which the play of presence and absence, the play of self-revelation and self-withholding, the play of imagination, is released from that repression that would subordinate it in the end to the ideal of sheer revelation, of pure presence" (D 11). This means that, for Husserl as well as for Kant, "there is no need to set imagination at a distance from metaphysics." On the contrary, for Husserl imagination becomes, while not exactly identical with theoretical reason as it is for Schelling, at least the condition of possibility of philosophy. Here also the relation between phenomenology and imagination has a twofold character, in the sense that not only is there a phenomenological theory of imagination, but phenomenology is in a way the work (or the play) of imagination.[22] The neutrality modification, which is "included in every abstaining-from-producing something, putting-something-out-of-action, 'parenthesizing' it"[23] and which can be universally applied to all mental processes, is the very source of the *epoche,* of this radical alteration of the natural positing that is the philosophical, or phenomenological, attitude.[24] And the same neutrality modification is also at work in the *Wesensschau,* in the eidetic seeing: To be able to "see" for example the species "red," it is necessary to start from the sensible intuition of an individual red; but the transmutation into eidetic seeing happens through a neutralization of this founding experience. So both the eidetic reduction and the transcendental reduction rely upon this fundamental "operation" of imagination, which is neutralization.[25]

The phenomenological theory of imagination is therefore a radical critique of the **spatial** interpretation of the dyadic schema of the difference between image and original, in which Sallis sees the fundamental structure of the field of metaphysics as a field of presence (D 6). Metaphysics can indeed be defined as a matter of eikastic imagination if we consider that what structures metaphysics is the drive to presence and the purpose of the reappropriation of an originary presence. This drive to presence however takes a **transcendental** form, in the sense that, as Sallis explains, the Socratic turn from the sensible things to the λόγοι has the meaning of a shifting away from the present things, recognized as images, to the originals which constitute their true foundation. This transcendental turn is all together a drive to presence and a drive to ground (D 14). But what is really metaphysical in it is the shifting away from the ambiguous and instable presence of the sensible and the seeking after the security of a full and accomplished presence. So that, starting from the same famous Platonic texts that are mentioned in "Imagination and Metaphysics"—the passage of the *Phaedo* (99 e) where Socrates explains why he must have recourse to the λόγοι, the allegory of the cave, and the scheme of the line in the *Republic*—we could also define metaphysics not so much as a drive to (true and eternal) presence but rather as an **evasion** from (sensible and temporal) presence.[26] This assumes that the sensible realm is a world of unreal "images" which have to be "transcended." But the movement of transcendence itself requires recourse to phantastic imagination as the power of making present what is not presently given to the senses. So that, as Sallis stresses, "Imagination both empowers and inhibits the metaphysical drive to presence and metaphysics must, accordingly, both appropriate and take distance from imagination" (D 7). This is particularly true in the case of Kant. On the one hand, (phantastic) imagination is required as the power of synthesis without which there would be no possibility of constituting objectivity, of articulating (sensible) presence into an objective unity (GR 162). But, on the other hand, (eikastic) imagination is the origin of the transcendental illusion by which we are illegitimately turning subjective ideas into objective beings, as is the case in the ontological proof of the existence of God, and "treating our thoughts as things and hypostatizing them," as Kant says (GR 160). Transcendental imagination, this power of originary exhibition which is purely productive, gathers not only the manifold of intuition into the unity of the categories, but it also gathers the manifold of all things into the unity of the transcendental ideas, which are, as Kant himself acknowledges, "bastards of imagination" (GR 161; D 33). Here it is also possible to say, as Husserl does, that fiction "is the source from which the cognition of 'eternal truths' is fed."[27]

However, concerning Plato and the opening of the χωρισμός between the sensible and the intelligible, the question has to be raised whether the "originals" are really forming another realm besides the gloomy world of the cave or whether they are nothing really existing outside the sensible world. If Plato must have recourse to an allegorical "story" in the *Republic,* it is perhaps because it is difficult to speak in a rational manner of the shadowy nature of the sensible which, like the image, possesses no positivity and is always in becoming. Merleau-Ponty has spoken in the same manner of the sensible, seeing in it not the positivity of a world of objects, but only the allusive presence of a Being that remains transcendent and distant.[28] The fact that Plato does not "believe" in the stories he tells and does not really consider the sensible world as a duplicate of the intelligible becomes quite clear in the *Parmenides,* with the third man's argument, which is a critique of the "vulgar" conception of εἰκασία as relation of resemblance between an original and a copy.[29] And if we effectively find a "movement of repression" of imagination in the Platonic texts (D 13), it is aimed at eikastic imagination and against those who not only deal in images, like the painters and the poets, but also against those who want to pass off images for realities, like the sophists, precisely because they are not able to **see**—for this requires the capacity of the eidetic look—the structural difference between the real and the imaginary. Are the sophists, whose rehabilitation has been undertaken nowadays by some of those who identify metaphysics and Platonism, really the thinkers of the reality of becoming, over against the metaphysical thinkers of the fiction of being? Or are they rather, as Heidegger pointed out, those who put an end to the astonishment of the thinkers facing the wonder of being by giving for everything ready-made explanations which could be understood by everybody?[30] Their denial of the Platonic χωρισμός in fact always takes the same form: It is the denial of the **temporal** "delicacy" of phenomenality, which is always hovering between being and nothingness and the affirmation of the positivity of the sensible, which allows them to identify images and things. While Plato considers the sensible as being as inconsistent as an image and tries to find a stable measure for it in looking away from the sensible into a universe of ideas, where no establishment is ever possible,[31] the sophist affirms that there are only images, but at the same time regards them as consistent things. This implies a blindness to anything else as positive, substantial, or spatial presence, a blindness to ideas—which is also a blindness to time and to the "creative" and not only destructive side of becoming—of which Husserl speaks when criticizing empiricism and its inability to see in ideas anything other than abstract constructs or "metaphysical hypostatizations," i.e., mental duplicates of empirical realities.[32]

The transcendental turn is always a turning away from realism and positivism; it is this turning to the "unreality" of being which was named philosophy and which involved as its very source the phantasmatic capacity of imagining. This is the reason why, as Sallis shows very clearly, imagination becomes explicitly the meaning of being in the first and still transcendental phase of Heidegger's thinking.[33] Sallis notes that there, as it was already clear in the Kantian schematism, the anticipatory character of imagination, which provides the horizon for all possible understanding and knowledge of what is, is determined by reference to time as constituting the universal form of phenomenality. But it is also there that, as Sallis notes, the effacement of imagination begins, because Heidegger stresses that, in the thinking of the identity of imagination and time, "the designation 'imagination' becomes of itself inappropriate" (E 108–9). Is this effacement necessary in order to think transcendence in a less metaphysical way and to leave behind the dyadic structure of the opposition of originary and vulgar time, as Sallis hints? (E 114, 116)[34] Or is it necessary for philosophical thinking to leave behind the dyadic structure of thinking **as such** in order to think the "sameness" of being and humanity in the *Ereignis*? Is the effacement of imagination as human faculty not required if mortality, understood as "being capable of death as death," is thought as the fundamental capacity of the human being and if mortal is now "the proper name of man"?[35] This last question, which I would like to leave unanswered ("hovering," that is to say, persisting **as** question), could in fact lead us again to the problem of Heidegger's relation to German idealism, which under the name of *Einbildung***skraft** thought the capacity of "holding opposites together in holding them apart" and the power of "sustaining death in its more than absolute alterity" (E 134).

Perhaps the time has come to think not so much the force as the delicacy of imagination, not so much its (dialectical) power of conjoining coincidence and opposition as its free playing beyond all "positive" objectivities. That is why, as written in "Image and Phenomenon," "The principle issue in the freeing of imaginality from objectivity is the granting of the delicacy of the image, that is the dissolving of the image as a quasi thing into the effervescent shining, that is the release of image into imaging" (D 74).

CHAPTER TWO

LEAPS OF IMAGINATION

Rodolphe Gasché

To conform with what John Sallis calls "the upward way of metaphysics," imagination "must be held within bounds, limited, constrained" by reason, whose supersensible nature secures its borders against any incursion by sensibility (S 121). Among the powers of the mind, Kant consistently describes the role of imagination as ancillary to reason, with the notable exception, for example, of his contention in the 1781 edition of *Critique of Pure Reason,* that the pure productive synthesis of imagination is prior to apperception and the ground of possibility of *all* knowledge.[1] The various, and, I would hold, non-unifiable accounts of imagination that appear throughout his works, agree in principle on only one thing— imagination is not an independent faculty. Its very intelligibility hinges on what it works to make either possible (cognition) or intuitable (ideas of reason). Sallis reads Kant's persistent subsumption of imagination to the faculties of understanding and reason as stemming from its power to space. Yet, Kant's own definitions of imagination as the power of synthesis in general,[2] of presentation (*Darstellung*),[3] of intuition without the presence of the object,[4] or of forming one image from several others—thus drawing on the semantics of *Einbildungskraft*— would, at first, seem to be at odds with such an understanding of that power. In addition, in light of the massive documentation to be found across all of Kant's writings attesting to imagination's subjection to reason, Sallis, by raising the question of an "abysmal imagination," an imagination excessive, as it were, so as to elide its domination by reason and to locate itself ἐπέκεινα τῆς οὐσίας (S 152,66), seems to argue for imagination's independence as a faculty. This question raises the possibility that a detachment of imagination from reason and presence be so radical as to cause it to drift away from any delimitation (S 130), or, to gesture towards Hegel, "as to exceed being regathered into the circle of self-presentation" (S 153).

In *Spacings,* Sallis provides no unitary theory of abysmal imagination. Although Sallis's readings of each thinker under discussion (Kant, Fichte, Hegel) yield a host of distinct spacing operations, their characteristic traits, as well as those of the manifold occasions and spaces in which they occur, are neither formalized nor drawn together. In the concluding chapter, Sallis even wonders whether the question of such an imagination can even be posed without immediately being recovered by spirit and reason. Sallis offers no response other than allowing the question to multiply itself within his inquiry. It is as though imagination, when addressed head-on by the question, escapes the dominating thrust of the question itself. Meeting the question of its abysmality, imagination spaces, displaces, dislocates itself in Sallis's text. Undoubtedly, such withdrawal is to be attributed neither to an allegedly unfathomable richness of imagination, nor to the identification of imagination as such a fundamental faculty that the finite mind could not hope to come to grips with it. Nor does the uncertainty that hovers around imagination derive from a failure, on Sallis's part, to penetrate its essence. Quite the contrary, the sharper his analyses become, the more Sallis postulates an increasing multitude of unexpected aspects of imagination that, more often than not, cannot be accounted for by the texts under scrutiny. A protean profusion of traits comes into view—especially in the case of Kant, where imagination divides into a seemingly endless array of types and where it is made to assume an equally great variety of tasks—that points to a limit very different from the one that marks the comprehension of riches, the fundamental, or the unfathomable. Abysmality and excess are the names for that limit in Sallis's work on imagination.

Yet how are we to conceive of such abysmality? Can one conceive of an abysmal imagination, in excess of spirit, without radically putting into question the traditional view that imagination is a faculty, not only in the sense of a distinct operation of the soul understood as a substance, as a function of the mind, as in Kant, but as a moment of subjective spirit as in Hegel? But if it is no longer an operation, function, or moment, what then is imagination, and in what way then is its abysmality to be understood? With these questions in mind, I turn to Kant's treatment of imagination. Given the limited space here at my disposal, rather than taking up the issue in the *Critiques,* I turn to *Anthropology from a Pragmatic Point of View.* Even so, I will only be able to formulate a skeleton of a question about imagination *itself* and to sketch out the outline of a response.

By general consensus, the *Anthropology* is Kant's most comprehensive exposition of the faculty of imagination. It may be argued that, in terms of its content or development, this text does not compare favorably with Kant's major works, that its empirical formulation excludes it from the realm of theoretical decision, or that its pragmatic orientation restricts the imagination that becomes thematic in it. However, I would contend that *Anthropology,* despite these limits, contains several new elements which make it possible not only to shed light on some of the difficulties encountered in Kant's treatment of imagination in his other works, but to help to elucidate imagination itself in an interesting and significant manner.[5]

Spacings, on one occasion, makes recourse to *Anthropology,* citing it as one of the places, in addition to the *Third Critique,* where Kant explicitly defines imagination as "the greatest faculty of sensibility" (S 114). Let me note from the outset that although Kant, in *Critique of Pure Reason,* had already shown with sufficient clarity that in the cognitive process understanding has no privilege over sensibility, *Anthropology* reinforces this position with its "Apology for Sensibility" and even assigns a positive value to certain kinds of delusive, deceptive sensibility, to appearances, in the sense of mere *Schein.* By establishing sensibility in its own right, Kant sets up the only condition under which sensibility can be recognized in its complex organization. It is against this background of a sensibility that differentiates into various interrelated parts that Kant's statement that imagination is the greatest faculty of sensibility must be read. Indeed, in contradistinction to sensibility proper, that is, to what Kant calls "sense" (*Sinn*), imagination is already a faculty (*ein Vermögen*), i.e., an active power very unlike the passive, merely receptive functions of sense; but activity, properly speaking, belongs to the faculty of the concepts. If imagination is a faculty—and moreover the greatest of sensibility, although it remains a sensible power—it is already capable of actively combining and separating intuitions. Thus, although imagination approximates understanding, it remains only an extreme limit of the sensible and, in order to make strict sense of experience and cognition, must still be kept distinct from understanding. From the start, then, the place of imagination is clearly circumscribed: it is part of sensibility, a kind of sensible, hence incomplete, "cognition." It is a part that is fully what it is only in its conjunction with understanding in the cognitive process. As Kant remarks, imagination "supplies the content of understanding, that is, content to its concepts for the sake of knowledge" (58).[6] Without the active help of this power, the properly active faculty, that is, understanding, would remain empty—and no cognition would occur.

After having distinguished imagination from sense, and having defined it as "intuition without the presence of the object" (40), in chapter 28 Kant divides it in the following way:

"The imagination (*facultas imaginandi*), as a faculty of perception without the presence of the object, is either productive, that is, a faculty of the original representation of the object (*exhibitio originaria*) (*ein Ver-*

mögen ursprünglicher Darstellung), which consequently precedes experience, or it is reproductive, that is, a faculty of derived representation (*exhibitio derivativa*), which recalls to mind a previous empirical perception. Pure perception of Space and Time belong to the productive faculty. . . . (56)

This definition of productive imagination looks like the productive, or transcendental, imagination defined in the First Critique; yet it is not the same. For it does not represent pure concepts, or ideas, but rather non-present objects. And although Kant's use of the term "poetical" (*dichtend*) to designate productive imagination insinuates that its art is akin to the "art [of schematism] concealed in the depths of the human soul,"[7] the art Kant has in mind in *Anthropology* is that of the artistic genius. Productive imagination here refers to an empirical, psychological power; yet, as I hope to show, the way this empirical power operates reveals certain traits and presuppositions that must have their corresponding structures in transcendental imagination. Let us therefore try to understand as clearly as possible what productive imagination achieves.

Like transcendental imagination, productive imagination *presents,* that is, renders present, effective, actual, not concepts of understanding, or ideas of reason, but non-present objects. And like transcendental imagination, productive imagination brings such presence about by means of pure perceptions of space and time. Yet, what are non-present (*ohne Gegenwart*) objects? To clarify the status of these objects, as well as the meaning in the given context of "originary presentation," it is imperative to note that, although productive or poetical imagination presents objects that are not present, "the productive faculty, however, is not creative (*schöpferisch*), because it does not have the power to produce a sense impression which has never occurred to our senses. One can always identify the material which gave rise to that impression" (57). Kant adds: "However great an artist the imagination may be, even if it be a sorceress, it still is not creative, but must gather the material from the senses" (58). It follows from this that the non-present objects that productive imagination presents are objects that, although merely 'imaginary,' have been composed of material drawn from the faculty of the senses. Productive imagination is poetical imagination in that it gives a reality of sorts to fictitious objects by forming them into sensible images composed of sensory material gathered by the senses. Kant writes that "imagination . . . seems to give a reality to its invented notions because of the analogy between them and real perceptions" (*vermöge der Analogie ihrer (gedichteten) Anschauungen mit wirklichen Wahrnehmungen, jenen Realität zu verschaffen scheint*) (58). Although productive imagination is 'only' the presentation of 'imaginary' objects—that is, of inventions by the poet's mind—this presentation is originary because it makes these objects present to begin with. Productive imagination is the power that allows for the *intuition* of fictitious objects; and, making these "objects of intuition," it makes them objects as such. Therefore, Kant can say of the empirical power in question that it precedes experience, as does transcendental intuition. But poetical imagination is not only an originary presentation; as is still to be seen, it can be original as well.

Since productive imagination is not creative, and must rely on material gathered from the senses to form its presenting images, imagination is an *imitative* faculty, as Hermann Mörchen has noted. A faculty of sensibility, imagination, although distinguished from sense perception, must, in conformity with the domain of passive receptivity to which it belongs, mimic cognition by the senses. Yet, as Mörchen also remarks, imitation "contains both the moment of passivity and activity."[8] In gathering the material for its originary presentations from the senses, imagination displays an ability that properly belongs to understanding—activity and spontaneity. How is it possible, one must ask, that a faculty that belongs entirely to the domain of the sensible can be active? Undoubtedly, by attributing qualities of spontaneity to productive imagination, Kant follows the lead of Aristotle, who, in *On the Soul,* determined imagination as an intermediate faculty. But Aristotle also acknowledges that imagination is not only a movement (unlike thinking), but that "this movement cannot exist apart from sensation." It is "a movement resulting from an actual exercise of a power of sense."[9] Yet despite its activity and the fact that no judgment is possible without it, imagination belongs *entirely* to the domain of the sensible. What, then, is the nature of that activity?

In *Anthropology* Kant writes that imagination "supplies the content of understanding, that is, content to its concepts for the sake of knowledge" (58). Productive imagination is patterned after this transcendental employment of imagination. It, too, appears to be the necessary active submission of content to concepts which understanding, despite the spontaneity of its sphere, cannot bring about all by itself. This is evident from Kant's definition of what constitutes the originality of productive imagination. "Originality," he writes, "(non-imitative production) of the imagination is called genius when it harmonizes with notions (*wenn sie zu Begriffen zusammenstimmt*)" (62). Productive imagination, that is, the rendering present of non-present objects, although dependent for its material on the faculty of the senses, can engender non-imitative, unique images. Both the genius and the fanatic (as well as the madman) are capable of originality. Yet only in the case of the genius do these formations harmonize with notions, that is, with concepts that guarantee the communicability and universality of these singular formations. Although Kant's distinction is pragmatic in intent, and agreement with concepts is the condition under which alone the unique formations of productive imagination can also be universally intelligible, suspension from concepts is the measure of productive imagination's own intelligibility. Only when harmonizing with concepts, and thus producing original formations for the sake of aesthetic consumption, is productive imagination in its own element. All other originality is, in its very meaning, dependent on such purposiveness. But, interestingly enough, Kant does not say that originality, to be genial, must harmonize with (*mit*) concepts; he literally writes that it must harmonize in such a way as to form concepts (*zu Begriffen zusammenstimmt*). Although this linguistic construction may certainly mean "with concepts," it also hints at an active according, or agreeing, of the original productions with themselves so as to form, to engender, concepts all by themselves, rather than submitting to already given ones. In the case of the genius, indeed, the new formations seem to accord so perfectly as to verge on becoming concepts themselves. If this is the case, the faculty of productive imagination becomes even more enigmatic. Can the active faculty of the passive domain of sensibility be spontaneous to the point of producing concepts? If, as we have seen, productive imagination mimics sensory cognition in that it must rely on material drawn from the senses, does this faculty also mimic understanding by engendering its own concepts? And in thus mimicking both sensory cognition and cognition properly speaking, does the intermediary faculty of imagination not also mimic reason? Yet, if this is so, is imagination a representative of reason in the domain of the sensible, or in excess of reason? Or rather, does the intermediary place occupied by imagination, its dependence on sensory cognition, understanding, and reason, not demonstrate its own nullity and utter lack of independence? The very possibility, necessity, and undecidability of these and other possible questions regarding the status of imagination in Kant would have to be addressed in itself. For the time being, we must inquire with Kant into the distinct varieties of productive imagination that, until now, have been dealt with only in general terms. As Kant sees it, "there are three distinct varieties of the sensory productive faculty (*des sinnlichen Dichtungsvermögens*). These are the pictorial (*bildende*) perception in space (*imaginatio plastica*), the associative (*beigesellende*) perception in time (*imaginatio associans*), and the sensory productive faculty of affinity (*Verwandtschaft*) based on the shared lineage of ideas from each other (*affinitas*)" (64). These distinctions will help us elucidate both how productive imagination can be said to be original to such a degree as to give rise to concepts and what concept means in this context.

In line with the claim that, as a faculty of original presentation, pure perceptions of space and time must belong to it, the first two kinds of productive imagination divide according to those pure forms. Yet, what about the third class based on "the shared lineage of ideas from each other"? In a manuscript written in his own hand, and which probably served as the blueprint for the published version of the *Anthropology*,—the Rostock manuscript—Kant at first called this third kind of productive imagination "the intellectual productive faculty of affinity (*das intellectuelle Dichtungvermögen der Verwandtschaft*)."[10] Although Kant subsequently crossed this formulation out because it did not render the nature—both intellectual and sensible—of this kind of imagination, it is indicative of the singular condition of this type of sensory productive faculty: It composes with an intellectual mode of production. In this extreme kind of the sensory faculty, categories—categories of relation, to be precise—are already at work. Before further delving into this third variety—also called "the sensory productive faculty of affinity"—we must, however, briefly outline the functions of the first two.

About "the pictorial (*der Bildung*) sensory productive faculty," Kant observes that "before the artist can depict (*darstellen*) a corporeal form (*Gestalt*) (palpable so to speak), he must have prepared it in his imagination. This form is an invention (*Dichtung*) which, when involuntary (as perhaps in a dream), is called fantasy and it is not to be associated with the artist; but if it is voluntary, it is called composition or discovery (*Erfindung*)" (65). In this first type of the sensory productive faculty of imagination, a shape (*Gestalt*) invented by the imagination, and which subsequently is to be presented in a corporeal form, is first formed (*gebildet*) so as permit its corporeal presentation. This formation of what is to be given a palpable shape takes place by means of the form of space. Through composition, i.e., through spatial arrangement and interconnection, that which is merely 'imaginary' is prepared (*verfertigt*) in view of its possible corporeal actualization.

"The associative sensory productive faculty's" law is defined as follows: "The law of association is that empirical perceptions, which frequently follow one another, create an acquired habit in the mind, so that when one perception is engendered, the associate one also arises" (66). Although the pragmatic thrust of the *Anthropology* restricts Kant to evaluating this faculty's role in social discourse formation, the function of this faculty (discussed in greater detail in the *First Critique*) is to assure the reproducibility of representations in view of the general task of imagination, namely "to bring the manifold of intuition into the form of an image." The associative sensory productive faculty provides the "subjective and *empirical* ground of reproduction according to rules," which thus permits "determinate connection of them ... [and not merely] accidental collocations."[11] Through temporalizing formation, the associative faculty shapes the representations before they can become elements of a well organized whole, such as a discourse with a beginning, middle, and end, for instance.

With this we come to the third variety of productive imagination, the one based on affinity (*Verwandtschaft*). Kant's definition of affinity explains not only why at one point he could have called this type of imagination an intellectual productive faculty, but also points to its singular achievement. He writes: "By affinity I understand the union by the derivation (*Abstammung*) of the manifold from a single foundation" (67). In contradistinction from association, which is limited to putting one representation with another (*beigesellen*), the sensory productive faculty of affinity unifies. In other words, it is involved in an operation that, ultimately and properly, is the power and responsibility of understanding. Yet, since imagination even in this extreme form, in which the realm of the sensible takes on a semblance of the domain of understanding, continues to belong to sensibility, the union in question, as well as the consequences that derive from it, cannot be that of the concept. As the definition of affinity shows, not only is the union in which the manifold becomes grounded entirely sensible (a genealogical ground, root, or stem) but the way in which it is realized—through filiation (*Abstammung*)—is sensible as well.

More precision is needed to describe the imagination's similarity to, and difference from, understanding. After having exhorted the inherent temptation of associative imagination to jump off (*Abspringen*), interrupt, and thus destroy the defining form of social conversation, Kant remarks that all conversation, and even silent thinking, requires "a theme according to which the manifold is ordered." Therefore, Kant continues, "the understanding must also be at work at the same time. Nevertheless, here the play of the imagination follows the rules of sensibility, which provides the material whose association is achieved without consciousness of the rule, consonant with the understanding (*dem Verstande gemäss*) but not derived from it" (67). Although such thematic ordering is an accomplishment of the sensory productive faculty of the third kind, the unity of the theme is already "*unity* of the concept, which [in this case, however] may be entitled *qualitative* unity, so far as we think by it only the unity in the combination of the manifold of our knowledge," according to the First Critique, where Kant evokes "the unity of the theme in a play, a speech, a story."[12] Lacking the consciousness of the rule, i.e., the self-awareness that comes with thinking (the concept), the unity produced by imagination based on affinity is nevertheless in accordance with the understanding. By deriving the manifold from a single foundation such as a theme, productive imagination mimics understanding; but, as a sensible faculty, it falls short of endowing its unity with the consciousness particular to thinking. The distinction between both functions of cognition is thus maintained. Again some questions suggest themselves: Since cognition is not possible without imagination's ordering of the manifold, is the active mimicry of this sensory faculty simply a sign of its being taken into service by the understanding? Yet what would such infinite plasticity of imagination reveal about imagination *itself*? Indeed, what is striking in this last, and extreme form of the sensory productive faculty is that, whether chaperoned or not, it is on the verge of no longer being itself, i.e., no longer being a sensory faculty. Yet what does such ability to transcend its own sensible nature—a transcendence that remains within the limits of the sensible—disclose about the very nature of imagination itself?

Before attempting to sketch out a possible answer to these questions, it is necessary to get a firmer grasp on the kind of unity here accomplished. We read that

> The word affinity, here reminds one of a catalytic interaction found in chemistry, an interaction analogous to an intellectual combination, which links two elements specifically distinct from each other, but intimately affecting each other and striving for unity with each other, whereby the combination creates a third entity that has properties which can only be brought about by the union of two heterogeneous elements.

Despite their dissimilarity, understanding and sensibility by themselves form a close union (*verschwistern sich*) for bringing about our cognition, as though one were begotten by the other, or as though both had a common origin, which is impossible; at least we cannot conceive how things so dissimilar could have sprung from one and the same source. (67–68)

What the above passage tells us is that by uniting the manifold according to a ground from which it becomes derived, the third kind of sensory productive imagination combines heterogeneous elements, thus bringing forth a third kind of entity, namely cognition. In this kind of imagination, cognition already occurs but remains cognition within sensory power, cognition of and by that power. It is a kind of cognition not derivative on understanding, the effect of an affinity that is only "analogous to an intellectual combination." And yet for it to be cognition in the first place, the affinity must bring together heterogeneous elements—sensibility and understanding. However, Kant describes this unification in sensible cognition in terms of a *Verschwisterung* of the so dissimilar faculties. In the unity of affinity, understanding and sensibility behave as if they were brother and sister, "as though (*als wenn*) one were begotten by the other, or as though both had a common origin (*von einem gemeinschaftlichen Stamme ihren Ursprung hätten*)." What occurs in sensible cognition is something which from the perspective of "human reason" (69) remains unfathomable. Seeking to understand what happens in such cognition, Reason loses itself in obscurity, Kant suggests. Indeed, the reciprocal generation of a brother by a sister, or the other way around, is as absurd as the idea that both "could have sprung from the same source (*Wurzel*)." And yet, the sensible paradigm of lineage, filiation, stem, and root, with all its contradictions, provides an effective unity of the manifold, one which secures productive imagination's success in achieving a degree of cognition. On the other hand, however, the unification brought about by this last kind of productive imagination is incomplete, only resembling the synthesis that the concept makes possible. It would thus seem that imagination remains subservient to understanding, or at best, on an equal footing with it. At its highest peak, imagination is determined by its cognitive success, by a task to which it must contribute, but which is, properly speaking, effectuated by another power.

Everything we have seen thus far shows imagination to be entirely restricted to the domain of the sensible. It is only the sensible's highest faculty, and a faculty to begin with only because it mimics understanding and reason, and does so, furthermore, in the service of these faculties. Although of the order of the sensible, it is parasitic even to its own realm, having little or nothing to claim for itself. How then can one talk about an abysmal imagination to begin with? On the contrary, imagination has shown itself to be a domesticated function of sensibility that acquires a degree of distinction only by successfully imitating sensibility, understanding, and reason. And yet, Sallis's question concerning the questionable possibility of asking a question about "abysmal imagination" here takes on an additional turn. As we recall, Sallis raised this question by noting the fact that imagination can always be dialectically thought to an end, such that, whatever abysmality it may have, it falls under the aegis of reason or spirit. To this consideration we now must add that of imagination's (almost) excessive plasticity. The question of imagination's abysmality now imposes itself as a direct consequence of its lack of status, of never being itself except when chaperoned by understanding and reason. And yet in spite of this absence of all independence, it plays an indispensable role, so indispensable indeed that it can be mistaken—that it mistakes itself—for a super faculty.

Imagination, thus, lacks an *itself* while at the same time performing operations without which the other faculties would remain empty or would be deprived of any bearing on cognition or moral action. While having the look, in its various efforts at mediation, of a union of the heterogeneous sources of cognition, it musters no autonomy for itself. If this then is the situation of imagination, to be not only a faculty of spacing, but to be dislocated from a space of its own, to lack any presence to itself, while simultaneously performing tasks ever so decisive for the other powers of the mind, does the question of imagination not have to address the economy that regulates its multiple functions *and* its simultaneous lack of an itself? As Sallis recalls, imagination is conspicuously absent from Kant's table of the faculties, say in *Critique of Judgement* (S 87). Of this faculty, which is denied the status of a faculty in spite of its originary and elemental accomplishments, one must account in a manner that explains this peculiar predicament. The only sufficient account, I would like to argue, arises out of an analysis of the structural traits that permit imagination to differentiate seemingly endlessly, if one follows *Anthropology,* into all its varieties, to perform the most decisive tasks in the most selfless manner, to relinquish the power that such performance bestows upon it in favor of the other faculties, etc. Establishing these traits and analyzing how they are linked illuminates a certain abysmality of imagination, one, moreover, that is thinkable, and can be accounted for only in structural terms.

In *Anthropology,* Kant's concerns are primarily pragmatic, that is, intent on determining in what ways the various facets of imagination can be enhanced in the perspective of what "man makes, can, or should make of himself as a freely acting being" (3). This pragmatic thrust explains, for instance, why *merely* reproductive, that is, involuntary imagination as it occurs in dreams, has no place in the otherwise quite comprehensive account of imagination found in this work. The scope of Kant's *Anthropology* also confines the meaning of such themes as *distraction (Zerstreuung),* and *jumping from (Abspringen),* broached explicitly, or in passing, to their pragmatic significance. And yet the pragmatic treatment of distraction and jumping off might offer some insights into the nature of imagination *as such.* Distraction, for example, appears to have an enlivening effect on the presentation by imagination of non-present objects. Kant writes: "Imagination is richer and more fertile with ideas (*Vorstellungen*) than sense is; and the imagination becomes, if coupled with passion, more lively when the object is absent than when it is present. This is evident when something happens which calls the idea of an object to mind which for a time seemed to be extinguished by distracting influences (*durch Zerstreuungen getilgt*)" (71). Does this statement, made in the context of a pragmatic evaluation of the sensory productive faculty of affinity, not hint at a constitutive role of distraction for a faculty that is to present non-present objects? Is imagination's animation as such not dependent on an extinguishing of objects by some sort of essential distraction? By contrast, jumping off, discussed by Kant in the context of the pragmatic evaluation of the sensory productive faculty of association, is not positively valorized. Indeed, to leap from a given subject to a heterogeneous one, to skip links in the chain of representations, is not only a danger inherent to association that is detrimental to social conversation, jumping off might well be the characteristic of mental disturbance (*Verrücktheit*) (118). But does such jumping off by a "roaming imagination" (67) not reveal something about imagination itself, or in general? Indeed, is it by pure coincidence that in the margins of the section on the sensory productive faculty of association in the Rostock manuscript of the *Anthropology,* Kant writes: "Jumping off from the subject matter of discourse, *facultas signatrix* belongs to associative imagination."[13] This contiguity of jumping off and *facultus signatrix* points perhaps to a much more essential role of *Abspringen* for imagination than the one discussed in the pragmatic evaluation of the power of association.

In the published version of the *Anthropology* from 1798, after his treatment of the reproductive forms of imagination, Kant comes to speak about the faculty of designation (*facultas signatrix*). The chapter "On the Faculty of Designation" argues that the association by the voluntary forms of reproductive imagination (memory and foreseeing) of empirical experiences of past, present, and future conditions is grounded in a special action of the mind called "designation" that is responsible for effecting the connections in question. Since Kant claimed in the Rostock manuscript that this faculty belongs to associating imagination, this chapter on designation is not only decisive for the understanding of reproductive but productive imagination as well. If this is so, it is because the faculty of designation is not merely a subdivision of imagination, another kind to be added to the already considerable list of imagination's varieties. It is, I would contend, an action by the mind present in all forms of imagination, one indeed that explains how imagination can be both the power of presentation and of bringing the manifold of intuition into the form of an image. To sustain this point, a patient analysis not only of this chapter on designation, but of the parallel chapter in *Critique of Judgement* "Of Beauty as the Symbol of Morality," would be required. Here, however, I must limit myself to following remarks: As Kant's definition of the faculty of designation shows—namely as "the faculty of understanding the present as a means of connecting the conception of what is foreseen with that of the past" (83)—designation is the power in reproductive imagination that permits the mind to interconnect its various experiences into a "coherent experience" (73). As Kant's expansions on jumping off insinuate, harmonization of representations with each other is also the aim of the associative sensory productive faculty, although this aim will only be successfully achieved in the sensory productive faculty of affinity. Now, in the chapter on the faculty of designation itself, such connection (*Verknüpfung*) is said to be the result of "designation (*signatio*), which is also called signalizing, of which the highest degree is called attribution (*Auszeichnung*)" (83). Although the perspective of this chapter is merely pragmatic, Kant's discussion of symbolic cognition and of language as signification of thought rests on the assumption not only that imagination is a presentative power, but that such presentation is a function of signs. To be able to present, imagination must not only interconnect the manifold of intuition and use it as a presentation of concepts or ideas. It must first and foremost shape the intuitions in such a manner that they can point at one another, and that their interconnected whole—the image—can refer to something other to begin with. It is obvious that this requirement is not only one for the pragmatically interesting types of imagination discussed in the *Anthropology,* but the very condition of possibility of imagination as such (transcendental and empirical). Imagination must be, in its most essential core, a faculty of designation, of signaling, such that intuitions point at other intuitions, and the whole they constitute, to something that is not of the order of the sensible. Mörchen has put it quite well: "Imagination as a faculty of designation is the power to understand an intuited existent as a sign that points away from itself; only because imagination is this power, it is also the power to produce a sign, to designate something. But this function of imagination presupposes that imagination has the possibility, by presenting up to the sign, to be in advance of itself, as it were, to precede itself; otherwise it would never be capable of understanding what the sign that points away from itself properly means."[14] Most fundamentally then, imagination is this: the power to make intuitions point away from themselves, and there must be such pointing away before imagination can divide into its various employments . Moreover—and with this I turn away from Mörchen's phenomenological and hermeneutical interpretation of imagination—as such a power, imagination cannot help but point away from *itself* as well. Always ahead of itself, this power of the sensible is by necessity understandable only through the powers that it serves, i.e., understanding and reason. Since imagination must interconnect and present, it is in *itself* nothing but the power to designate, a power that can only be designated by pointing ahead of itself to the other faculties. With this, do we not touch upon the enigma of imagination's abysmality? Must it not be understood in terms of such pointing away, a pointing that ultimately allows for no *itself* anymore? But is such structural abysmality, or excessive spacing for that matter, not merely the minimal condition under which imagination can perform all its positive and seminal tasks? And hence in its very abysmality still remain bound up with understanding and reason?

As Kant's admonitions against jumping off demonstrate, imagination always risks running "from hundreds into thousands so rapidly that it seems we have completely skipped certain links in the chain of perceptions, although we are merely not conscious of them" (66). Such jumping off in no way interrupts imagination's connecting actions. But is not jumping off (as well as distraction) a possibility rooted in the very power of designation, of making things or intuitions point away from themselves? Is it not, at first, a modality of designation? Yet, pointing away from self harbors as such the possibility of failing to connect. Indeed, *Abspringen, Absprung,* also means to take off, come off, fly off, break, drop out. Because imagination must on its most fundamental level turn intuitions into signs, they can always fail to designate and "to bring [in tumultuous madness, for instance] ideas into mere coherence necessary for the possibility of experience" (112). Jumping off, in this latter sense, as a possibility inscribed into the very base power of imagination, into the power of pointing away from itself, situates imagination's abysmality beyond the circle of appropriation in which it would simply represent a condition of possibility for all of imagination's crucial tasks. The possibility of merely leaping off as a structural trait of (productive) abysmality—as something that is always possible, and that hence must be accounted for—prevents the abysmality of imagination from offering itself up without reserve to the powers to which it itself points and which it serves. Imagination holds the possibility in reserve that, in pointing away, it *could* not point at all, or that it could point otherwise, otherwise than required by understanding and reason. Conjoined to abysmality as a condition of possibility for imagination's multifarious tasks, the possibility of failing to point brings an abysmality of imagination in view that escapes the logic of appropriation. It is an abysmality that is thinkable, whose structural traits can be clearly spelled out, whose bottomless flight is the result of a possibility that necessarily comes with the designating power of imagination. Yet here too, we must ask, with Sallis, whether this abysmal imagination can be questioned at all. Is it possible to address such abysmality by, or in, a question? Is this abysmality not rather what bottoms out the question? Yet while such excessive abysmality, excessive to the point of being radically detached from presence, chokes off the question, it *points*—perhaps, although always risking being cut off—to another kind of thinking. Does it not broach, to quote Sallis, "a wonder that one could never aspire to surpass" (S 157), a wonder to be reflected in a new, very new, kind of thinking?

CHAPTER THREE

TENSE*

Jacques Derrida

Translated by D.F. Krell

I. ECONOMY

Let us imagine. Let us imagine that we are dreaming. We are dreaming, in French, of inventing for John Sallis an *autre temps.* (I ask the translator to leave these two last words in their original language.)

Unless—and we are now in the time of the dream—unless he has already done it himself. Unless John Sallis has already invented an *autre temps,* discreetly, after his own fashion—that is to say, by means of a most economical gesture—

---

*The word *tense* is not French but English. When the French speak of the tense of a verb, they say *temps;* when they speak of a person's being tense or a rope's being taut, they say *tendu.* Derrida's title is therefore written in English. Quite often, in fact, Derrida writes in English in his otherwise French text, even though I have spared the reader endless brackets containing the phrase "in English in original." The title "Tense" may have to do with either time as such or the "time" or tense of verbs; it may also have to do with tautness, or all of these together: time, tense, and tension, suspense and suspension. "Tense" may have to do with the Nietzschean tension between force and the play of forces in John Sallis's thought, particularly in its shifts, oscillations, and hoverings.

I am grateful to have had the opportunity to translate the text *of* a friend *for* a friend, and thus to have been able to make my own modest contribution—*il y a là CALypso*—to this volume. And, once again, my thanks to Michael Naas.—TR.

and this by giving us to think that it is as risky to determine time as it is to determine the imagination. The moment it is a matter of imagining time, imagining may perhaps mean something altogether different from what we generally believe it to mean. Unless imagining, in whatever sense, is always a matter of time.

Let us imagine, then, that we are dreaming. Since Plato, since Descartes, the hypothesis of the dream represents a noble tradition in philosophy. However, since we are talking of time, we ought to ask ourselves to what time a dream may belong. Would it be a time homogeneous with that of consciousness? Would it still be a time, or would it be some atemporality of the unconscious, for example, the sort of atemporality in which Freudian discourse always gets caught up? Or, yet again, some other temporal structure, more heterogeneous and more difficult to describe?

Let us leave these questions hanging for the moment; let us grant them the time of suspense.

Who could imagine an *autre temps?* Who else? And when? What does *when* mean, *if l'autre temps* is not yet nameable, *from the instant* it refuses to submit to a concept, *all the while* we are still asking about it? One would like to know at what moment, during what epoch, and according to what rhythm the time could arrive for inventing an *autre temps.* One would have to think another temporality, another process of temporalization, or again, another epoch of history—and, first of all, another language in which to say these things, another time of the *verbe* (at the same time *verbum,* λόγος, speech, speech act, and tense or verb). For that, one could no longer be content to describe or analyze: one would have to *make* something *come* [*faire venir*]. Not merely to produce, in the sense by which to produce (*pro-ducere*) consists of conducting *what was already there* to the fore, *to the forefront,* that is, to the very first position, but to make something advene there where it *was not.* Further, to *make* something advene should always come back to *letting* it advene: what comes cannot be decided, cannot be by definition; that simply isn't done; it arrives, and one *can* and *should* only let it arrive; doubtless, one would not know how to *produce* it. And since we have only now in some sense set aside, or at least suspended or suspected, this value of "production," let us note in passing that the modern notion of the imagination, notably in its Kantian or post-Kantian provenance, remains deeply tied to the value of production or to the opposition between the productive and the re-productive, between the *power* to produce and the *power* to re-produce.[1] We shall leave all these potential questions in suspense; but *puissance,* as power and possibility, and *suspense* will doubtless be our themes, and precisely where they can no longer be separated from the imagination.

Thus one ought to *imagine* not only that which *is not, not yet or no longer,* but also that which no longer bears any relation to the "is," to the meaning of being as determined by the grammar of this verb, in particular by its *temps* (tense). Will this still be to imagine? Or will it be the sole condition for imagination to begin, and to begin to let itself be thought? Would not the condition of imagination be a certain thread tied between nonbeing (the beyond of being) and time?

As we are in process of dreaming, one might think while dreaming that the time of the dream is absolutely heterogeneous with the time of wakefulness and even with the time of an existence (let us call it *Dasein,* by way of example) that is no longer simply aligned with the consciousness or ego of a subject. Thus the existential analyses of time—to the extent that they remain, as it seems to me, mute or spellbound with regard to oneiric temporality (and thus phantastic or phantasmatic temporality, fictive temporality, and by that very fact the virtual temporality of the poetic or literary, and so on)—also remain surreptitiously regulated by the time of presence-to-self as wakefulness and self-consciousness, no matter how vigorous the denials. (The Heideggerian concept of "testimony" [*Bezeugung*] in *Sein und Zeit* would here play the role of mediator between a phenomenology of consciousness, that of Husserl, and the phenomenology that still governs the existential analysis of *Sein und Zeit*). It is a certain phantasticity (of which the oneiric would here be an example) that is misunderstood or reduced every time. And yet the great thinkers of time (Kant, Hegel, and Heidegger, for example), were also thinkers of the imagination (as productive and reproductive) or of the transcendental fancy [*phantastique*]. What, then, would the misunderstanding be, if there ever were one?

Here you are playing with a French word, but without playing, let us never play, the word *temps,* in order to designate two in one, and while dreaming you are already crossing the border between two languages: *time* and *tense.* Therefore let us say more strictly that we are imagining, dreaming also of inventing another grammatical modality, another category of "verbal time" (tense), in order to describe John Sallis's gesture of thought, the gesture that is most his own and is no doubt inimitable. What would be hard to imitate here would be not so much a "logical" schema, the "conceptual" content, the "philosophical" theme or gesture of a procedure. The philosophical is always *reproducible.* And it is precisely the delimitation of philosophy, a certain end of philosophy, that *interests* Sallis on the site he inhabits, in the midst of the milieu in which he finds himself, the place where he insists on being, the place where he recognizes himself. Such a limit might also be a threshold. What is inimitable would thus derive more from the modality, quality, or tonality of an *insistence on thinking* the dream and this *autre temps,* and thus on making it *exist* with a singular *intensity.* Insistence and intensity—these are the things that count here. One would have said not long ago that what counts is the style, but here I would rather invoke the singularity of the event, of the idiom or rhythm, and also, for the intensity of the insistence, a manner of persisting and persevering in the same place, the place of the taking-place. These are the things to be taken into account. Yet how to take into account the intense, or an *intense insistence?* What precisely does *intense* mean; and, above all, how are we to calculate intensity? How to describe the concentrated, serene sobriety of this Sallisian writing? It is precisely a writing of intimidating *economy:* a knowledge deployed in filigree, faithful to all the folds in the very moment that marks the most audacious of its prudent moves. The word *economy* is risky, I know, but

I will take the risk where the meaning of such a word holds us at the limit of the calculable and the incalculable. It also refers to what Freud made the word say: with regard to cathexes [*investissements,* literally, "investments"], the economic point of view takes into account simultaneously their movement, their variable *intensity,* and above all the *tension* in their antagonisms, contradictions, and all the conflicts that dialectically institute them (no cathexis without a countercathexis). Although (or, if you prefer, because) Sallis never or almost never refers directly to Freud, I will run a second risk. Following the *economic* point of view, and playing with the metapsychological lexicon, I will speak later of a *dynamic* point of view, and finally of a *topical* point of view.

Thus we have only now, whether wittingly or not, broached a question one might entitle, albeit only in French, "*l'invention d'un temps,*" or "*temps et invention,*" or again "*le temps pour l'invention.*" If one takes *invention* to be a discovery of truth or the arrival (the making—or letting—come, as event) of what is not, of what is not yet, then in each case the word engages something one may name *imagination.* "Let us imagine," we said at the outset. Imagination furnishes at least an image of that—a good or bad image, a more or less trustworthy image. Thus it is in the first place a matter of the imagination, of the *place* of the imagination. It is well-known that John Sallis, among his other achievements, has shown the rare lucidity required to situate the enigmatic stakes of the imagination, that is to say, the stakes of this apparently classical concept in the history of philosophy. He will have situated it for every meditation on the ends of metaphysics, for the auto- (or hetero-) interpretation of metaphysics and of its "own" limits. Thus it is a matter of the imagination and even, to be more precise, employing a word that will become clear (unless it makes matters still more obscure), a matter of a certain "shift" of imagination, a "shift" in this phantastic history of imagination that Sallis has recounted to us and taught us. (What is a "shift"? Is it more than a making explicit, a thematization of what was already there, already possible? Is it a mutation, change, turning, displacement, rupture, restructuring, deconstruction—all of these under the inventive form of an event of revelation, inauguration, or transformation? Knowing already that I will have no reply to this series of questions, I am hurrying to pose or depose them here; or rather to leave them once again in suspense, *hovering.*)

Thus we find ourselves drawn back into the vicinity that John Sallis himself has not ceased to revisit, the history of imagination (εἰκασία, φαντασία, *Einbildungskraft,* etc., from Aristotle to Kant, Hegel, and beyond), and above all the Kantian schema of the transcendental imagination, this place of time, in some sense, along with its Heideggerian "repetition," and so on.

Yet at the same time this invention of an *autre temps* ought to *engage* us. And engage us in a contradiction one would need to cross over (second crossing, *double crossing,* after that of the frontier between two or more languages). For it will never suffice to describe the *autre-temps*—time and *tense*—that receives the gesture of Sallis's thought as he is on his way toward them, calling them, inviting them, receiving them as well: letting them come to him. This double invitation, the invention of which we are speaking, ought *at once, at the same time* (ἅμα, simultaneously) to reveal or discover what we find already there (the movement of truth as memory), all the while granting place to an absolutely inaugural event (another status of truth as the quality of inauguration). However, that is not all. This double invention ought not to limit itself to the *modality* of a philosophical writing—not merely philosophical, because it may be a matter of metaphysics *and its ends* in this passage from one *temps* to another, from one "verbal" modality to another—here, the writing of John Sallis. The double invention should affect writing itself, thoughtful writing, which, in order to take it into account, would take into its ken and keep, precisely here, the writing of John Sallis. Without imitating him, one would nevertheless have to write *like him* in order to write about him, one would have *to be of his time* and to take part in the double invitation. I will have given up on this ahead of time, but I wanted to begin with this avowal, leaving at least a trace of it here.

Those who, like me, read and admire him doubtless will not have failed to observe his openly declared preference for and attachment to titles that in *his* language end in *-ing*. Titles that seem to play with the presenc(ing) of the present (present participle or gerund, verb or nominalization of the verb). To be sure, it is a manner of treating *temps* (time and tense). This preference shows itself first of all from one book to another (*The Gathering of Reason, Spacings—, Crossings . . . ,* "Doublings," "Translating Ecstasy," and so on). It also intervenes in any given book: "Clearing(s)," in *Delimitations,* a nominative title like the others, which itself says also at one and the same time (the two *at the same time,* ἅμα, simultaneously; this gathered duplicity, the singular *both* is in some way marked in the plural itself) the act of delimiting and the effect that remains after the operation: delimitation as the object or result of an act, *auto*-delimitation; "Tunnelings—," "Hoverings—," "Enroutings—," "Tremorings—," "Ending(s)—." The mark of the plural most often comes to confirm and to complicate still further the regularity of that which plays and is at stake, *se joue,* in this accident of English grammar. Not that Sallis is content simply to play with it. Noun and verb at once, gerund and noun, thing and process, arrest or stasis and uninterrupted continuity of a movement, being and becoming, agent and patient, attribute too at times, and thus by that very fact subject and object: *between the two and beyond the two. Between two and beyond two modalities of the presenc(ing) of the present.* One would have to take note of this strange topology, take note of the fact that it *takes place* while it *grants place.* Economy and topology of the event.

What happens with *le temps* (time) when *le temps* of a verb (tense) lends itself to nominalization? And when that seems to affect the very presenc(ing) of the present? Within presence, yet also at the same stroke beyond presence, in order to be in between two forms of presence itself? In fact, it is as though we had to do with an auto-affection of language within language. We have already begun to become interested in imagination and in time, that is, in the structure of auto-affection that Heidegger will have analyzed so powerfully in his Kant book. One scarcely displaces the question by illustrating it—toward ends that are less pedagogically motivated than it may seem—through the example of this strange grammar, this singular possibility of time and of the verbal mode. Our attention to this matter should not be diverted by the fact that many have abused it in recent years in the production of not-so-very-inventive titles, titles of books and articles, it being the great merit of John Sallis that he has never bowed to such facile productions. Let us take an example: someone proposes to hold a discourse on "writing architecture." What will that involve? To write architecture? The verb here is obviously transitive, writing being a present action, whether punctuated or continuous, and architecture the object-complement of this supposed agent, the subject behind its verb. Or will it rather involve a writing architecture, in such a way that architecture operates, acts, and itself writes? What was earlier the object now becomes the subject, thereby affecting itself from one reading to the next. In both cases, the time is that of a present; and the fold of auto-affection, implied and capitalized, reverts to the fact that the object can become the subject of that of which it is the object, that it can touch itself, reflect itself, examine itself, itself affect itself. When the potential of this auto-affection is concentrated in a gerund ("Crossings," "Spacings," etc.), but also when it is multiplied regularly in a plural; when such a word designates at once an ongoing (present) operation and its own effect (that is, something that presupposes the present past, already past)—whenever this occurs, all oppositional logic sees itself suspended (I would say, as Sallis does, sees itself "hovering") between verb and noun, subject and object, active and passive, the present and its own past. Consequently it is suspended between an incalculable number of other poles,—incalculable because the arithmetical itself, the order of 1, 2, 3, is found to be gravely perturbed by it. Economy of the incalculable, incalculable economy.

Perhaps this is what is happening in the case of John Sallis: with, in, thanks to, and through Sallis's "writing" or "writings." And "writing" would be a remarkable example of the *temps* (time and tense) of an ambiguous present that floats between noun and verb. And what happens if I now write "Writing John Sallis" or "Writing 'John Sallis'"? And if, in the face of everything that is destabilized and becomes less and less trustworthy in all the oppositional categories of grammar or of classical logic (noun or verb, subject or attribute, subject or object, active or passive, present or nonpresent, self or other, etc.), I felt obliged to write all these word-concepts under erasure? And not only to *write them under erasure,* as Sallis himself demands at the end of "Imagination and Metaphysics" ("Writing under erasure, attending to the subtlety and risk of the move, one might then broach the demands of a logic of imagination" [D 15]), but to write under erasure the word *écriture* (writing) itself? Perhaps that is the profound logic of Sallis's deconstructive, hyperdeconstructive, even metadeconstructive gesture: the erasure of "writing," as we shall see, attains therein its extreme coherence.

I could have taken another example. I shall say nothing about it for the moment, but, as I shall attempt to show, it could have furnished the subtitle of these modest reflections: "Deconstructing Metaphysics."

Thus John Sallis is not content to play. He no doubt finds, discovers, invents. His thought is in the strongest and most enigmatic sense of the word *imaginative,* not imaginary—note the difference, if difference there be. That would be his signature, and yet he finds what is already found in a language as a singular and latent possibility. For one does not fortuitously encounter the *power* of a language as though it were a tool lying abandoned on the building site, a tool with which one handily produces unsuspected effects. The economy of language here keeps in reserve the very thing it gives us to think, the moment we turn our thoughts toward heeding it. That does not mean that "this very thing" is "within" language or is reducible to a linguistic phenomenon. Sallis is not content merely to exhibit a possibility that was found to be waiting, a possibility that others, as we know, have used and abused in a quite mechanical way, in a technique of titles that in effect permits this grammatical suspense. No, because the gesture that is properly idiomatic with Sallis—at least, this is the gesture I would like to acknowledge and give us to understand—consists in situating, inscribing, let me say more precisely, *de-limiting* within a *single* "grammar" *the* singular figure of metaphysics in its "truth," nothing less than that. There, where it is a matter of the presenc(ing) of the present, that is, of the being. I recall in passing, without wishing to reduce one example to the other, that one of the decisive moments of *Heidegger's* meditation on the mystery of being and the presencing of what is present traverses this inflection of the Greek ὄν: Under the ambiguity [*Zwiefalt*] of the participial signification of the ὄν there hides in retreat [*verbirgt sich: est en retrait*] the difference between 'being' and 'the being' [*der Unterschied von 'seiend' und 'Seiendem*],[2] that is to say, the difference between the being *tout court,* if one may say so, and the being in its being (insofar as it is).

A strange topology, therefore. Is it still a topology of being? This grammatical form marks the very thing that is found *between* two and *beyond* the two, perhaps *beyond the two* in general, indeed, beyond the three as the dialectical resource of the opposition between one and one, one and two. How can this *between* (the two) be a *beyond the two?* This, in effect, is the question that never subsides in me when I am reading Sallis. Let us not hasten to speak of a middle voice or of a third voice, but rather, with John Llewelyn, of "Something Like the Middle Voice."[3] It is true that in this tremulous state *between two* possibilities the question of the *third* becomes inevitable in all its forms. Inevitable, like a destiny, as that which desire desires not to desire but represses as the very thing (μοῖρα, ἀνάγκη, *fatum,* necessity, law) from which it derives its force and its proper possibility. The Third: we would immediately have to say, in English, *the Third One,* in order to let the

hesitation oscillate between the One and the Three. The Third One—is it someone, some One? The One of the Third—is it that which participates in or proceeds
from *both* the One *and* the Two, *or* the One *or* the Two, or again, *neither* the one
nor the other? And would this "neither the one nor the other" still be a relation, or
would it be the without-relation of the altogether other?

We know that Sallis's ceaseless meditation on time and on the tenses of time
[*sur les temps du temps*], at least on the path of thought he has followed from *Delimitations* to *Spacings, Crossings,* and *Echoes,* cannot easily be separated from a
genealogy of the imagination, and of imagination in its two senses, assuming that
the distinction between the two can ever be pure: *on the one hand,* imagination as
reproduction or production of the image (the copy, the double, the representation),
imagination that invents only by reflecting what it finds already there; and *on the
other hand,* the imagination that invents by producing what never was present,
thus hesitating between fiction and the event (and therefore prodding us to ask ourselves whether every event is not meant to risk fiction). Here one of the great questions concerning the imagination is whether its concept is totally determined,
contained, and enclosed in a history of metaphysics; or whether "on the contrary,"
as Sallis himself suggests, a "closure of metaphysics" liberates the field or the play
of imagination.[4] Naturally, that cannot be a simple alternative. There is no *one* concept of the imagination, one sole homogeneous concept that would be interior *or*
exterior to the closure of *the one sole* metaphysics, itself unique and self-identical.
We do not possess *the* concept of metaphysics and *the* concept of imagination; we
have movements and tasks, an economy of mutations and displacements, of
processes, of phases and multiple phrases that are irreducibly heterogeneous, in
which these concepts are formed—and in which they deform the nonidentity-to-
self that institutes and constitutes them. One of the *major, exemplary interests* of
the Sallisian gesture is to follow the historical thread of the lexicon as well as of
the *multiple* concepts of the imagination in order to think not only what "imagining" might mean across many languages and diverse discursive contexts (and in
the first place that context we call "philosophy"), but also what "metaphysics"
might mean, "the" metaphysical, closure or the end, self-relation, the incalculable
economy of said metaphysics, which is also to say, of said deconstruction of metaphysics. Concerning each of these terms one ought to pose again and again the
same question: Is there one of them, one concept (of metaphysics, of the imagination, for example; but also of deconstruction), one sole one, one that would be
the sole major one? Is it identifiable, and in the first place is it identical to itself,
economical, and so on?

We have only now referred to an "exemplary interest" in the double sense of
our theme: it provides us with the best example of a procedure, but there would be
other examples of an analogous demonstration in Sallis's works. Alas, the limits
of this essay will not permit me to do them justice. For these very preliminary remarks, I prefer to keep to the very essay—itself liminal but also seminal, it seems
to me—that opens *Delimitations,* "Imagination and Metaphysics." It will remain

for us, among other things, to follow there the labyrinthine threads that Sallis holds well in his hands, in order to guide us through the richness and diversity of his works.

II. DYNAMICS

Does not imagination, for metaphysics, possess right from the start all the traits of the great Third? Instead of thinking the imagination as the place or faculty of re-productive or fictive images (as εἰκασία or φαντασία), are we not better advised to determine it first of all more abstractly on the basis of this "more than two" of the "between two"? "Imagination is the great mediator," writes Sallis, describing a line of thought that would extend, let us say, from Plato to Pico della Mirandola (D 8). Pico insists on the mediating *power* of the imagination; in truth, on a power that assures imagination its *place,* its *lieu* as *milieu.* In all the senses of this term, the imagination constitutes a *milieu,* an elementary medium *in the middle,* between two. Pico della Mirandola: "Since the imagination itself is midway between in-corporeal and corporeal nature, and is the medium through which they are joined, it is difficult to grasp its nature through philosophy" (D 9).

"It is difficult. . . . " The avowal of this difficulty may take more than one form. Sallis interrogates these guises, without violence, but with an unceasing constancy and a dogged vigilance. And each time it is the destiny of metaphysics that he identifies. It thus befalls him to have recourse to the psychoanalytico-political rhetoric of *repression* [refoulement], *suppression* [repression], and *power* [pouvoir]. However, before calling them "psychoanalytical" or "political," one must continue to try to grasp their metaphysical essence. In effect, how can we forget that the code of such notions pertains first of all to the history of meta-physics itself?

Metaphysics would *at one and the same time* like to *exclude and preserve* the equivocal third represented by the imagination; it would be metaphysics by this very trait, in the contradiction of this very equivocity. This third, this imagination, is a parasite that would have to be expunged, but also a resource, a source of la-bor, a faculty or, to be precise, a *power.* As a result, metaphysics constitutes itself by dividing itself. Perhaps metaphysics is only this rapport divided in itself, this partition of itself, its self riven by the rhythmic phases of a mitosis. At the same stroke, however, the concept of its end or closure becomes problematic; it remains difficult to identify such closure on an indivisible line. Concerning these limits, and thus of the *straightforward possibility of a deconstruction* that occupies itself with a proffered limitrophy of metaphysics, Sallis's disquiet is never appeased. In my view, that disquiet remains profoundly necessary. For metaphysics divides it-self, practically impugns its proper identity, by trying to suppress or repress the very thing from which it derives its power and its rights. That is to say, translating into French a certain "empowering," metaphysics represses its own *capacitation* [habilité]. It thus turns its power back upon its own proper power. It would be a power worked by a counterpower. But a counterpower that it would bear within itself. Thus a counterpower that it itself *is* and on the basis of which it will ultimately be instituted. The origin and the end of metaphysics would be the possibility of the counterpower, its very *possibility as power* and as faculty (*Möglichkeit* and *Vermögen,* the two modes of which metaphysics is *capable,* the two modes of what remains *possible* for it, or of what renders it *possible:* metaphysics as *dynamics,* indeed, as *dynasty*). It would be necessary to think the "phantasms" of beginning and end in terms of this dynamology of the counterpower, and not the other way around. (The word *phantasm* imposes itself here perhaps by reason of its relation to the imagination as φαντασία.)

The language of *capacitation* [l'habilitation] says at one and the same time right and power [*le droit et le pouvoir*], the force of law. It first imposes itself on Sallis's remarkable reading in order to describe what appears as something we might call the Mirandolian moment, that is, the moment of Mirandola's treatise *On the Imagination,* composed in 1500, a treatise that would mark a turning (shift) from the eikastic to the phantastic imagination.

If in its Platonic moment the imagination already "both empowers and inhibits the metaphysical drive to presence" (D 7), and if, in consequence, metaphysics is at one and the same time to appropriate imagination to itself and disabuse itself of it, this trait remains unchanged in Pico della Mirandola. He calls the imagination to judgment, condemns it in some sense in the name of the law, ("we should pass sentence upon the treacherous imagination"); yet in so doing he pronounces judgment on a power of corruption that is nevertheless the philosophic power itself. He passes judgment on himself, somewhat as though he were priming, initiating "within" himself—economically—the deconstruction that one will "later" believe one can aim against him. Thus the heterogeneity to self of *the* metaphysical is announced or confirmed, its plurality or its internal limit; and, in that very step, all the paradoxes of its end or closure, the aneconomy of its economy.

Let us pursue for a moment this rhetoric of power, of *repression* or *suppression.* Here too we have two words in French (I ask the translator to keep them distinct) for two different concepts in the Freudian text: *Verdrängung, refoulement,* repression; *Unterdrückung, repression,* suppression.** This distinction shelters matters that are by no means negligible, matters in which much more is at stake than mere terminology, for what I am proposing to call a "dynamology" and for interpretation of the relationship between the metaphysics we have been discussing and this counterpower. However, here we can unfortunately only point toward what is at stake. In the Platonic text, the imagination would have a double effect: capacitating (*habiliter,* "empowering") *and* inhibiting, debilitating, or in-

---

** See the discussion in J. Laplanche and J.-B. Pontalis, *Das Vokabular der Psychoanalyse,* trans. from the French by Emma Moersch (Frankfurt am Main: Suhrkamp, 1972), pp. 570–71.—Trans.

capacitating the drive to presence. The decisive turning ("shift"), of which Pico della Mirandola gives the clearest indication in his treatise *On the Imagination,* consists in identifying a "power" of the soul, the φαντασία, and in passing from the eikastic to the phantastic imagination. The two Latin words *imaginatio* and *phantasia* translate the Greek φαντασία, while εἰκασία, as Sallis notes, remains "virtually untranslated" (D 7). In what does such a turning, such a mutation, consist? (Here Sallis has recourse several times to the word *shift*.[5])

Such a *power* would be spiritual. A spiritual nature, in imitation of God himself, would communicate it to the inferior world. A transfer of power, then, and a transfer of spirit: "For whatever the object of sensation, and that means for everything corporeal which can be perceived or felt by any sense, the object produces, insofar as it can, a likeness and image of itself, in imitation of incorporeal and spiritual nature. This spiritual nature communicates its power to the inferior world of imitation of God himself, who in his infinite goodness, spread far and wide, has established and preserves the universe." (D 7–8, citing Pico.)

The phantastic imagination no longer proceeds from the sensibility or the body. It is no longer empirical. It engages the soul and spirit. Spirit is a power; power is an affair of the soul. The phantastic imagination, elaborates Sallis, is a "power of the soul." As such, it intervenes in all acts of knowing. It is not a faculty or power among others; it is at work in *all* the remaining powers, at least in order to *aid* or *supplement* them. It renders power possible; it is *able*; it is *capable of power.* It is able to aid or supplement, serve or furnish—but with a view to reaching a *natural* destination. Here *natural* also means *theological,* which suggests that the *natural, psychic,* or *spiritual* power (for here they are all the same) is divided and is insufficient to itself. It is not what it is, is not totally present to itself. In itself it is lacking; it fails to find itself. It is able not to be able; it is able (on the basis of its) being unable. It is capable of this, liable to it. It is affected by a lack that it cannot even inscribe in itself—a lack, however, that capacitates it and causes it to emerge. Its economy as well as its dynamics lodge within themselves the (incalculable) possibility of the incalculable, and thus a singular debility, an essential impotence—one could also say, an irreducible finitude.

Is this an abusive interpretation of the words I am about to underline, that is, I myself interpreting Sallis's interpretation of Mirandola's interpretation of Plato and Aristotle? Allow me to cite a long passage from Sallis, placing an occasional accent here and there:

> . . . Pico's text has begun by reenacting the *shift* away from εἰκασία. A *new, more controlled beginning is made,* and now the authority of Aristotle is explicitly invoked. Now the constitution of the field of metaphysics, its structuring, hardly comes into question. Instead, the investigation centers on imagination—phantastic imagination—as a *power of the soul.* As such, imagination proves to be essential to all knowledge,

an *ally* that must come to the *aid* of all other human *powers* if they are
not to *fail* in the function bestowed upon them by nature. As Pico writes,
actually *shifting* at this point in his text to the word *phantasia:* "Nor
could the soul, fettered as it is to the body, opine, know, or comprehend
at all, if phantasy were not constantly to *supply* it with the images themselves." Imagination is the great *mediator:* It *receives* the impressions
of objects from the senses, retains them within itself, and renders them
purer before passing them on to the *higher powers* of the soul. As in the
Platonic texts, imagination *mediates* the ascent from the sensible,
though now it is a *mediation withdrawn* into the soul rather than one that
draws the soul into a *dyadically structured field of presence.* (D 8)

In what, then, does this "shift" consist? And what are its effects on the divisible, dyadic, mitotic structure of the metaphysical field, which is also to say, its effects on the closure of that field? The retreat ("withdrawing") by which the
imagination, returning to the inside of the soul, interiorizes itself by spiritualizing
itself, far from depriving it of its mediating *power,* on the contrary augments that
power. In exercising such power, the imagination plays a role whose significations
merit analysis in all their figurations. Such analysis is necessary if one wishes to
understand better the movement of "repression" that Sallis goes on to pursue as
the proper gesture of metaphysics. Presupposing always the connection between
soul and body, the imagination, remaining a matter of the body, becomes a "power
of the soul" to the extent that this connection of soul and body signifies a swooning, a lack, an insufficiency, the possibility of default or fault ("*to fail* in the function bestowed on them by nature") in that which is granted by nature (in truth, by
God). Yet such swooning, such finitude, marked by the passivity in sensible receptivity, is also the condition of imagination's supplementation, which furnishes
("supplies") the images, assists ("aids") and allies itself, in the double sense of alliance and alloy, with the superior powers of the soul. It is an auxiliary, but an indispensable auxiliary, a domestic; it is an essential supplement, not an accidental
one. Thus one can say that imagination is at once passive (in that it furnishes the
sensible image) and active (in that it helps to produce knowledge, proceeding from
within the soul as well as from without), and that it therefore prefigures the function of transcendental imagination such as it is described in the *Critique of Pure
Reason.* Above all, imagination recalls the nonpresence to self of the soul, this in-
carnate finitude that inscribes inadequacy into the center of the "power of the
soul," a sort of *unpower* [impuissance] that is nothing other than a division within
self-presence. Paradoxically, it is this unpower that proceeds to produce the suppressive superpower of metaphysics and that inscribes in Sallis's work or in his
"deconstructive" strategy—I would even say, in his hyperdeconstructive strategy—a necessary and recurrent motif, namely, that of a metaphysics whose limit,
end, or border is less a line of circumscription than a labor of antagonistic forces

traversing the "inside" (which is thus no longer an "inside") of the metaphysics that is under discussion. At bottom, if one accelerates the movement a bit, it all tends to render problematic the very name "metaphysics" itself, down to the presumed identity of its very concept.

That, in short, would be the Sallisian operation. It would constitute merely one example among others: broaching a procedure of the deconstruction of metaphysics, which by way of a certain genealogy of the imagination leads us by assured steps toward a radical dislocation of the very identity of metaphysics, an identity that certain types of deconstruction at least provisionally seem to presuppose. From this point on, it is a certain idea of deconstruction that is at stake, perhaps "deconstruction itself," as if such a thing existed that could claim for itself the stable identity of a project. It is Deconstruction Itself that would in turn find itself destabilized, disseminated, delivered over to its precarious, ruinous existence, to itself as a *ruin,* indeed, to its impossibility, *its possibility as impossibility.* (That is to say, I am often tempted to suggest, deconstruction is delivered over "to itself," its possibility being confounded with the experience of its impossibility, that is, with the very experience of the impossible in general: of the impossible as unpower or im-potence.) Let the avowed and compulsive enemies of Deconstruction Itself take note. Let them rejoice over it too soon, or suffer disquiet on account of it once again: in the thoughtful and rigorous vigilance of John Sallis there is more menace held in intense suspense ("hovering") over such a Deconstruction, if it exists, than in the more or less journalistic aggressions to which, it is true, more professors than professional journalists are surrendering themselves.

How does this question of possibility, such as we have only now broached it, relate to that of power?

It is by reason of the impotence of philosophy, of knowledge or of metaphysics, that the imagination is "empowering" for it. ("Philosophy itself, empowered by imagination . . . ," " . . . for imagination, empowering knowledge . . . ," "His [Pico's] metaphysics of imagination, i.e., his metaphysical theory regarding the nature of imagination, belongs to metaphysics, to metaphysics as empowered by imagination . . . ," and so on [D 9].)

However, metaphysics, "the" metaphysical (and from now on its identity is for us but a fiction or a simulacrum), as though it wanted to efface the signs of this unpower and this finitude, "suppresses" or "represses" the very thing that supplements it. It is nothing but this suppressive repression. All the turnings ("shifts") of its history, that is, of the constitution of its field, are (relatively) specific moments or (relatively) original determinations of this "repression" and thus of the exercise of this counterpower (of power against power).

Let us try to isolate and underline a paradox on the "inside," if one can say so, of this history of suppressive repression. It will perhaps allow us to perceive more sharply the originality of the Sallisian approach along the edges of the end— or rather the "ends"—of metaphysics, on the very verge of its confines. It is a matter of Kant's situation. Apparently, at least, the Kantian moment, along with every-thing that is inherited from that moment, is defined by a double gesture that, in truth, reverts to the same: passage from the eikastic to the phantastic imagination and release of the suppressive repression of the imagination. Prior to him, from Plato to Pico, the "repression" continues to work its effects in the direction of an imagination that at once "empowers" and "corrupts" philosophy. For Pico, "meta-physics itself is genuinely realized, is genuinely metaphysics itself, only in that do-main in which imagination is repressed" (D 13). To be sure, the quasi-political dimension of the figure (*refoulement* as "repression"), this energetic connotation of the act of power (at once ἐνέργεια and δύναμις: Sallis often speaks of a "dy-namics" [D 3, 9, 11, 12, 13, 14]) reflects Pico's rhetoric. The latter privileges the "power" of the soul, inasmuch as such power can "dominate" the phantastic imag-ination. The intellect can and must in this way protect its "domain," by grace of a sort of military or police power, after having pulled back into its palace or citadel. It is also a matter of exercising an authority or a force of law, of a territorial or re-gional dominion. I emphasize the following words: "Pico outlines this *domain* in his conception of *intellectus,* that highest *power* of the soul, the *power* by which one can contemplate those purely intelligible things that are absolutely removed from the *region* of sense. Within this *domain* of intellectual contemplation, one is able, in Pico's telling phrase, to '*dominate* phantasy.' He continues: 'When the soul has withdrawn itself into the intellect, there, as in its own protected *palace* and enclosed *citadel,* it reposes and is perfected' " (D 13).

(Let it be said in passing, and parenthetically, that one could show how the Sallisian meditation on the imagination and its role with regard to metaphysics also thematizes this foyer of δύναμις: power, possibility, puissance, force, ca-pacitation, empowering, suppression, etc.—this foyer of potential δύναμις or of δύναμις in act (ἐνέργεια). As an operative concept in the genealogy of the imag-ination, δύναμις (with its entire semantic network) is *also,* virtually, potentially, a thematic concept. Sallis's entire discourse can *also* be read as a discourse *on* the *possible, power, force,* and so on. For the moment, let us draw only a provisional and general consequence, a formalizing consequence: the opposition between an operative and a thematic concept (such as Fink, for example, has proposed) per-tains in only a limited way to all deconstructive genealogy. The quasi-systematic connection of a network causes every operative or lateral (precisely, potential) concept to play an essential and indispensable role in the functioning of the dis-positive—here, for example, the concept δύναμις—and thus can come to occupy the determining position, the thetic or thematic position. Any concept or word whatsoever can assume the function of the guiding thread, or, if one prefers this figure, the function of the deconstructive lever, thus receiving the privilege that is here accorded to the imagination. It is enough if we imagine, if we prove the imag-ination by putting it to the test [*faire preuve d'imagination*], as one would say in French. The privilege accorded in a deconstructive operation to this or that concept, word, or syntagma is always "contextual" and "strategic." As with every privilege that one accords, in order to privilege whatever it may be, that of the quasi-guiding thread or of the provisional lever is subjected to the law of singularity. No rational and universal justification can be given for it, argued of it, demonstrated with regard to it, outside such contextuality. Such contextuality remains strategic, singular, and mobile, hence relatively and provisionally stabilizable. One of the redoubtable consequences of this would be what Sallis will say of the imagination, of the name *imagination,* to wit, that "perhaps" it is "the meaning of Being" (E 97). *Perhaps* is doubtless the most important word here. Yet what happens when one says "perhaps" [*peut-être*] with regard to the name of being [*être*]? We shall come back to this.)

Even though Pico performs this "shift away" from εἰκασία to φαντασία, thus distancing himself from Plato, he repeats a movement of "repression" that was *already at work* in Plato—"at work," that is to say, already active, as is always the case, under the *double form of force and play:* "The movement of repression is also in force in the Platonic texts—or rather, one might say, at *play* in them, since it is rarely traced in those texts without being set within a dialogical play of the utmost subtlety and irony" (D 13). This alliance of force and play always commands Sallis's attention; yet it also imprints a Nietzschean aspect on his thought. To be sure, Sallis is not "Nietzschean," supposing that such a hypothesis would make any sense at all. However, his rapport with Nietzsche is, let us say, of a remarkable intensity and lucidity. And in playing with homonymy, my title alluded precisely to this crossing of Nietzschean motifs, from the values that I nickname "dynamological"—intensity, tension (tense, taut), force, and play—up to the discreetly polemical tension of a philosophy that goes to war only on doves' feet.

The dynamics of suppressive repression are thus apparently coextensive with all metaphysics, eliding themselves with the very exercise of its power: power-against-power, which presupposes "within" itself a difference of force. As for this constitutive co-extensivity of metaphysics and the suppression of the imagination, it seems that Sallis never doubts it. If Platonic subtlety and irony could indeed once again complicate things, they tend to disappear in the aftermath. Suppression asserts itself ever more seriously, and without folds or feints: "In the discourse woven by the history of metaphysics, however, such subtlety and irony tend to disappear more irrevocably, to disappear in favor of a massive repression of imagination. It is a matter of *stabilizing* the otherwise dynamic relation between imagination and metaphysics" (D 14, my emphasis).

I have just now underlined one word, perhaps forcing matters a bit. Yet I continue to believe that there is no reading that does not force things, the question of the *fitting* forcing of them remaining open for essential reasons. I have therefore underlined this allusion to stabilization ("stabilizing"): if the presumed unity of metaphysics is only a conflict of powers, of forces and suppressive counterforces, then this movement has neither beginning nor end, knows no definitive interruption, no trenchant rupture, but only moments of *more or less stable* stabili*zation*. In contrast to stability, which one can always take to be essential or natural, a stabili*zation* takes shape only against the backdrop of an instability or a destabilization that is always possible: not simply a pure chaos but a chaoti*zation*, if I may say so, a becoming or re-becoming chaotic whose menace (which can also assume the form of chance or opportunity) must always announce itself. Such an announcement remains without any assignable status. The concept of stability (*sto, stare, stabilis,* stance, station, etc.) cannot be dissociated from a certain semantics of being, inasmuch as being stays and stands.[6] Stabilization against the background of destabilization puts every ontological assurance in question. The radical in-stability against whose background (without ground) this history of suppression emerges (as power against power) could no longer "be" an instability as a movement of being (as stance or estance, existence or resistance, etc.); rather, it would be "being" and "being thought" as an un-being [*in-être*], an un-presence, a nonbeing that would no longer even "be" absence, nihilation, negation of being or the stance. It is toward this limit that I would like to orient my reflections on the imagination of an *autre temps* (time), as of an *autre temps du verbe* (tense), of a *temps* that not only would no longer be the sole modification of a present now (that has become, i.e., come to be past—or that is to come, i.e., future) but would in fact *remain without any relation at all* to the presence of the present or to any stance or estance of being in general.

In what way does this thought of the possible, of power and counterpower, get us under way in such a direction—which for all the reasons that announce themselves here cannot be a direction, the rectitude of a way or a method, much less the orthothetic or orthoteleological address of a destination? Why, at bottom, is this a "dynamics" that tends to exceed metaphysics all the while making it possible as and within the horizon of a history of being? In what way is "force," as force of imagination and imagination of force, ultimately the very thing that withdraws from being, which is to say, also from nonbeing?

The joint history of metaphysics and imagination would play itself out within, and revolve about the axis of, the "dynamic" exercise of a power or possibility as "repression" (here I use the English word, in order thereby to associate the values of repression, *Verdrängung,* and suppression, *Unterdrückung*), that is to say, of a counterpower that pluralizes apriori within a difference of force the very identity of that which it institutes.

Naturally, if the interpretation proposed here always risks forcing things, it nevertheless ought to take into account *two indices.* On the one hand, it would force matters on the subject of a discourse that is on the subject of force itself (Sallis's discourse, I insist once again, is here a dynamics, more precisely, a dynamology). Here it is a matter of a discourse for which the difference of forces remains an ultimate reference, authorizing no metalanguage concerning it. On the other hand, with all the ambiguity that English confers on it, preserving some trace of the passage of psychoanalysis, even if psychoanalysis is not mentioned thematically, the word "repression" recurs throughout "Imagination and Metaphysics."

Let us take up several examples in a movement of Sallis's very complex and, as it were, spiral argumentation. It is still this same text, "Imagination and Metaphysics," that occupies us here, a text whose dominant code remains very much that of power ("power," "empowering," "dynamics," etc.). On the one hand, one might well gain the impression that a suppression of imagination remains at work and stabilizes itself from Plato to Pico, in order later to be lifted by Kant. To be sure, that is not a mere appearance; yet to hold fast to such a stabilization would be to simplify matters. In the first place, the Kantian "shift" preserves "a trace of the dynamics that governed the Platonic conception in its relation to metaphysics and to the field of metaphysics" (D 11). For the Kantian imagination, like the Platonic eikastic imagination, represents to intuition an object that is not present. It therefore remains to this extent a faculty that is bound up with the possibility of presenting the absent, that which at once "empowers and inhibits the metaphysical drive to presence" (D 11). Of course, this *double law,* which concerns the relationship between the presence and absence of the present, cannot but imply an ontological interpretation of time. In this sense, Kant confirms and stabilizes the Platonic "repression." However, on the other hand, Kantian critique situates the imagination (as faculty or power, *Einbildungskraft*) in a field that is no longer "simply governed" by the drive to presence in its intelligible or originary form, the form of the thing-in-itself, which assures classical metaphysics its τέλος. To this extent the "repression" of the Platonic sort, as it was relayed or mediated by the phantasiological displacement introduced by Pico, would be found to be alleviated by Kantian critique: "The field of metaphysics as reconstituted in the *Critique of Pure Reason* is a field in which the play of presence and absence, the play of self-revelation and self-withholding, the play of imagination, is released from that repression that would subordinate it in the end to the ideal of sheer revelation, of pure essence" (D 11). Such suspension of the suppressive dynamics corresponds to an appropriation of the imagination. The latter is no longer held at a distance by Kant, nor will it be by the great English Romantics, or by Schelling, who will identify it with the very movement of philosophical reason.

However, the analysis does not stop there. For, in truth, this alleviation of the suppression, this reappropriation of the imagination in the *Critique of Pure Reason,* finds itself in turn limited and once again put into question by practical reason. Capacitating and rehabilitated, the empowering power of the imagination finds itself in its turn disqualified and *excluded* from the "domain," in other words, from the dynasty, from the field of power that is practical reason. This time the suppression takes the form of "exclusion," as the following passage (the underlinings are mine) indicates: "However much imagination, extending between sensible and intelligible, can *empower* theoretical reason and *make it possible* to delimit a metaphysics of nature, imagination is, on the other hand, that *power* which, perhaps most of all, must be rigorously *excluded* from the *domain* of reason's practical employment" (D 12). In other words, such an "exclusion" repeats and confirms the classical suppression (from Plato to Pico). The "dynamics of the relation" between metaphysics and imagination remains the same: "However much imagination is appropriated to theoretical reason, to the metaphysics of nature, it is with equal rigor excluded, distanced, from practical reason, from the metaphysics of morals. For critical metaphysics as a whole, the dynamics of the relation between imagination and metaphysics remains essentially the same as that traced in the texts of Plato and Pico" (D 12).

Thus what remains permanent and self-identical ("the same") across the turnings or mutations ("shifts") whose importance Sallis never seeks to minimize is the possibility of stabilizing or restabilizing the dynamic relation between metaphysics and imagination. Such stabilization, which I earlier suggested rises against a background without ground, coming to stand in truth in the abyss of an instability that is no longer subsumed under the agency of being, compels a question: How can this stabilization now be dissociated from both the imagination and the law of suppression (power-against-power) that scans its entire history? Before we begin to imagine where such an hypothesis or question might lead us, let us assure ourselves, reading Sallis's text quite closely, of what binds together the dynamics of repression (whether exercised or alleviated), stabilization (without being), and imagination as history (the divided, hence divisible history) of "the" metaphysical as such. Let us note at the outset the necessary connection between this dynamology and a strategy, a calculus of the relation of forces and of the opportunity for moments of stabilization, the equivalents of an epoch (ἐποχή) during which suppressive violence is, as it were, *suspended* ("hovering," I would say, forcing a bit perhaps Sallis's intent). Sallis's strategy is ultimately regulated (such would be my hypothesis) by the moment at which the strategy is suspended, without ceasing altogether to exercise its effects, but *in the end coming to appear,* coming to appear as what it is or will have been, as such, *as* strategy. Is a strategy disarmed when it exhibits itself? Nothing is less certain than that.

> One can perhaps discern this moment most distinctly, most thoroughly separated, in reference to the specific form which the dynamics assumes in critique. In the Kantian conception of practical reason there is operative not only a distancing of metaphysics from imagination but also a rigorous stabilizing of that distance, a setting of practical reason in a domain in which it would be essentially free of imagination. . . . That moment of the metaphysical project that I want now to make explicit can thus be characterized as a certain *stabilizing* of the otherwise *dynamic* relation between imagination and metaphysics. It is a matter of positing a refuge beyond the play of imagination, a refuge in which pure presence would be protected from the threat of imagination. It is a matter of

decisively limiting the *dynamic* relation between imagination and metaphysics by means of a repression of imagination. This moment is constantly in force in Pico's text and is precisely what allows him to pass
so lightly over the positive role which imagination plays in metaphysics.
He can pass beyond this role because metaphysics itself is genuinely realized, is genuinely metaphysics itself, only in that domain in which
imagination is repressed. Pico outlines this domain in his conception of
intellectus, that highest power of the soul, the power by which one can
contemplate those purely intelligible things that are absolutely removed
from the region of sense. . . . This movement of repression is also in
force in the Platonic texts. . . . (D 12–13, my emphases)

And after having marked the continuity of this suppression, from Aristotle to
Hegel, right up to the *end* or *closure* of metaphysics (these two terms, *end* and *closure,* here seem synonymous), Sallis insists on this "drive" or pulsion (*Trieb*). This
word, like that of "repression," and *a fortiori* an expression such as "return of the
repressed," continues to signal in the direction of a certain lexicon of psychoanalysis, even though that term, like the name of Freud, is (or so it seems to me)
never pronounced in the book.

Metaphysics as such is drive to presence, drive to ground, and the repression of imagination belongs integrally to it. And yet, I have deliberately kept this moment detached from a certain field, a field in which
obtains the dynamic relation between imagination and metaphysics. I
have kept it detached because it is precisely the moment that gets detached at the end of metaphysics, in that closure of metaphysics announced most forcefully by Nietzsche and analyzed most thoroughly in
recent Continental thought. In this end, this closure, that strategy by
which the dynamic relation between imagination and metaphysics was
stabilized, that strategy by which imagination was finally repressed,
comes to show itself precisely as a *strategy.* The closure of metaphysics
is precisely the emptying of every refuge in which pure intelligibility
might find protection from the threat of imagination. The end of metaphysics is, then, the release of imagination into the entire field, the return of the repressed. (D 14–15)

We must proceed with patience here, in order to analyze the paradox of a
strategy. This strategy is at once, on the one hand, that of metaphysics itself, as we
have only now read, inasmuch as metaphysics suppresses the imagination, and, on
the other hand, the strategy of John Sallis, treating imagination in terms of the
"return of the repressed." An intricate strategy is indispensable on his part, and he
expresses this quite clearly ("And yet, I have deliberately kept this moment detached . . . ," etc.). For if he were content with a simple gesture, the conclusion of

the demonstration would be the exact inverse of the one that is quite clearly under investigation. In effect, if "the release of the imagination" as "return of the repressed" were the accomplishment or the liberation of a metaphysical consciousness, a consciousness of metaphysics disengaged at last from all "repression" (*refoulement* or *Verdrängung,* and suppression [*repression*] or *Unterdrückung*), then this would be the triumph of the "drive to presence"; it would be that teleological plentitude precisely in whose name the "repression" was exercised. Because that is out of the question, it must be that the "return of the repressed" is not fully accomplished. A certain repression must continue to exercise itself; in short, there is no pure end of metaphysics, but only a new stabilization of the suppression and a new structure of the metaphysical field. For the imagination, thus "released," must no longer respond either to the "drive to presence" or to its symmetrical contrary, which would be turned in the direction of simple absence. The new stabilization must no longer be ordered by the τέλος of being, as stance of the presenc(ing) of the present or of the presenc(ing) of absence. Once liberated, hypothetically, from metaphysical "repression," imagination can and should no longer be *the same,* have the *same status* as the one assigned it by the metaphysics we have been discussing. Should not its relation to time—for example, to the present, and to the presence of the present—be altogether other?

It is the disquiet of this question that I believe I can sense in Sallis's "strategy" the moment it has taken note of the "return of the repressed." Indeed, Sallis adds: "And yet, the field does not remain the same; it is not, as I pretended earlier, merely the field of metaphysics without its final moment. For that final moment, the τέλος of originary presence, is precisely what orients the field of metaphysics. Once that moment is detached, the field is no longer simply a field of presence, a field oriented to presence" (D 15).

"*No longer simply* a field of presence." Yet "no longer simply" something altogether other. Well, then, what?

III. TOPIC

If I have no answer to this question, it is no doubt a weakness on my part. Yet it is also for another reason, one which, I believe, is more interesting. The response to this question, once put in motion and set to work, can only be the singular deployment of the Sallisian field of writing in all its intensity, the relatively stabilizable signature (under erasure, if you like) of John Sallis himself. Not his thesis, but a tension and an intensity—along with the *temps* of his signature. Why that?

There is a thetic response in all these texts, to be sure; a thesis of John Sallis; a coherent ensemble of pronouncements presented as the definition of this new "field" that is "no longer simply a field of presence, a field oriented to presence." This thetic response is readable in, among other places, the two final pages of

"Imagination and Metaphysics." It is very well defined there, even if it takes the figure of suspense: the *figurative* model will be "the flight of fancy, the flight of the dove"; it is the instruction, the conclusion in the form of the lesson we ought to grasp ("we must learn"): we ought to learn to "*hover* between heaven and earth." The conceptual and less figurative form of this thesis confirms the gesture of *The Gathering of Reason,* and not only the article "The Gathering of Reason" in *Delimitations,* where, as he does more than once, Sallis puts in play and, if one may say so, analyzes in a thematic way the phenomenon of his signature or of a supplement of signature (D 29 ff.). I am referring to the concept of gathering, reassembling [*rassemblement*[7]], and of gathering by *mixture* [mixité†], the mixture that characterizes the moments of the Kantian subversion ("encroachment," "transgression," "abyss"), moments in terms of which Sallis thinks the limit of metaphysics. Now, the concept of gathering or of participative mixture is very much the most decisive response, offered again and again, and in thetic form, to the question as to what this *field* that is no longer "simply a field of presence" can be. Further, the very concept of the "field," which Sallis never renounces, never even dreams of renouncing, as it seems to me (but why? that is a question I would like to ask him), implies in the final analysis that the strongest force in the conflict or in the differences of forces is a force of gathering; and that, in the end, force and force-of-gathering are at bottom synonymous (but why? why not the contrary just as well? why not force of dissociation, dissociation in the gathering, or gathering in and of disjunction?—that is a series of questions I would like to ask him). A gathering, here, this time, of "traces or residues" of what metaphysics has dissociated; a gathering in view of what Sallis does not hesitate to name—as though it were a systematic project or a theoretical program—a "logic of imagination" to come:

> More precisely (perhaps), it would be a matter of taking the directional, oriented character and the reiterably dyadic character of the field as traces or residues of what metaphysics began by calling λόγος and εἰκασία and ended by calling reason and imagination. It would be a matter of venturing, beyond the closure of metaphysics, to reassemble these moments which metaphysics from its beginning has set apart. *Writing under erasure,* attending to the subtlety and risk of the move, one might then broach the demands of a logic of imagination. (D 15, my emphases)

This imagination or its "logic," and no one will have demonstrated this better than Sallis, is destined to be borne beyond the dyad and the opposition

---

†*Mixité* normally means coeducation (the mix of genders in a school) or comprehensive education (the mix of programs of study).—TR.

presence/absence, with all that this opposition entails (in particular, "logic" and "ontology"). That is the very thing that essentially prevents these pronouncements from presenting themselves in the stable presence of a thesis, or from gathering themselves into a logic that is presentable in the form of a program, project, or blue print. The *temps* of this "gathering" must be altogether other, if it takes place at all. It pertains to a strategy of signature, a strategy whose events form an open series, at once concatenated and discontinuous. There is always more than one event; each one is divided in its signature. This originary multiplicity forms what I have attempted to define elsewhere, with regard to Levinas, as *seriature*.†† Such an open series of events proceeds from neither presence nor absence, from neither substance nor subject, thus from neither theme nor thesis, but from the intensity of a "*temps*" (*time* and *tense*) that neither the logic of the dyad nor even perhaps that of the mix or of participation would know how to circumscribe, prescribe, describe, or scribe. Perhaps not even the logic of bastardy.

Why is the motif of bastardy particularly important here? Because on it converge the questions of, on the one hand, legitimacy, of the name or of signature and, on the other, the mix of participation.[8] (That is to say, the mix of that which is *neither one nor the other* while being *both one and the other,* in this impure place of two filiations whose convergence can only be in some sense normal and acknowledged.) One recalls the many Platonic figures of bastardy.[9] And Sallis refers (in a manner that in my view is decisive) to what Kant calls "a bastard of imagination."[10] If one holds to the thetic (or, if you prefer, semantic and conceptual) form of the problem of bastardy, such as it is repeated here, the oscillation would remain in suspense between a bastardy of mediative participation, of mixture (μέθεξις) between two (between the one and the two) and a bastardy whose third would be radically heterogeneous with regard to the two originary terms or to the couple from which it *seems* to issue, even if illegitimately. Such a filiation would in truth be a fiction to which one would have to adhere for reasons of "logic," "dialectic," or rhetorical, thetic, or thematic "presentation."

In order to give at least a quasi-paradigm of this law or of this place of thought,[11] we could once again invoke Plato, who remains an inexhaustible source, especially for Sallis. And in Plato there are at least three instances of the *matrix* that one must be able to distinguish.

1. There is first of all the enormous issue of participation (μέθεξις) and of interweaving (συμπλοκή), that is to say, of dialectic itself. Here it is each time a matter of what *is* without being anything other than what it is, but in the mode of both/and, the mode of crossing.

2. Let us insist even more on another discursive matrix, the one that opens the entire Plotinian, Neo-Platonic tradition, namely, what is called *negative theology.*

---

††See the notions of *série, sérialité, and sériature* in "En ce moment même dans cet ouvrage me voici," in *Psyché: Inventions de l'autre* (Paris: Galilée. 1987), pp. 159–202, esp. pp. 162, 165, 175, 180, and 189 ff.—TR.

This matrix is not necessarily or intrinsically bound up with the first (dialectic and participation) in Plato: it is the matrix of the Good as ἐπέκεινα τῆς οὐσίας. It can interrupt dialectic, participation, and even ontology. One recalls the role it has played through Heidegger and Levinas. Sallis refers to it more than once as the very thing that already in Plato marks what is in excess with regard to metaphysics. But an excess that is also hyperbole itself, the *nec plus ultra* of metaphysics, when it attains the summit of its accomplishment (already with the Greeks). It is thus that with regard to Dionysos, to the "without measure" (*das Maßlose*) or the abyss, and echoing the marvelous chapter on *das Maßlose* that opens *Crossings,* Sallis outlines a paradox by associating the figure of Dionysos to the movement that carries or transports one ἐπέκεινα τῆς οὐσίας. The Dionysian figure, which "could be considered the most perfectly metaphysical, the original *an sich,* so compactly an original, so thoroughly *an sich* as to withhold itself from direct disclosure in an image," is also the figure that exceeds metaphysics. It thus gives us to think that metaphysics bears in itself its own excess, if we can put the matter this way, carrying its limit (if such a thing is possible), and that also means carrying its transgression within itself, in an inside that is therefore its own outside. It is the effect of "resounding": "And yet, by virtue of this very withdrawing, it can also be considered an excessive figure, one that exceeds the circuit of metaphysics, a figure in excess of metaphysics, resounding from beyond closure, ἐπέκεινα τῆς οὐσίας."[12]

Elsewhere, in a different context, the beyond-being (ἐπέκεινα τῆς οὐσίας) is evoked in the neighborhood of a question that cannot remain foreign to that of the signature. And we could even add: the signature as writing (no signature without writing), as writing (of) the "I" (no signature that would refrain from saying, posing, or marking "I," "as for me, I . . ."), an "I" whose very being can be written (and thus signed, represented even by a proper name) only under erasure: "And one would need to be attentive to the recoil of the said upon the saying, crossing out the 'is,' writing it under erasure. One would need to write: the I is beyond being—thereby contesting while also confirming what Fichte says about the word 'being,' that without it 'no language would be possible'."[13]

We have only now experienced the necessity of such passage beyond being in the form of a movement that would be borne beyond opposition, beginning with the opposition of presence and absence. Erasure limns its graphic and spatial emblem: neither present nor absent, at once present and absent. Now, this is very much the power assigned by the tradition, the tradition that Sallis has so powerfully interrogated, to the imagination. What, then, is the relation between the motif of the ἐπέκεινα τῆς οὐσίας, the imagination, and *espacement* (spacing)? In order to approach slowly the question that I would also like to leave in suspense here, let us first recall the series of rigorous shifts [*glissements*] by which Sallis sets in place, if one can put it this way, the links in the chain of an equation—more or less metonymic and more or less stabilized in its flow: imagination = ἐπέκεινα τῆς οὐσίας = spacing. In order to approach this question, let us first refer, among other places, to what is said about Fichte in "Hoverings" (in *Spacings*). In the course of a fine analysis, the very concept of "hovering" takes up the position of a translation with regard to a certain Fichtean *Schweben,* to wit, the suspensive oscillation of the power of the imagination (*das Vermögen der Einbildungskraft*), and of the productive imagination, which is creative (*schaffenden*) and not merely re-productive (thus eikastic). This oscillation is borne beyond all oppositions and therefore operates as a kind of spacing, the interval between two, in the middle of two, as the very spacing of truth, Sallis goes so far as to say. He cites Fichte: "Imagination is a power that hovers [*schwebt*] in the middle between determination and nondetermination, between finite and infinite" (S 64). The analysis he goes on to propose concerning Fichte's project leads him quite naturally, among other places, to this definition of the imagination as "power of spacing": "Imagination is the power of spacing those oppositions that can be neither dissolved nor eliminated from theoretical knowledge. Imagination is the spacing of truth" (S 64). In the serenity of its daring, the force of this formulation gives us much to think about. In particular concerning the essence (without essence, beyond essence) of a *power,* of the power of which this imagination consists. One may ask not only what is, what *can* be or *may* be [peut *être*], what ought to be, must be, should be [doit *être*] a power that *can* and that "empowers" beyond being; yet also, and here at one stroke, whether this power of imagination, as the "power of spacing" the oppositions, proceeds from "spacing" (spacing being itself a power, a puissance, a δύναμις), or whether it is at the origin of spacing. All of which reverts to asking about the relationship of genealogy or of predication between potency and spacing. No less remarkable here is the thesis concerning the theoretical—"theoretical knowledge": it is defined as that which the power of spacing is unable to attain, in order there to dissolve or eliminate the conceptual oppositions that all knowing requires—limits of the imagination, limits of its power of spacing, limits also of deconstruction as suspension of oppositions. A limit, ultimately, of the imagination as "the spacing of truth." This limit is not negative. First of all because it renders possible cognition, theory, determination, meaning, moments of enlightenment, and so on. Then it is this limit, to wit, an impossibility, that gives us most to think about when it comes to power or possibility. And deconstruction too—contrary to what is often said about it—is the experience of an impossibility.

   Such would be the stakes of a *reinscription* of the imagination such as Sallis is attempting. Those stakes are nowhere better played out, it seems to me, than in the "perhaps" that at the outset of "Imagination—the Meaning of Being?" once again suspends the "first move toward reinscribing imagination":

   Is the meaning of Being not, then, a matter of imagination? Is it not imagination that in its flight opens to the shining of the beautiful? Is it not imagination that in its hovering spans the gigantic space of *sense,* thus gathering now what would previously have been called the horizon, the meaning of Being? Is imagination not precisely this gathering? Is imagination not the meaning of Being?

Must imagination not prove to be the meaning of Being once phenomenology is thought through to its end, to an end that, in more than one way, exceeds the project of fundamental ontology?

Perhaps. (E 97)

To be sure, all these questions remain in suspense, notably those that concern the oscillating relation between "power" and "spacing" in the imagination as "power of spacing." Yet must not one say rather that they give us to think about what it is that constitutes their strange element, the very suspension of "hovering" itself—concerning which we cannot decide if it is here a figure or a concept—whether animal, human, or divine—between sky and earth, in a site without repose, within and without a strange habitation, neither nomadic nor sedentary: ἐπέκεινα τῆς οὐσίας? "The circle(s) of reason would, then, have been redrawn as the displaced circling of imagination, withdrawn from being and ground, drawn into the spacing of oppositions. Philosophy would end—or be denied an end—with imagination hovering ἐπέκεινα τῆς οὐσίας, hovering between heaven and earth, a dove" (S 66).

3. We invoked three Platonic matrices. The third would have for its name χώρα, the singular place of this place (after economy and dynamics, topology), and this spacing concerning which *Timaeus* tells us or at least suggests some things that I will here simplify to an extreme.[14]

A. χώρα is a third, or a third term, which seems to participate in two others (sensible and intelligible, copy and model, icon and paradigm), but which could also equally as well be neither the one nor the other.

B. One can therefore speak of it only in images, tropes, and metaphors—in accord with an imagination concerning which it would be difficult to know whether it is eikastic or phantastic; and concerning which it would even be difficult to know whether it is still imagination in general; and even whether it provides a place for something like "images" in the rhetorical sense of tropes, metaphors, and so on; and among those ventured figures one finds, quite close to the matrix, precisely that of the nurse. Return to the dream, then, the dream that we never abandoned, for still "we are imagining that we are dreaming." We recall that Plato says of χώρα that we perceive it as in a dream (*Timaeus* 52 b–c).

C. From the moment there is nothing but images, and from the moment there is no image for χώρα, the power of imagination as "power of spacing" finds in χώρα (that is, in the place of espacement itself) at once its ultimate resource and its ultimate limit, its condition of possibility *and* of impossibility, its possibility as impossibility, its power as un-power.

And yet why does not Plato say that χώρα is ἐπέκεινα τῆς οὐσίας? Why is that so difficult to say and to think?

Everything seems to come to pass as if "hovering" received its suspense, not only as power of imagination ἐπέκεινα τῆς οὐσίας, but also *between* this power of the imagination, as imagination, and the singularity of the place called χώρα. For although neither the one nor the other is any given thing, they will never be "the same thing." Whether one determines it still as the Good (Plato), as the One (Plotinus), as the pole of the transcendence of Dasein (Heidegger), or as the movement toward the altogether other (Levinas), what is said to be ἐπέκεινα τῆς οὐσίας continues to orient a space, a "field," as Sallis would perhaps say (whether a field of ethics or of politics, of existence or of historicity, of humanity, teleology, or theology matters little here); it will never possess the untamed nature or the virginity that is at once a-human and a-theological of the χώρα. The altogether other, as χώρα (the third as neither the one nor the other) does not yet possess the phenomenality of any visage, nor can it ever have such a visage, neither that of God nor that of man. That it gives place by withdrawing from that place, from names, visages, images—therein consists the least puissant and yet most invulnerable of powers.

What χώρα eludes, beyond the beyond of being, is everything that, presupposing it, can only be posed, inscribed, or received in it. Beyond all the pairs, in particular that of presence and absence, and thus beyond a *temps* interpreted in terms of the pair presence/absence, what is thus posed in the presupposition cannot be a thesis or a theme. It can at the very most stabilize itself for a time, according to an *autre temps,* in the name or in the concept.

I am grateful to John Sallis because he has helped me approach the nonproximity of this place that renders at once possible and impossible everything that comes to situate (pose, inscribe, receive) itself in it. In the vicinities of this place, where it is opened and offered, granted in accord with an *autre temps* (time and tense), granted in an accord that is to be found at one and the same time in the registers of the gift and of grammatical writing—it is there that I believe I can descry, receiving it also as a present, but beyond all thesis, the *rare intensity* of such a signature.

CHAPTER FOUR

IMADGINATION

John Llewelyn

> Is imagination not the meaning of being?
> —John Sallis

I

Might imagination be congenitally mad? Might it be intrinsically out of its mind? Imagination, madness, and the relation between the two are topics to which the writings of John Sallis repeatedly return. A biographical note to one of his essays states that his recent work "ventures a recovery of imagination within the contemporary context of deconstruction and post-Heideggerian thinking."[1] But a book of his published ten years earlier has as its epigraph the following sentence from Rousseau's *Émile:* "C'est l'imagination qui étend pour nous la mesure des possibles soit en bien soit en mal, et qui par conséquent excite et nourrit les désirs par l'espoir de les satisfaire" (GRix). We may well wonder what measure the imagination could be discovered to extend to us when we learn from the page facing the one on which this epigaph is printed that a chapter in the book is headed "Reason, Imagination, Madness." We know that we shall still be asking this question when we take up *Spacings—of Reason and Imagination,* a book whose date of publication is between those of the other two works by Sallis so far mentioned, and glance ahead to that book's end, if it is one, where, in a chapter entitled "Ending(s)," the author risks wondering "whether imagination can detach itself from presence so disruptively as to exceed being regathered into the circle of self-presentation. Can imagination be so disruptively detached as to be in excess of spirit?" Must we follow in the circle of §408 of the *Encyclopaedia,* Sallis asks, where Hegel deals with cases of imagination apparently afflicted by madness, *Verrücktheit,* either by excluding them from psychology as incurable physiological disease, hence no threat to the totalizing power of rationality, or by including them as only apparently unamenable to reason but in fact susceptible to treatment by rational measures such as that of the acting cure which Hegel describes thus:

If someone imagines he is dead, don't tell him he must be mad; humour him rather, as did the person who took him in his coffin to where there lay also in a coffin a third person who, acting as though he has been in the realm of death long enough to know what to expect, after a while sat up and partook of food. The first man was induced to follow his example and consequently was cured.

Sallis wonders whether this story illustrates too dismissive an estimation of the wonder in which philosophy is supposed to begin. He wonders whether, against Hegel, there may be a residue of wonder which philosophy cannot dismiss and which cannot be put into words or concepts as readily as the insane "dead" person in Hegel's parable is spirited into sane life. May there not be a reserve of sensible images which, without being alienated from reason as non-rational or irrational, resist being raised from the dark pit of unconscious memory (*Erinnerung*) to be commemorated publicly in, as it were the pyramid of a universal sign?

Against Hegel, in allowing this question to "multiply" (S 155), Sallis must be on guard against "against." In the concern he shares with Nietzsche to give sensibility its due, he will not want to expose himself to the trap Heidegger says Nietzsche sometimes falls into of only confirming Platonist grading when he describes his overturning of Platonism as an *Umdrehung* that stands Plato's statements on their heads. Platonism can be superseded only by *Herausdrehung,* a twisting free. That this is so becomes clear to Heidegger's Nietzsche only when at the end of his life, like his Empedocles at the edge of the abyss, Nietzsche becomes mad. It becomes clear to Sallis's Nietzsche even before *The Birth of Tragedy,* in the birth of tragedy from the crossing of Dionysus and Apollo (C 5). Reading Sallis, it becomes clear to us that the outcome, let us not say *Resultat,* of such a twisting free must itself be twisted and tormented, let us say mad. This becomes clear as he thinks with Nietzsche and with Heidegger, but also sometimes almost without Heidegger (E 97), and therefore with and without Kant and Fichte and Schelling. Following Sallis, and for the most part oscillating between Heidegger and Kant, the following pages will show that the twisted outcome of this twisting free is imagination with a difference, imagination where the classically parallel lines of sensibility and intellect or reason wind up being crossed, imagination that rewrites itself with a "d" for differance and death that sets imagination at naught.

Lest this reinscription be read as a prescription for irrationality, it will be salutary to remember that the chiasm of the optic nerves is a condition of seeing straight. Sallis is not giving reasons for the rejection of reason or meaning, what-ever that might mean. Nor is he falling into that other now familiar trap of subor-dinating reason to unreason. With the reinscription of imagination we have also reinscribed reason. And sensibility. And meaning or sense.

In what sense sense? In the double sense of sense and *sens* and *Sinn* that are at one and the same time the sensibility and the intelligible or conceptual meaning which coincide in the conceptual sensibility of the schemata of the Kantian tran-scendental imagination through which, as argued in the first of the Critiques, the objectivity of objects in space is articulated in time, in the rational sensibility (re-spect) treated in this second and in the aesthetic ideas treated in the third. Because this transcendental imagining, *wähnen,* is undecidably both in and out of its senses, its ambiguous meaning, *Sinn,* is a *Wahnsinn,* a madness, in which the imagination points in opposite directions at once. Hence on the one hand Kant sometimes iden-tifies the imagination with intuition, and on the other he sometimes identifies it with the understanding. This twofold elision is facilitated by and reflected in his speaking of apprehension in intuition, reproduction in imagination, and recogni-tion in a concept as a threefold synthesis, as though each is an aspect of a complex whole, so that each so-called faculty or function is a function of the others. Kant's singling out of reproduction as a power specifically of imagination reflects a du-ality in the history of philosophy according to which memory is sometimes listed as a faculty in its own right and sometimes subsumed under imagination as one of the ways in which the latter represents something absent. What he thus singles out as reproductive imagination is sometimes empirical or associative imagination. But his Critical doctrine of time as a pure *a priori* form of sensibility requires a re-productive imagination which is, however paradoxical it may seem, an aspect of pure, transcendental productive imagination.

Heidegger believes that Kant's doctrine meets this requirement. If it did not, it would be exposed to the danger of putting the clock back to the pre-Critical doc-trine of his *Thoughts on the True Estimation of Living Forces* (1747), which main-tains that the existence and structure of time and space are contingent on whatever laws of interaction among substances obtain in, to speak naïvely but significantly, whatever epoch of cosmic time we, to speak with Heidegger, find ourselves thrown. However, this danger may be one of those dangers through which Hölder-lin and, following him, Heidegger say that the chance of rescue is increased. Here the rescue would be the rescue of Heidegger and his readers from the danger of fail-ing to see that fundamental ontology must be supplemented by metontology. That Heidegger would regard this failure as in part a repetition of Kant's failure to see that temporal schematism requires supplementation by spatial schematism is con-firmed by Heidegger's declaration in "Time and Being" that the attempt made in §70 of *Being and Time* to trace spatiality back to temporality cannot be sustained.[2]

On the page of *Echoes* where reference is made to this repudiation, Sallis ar-gues that the turning toward spatiality demands not simply a turning *from* the question of being that defines fundamental ontology to the question of beings as a whole with which metontology is occupied, but an *Umschlag* or *metabolé*, which is a violent turning *of* the former question *into* the latter (E 115). A clue to what this means is given when Heidegger compares what he calls metontology to what Aristotle calles *theologiké*, the contemplation of "what simply is—the heavens: the encompassing and overpowering, that under which and at which we are thrown, by which we are benumbed and overtaken, the overwhelming." Does not Heidegger tell us already in "What is Metaphysics?" that we shall be awakened from our dogmatic numbness to the urgency and agency of the question of the meaning of being as such only through being benumbed, overtaken, and overwhelmed by the wonder that there is a cosmos rather than nothing? Now the Postcript added to the 1943 edition of "What is Metaphysics?", after fumblings in earlier editions, affirms both that being cannot hold sway without beings and that beings cannot be given their due as such unless we experience the force and drive or drift of the question of being; hence the shock of the realization that the totality of beings is in place of nothing. In the existential analytic of *Being and Time* the place of the experience of the *Anstoss* of this, let us say, meontological difference between there being the totality of what is and there being nothing is the there-being of Dasein in its being toward its death. This experience checks rather than stops Dasein in its tracks, for Dasein is always underway. The experience is an *Erfahrung,* not an *Erlebnis.* Not a lived-through event in its life, but the way of Dasein's being on its way—on its way toward naught. This endingness without end of the to-be-there means that the intentionality of the meaning of being, if we dare employ here "the very last word to be used as a phenomenological slogan",[3] is an intentionality without an intentional object, transcendence via things toward nothingness and so toward being. Recognition of what Heidegger will call the ontological difference between beings and being implies that the *Sinn von Sein* is not an accusative. It is, however, accusatory, insofar as my recognition of the force of the ontological difference is an acknowledgement of an original ontological guilt, a hearkening to the call of conscience. Recognition is not cognition here, any more than acknowledgement is knowledge. Not certainty, but certification is what is here at stake—not wisdom, but witness. Attestation, *Bezeugung,* Heidegger's word for Dasein's ontic testification to the possibility of its authenticity.

> And yet, though indeed anticipating the radical overturning broached in the draft of metontology, the turn back to beings, clearly the turn to conscience is, in the end, governed largely by the project and the directionality of fundamental ontology; it is a turn back that is, quite decisively, for the sake of the advance toward the beyond of Being (E 147).

That is, it is a turn back toward time, hence back to the topic of the Kantian transcendental *Ein-bildungskraft,* with the difference that, whereas Kant founds the *Ein-heit* that the imagination achieves on a threefold synthesis, each fold of which, at least according to the interpretation given in *Kant and the Problem of Metaphysics,* corresponds to one of the three ecstases of time, this unity is founded according to the fundamental ontology of *Being and Time* on the threefold existential structure of care. However, this structure is destined to destructuration. Attesting is a testing to destruction. Just as from the beginning the history of being is marked by an epochal passing away that may be a passage to another beginning, destruction is of the essence of Dasein's existential structure or, more precisely, χίνησις (S 105), *Bewegung.* It is a foundation found(er)ed on an abyss, a *Grund* grounded in an *Abgrund,* what we might call a principle of deficient reason that destabilizes the principle of sufficient reason, turning it into what is literally a *Satz vom Grund.* For *Sorge,* the principle of Dasein's unity, goes with, presupposes,[4] Dasein's being a whole, and this is made possible by Dasein's being toward death, the condition of all its possibilities, itself the metapossibility of impossibility, literally a *Vor-aus-setzung* that stretches the imagination beyond the breaking point. For death stretches the imagination beyond the concept and beyond the *Bild* understood as schema further than the *Bild* understood as schema is stretched beyond the *Bild* understood as image. Death stretches the imagination to the limit at which the totality of there-being is not all there, to the limit which is also a beyond of limit, where being-there is intrinsically extrinsic to itself, *ent-setzt,* de-posed.

Therefore, insofar as the Kantian transcendental imagination is taken by Heidegger as a clue only to an analysis of Dasein's temporality, it will leave untouched the problem of the spatiality of beings as a whole. Metontology would face up to this problem when metaphysics remembers that the factical existence of Dasein and the factual extantness of un-Daseinish beings are presupposed by the possibility of Dasein and of the *Reich* of the world across which Dasein, the being of *Ent-fernung,* distancing and de-distancing, reaches, *reicht,* toward its death and the possibility of a remembrance of the ontological and meontological differences.

If the investigation of these differences has to be allocated either to fundamental ontology or to metontology, it seems that it would not figure on the agenda of the latter. This is why it was said above that the failure to keep in mind the difference between fundamental ontology and metontology can be regarded by Heidegger only as up to a point a repetition of Kant's failure to grasp that temporal schematism calls to be supplemented by spatial schematism. Heidegger adapts Kant's doctrine of schematism to what he is still calling fundamental ontology in 1929, after this had been distinguished from metontology the year before. And, as Sallis brings out, metontology is introduced, though not by name, into the *Introduction (in)to Metaphysics* of 1935, by which date Heidegger is less inclined to mention fundamental ontology and the imagination by name. A place for metontology is prepared when in *The Basic Problems of Phenomenology,* in words that correspond to those in the antepenultimate paragraph of the first division of *Being and Time* and respond to the claims of German and Irish idealism, "World is only, if, and as long as a Dasein exists (*existiert*). Nature can also be (*sein*) when no Dasein exists".[5] In other words, whereas being-in-the-world belongs to the being of Dasein, it does not belong to the being of rocks, stones, trees, and all entities studied by the natural sciences, though these are necessarily in a world once they are discovered (*entdeckt*). This also raises the question of the totality of Dasein's being-in-the-world toward its death. Philosophy must ask about the totality of nature—and indeed of cultural and historical entities whose coming to be necessarily belongs to a world yet whose passing away is possible when there is no longer Dasein, hence no longer being-in-the-world. The philosophy which asks these two questions is called metaphysics in *The Metaphysical Foundations of Logic*. It would be shortsighted to suppose that whereas the first question is a question for fundamental ontology; the second question, the metontological one, is a metaphysical one in the traditional sense. If the first one is not this, then neither can the second one be; for, as we have noted, what Heidegger projects is a radicalization of fundamental ontology which produces a metontology by "an overturning of ontology out of its very self."[6]

As we have also noted, following Sallis, Heidegger ceases to employ the words metontology and imagination. We have seen how these notions are connected through the linkage of imagination and totality through mortality, a linkage indicated in Sallis's chapter titles "Imagination—the Meaning of Being?" and "Mortality and Imagination—the Proper Name of Man." Still following Sallis's indications and oscillations between Heidegger and Kant, the remainder of this essay will adumbrate grounds for thinking that Heidegger continues to be preoccupied with the topics of metontology and imagination even after he no longer favours these names and that imagination as he and a certain Kant treat it is imagination treated as if mad.

II

Mortals make moral claims. They also make moral climates. Moral climates do not fall readymade from the sky, and moral climates are mortal. They are cultural institutions whose decay and passing away, unlike human artifacts like hammers, are no less tied to the being-there of historical Dasein than is their being instituted. This does not mean that moralities do not embrace and are not embraced by things that belong to nature, things that include among them the bodies that for a while survive human death. By morality here is meant an ethos in the broad sense which that word has in the "Letter on Humanism." It is of ethos that "The Origin of the Work of Art" speaks when it refers to the different styles and measures according to which the world, which is "the clearing of the paths of the essential guiding directions with which all decision complies (*fügt*)," "lets beings attain to the Open of their paths" where "each being emerges in its own way."[7] Each being is a being of a regioning of what in later essays and lectures Heidegger calls the fourfold, the gathering together, still each in its own way letting beings be, of mortals, immortals, sky, and earth. World is worlding, the fourfold regioning and fouring, *Vierung,* as these late essays and lectures say. It is still the measure and pattern or patron, the πέρας and δική or ground of justice and order (*Fügung*). Fourfold regioning is, in Rousseau's phrase, "the measure of what is possible in matters either of good or evil," the measure by which is decided "what is holy and what is unholy, what great and what small, what brave and what cowardly, what lofty and what slight, what master and what slave."[8] It determines the limits of all that is, which, we might speculate, is the topic or at least the heir to the topic of what Heidegger may have meant by metontology. In so doing it determines also the limits of what is no longer called fundamental ontology, and its relationship to this is described by what is no longer called metaphysics or ontology and could now perhaps be called ecology.

Observe that when Heidegger refers to what is holy, great, etc., and what is not, he is speaking of what may be up for decision, and writes that "Every decision, however, bases itself on something not mastered, something concealed, confusing; else it would never be a decision." This *Nichtbewältigtes, Verborgenes, Beirrendes* he calls earth. In "The Origin of the Work of Art," dating from the mid-1930s, earth duals with world in the Open. In the texts of the 1950s this twofold is articulated into a fourfold in which earth is one member among four and so apparently more restricted in its scope. And the task previously performed by the expressions World, Open, and Clearing is distributed among a multiplicity of expressions connoting various temporal and/or spatial notions, among them verbal *Vierung* and *Verweilen,* along with *Ort, Stätte, Raum, Stelle.* This is to be expected, given that the earlier text is focused on the question of truth and we are told that the holding sway of truth (truth's *Wesen* or *Wesung,* which could also, perhaps, be thought of as a *Schweben,* an oscillation, suspense—or hovering) is the open middle between the unconcealing or clearing of world and the concealing of earth, the betwixt of the lethic and the privative a-lethic which the work of that extra-special thing, the great *Kunst ding,* par excellence displays. The later texts in question are not concerned especially with the work of art, but with artifacts of other kinds and with things of nature. They return to the question "What is a thing?" which Heidegger had asked in a book with that title, based on lectures contemporary with those published under the heading "The Origin of the Work of Art."

What is a Thing? returns to Kant, but to the logical doctrines of the first Critique, not to the parts dealing with schematism and the imagination with which *Kant and the Problem of Metaphysics* had been especially concerned. Heidegger's return to the question "What is a Thing?" in the 1950s is also in its way a return to Kant. It does not, however, return to a Kant for whom space and time are *a pri-*

ori forms with which sensibility anticipates the experience of things, but to the pre-Critical Kant to whom we previously referred except that whereas in his *Thoughts on the True Estimation of Living Forces,* space and time are epiphenomenal to the active forces of non-spatial substances, so that "Things can actually exist and yet not be present anywhere in the world,"⁹ in Heidegger's account of the thing as a four-in-one, the thingness of a thing is its where-and-when, and its four-dimensional where-and-when is the thing's distinctive way of letting other things be. It is difficult to see how matters could have been otherwise without denying that the meaning of being is time or/and withdrawing the analysis of time-space which is outlined in *Beiträge zur Philosophie* and which, although supplemented, seems not to be abandoned in the lecture on "Time and Being," delivered in 1962.

The first Critique teaches that for human experience the modalities of temporality, namely permanence, succession, and coexistence, are inseparable from the dynamic principles of the three Analogies. "The Thing" and "Building Dwelling Thinking" step back to but also beyond Kant by proposing that this particular teaching regarding experience calls to be grounded in the premathematical and more generally prescientific prescience of the ways of being and interplay, which these essays describe "poetically." Consequently, corresponding to Kant's assertion that the experience of the sequence of events is not independent of the concept of cause is Heidegger's assertion that experience is dependent upon a biding or whiling, *Verweilen,* whose *weilen* means staying, but whose *weil* could mean because.¹⁰ In other words, there would be an anticipation here too of Kant's teaching that the concept of substance, whose special schema is permanence, is implicated with the concept of causality, the special schema of which is succession. The French *chose* we are told, is etymologically connected with *causa,* and the German *Ding* with *bedingt.* How Heidegger would ground the concept of community and the schema of coexistence is not a question we need go into here, as long as we remember Kant's discovery that the schematized concept of community cannot enter our experience without the assumption of space. We have already remarked that there is a parallel for this in the history of Heidegger's thinking. His discovery is articulated in his reflections on time-space, in his demonstration in "Building Dwelling Thinking" (without benefit of commas) that the middle term of these three is indeed a middle in the sense that the other two belong to each other through belonging to it, and in his interpretation of the thing as an intersection of the regions of the fourfold which gives rise to locality or neighbourhood, *Ort* or *Ortschaft,* which in turn makes possible place, *Stätte,* positions, *Stellen,* and space. To cite words saying what is said in another of Sallis's epigraphs, that of *Delimitations:*

> *Raum* means a place cleared or freed for settlement and lodging. A space is something for which room has been made, something that is cleared and freed, namely within a boundary, Greek πέρας. A boundary is not that at which something stops but, as the Greeks recognized, a bound-

ary is that from which *the presencing (Wesen) of something begins . . .*
Accordingly spaces receive their being (Wesen) from locations and not
from Space.[11]

Location and whiling or biding are Heideggerian σχήματα, this Greek noun
being cognate with the verb ἔχω, among the meanings of which are to house and
to dwell, to be on home ground. They are the ground of homogeneous space and
time in an extremely eccentric way, as Sallis brings out through what Heidegger
writes in the section of *Beiträge zur Philosophie* on time-space. In light of what
Heidegger says about the withdrawal of earth in "The Origin of the Work of Art,"
we are prepared for the "leap from the ground" of what we have called the principle of deficient reason once we learn that in the *Beiträge zur Philosophie*, a long
section of which is entitled *Der Sprung*, ground or reason is itself grounded in
earth—grounded therefore as disgrounded. Not ungrounded, which would be to
replace ground by its simple opposite and by the negative emptiness of place.
Grund and *Ab-grund* (not *Un-grund*) cross and supplement each other chiastically.
They make up for each other's deficiencies in a way that recognizes the deficiency
of the principle of sufficient reason. The negative emptiness of absence of occu-
pants from the homogeneous space and time of calculable measure is not the orig-
inative, *ur-sprünglich*, emptiness of the Heideggerianly schematized time-space.
This dis-groundingly grounding "first clearing of the Open"[12] is the *Ursprung*, the
first fissure—for a *Sprung* is a crack or cis(s)ion or *Scheide* as well as a leap and
a source,[13] the first scissure of a jarring ajarness, an *Aufklaffung*, a seismic sagging
and giving way, a *Versagung* of the ground which both donates Dasein's way and
at the same time defers Dasein's arrival at a destination. The *Ab-grund* of *Grund*
is *Wegbleiben* and *Weg-bleiben*, both staying away and staying a way.[14] Always
underway, Dasein's striving thither, its *Hinwollen*, as Heidegger says, its *Streben*,
as Fichte and Schelling say, its *Bestreben*, as Kant says,[15] is checked by an *Anstoss*,
as Heidegger says,[16] following Fichte and Schelling, an *Abstossen*, as Kant says.[17]
This is not however the resistance (for *Versagung* is also resistance) of an object,
but of an obstacle which is no such thing, no thing whatsoever, but being. This resistance of non-resistance, this de-limitation of delimitation, takes place, and takes
place away, at the no-man's land where the call of being, the voice of Dasein's
conscience which comes overcomingly from him as though from inside and from
out (OE *fram*, from which English gets "from"), is met by Dasein's heedful or
heedless response. This place is the place of displacement and of the moment of
decision, *Entscheidung*.

Heidegger says that this *Augenblick* is the moment and movement of
Ereignen. It corresponds in Kant to the moment of imagination which is suspended
and wavers between sensibility and understanding, which in parts of the first Critique appears to become understanding and which in parts of the third Critique,
those parts where it leans on the second Critique and where aesthetic judgement

answers to an echo of the moral law, will often be difficult to tell apart from reason. Imagination. Kant's later writings retain the word, despite its not being employed as a name for one of the faculties listed in the Preface to the third Critique, as noted by Sallis (S 87), who wants to retain it too. Although it occurs in Heidegger's later writings,[18] it is employed much more sparingly than in his earlier ones. This and the fact that the decreasing frequency of its use coincides with the increasing frequency of occurrence of the word *Ereignis* could be interpreted as a sign that he continues to be preoccupied with what goes under (in) the name of imagination in Kant and the German Idealists on whom he is lecturing at the end of the 1920s and the beginning of the 1930s: the complicitous manifold of the proto-theoretical, proto-ethical, proto-legal, proto-political, proto-poietic and proto-aesthetic *Einbildungskraft*. Might it not be this that is sealed in the name *Ereignis?* Might not *Ereignen* be the schematizing whose artful schemings are concealed in the depths of the *Da* and *Seyn* whose cunning or cunnyng philopolemical maneuverings (*Handgriffe*) are the shifting ground which juts through, performs, and prepares the way for (*bewegt*) the handwork (*Handwerk*) Kant identifies with the action (*Handlung*) of "I think" and whose overtures we are hardly likely ever to persuade mother nature, mother Isis, to lay bare to our eyes?[19] Might it not be to this, imagination differently imagined so differently named, no longer named as a human faculty but as the advening of φύσις as being as such, might it not be to this that is made the sacrifice of understanding and of the understanding of being named in the title of a chapter in *Echoes?* That chapter marks the stages of this sacrifice beginning with "What is Metaphysics?," the Postscript of "What is Metaphysics?," the *Introduction to Metaphysics,* and *"Zur Kritik der Vorlesung."* This last undated note is a criticism of the too Critical manner of questioning adopted in the *Introduction*. It calls for a passage *vom Seinsverständnis zu Seinsgeschehnis.*[20] But *Seinsgeschehnis* is a synonym or pseudonym for *Ereignis.*

In the *Beiträge zur Philosophie,* subtitled *Vom Ereignis,* and in what should perhaps be re-titled "The Primal Split of the Work of Art," earth, although reserved, nevertheless juts or towers through the Open and through the world, and as closing rises up, even—for *aufgehen* can have this sense when said, for example, of a door—*opens.*[21] Reciprocally, as we have seen, world grounds and disgrounds itself, constructing (*bildend*) itself and deconstructing itself in earth. But, because *Ab-grund* is not to be confused with *Un-grund,* there is no logical product by dialectical determinate negation in which these movements come to rest. It is not as though a deep, dark inside is opposed to an outside that is all light. Although, as just indicated, Heidegger may have more than one view of the matter, the chasm we have been locating in *terra infirma* is not something already there independent of earth's chiasm with world. It is not a something present or absent, hence it is not something that could be represented to our view or imagined, any more than is imagination itself, which is not a self, not something that "is" or, it should be added, "is not," any more than "is" the *Es* of the statement regarding

Ereignis in "Time and Being" that *Es gibt* and that what gives is time and being. Saying *Es ist* would be a *Ver-sagen,* a mis-saying where there would be a more serious breakdown of predication than when we say *Es regnet,* "It is raining," and suppose there must be another entity denoted by this *Es* or "it." Although it is only the rain that raineth everyday, it is appropriate to refer to it by "it." Of appropriation, *Ereignis,* we can say with truth rather than mere correctness neither *Es ist* nor *Es gibt,* but only *Das Ereignis ereignet.*[22]

III

Die Einbildung bildet ein. It prevails as *In-eins-bildung,* but also as *Bildung in zwei.* At the unstill point where—to cite a third epigraph from Sallis, this time his echo in *Echoes* of Heraclitus Fragment 60—the way up and the way down are the same, there happens the philo-polemic of the sway of the truth of ἀ-λήθεια (Heraclitus Fragments 8, 80), whose hyphen hints, *winkt,* not at an interval, but at an oscillation in the very *Wesung* or sway of truth as concealing-unconcealing without interval (Heraclitus Fragment 123). This swaying, *Schwingen,*[23] is the crossing of the betwixt where/when timing and spacing belong to each other chiastically. There is not a synthesis but a chiasmus because separateness is preserved. For although space allows time, unlike time it is never enrapturing, *entrückend;* and although time allows space, unlike space it is never encapturing, *berückend.*[24] By comparison with the homogeneous space and time of the transcendental imagination in Kant, this imagination is *verrückt,* mad or, as is said of a clock, put back, regulated, deregulated, deranged, changed. "Mad" derives from the past participles of verbs with the Indogermanic root *mei-,* meaning altered or changed. Compare the Latin *mutatus* and *motus,* moved, stirred, set in motion, shaken, disturbed, removed, caused to waver, dislodged, displaced; that is to say, once again, *verrückt,* as when Heidegger describes as displacement, *Verrückung,* the alienation from our accustomed relations to world and earth brought about by the *Anstoss* of our being struck by the "that it is" of and brought out by the work of art.[25]

IV

The working hypothesis of the final section of this essay is that "The Origin of the Work of Art" is a repetition of the *Critique of Aesthetic Judgement,* especially of what is written there about the imagination and the sublime. The absence of the word sublime from these lectures no more counts against the plausibility of this hypothesis than does the absence from it of the word *imagination.* And it is a hypothesis that impels us to take notice, all too briefly, of some of the remarks Sallis makes in the chapter on the third Critique in *Spacings,* which is entitled

"Tremorings" and is ambiguously subtitled "Withdrawals of the Sublime." These very withdrawals of the sublime confirm the plausibility of our hypothesis, and turning to consider Sallis's remarks on them enables us to return now at the end of our own remarks to clarify and respond affirmatively to our and Sallis's opening question as to whether the imagination is mad.

That opening question was whether imagination might be congenitally mad. Could imagination be uncontrollable by reason, not because imagination is in a coffer isolated from reason so that, no matter how diseased the imagination may be, reason remains safe and sound, but because reason participates in imagination so that reason is congenitally mad? Sallis's hypothesis is that it could. The plausibility of his hypothesis is a corollary of the plausibility of the hypotheses that, while in *Kant and the Problem of Metaphysics* Heidegger is giving a "destructive" reading of the doctrine of imagination and related doctrines presented by Kant in the first and second Critiques, in "The Origin of the Work of Art" he is doing likewise for the doctrine of imagination presented in the third.

Toward the end of his discussion of the doctrine of the sublime presented in the third Critique, Sallis proposes "tremoring" to mark the rapid oscillation between repulsion and attraction in the complex feeling of the sublime. We are pained by and recoil from a sensible object of nature, of "nature itself in its totality", φύσις-Isis,[26] or of art, when the comprehension of it as a whole exceeds the imagination and the imagination fears to lose itself as though in an abyss. However, once the difference between the subject's sensibility and the object that the imagination strives unsuccessfully to comprehend becomes the schematization of the difference between a striving of imagination and an idea of a totality controlled by a law of reason, the moral law which is the subject's own freedom, "here there is the same amount of attraction as there was repulsion for the mere sensibility."[27] Thus "especially in its beginning," as Kant writes, the "tremoring"—so called by Sallis because the word itself hovers between the "trembling" of the subject and the "tremor" objectively considered—oscillates or hovers. This hovering continues as long as something is felt to be sublime; for without a sensible object to occasion it, the feeling of sublimity would give way to some other feeling, for instance the feeling of respect. But especially in its end, as we might say, the object of the feeling withdraws from the abyss toward reason, the subject's own ground. This movement of partial polarization takes the direction opposite to that which is found to be decisive in Heidegger's account of what, following Kant, he calls *das eigentliche Selbst.*[28]

Opposite? Decisive? Not simply opposite, because the difference between the *Grund* and the *Abgrund* to which Heidegger and the work of great art would have us attend cannot be the difference between sensibility and reason if it is, to speak with Schelling, the indifference of ground or reason and abyss within the time-space of which must take place any distinguishing between faculties of the mind, between special areas of philosophy, science, etc., and between theory, practice, and production. Not simply decisive, because these last-mentioned distinctions are distinctions in an *Entscheidungsraum* in which choices are to be made among ontic or existentiell alternatives.[29] Prior to such decisions is the *Entscheidungsraum,* which takes choosing away even though it makes place for the whether-or of regulation and law, "for decision what is holy and what unholy, what great and what small . . ." etc.,[30] and even though its priority over such whether-or questions and the way it lets us "restrain all usual doing and prizing, knowing and looking[31] can be brought out through asking whether-or questions calling for such decisions as *"whether* man wants to remain 'subject' *or* whether he grounds Da-sein."[32] What if this grounding is abyssal? What if decision is grounded in discission? As the cission between sensibility and reason would be if imagination, although sometimes said by Kant to be a component along with sensation of the faculty of knowledge,[33] sometimes assimilated to understanding and sometimes said to be a faculty along with and between sensibility and understanding, were, as he also says, the common root not just of sensibility and understanding, but of sensibility and reason. What if, instead of remaining subject, imagination is "the openness of existent *Dasein*" (GR 175), as, without being so named, it begins to become when *Da* and *Sein* are interpreted through the time-generative functions (*Handlungen*) attributed to the productive imagination by Kant and supplemented by Heidegger from the 1930s on with a multiplicity of topologies which he might well have brought together under the title *Being and Space* or "Space and Being"? When the productive imagination of the first Critique is pro-duced as it is in the third, it is still less likely that the root of reason can be under reason's control. Because no concept of the understanding can comprehend what in the critique of aesthetic judgement—by analogy with the schematic sensible concepts of the critique of knowledge and the rational sensibility of the critique of practice—Kant calls aesthetic ideas, Sallis can justly say: "Now imagination is so freed from the rule of understanding that, conversely, it can govern understanding—though in its own playful way—by provoking thought" (GR 173). But can it govern reason, and can it do so without reason's being lost?

Although according to Kant the feeling of beauty is restful whereas the feeling of sublimity is an e-motion in that the mind feels itself set in motion and depends on an unceasing oscillation,[34] the feeling of sublimity is directed toward the putatively stable center of rationality, legality, and freedom which is (re)presented by the aesthetic idea. If the fact that the aesthetic idea is itself a product of the imagination's *free* play should lead us to suspect that imagination is an exercise of reason, we should be prepared to admit that reason is an exercise of imagination when we remember that Kant has said, in a sentence reproduced by Sallis from the first Critique: "This *unconditioned* is always contained in the *absolute totality of the series* as represented in imagination" (GR 162).[35] That is to say, the idea of absolute totality is both an idea of reason and an idea of imagination. Furthermore, this involvement of the imagination is not limited to the moment in which we succumb to transcendental illusion, the illusion which might be compared to the inclination to mistake for something outside us what is only in our mind and which, Kant says in the *Anthropology*, "accounts for the giddiness that comes over us when we look into a chasm (*Abgrund*)."[36] The *Anthropology* says that some mentally sick people (*einige Gemüthskranken*) have a fear that they may throw themselves into the abyss. The *Critique of Judgement* ascribes to the imagination the fear of giving way to this inclination.[37] Just as this inclination is not restricted to the mentally deranged persons referred to in this section of the *Anthropology*, so transcendental illusion is "inseparable from human reason."[38] It is therefore inseparable from human imagination; for the so-called ideas of reason, in which the illusion has its source, are inseparable from imagination, Kant concedes (B 444). Sallis is thus right when he says that Kant's heading oversimplifies when it claims "Pure Reason as the Seat of Transcendental Illusion." Besides, although the illusion which Kant says is inseparable from human reason is regarded as a propensity which, although ineliminable, can be guarded against provided we remember that the ideas are employed rationally only when they are employed regulatively, what could that employment be except an employment of imagination if it is a gathering of reason that gathers hermeneutically *as if* in a *focus imaginarius?* It is as if imagination were the vertiginous abyss in reason's ground, in sanity.

CHAPTER FIVE

IN THE INTEREST OF JUSTICE TO ART

Charles E. Scott

"For you can tell a true war story only if it embarrasses you. If you don't care for obscenity, you don't care for the truth; if you don't care for the truth, watch how you vote."
—Tim O'Brien, *The Things They Carried*[1]

John Sallis draws the lines of his thought with a fineness that reminds me of the lines in a Japanese painting. There appear to be no excess. Each mark is exacting, exactly meant, placed with a very fine brush, leaving aside clutter and wasted movement. Among us who premeditate everything, he stands out for his precision and clarity of purpose, for his forethought that demands quiet patience and elimination of each word and innuendo that do not count towards a presentation of precise meaning and simple determination. But like in a Japanese painting there is also in his writings a planned imperfection that in the precision of its placement opens us to much more than we can see and Sallis can plan. The lines themselves, by the imperfection and in their spareness, come to bear far more than their lightness at first announced. The more he withdraws the impact of thought in its force of theory, the more something else seems to weigh in upon us; and before we know what it could be, we sense that something born of error, something of enormous finitude has left us shaken in its wake as we read.

There is an elusiveness in Sallis's thought that will not come out by direct description. It happens in yoked, unreconciled opposites and in breakage of connections. I cannot be true to the elusiveness—I cannot follow it or present it properly—only by speaking about it. In an effort to be true to this dimension of Sallis's thinking, I will allow an invasion into my narrative by another narrative that is as foreign to my words as it is to Sallis's.[2] The interruptions, which I believe that Sallis will welcome as a certain dissonance, are from Tim O'Brien's *The Things They Carried,* a recent book on memories of the war in Vietnam, that attempts to be true to what happened to some of the people there. O'Brien speaks of true war stories, of how they often have to lie by some standards if they are to be true. In the interruptions and in what he says—and above all in yoking the differences and oppositions that the interruptions introduce to my thought and to Sallis's, which seem to come from a world radically different from that of a footsoldier in Vietnam—we might find a mimesis of the mimesis in Sallis's thought, a yoking of opposites that reveals both error and truth other to what I say about them.

In any war story, but especially a true one, it's difficult to separate what happened from what seemed to happen. What seems to happen becomes its own happening and has to be told that way. The angles of vision are skewed. When a boobytrap explodes, you close your eyes and duck and float outside yourself. When a guy dies, like Curt Lemon, you look away and then look back for a moment and then look away again. The picture gets jumbled; you tend to miss a lot. And then afterward, when you go to tell about it, there is always that surreal seemingness, which makes the story untrue, but which in fact represents the hard and exact truth as it seemed.

The word *imagination* organizes a major portion of Sallis' thought. A cursory glance at his work up to now could give one the impression that he wants to trace the imaginative variations on imagination that have developed in Western thought. We might expect that his scholarship will culminate with a major volume on this subject, one that connects Plato and Nietzsche, Fichte and Husserl, Aristotle and Heidegger, the pre-Socratics and Derrida in a major tour de force that shows linkage and subtle influence often where one does not expect it, a work that establishes the Western experience of the imaginative basis for all thought. But Sallis will not write such a book because his thought is itself mimetic, and mimesis as he undergoes it renounces its completion in this kind of descriptive undertaking.

As I turn to his thought, I must give two other cautionary statements. I have already cautioned us against assuming too quickly that Sallis's thought is descriptive in an ordinary sense of that word. I have said that something in it is born of error. *In many cases a true war story cannot be believed. If you believe it, be skeptical. It's a question of credibility. Often the crazy stuff is true and the normal stuff isn't, because the normal stuff is necessary to make you believe the truly incredible craziness.* A second caution addresses mimetic movement, which occurs as Sallis writes about mimesis. One of his favored words, *doubling,* arises from his own thought as well as from the historical movement of mimesis. He allows mimetic movement to happen as he thinks about mimetic movement. This is doubling without a completing synthesis. *In other cases you can't even tell a true war story. Sometimes it's just beyond telling.* Sallis's departure from Hegel pervades his own logic. It is not a logic of higher syntheses among opposites but rather a logic of what he calls monstrosity. It is logic that holds opposites together in aporetic structures that lack a synthesis of higher identity. In Sallis's thought mimesis is a movement without identity, a movement of displacement in the sense of his words, one that does not allow completion in definition, image, or system. We should thus be prepared to find in his thinking more than accounts of how the concepts and images of mimesis lead away from the fixture that Western thought has given them. We should be prepared also to find that the finely placed error, which is at first barely perceptible in the texture of his work, comes to figure, as we draw near to it, a monstrous thing within the context of proper identity and good sense. I shall later show how Sallis's thought includes mimesis of mimesis, which is very different from conceptual clarity about mimesis, and that this movement, this mimetics, is the distortion that I have forecast.

Finally, a caution about the historicity of Sallis's thought. If we were to place him within a departmental structure, we would accurately assign him to a position in the history of philosophy. We would smile apologetically, in an American way, if someone asked about high medieval thought, and say that his primary strengths are in ancient, modern, nineteenth-century, and twentieth-century thought, and having said that, we would rest our case. Privately we would suspect that sooner or later he will examine mimesis and imagination in Aquinas, perhaps in Bernard and Francis of Assisi, but for now we need to recognize only that Sallis always thinks in a historical context, that *imagination* means for him a certain movement within texts, within works of art and thought, and does not name a transhistorical faculty. Included in his appreciative work on Kant's thought, for example, is a thorough undercutting of any claim that would make imagination a faculty or part of a faculty or a transcendental power or the spontaneous assertion of reason. In order to address imagination, we address texts, their interplay, the subtle exercise of movements of thoughts, meanings, and images, and, above all, the work of little noted oppositions that maintain aporetic connections and disrupt texts in their claims of noncontradiction and adequate conceptual definition. Mimetic thought, we shall see, disrupts the identities that is discloses; and in this claim we will find far more of Dionysus than Sallis's Apollinian style suggests is there. *In war you lose your sense of the definite, hence your sense of truth itself, and therefore it's safe to say that in a true war story nothing is ever absolutely true.*

In *Echoes* Sallis says that *echo* is "an original divergence from an original," (E 5) and this statement accurately describes Sallis's own work in the history of philosophy. The way in which he repeats the theories and claims made about imagination in western philosophical texts returns us to what would be originals if they were not themselves echoes. In this re-sounding process he does not follow a thread that guides him to a definitive essence or to a primordial presence that has been badly represented; he finds, rather, multiple and undecided images and structures of thought that are marked by breaks in continuous sound and by spacings of no sound and no meaning, like a canyon of echoes that leaves one stunned by silence that is as audible as the sounds resounding in the empty hollow. By this image I speak of Sallis's encounter with the history of philosophy and the hearing of his own words within it. There is always, in his words, "a fugitive effect" that accompanies the texts and the "beauty of their rigor" that gives us to think as we do.[3]

Secondly, we can say about the historical dimension of his work that Sallis finds many broken narratives. His chosen texts are not isolated from one another, but they are not connected by a line of ascending development or progress. Rather they are joined by images whose relations are not found in a unified faculty of imagination but in their appearing. Sallis is thoroughly phenomenological in his locating images in their appearing and in his redetermining the thought of imagination by the thought of mimesis whereby images come to appear in a mimetic relation that reveals only mimetic movement, only imaginal transmission in imaginal appearance. This is an aspect of the Apollinian dimension of his thought. The history of imagination, if we may call it that, is thus one of multiple imaginal transfers without a connecting tissue other than that of the textual appearance of images and their mimetic movement. Something different from historiography is needed if we are to uncover an imaginal history, something more like mimetic thought and more than a scholarly presentation of the developing meanings of images and imagination.

Let us begin by looking at a theoretical movement in Sallis's work on imagination and mimesis. This movement is determined by his showing in multiple studies the loss of an aspect of mimesis in a variety of claims about mimesis. It is constituted by critical studies in which he shows that opposites are preserved in their opposition in mimetic movement even though this aporetic dimension of mimesis is usually overlooked. For example, the opposites of distortion of truth and disclosure of truth are held together in Plato's thought in *The Republic*. In Book X Socrates banishes the unapologetic poet from the polis because the poet provides mirroring images in the name of truth and separates people from what is really real. By giving people images the poet gives them only imperfect copies of reality as sustenance for their souls. But at the end of the dialogue Socrates becomes a poet as he tells the myth of Er in order to disclose imaginatively a dimension of truth to which the dialogue has given us partial access. In the dialogue poetry as falsification and the occasion of corruption is held together with poetry as a disclosure of truth for which our souls are made. We have in this opposition a problem that will surface repeatedly in Western thought as suspicion of the poet and as the experience that poetry discloses truth; and we have an instance of thought's holding together an opposition, a holding which is itself a mimetic movement. Let's consider this movement.

We shall look, by Sallis's reading, through Nietzsche's eyes at the Apollinian and Dionysian powers in the Greek experience of tragedy. I begin with this account because in it we will find, not only an original reading of parts of *The Birth of Tragedy,* but also a mimesis on Sallis's part in his relation to Nietzsche's mimetic thought of mimesis in Greek tragedy.[4] On Nietzsche's account *Apollo* names first a power of nature that is not mediated by art. It is found primarily in dreams, in dream images which arrest people in the immediacy of their shining. In this immediacy, however, there is also distancing or what Sallis will call in other contexts "spacing": the dream image gives the immediate sense of appearance rather than of an encounter with something original. Sallis calls this distancing effect a betrayal of the shining image because in the sense of appearance the dream image, far from being totally absorbing, is demarcated as an image and as over against the dreamer. The distance allows for both contemplation and interruption on the part of other powers. In its individuation process dream imaging sets itself apart from the dreamer and gives availability for both objectification and the coming of something other to the Apollinian. Further, as demarcated the image suggests something that is imaged or mirrored, something original. But within the Apollinian power the image, not the original, is the site of perfection. Images are given archetypal status, given a truth that is cleansed of everyday partiality and corruption. Perfection is not found in an original that is mirrored but in the mirroring that elevates images. We should emphasize the image's singularity that comes at the cost of an individual's total involvement, a cost that Sallis calls "betrayal" and this cost is the price of perfection. Apollo's shining and healing power comes with the vulnerability of suspension, an absence of an anchoring original that might provide perfection before appearing. I repeat: Apollo's power is found in the dream world, and his healing will have a dream status in the midst of corruption and suffering. Within this thought—and I believe that it is a thought pervasive of Sallis's work—when we deal with appearances and images, and hence when we deal with the imagination, we have to do with the coming of what has not previously been real or true, with something that brings optionality with it as it gives identity, discreteness, and individuation. If you read Sallis's work, as I do, as a masterful accomplishment of discretion, discreteness, identification, and demarcation, you will see that his acceptance of the Apollinian power at work in his thought comes to an acceptance—a happy acceptance, I believe—of a high degree of vulnerability, quite the opposite of finality, at the heart of his careful structures of thought. *You can tell a true war story by the way it never seems to end. Not then, not ever.* But I am getting ahead of the images that I wish to present to you.

A second power of nature that Nietzsche accounts in *The Birth of Tragedy* is named *Dionysian.* This power reunites individuals with nature and in that process obliterates their individuality. Return to nature is indeed a return, a recoiling back into a way of being from which human beings have only partially departed. Hence, Dionysos indicates both an animal-like nurturance that touches and soothes us in our natures while preparing to dismember and consume us. Of all the gods, Dionysos is said to be the most gentle and the most terrible to human beings. His gentleness is found in our touch through his power with our nonhuman dimension. His terribleness is found in our loss of individuation, of our selves, in this touch and return. Hence, there is an ecstatic moment for humans in the excess of Dionysos's power. In his moment we are outside the limits, the images, that define us and give us to be as we are. But that excess, that outside, is no *place*, no region of identity, no 'itself' to which beings return. The 'nature' to which Dionysos returns us is mere excess where nothing dwells. In Dionysian ecstasy people are outside of being as well as being outside of themselves. Dismemberment leads to nothing. Hence the wisdom of Silenus who gave words to the terror and consequent discouragement of Dionysian excess: It is better for people not to be born, or, having come into life, it is better that we die soon, for Dionysian ecstasy is of our lives and destiny.

These two powers in Greek experience—the Apollinian and Dionysian— precede art. Tragedy, in Nietzsche's account, is a mimesis of them both—Sallis calls it a double mimesis. The Dionysian mimesis in tragedy occurs without images and without truth in the music of the chorus, which gives birth to the space of the tragic scene. The chorus discharges itself in an Apollinian scene which gives scenic determination to this musical discharge, and the tragedy takes place between the chorus and the scene as the chorus repeats the scene and the scene is enlivened by images that return to the music of the chorus. The Apollinian mimesis occurs in the scenic images of the play. Through the play's images both Apollo and Dionysos are given presence in a formation of destiny and character. Our emphasis is on the double mimesis that occurs in tragedy vis-à-vis the Apollinian and Dionysian powers. In this mirroring the Apollinian makes the Dionysian endurable by supplementing Silenic "wisdom" with the drama's sublimeness, capturing, as it were, Dionysian excess and ecstasy, its overwhelming power beyond an individual's reach, in a sublime presentation that makes us feel participant in a primordial struggle and gives truth instead of disjointure, joy instead of terror. *At the hour of dusk you sit at your foxhole and look out over a wide river turning pinkish red, and at the mountains beyond, and although in the morning you must cross the river and do terrible things and maybe die, even so, you find yourself studying to find the fine colors on the river, you feel wonder and awe at the setting sun, and you are filled with a hard, aching love for how the world could be and always should be, but now is not.* But Sallis calls this a monstrous accomplishment and thereby sets himself at some distance from the image that he contemplates. Greek tragedy is "monstrous" in the "yoking" together of a double mimesis in the tragic dream. The dream relieves us of Silenus's pessimism; but in giving us joy it also gives us the pain not only of inevitable failure, but the pain as well of the unresolvable conflict of two terrible opposites: the appearing of truth only by image and the withdrawal from the truth of appearing, namely, the disclosure of the Dionysian power of life. We could add, although Sallis does not say this, that the Apollinian moment of victory within tragedy, a victory that comes in giving form, truth, and determination to Dionysian power, is itself empowered by a will to dominance that will later be thought by Nietzsche as the will to power in the form of the ascetic ideal. This will to dominate the Dionysian is a second betrayal of the Apollinian. In tragedy the Apollinian is given force by incorporating Dionysian power toward domination which dissolves Apollinian truth even in Apollo's impetus that produces truth. More than shining takes place in tragic discourse—we have a shining that dominates, that momentarily overcomes the consuming maul of the Dionysian. So in the art of tragedy we have in Apollo something monstrous: a power to give appearances that by its dominance discloses in its formation and hence in its overcoming of the Dionysian the operation of Dionysian power that withdraws from appearances and in its withdrawal dominates Apollo. This second dominance by Dionysos is much clearer from the retrospect of Nietzsche's fully developed thought of will to power, but even in *The Birth of Tragedy* we can glimpse the birth of a monster in Apollo's image.

The first double mimesis that we have specified is that, in tragedy, of the two forces of nature, the Apollinian and Dionysian; Nietzsche's own thought is mimetic as he determines this mimesis. We might show how Nietzsche's thought is mimetic vis-à-vis Apollo and Dionysos, how his thought is formed like the formation of Greek tragedy, not, however, in a mimesis of powers of nature but rather in a mimesis of tragic art. Sallis, however, shows first that Nietzsche's thought—as a philosophy of art—follows the loss of tragedy which takes place in the traditional development of Socratic thought, or Socratism, and shows further that Nietzsche's thought follows as well a Dionysian displacement of Socratic philosophy in a return to tragedy. It places itself in philosophy and "slides" or "drifts" away from philosophy toward art. What kind of movement is this? By describing Greek tragedy in its formation, Nietzsche gives us a theory of Greek art, one that is designed to clarify Greek tragedy and to let it shine forth in its own appearance. By this theoretical intention his thought follows the Apollinian. It provides the "metaphysical comfort" of an understanding of this drama, places Greek tragedy in a carefully determined way in its yoking of the two opposing powers, and makes claims to a certain accuracy of presentation. In that process his thought also dominates Greek tragedy, finds it at a distance that makes possible its contemplation, and establishes its own dynamism by a definitive gathering of those opposites in a body of concepts and images. We follow Nietzsche as he follows Apollo in letting Greek tragedy shine as it is re-imaged in theoretical presentation. But there is also a Dionysian moment. Nietzsche "slides away" from theory and philosophy of art as he allows Wagner's music to guide his thought. Nietzsche's attunement to music in his philosophy of art displaces that very philosophy. There is no truth in music as he hears it. In music there is a movement toward dissolution of all images and words. Just as in Greek tragedy the chorus brings music to bear in the coming of dramatic images and both inaugurates a space for them and tends to return them to imagelessness, so Nietzsche's thought tends to unhinge its own theoretical connections by recoiling to music at the heart of its own conceptualization and attunement. Nietzsche hears the dismembering of his careful construction in the power of music to withdraw from the images that have presented this power. The care with which his philosophy of art has explained tragedy includes something that exceeds explanation and theoretical connections; in this moment Nietzsche not only delimits his own presentation by setting it in the context of music, he also thinks Dionysian power mimetically in presenting what exceeds the appearance of images and undermines the truth of what he says and the way he says it. His thought, in this double movement, yokes together Socratism and the Dionysian power of Greek tragedy. As well as being a philosophy about mimesis, it in this mimesis escapes the boundaries of philosophy.

Mitchell Sanders was right. For the common soldier at least, war has the feel—the spiritual texture—of a great ghostly fog, thick and permanent. There is no clarity. Everything swirls. The old rules are no longer binding, the old truths no longer true. Right spills over into wrong. Order blends into chaos, love into hate, ugliness into beauty, law into anarchy, servility into savagery. The vapors suck you in. You can't tell where you are, or why you're there, and the only certainty is overwhelming ambiguity.

Allow me to underscore the double movement of mimesis as I continue to think philosophically about mimesis: on the one hand, like an echo, mimetic activity brings images to appearance, in this case images of images. It does not merely copy an image. Mimetic activity re-imagines images in a movement of imagination that is at a clear remove from whatever is re-imagined. This mimetic Apollinian imagining can clarify, can establish a certain normative perfection of the image, can dominate whatever is excessive and corruptive of the image, and can give us something like an archetypal appearance that defines in this case Greek tragedy. On the other hand, this mimesis follows after an excess that is not subject to the process of appearing. In this mimesis a space of difference not only betrays the insistence of the image in its appearance; this space allows the image its determinateness and also threatens in its lack of imaginal determination the image's determinateness. It is a space of indeterminateness that interrupts the shining determination that transpires with it, a difference to image that is yoked with the image. In this theory, spatial difference refuses the imagery that we are now giving to it. Even the image of Dionysos is threatened in Nietzsche's appeal to music, for example. In mimesis all images move toward dissolution. Theory as such is placed in jeopardy by the mark of Dionysos that Nietzsche's account has so carefully figured into its construction. When we reach this point, we can say that the image of mimesis as a yoking of opposites suggests a movement of falling apart from which it itself is not immune; and within the thought of noncontradiction by which we have defined the opposites, we undergo a sense of things falling apart at the core of the meanings that we have established. Something in the theory of mimesis fails to make sense. Not only is the yoking of opposites "monstrous"—something in the yoking itself is monstrous, like a gaping mouth beyond which is something like vacuum without concentricity, like no place with nothing to give horizon or appearance.

At this point we could follow Nietzsche as he transforms Socratism into philosophy that begins to think in the collapse of a theological center, a Dionysian collapse that in its Dionysian dimension allows a reformation of philosophy into tragic thought with full attention to the Dionysian power of self-overcoming. But let us instead turn to Sallis's presentation of Nietzsche's mimetic thought. I have given, partially and imperfectly, part of the structure of descriptive care with which he provided a reading of *The Birth of Tragedy*. Those who know Sallis's work can fill in some of the spaces I have left by imagining his texts and lectures, their shining clarity, the compelling quality of their delimitations, and the exactness of movement from thought to thought and image to image. Most readers have learned from his scholarship and his insights into texts and have related to his writings as to a teacher who opens up texts with originality and gives them a new life for one's own thought. *You can tell a true war story by the questions you ask. . . . the answer matters.* But other to his scholarship and Apollinian determinations and throughout his readings and interpretations something has hovered from the beginning that I believe has both perplexed and moved Sallis as a philosopher. Even before his first graduate work in mathematics and his early interest in logic, we can imagine that he was moved by a passion for the clarity of abstract relations. It is no accident that *shining* plays both an organizational and an affective part within his thought. I believe that he has always wanted that bright serenity and presentational unclutteredness that abide in platonic thought and wisdom, the loss of which defines the unshining world of ordinary confusion and stress. But something else hovers there—something not shining—as Sallis thinks, not like a distracting background noise but like a withdrawal of delimitation that gives infinite indefiniteness within the most sharply drawn conceptualization. . . . *but I could tell how desperately Sanders wanted me to believe him, his frustration at not getting the details right, not quite pinning down the final and definitive truth.*

Heidegger speaks to Sallis like an intimate whisper when he thinks the ending of metaphysics in the finest self-expressions of metaphysics. This ending occurs in the appearances of things, in, for example, the spaces that pervade the synthesis of experience and the coming of beings to determinations that are always within an ungraspable horizon which at once delimits them and withdraws from them. No identity appears in singularity for Sallis. Each thing in its being is confounded by opposites in its coming to be and persisting in its being, by such opposites as shining and darkness, noncontradiction and contradiction, truth and nontruth, revealing and concealing, healing and corruption, delimitation and spacing. Mimetic appearing is not only shining, it is not neat and clean for Sallis; hence he finds it monstrous.

In his reading of *The Birth of Tragedy,* for example, the yoking of the opposites, Apollo and Dionysos, is unyoked in Sallis's way of thinking of the sublime. The movements are these: first, Sallis identifies the sublime as the truth of tragedy. In sublimeness the excess of the Dionysian is yoked to the truth-giving determination of the Apollinian in a mood of elevation that reveals Dionysos's terrible inevitability and untruth in the disclosive truth of tragedy. In this disclosure the mood of terror and madness that accompanies Silenus's "wisdom" is converted into the "metaphysical comfort" of cosmic participation and joy that accompany tragic appearance. Second, by identifying the sublime and the truth of tragedy, Sallis disrupts its metaphysical comfort by the disturbing realization that such comfort is provided by images that are themselves ungrounded by anything original beyond image. Sallis yokes the sublime to its own internal incoherence, absences sublimeness from both rational ground and ontological grounding in something like will-to-power or some infinite imaginal agency. He thereby decisively interrupts the joy of sublimeness and qualifies it with questions and with the dismembering coming of nonappearance. The arising of non-arising of which Heidegger speaks in his account of the Anaximander Fragment comes to mind. In Sallis's reading of *The Birth of Tragedy* sublimeness also arises nonsublimely, without metaphysical comfort, unmarked in its fragile construction by human participation in a cosmic drama. *A true war story is never moral. It does not instruct, nor encourage virtue, nor suggest models of proper human behavior, nor restrain men from doing the things men have always done. If the story is moral do not believe it. If at the end of a war story you feel uplifted, or if you feel that some small bit of rectitude has been salvaged from the larger waste, then you have been made a victim of a very old and terrible lie.* The non-arising of the sublime comes with its arising in a moment of Sallis's thought. Third, and as an elaboration of the previous thought, Sallis yokes the sublime its unyoking. The sublime falls apart in his thought as a mimetic construction of terrible metaphysical comfort. These images of images deconstruct the originary nature that allowed them the appearance of sublimeness. The spacing that has allowed Sallis his contemplative distance, the spacing that he thinks as he forms the images under the rule of mimesis, gives the power of sublimeness to expire in his thought of it. Sallis's thought is mimetic of the movement of the tragic sublime. Now we have the sublime not as an originary presence, but as a mimetic echo that is echoed in its falling apart in Sallis's image of it. This is the most radical moment. Out of this unyoking in Sallis's thought another thought might arise. It might be tragic thought as distinct to thought about tragedy, thought that is not in Sallis's Apollinian voice, thought that probably strikes Sallis as strange—an echo of something other to *his* thinking in his thinking, Dionysian mimesis in the extreme, as the order of the sublime, the order of tragedy, the order of Nietzsche's crafted philosophy, and the order of Sallis's own thinking fall apart in the images by which they appear, not only something about dissonance, but a hovering dissonance, mimetic of the dissonance about which Sallis speaks coherently, dissonance in the good sense by which Sallis teaches us about Nietzsche's *The Birth of Tragedy*.

I listen for the laughter and the sounds of dissolution that this opening allows. I have followed Sallis in the serenity of his ordered images; at the apex of his account, like the single note of an oboe into which my hearing enters, comes suddenly an opening so harsh, a playing out of the presence of the previous order so stark, that I hear in it the collapse of the order of Sallis's thought. That he might have planned it this way does not diminish the strangeness of the sounds that emerge, for in *this* mimetic moment the abstractness of Sallis's thought, its descriptive accuracy about imagination's holding opposites together, its synthetic power to join together the opposites of appearing and disappearing, all collapse in an unhinging movement that is not unlike "dithyrambic madness." In this moment there is no tragedy. There is a dissolution of tragedy. The comfort of Sallis's clarity ceases in this moment without promise of a comfortable return. Almost like a Buddha, Sallis seems calm as he pronounces "monstrous" while the unyoking continues. I find neither love nor hate, neither attraction nor rage in this moment, but an unyoking that Sallis will yoke again as he imagines a theory of imaginative yoking of opposites, almost as though the mimetic moment did not linger, a moment usually unsensed by those who hear him think.

"You just don't know," she said. "You hide in this little fortress, behind wire and sand bags, and you don't know what its all about. Sometimes I want to eat this place. Vietnam. I want to swallow the whole country—the dirt, the death—I just want to eat it and have it there inside me. That's how I feel. It's like . . . this appetite. I get scared sometimes—lots of times—but it's not bad. You know? I feel close to myself. When I am out there at night, I feel close to my own body, I can feel my blood moving, my skin and my fingernails, everything, it's like I'm full of electricity and I'm glowing in the dark—I'm on fire almost—I'm burning away into nothing—but it doesn't matter because I know exactly who I am. You can't feel like that anywhere else."

What kind of thought is this? You can see how far removed from commentary it is in its mimetic movement, how it redetermines the texts about mimesis in its own adherence to the powers, disclosures, and concealments that play in those texts. We can expect Sallis to intensify the mimetic as he shows how imagination has worked in western thought and art. He calls this way of thinking poetic and means a mimetic manner of thinking that thinks the movement that it writes about from the "standpoint of the poets" rather than from the standpoint of philosophers. We know now that it is an oppositional thinking that releases itself from the passion for synthesis that also animates it, that it is not finally regulated by the principles of identity and noncontradiction, and that it gives a space of indeterminate distance as it comes to know the indeterminate in images and concepts that undermine that very knowledge. We have seen within a Nietzschean context that a war of structure, shining, dehiscence, and concealment takes place in Sallis's thought.

I would like to close with an image that is admittedly speculative. It is the image of the poetic thinker, one toward which Sallis has directed us in his more recent writings. The scene of this image is set by the priority of presence in the traditional thought of mimesis. Mimesis has been thought traditionally as an activity that presents something original in images from which the original withdraws. Thus conceived, imagery has both a disclosive and a distorting dimension. Imagining is said to present and to make available something originally present, but the imaginal presentation, the very activity of mimesis, fails to bring the original to full presence. The image, in thus concealing the original that it presents, is repeatedly judged to be inferior to some other activity that makes the original present in its full disclosure, in, for example, spirit that is in and for itself or in rational intuition or in practical activity that deals with political reality without absorption in abstraction. By the standards of full presence mimetic activity, in its instability and imaginal quality, is either deceptive or incomplete. "Under the demand for presence," Sallis says, "mimesis cannot but be effaced. . . . "[5]

In a move similar to Nietzsche's toward a tragic philosophy, Sallis turns to art, to the field opened up by mimesis. "One might venture such a move," Sallis says, "in the interest of justice to art, in behalf of art itself, art proper, which one would then want to distinguish from the improper determination brought to bear upon it in the history of metaphysics. But one might also so venture still in the name of philosophy, justifying the break by appeal to the necessity of *questioning* of privilege of presence."[6] In this move mimetic relation is the scene of origination and withdrawal from origination: there is no non-mimetic original that is copied and lost in its presentation. The scene is turned from one of presence to one of the ending of presence, and this thinking at the end of presence is governed by questioning the priority of presence and by giving priority to the work of art. The scene is then the space of manifestation in which differences are gathered, in which masking and concealing are in the coming of things to presence, in which presence comes to be lost, and in which nothing present seems to hover throughout the space of differences. *And in the end, of course, a true war story is never about war. It's about sunlight, it's about the special way that dawn spreads out on a river when you know you must cross the river and march into mountains and do things you are afraid to do. It's about love and memory. It's about sorrow. It's about sisters who never write back and people who never listen.* Sallis says "In every case, the work of art gathers opposites in their opposition; it presents what cannot be simply present together, issuing thus in a presentation that borders on impossibility, on contradiction."[7]

The work of this thought will need to be a mimesis of the work of art. It will need to be a gathering of opposites. It will be in a voice strange to Sallis, an almost impossible voice, I believe he would say, one that echoes more than he could say or want to say. The work of art in the work of thought by a questioning of presence, a mimesis of depresencing in the coming of things. I believe that for Sallis the issue of doing justice to art is one of bringing to thought a vitality that is traced in the traditional instability of mimesis.

. . . *Any soldier will tell you, if he tells you the truth, that proximity to death brings with it a corresponding proximity to life. After a firefight there is the immense pleasure of aliveness. The trees are alive. The grass, the soil—everything. All around things are purely living, and you among them, and the aliveness makes you tremble. . . . though it's odd, you're never more alive than when you're almost dead. You recognize what's valuable. Freshly, as if for the first time, you love what's best in yourself and in the world, all that might be lost.*

I have attempted to follow Sallis's thinking in this short moment as it has driven me again to the mimesis of texts. I have felt the overturning that occurs as he reads. I have ended where I would now begin, with the esteem for things that can come with the quiet and severe stalling of our ethical and political assertions. I share what I take to be Sallis's hope that by this stalling a beginning emerges in the ending of the dominion of presence. I share his persuasion that a transformation in the use of beings can transpire in a transformation of thinking, that the so-called aesthetic involves an enactment that is not aesthetic at all, when *aesthetic* is taken in its traditional senses. I see in his work the possibility of a reversal in which art comes with new politics and in which we may know that our usual understanding of politics necessitates, surprisingly, a drastic separation from what we have usually taken to be true, and a reunion, if we may call it that, with something that comes with art in its imaginative, mimetic work. *In a true war story, if there's a moral at all, it's like the thread that makes the cloth. You can't tease it out. You can't extract the meaning without unraveling the deeper meaning. And in the end, really, there's nothing much to say about a true war story, except maybe, 'oh'.* I wonder if Sallis also experiences limitations to art and the artist as he turns into them. Is there also a turning out and away from them, *that* kind of merciless Dionysian tenderness? How does the other to art take place in poetic mimesis? Only as ecstasy or as something fallen? Or does the other to art speak too of an opening, maulish to his thought, that depresents the play of light and shadow in, for example, Monet's haystacks, and disfigures the delicacy that has drawn Sallis to the poet's standpoint? Is he drawn beyond art in being drawn to it? Beyond good and evil, does a beyond-art occur that twists art to something political? Is he turning to a different politics as he turns out of aesthetics in the interest of doing justice to art?

CHAPTER SIX

THE WORK OF ART AS THE
REVERSE OF THE WORLD

Eliane Escoubas

Translated by Ashraf Noor

W hen the writings of John Sallis turn to the work of art—and especially to the pictorial work of art—two dimensions of his thought stand out: the *spatial* metaphors in his thinking and the work of *doubling*. This is the case, not only when the work of art forms the object of an explicit and direct elaboration, in texts which are specifically devoted to it, but also, in many other texts which are not explicitly devoted to art, when they are in some way placed under the sign of art and are inscribed in an indirect fashion into the horizon of the visual and pictorial work of art. Let me thus introduce the question of the work of art in Sallis's writings by making two opening remarks.

(1) Art occurs as a metaphor for the work of thought in numerous texts by Sallis. Is it not, indeed, noteworthy that the titles of several books and of other texts by Sallis use spatial metaphors which indicate an opening towards the pictorial arts, those which Kant designates as figural and which bear on the work of pictorial art in condensed form?

For example, *Spacings,* with its four chapters "Tunnelings," "Hoverings," "Enroutings," "Tremorings," uses terms which express the figures or the events proper to spatiality, that is, modes of dwelling in space. Similarly *Delimitations,* with the double play of "CLosure" and "Openings," as well as *Crossings,* with its subtitle *Nietzsche and the Space of Tragedy,* make use of spatial terms. And this is also true of *Echoes,* where one hears a duplication and at the same time a play of resonance/reflection—in other words, a double space: a space according to rhythm and a space according to imitation. On the other hand, two terms traverse all of Sallis's texts, where they constitute the problematic knot of thought, the place where philosophical questioning engenders itself: *threshold,* where at the same time the moment of limit and the moment of return, of reversal, show themselves, and *gathering,* where the mode of thought's questioning shows itself. Now, threshold and gathering both imply a space and a play of space, a "thinking" which is a "dwelling."

It is thus a question of spatial metaphors imported into a general question of the determination of thought in the epoch which Sallis designates as that of "the end of metaphysics." Metaphors, then, or rather figures of thought where the figurative is constitutive of the very thing of which it seems to be merely the figure, where the figurative is thus originary. Following Derrida, one could say that there is a question of supplement here, of the supplement as origin.

We shall thus make the hypothesis that an invisible thread ties together and marks the texts of Sallis. This invisible thread is a "supplement of the origin"; and this supplement of the origin has its place in the work of art whose essence is the working of space: the pictorial work of art, the painting. More than a metaphor, the pictorial work of art is the presentation (*Darstellung*) of the very mode of thought and of writing in the epoch of the "end of metaphysics."

(2) Another term, another metaphor, seems to me to have a bearing on the task of analysis and of deconstruction which Sallis carries out: the term *doubling,* which traverses all the texts and ensures the task of deconstruction throughout. Now, the "doubling" is the carrying out of the pictorial work of art; it bears at the same time the "realization" and the "critique" of the pictorial work of art. It is, as one could put it in a single expression, the critical realization of painting. I shall restrict myself to giving two examples to show that "doubling" is the task of deconstruction throughout.

First of all, the term *echoes* announces in itself a doubling; and this doubling expresses itself as a reversal. The end of chapter IV of *Echoes* ("Imagination— The Meaning of Being?") states this explicitly: "The Heideggerian case is of course different: the very plan for the demolition of the edifice of fundamental ontology is already sketched in this text. The question is only whether, in his case as in Kant's, imagination does not chart the way from ground to abyss" (E 117). This expression—"from ground to abyss"—describes simultaneously the *echo* and the *doubling.* They both say the same thing: the transformation of *ground* into *abyss.* This expression perhaps also describes, as we shall see, the essence of the work of art and particularly of painting.

"Doubling" is also the issue at the end of chapter V of *Echoes,* entitled "Mortality and Imagination: The Proper Name of Man." The French version of this text adds a phrase which the English text does not have. The English text ends with: "for imagination would say differently that coincidence of ownness and otherness that is mortality" (E 138). The French text has: *"car l'imagination dit autrement cette coincidence d'appartenance-en-propre et d'alterité qu'est la mort. Il s' agirait alors de doubler le nom doublement propre de l'homme."*[1] This last sentence, which is missing in the English text, expresses a doubling and a double doubling. And the doubling as said in French is divorced of any repetition.

Thus, in my view, the spatial metaphors of thought and the work of *doubling*—which is always at the same time a *reversal*—open the dimension of the work of art, and particularly of painting, in Sallis's work.

*   *   *

We shall now analyze three texts in which painting forms the explicit object of Sallis's thought. Three stages of choice: Monet's impressionism, Kandinsky's abstract art, and Mimmo Paladino's contemporary art. Three ways in which Sallis describes the doubling: from ground to abyss.

Monet and Impressionism.[2]

Under the heading "Shades of Time" Sallis describes Monet's series of paintings that depict haystacks, focusing on those exhibited at the Art Institute of Chicago during the summer of 1990. This exhibition recalls—though not duplicating exactly—the one which took place one hundred years earlier, during Monet's lifetime, at Durand-Ruel in Paris, in May of 1891.

The core of Sallis's analysis lies in the theme of *doublement* (doubling). The series is a mode of doubling, or, to put it inversely, the doubling gives rise to the series.

How do Monet's haystacks in fact present themselves? The series of haystacks are actually a series of variations. One knows that Monet painted the haystacks at different times of the day (in the morning, at midday, at sunset) and in different seasons (in summer, at times of snow, etc.). There are, however, also variations of point of view. On the paintings which represent two haystacks, the distance between these varies from one painting to the other—the small haystack is nearer or farther away from us than the large one, the large haystack partially hides the small one, or they are, in contradistinction, very far apart from each other—as if Monet had turned these haystacks around by changing the position of his easel.

What thematic consequences does Sallis draw from these observations? (1) "Beyond the painting there is nothing. This is not of course to say that no mimesis is in play. . . ."3 *Nothing.* The work in a series puts an end to the domination of the objective referent. Impressionism suppresses the object and paints the impression in place of it. It carries out a rehabilitation of the sensible world which is close to the one effected by Nietzsche. It is not surprising that Kandinsky, upon seeing a haystack painted by Monet in an exhibition in Moscow, spoke of a "confused feeling that the subject was lacking in this painting."4 (2) "In such impressionism things are painted as they show themselves rather than as sensible images that would present a meaning transcending the sensible presentation."5

That which the pictures of haystacks present is the "self-manifestation" of things, the visibility of the visible—not what things are. That which Monet paints is the appearing of what appears. In Monet "appearing" is composed of diverse kinds of light. Monet does not paint objects, but light as envelope and shining; or perhaps one could say: objects which have become light. Thus Sallis writes that the haystacks are mirrors and fulcra, transitory objects. As fragments of light, the haystacks lose their character of being haystacks, that "everything is dissolved into shining . . . ; virtually every thing has disappeared into a spread of fading light."6

In this way shade conquers the object. Shade becomes the symptom of the radiance of light. Shade as a reversal of light is its "reflexion," a transformation from ground to abyss.

What, then, is the "doubling" of impressionism? What are its features? It is the double play of the disappearance of the object and the enacting of light as the appearing of what appears. Sallis calls this double play: "adumbration."

A reversal is thus carried out by which shade becomes more real than that which is real. It is precisely through the shade of the haystacks that reality becomes visible. It is as a reversal that the world enters on the scene in painting, in the impressionist painting of Monet.

What is this "reality" which realizes the doubling and the reversal of the world in painting? This reality is *time.* That which Monet's pictures render visible is time, and the haystacks are like sundials. The appearing is an appearing of time, and *adumbration* is the mode of the advent of time in painting.

Thus the whole of Sallis's analysis of the theme of Monet's haystacks has "a new interpretation of the sensible" as a guiding thread,7 the liberation of the sensible from its subservience to the intelligible. And this is carried out by time's becoming visible—a time which, by its doubling and its reversal in adumbration, constitutes the space of the impressionist painting. Adumbration is the essence of painting.

Kandinsky and the Thresholds of Abstract Art.8

It is not surprising that Sallis is interested in Kandinsky, for in Kandinsky's work the disappearance of the object is accomplished. In Kandinsky the abstract mode of appearing enters the scene of painting. Kandinsky himself calls this "the pure art."

The guiding theme of Sallis's analysis here is again that of "doubling": "from one doubling to another" and also: "Passage across the threshold is a movement from one doubling to another." And this passage is incessant, for doubling "is itself, in turn, a movement across a certain threshold."[9] From now on doubling and threshold redouble or duplicate each other.

Abstraction, "the pure art," is not the elimination of all doubling (i.e., of all mimesis). It is not a question of making an ornament of painting; it is "never a matter of purging art of all doubling"[10]—and abstract painting is not "like a necktie or a carpet." Rather it is a matter of passing from one doubling to another, from doubling by reproduction to "spiritual doubling," in other words from the doubling of nature to doubling "from another origin"; and this "other origin" is what Kandinsky names "internal necessity." "Internal necessity" is a turn inward, a spiritual vibration—or that which the German word *Stimmung* evokes.

What Sallis finds, then, in Kandinsky is "a renewed interrogation of doubling," a doubling that would twist free of the all-too-metaphysical oppositions between inner and outer, between spirit and nature."[11] It is a matter of suspending the dualistic schema itself and of posing the threshold *as threshold,* where there is no longer inside or outside. Only the threshold. The doubling is the threshold itself.

Mimmo Paladino and Contemporary Art.[12]

If Sallis finds the withdrawal from the object in Monet and in Kandinsky, he encounters another withdrawal in Mimmo Paladino: the withdrawal from language.

Sallis is interested in a series of paintings by Mimmo Paladino, the series EN DO RE, in which the individual paintings are at first left without titles and then reproduced with the title "untitled." Here language withdraws in a double manner; it comments on its own absence, it enunciates its own absence.

What remains when the enunciation of that which appears disappears? What remains are images. Sallis cites Mimmo Paladino's expression: "What I was looking for was images."

What remains when images remain? Sallis answers: "the pure visibility of the work." One thus arrives at a new definition of the notion of image. The image is no longer determined as reproduction and resemblance but as the "pure visibility of the work." What does the painting paint when it "looks for" images? It paints visibility as such.

The pictorial image, the painting, does not show what it shows, but it shows the showing itself. It shows what it conceals, and it conceals what it shows. It stays wholly within the play of appearing as disappearing and of disappearing as appearing: It lets the disappearing appear. It is thus, once again, a question of another mode of doubling.

Three definitions or observations, then, come into play in Sallis's analysis: (1) Mimmo Paladino's images are masks: "they are recondite images." A mask is an appearing which conceals. And precisely because they are masks, the images are not fixed; they are "passing images." From now on another logos enters the scene, the reversal of the traditional logos, a logos of the mask and of transition, a nomadic logos. (2) The work of Mimmo Paladino's painting is the carrying out of a superimposing of surfaces. The image which is the painting reduplicates the painting by the introduction of another painting that is superimposed onto the surface of the image: an obfuscating panel. A painting conceals or covers a painting. The superimposition of surfaces joins itself to the opening of the frame which is effected by Mimmo Paladino. There is thus a double play of open and complete closure. (3) The work of supplementarity is added to this. The painting is enlarged, extended by a portion which is added to it from the exterior, added as an excrescence. This is an addition which dismantles the painting, which subtracts from it any possible or presumed unity. The dis-unity, the dis-integrity, of the painting is what this enlargement reveals. Mimmo Paladino's painting thus bears a strategy of the *reversal* of values.

The non-fixity of images is the object of painting here. Painting paints the non-fixed: "The logic of this painting is such as to produce a reversal, gathering the passing images into an image of passing."[13] And "the image of passing" is radiated by the work itself. This is why the series which is most characteristic of Mimmo Paladino's painting is without a doubt the one whose title barely resonates in the silence: *On Tip-toe.*

*   *   *

I should like to parallel or echo these analyses of painting with two pieces of philosophical work by Sallis, one concerning the imagination and the sublime in Kant (from *Spacings*) and the other concerning Heidegger's *The Origin of the Work of Art* (from *Echoes—After Heidegger*).

The hypothesis of my reading of "Tremorings" (chapter IV of *Spacings*) is the following: The two themes which, according to Sallis, are constitutive of the pictorial work of art, of the painting—the doubling and the reversal of the world (that is, the inobjectivity of the work of art)—are the same ones that are constitutive of the sublime in Kant. The only difference is that in Kant the doubling-reversal is maintained within the opposition of the sensible and the supersensible, an opposition which does not operate at the center of the work of art.

Let us outline the principle features of the sublime in "Tremorings" (chapter IV of *Spacings*). First, there is the withdrawal of the object. Nothing is sublime, just as nothing is beautiful. The sublime is not, anymore than is the beautiful, a determination of the object. The reflective judgment which announces the sublime as well as the beautiful is withdrawn into the subject and applies the subject's power of schematization, that is to say, the imagination.

Yet the sublime goes beyond the beautiful: While the beautiful is such because of its form, the sublime is amorphous. To the inobjectivity of the beautiful the sublime adds the unlimitedness of nature in its two modes, mathematical and dynamical (magnitude and power). The *abyss* of the sublime (the amorphous) is substituted for the *ground* of the beautiful (form).

Secondly the imagination which is put into effect in the sublime is the faculty of "negative presentation." The imagination is the faculty of disclosure. ("Disclosure is the site of the sublime" [S 111].) Yet Sallis's analysis shows that, as the faculty of the sublime, the imagination is the faculty of the supersensible and that it is thus a faculty of the *repression of images:* "a repression of images in favor of that merely negative presentation of the supersensible" (S 121).

Yet does not another notion of image emerge here, an "image" of "another origin"? Is not the repression of images the repression of images only insofar as they are copies or reproductions of something which is already given? Does it not, on the contrary, leave room for an image of another type, which does not have the function of imitating but of appearing? Thus "the agency of the disclosure is indeed imagination" (S 124)—and the disclosure is a reversal of the world.

Put more succinctly: Sallis's text now effects a generalization of doubling; the twofoldness of pleasure and pain is superposed onto the scission of nature-man and sensible-supersensible. In order to explain this twofoldness, Sallis effects an exercise of language. On the basis of "trembling" (as the subject orientation) and of "tremor" (the object orientation), he fabricates the word *tremoring* as a translation of the German word *Erschütterung;* and he defines *tremoring* "as alternation or drift between ground and abyss." Thus, one has here the doubling and the reversal, interlaced and indissociable.

If, then, the sublime is an "imaginal supplement," can one not employ the same expression for the work of art and particularly for the painting of Monet, of Kandinsky, of Mimmo Paladino, i.e., an imaginal supplement that is a doubling between ground and abyss?

Let us now look briefly at "Poetics" (chapter VII of *Echoes*), which deals with Heidegger's *Origin of the Work of Art.* This begins in the following manner: "Art, too, is a way in which truth happens. If such happening should prove to be essentially poetic, then to think art would be to think the poetic, to think poetry" (E 169). One can recognize two Heideggerian themes here: art as "truth's putting itself in(to) (the) work" (*das sich-ins-Werk-Setzen der Wahrheit*) and art as essentially poetry ("all art is essentially poetry").

Sallis takes the Greek word ποίησις as the point of departure for his analysis of Heidegger. Ποίησις is production, that is to say τέχνη, that is to say manifestation. Ποίησις: "it is a matter of bringing something into manifestness

(*Hervor-bringen in die Offenbarkeit*)" (E 171)—and he arrives quickly at the knot of the question.

The knot of the question consists in this: *In Heidegger the doubling is a circling* (E 172). Everything will hinge on this Heideggerian elaboration of doubling or circling. The first circle is that of the artist and the work (each is in turn the origin of the other). The second circle is that of art and of the work of art. Now, this second circle is, in Sallis's analysis, the circle of μίμησις, where μίμησις serves to name the connection by which Heidegger thinks "the necessity of the doubling return from the truth of Being back to beings."

From now on works of art are and are not things. The shoes painted by Van Gogh "serve to disclose what the shoes are in truth." It is the same in the case of the Greek temple. One thus has to take the Heideggerian expression "happening of truth" in a "double sense": "truth's putting itself to work in putting itself into the work of art" (E 174). And this says the same as "the Being of beings comes into the steadiness of its shining (*Das Sein des Seienden kommt in das Ständige seines Scheinens*)" (E 175).

The question which Sallis poses, then, is the following: Is it possible to think μίμησις ontologically? Here one has to think the relation between world and earth: "But how do world and earth belong together such that the setting up of world and the setting forth of earth can belong together in the unity of the work? Heidegger's answer is decisive: World and earth belong together in *opposition*" (E 177,178). *Opposition* names the German *Streit* and the Greek πόλεμος.

This opposition, which is in the interior of circling and at one with it, is what Sallis names doubly: doubling-reversal. It is what Sallis calls a new mimesis: "It would be a mimesis that would take place in and as the *Gestalt* in which truth would be set into the work, placed there, without having preceded the work and yet in such a way as to be doubled in the play of reciprocity between the work of art and the strife of world and earth. It is in this doubling that mimesis can be rethought and reinscribed within Heidegger's poetics" (E 185).

Is not the ultimate goal of Sallis's *doubling* the reintroduction of μίμησις in *The Origin of the Work of Art,* while fundamentally disturbing the sense of μίμησις, where mimesis becomes pure "reversal"?

* * *

Doubling and reversal are characteristic of painting. Modern painting in the thought of Sallis also reveals itself in three modes, which are modes of doubling and of reversal: Monet's impressionism, Kandinsky's abstraction, and Mimmo Paladino's "passing images."

I should like to confront Carazan's dream, which Kant relates and which Sallis cites at the beginning of "Tremorings," with a story by Italo Calvino that seems to reflect the theme of Sallis's analysis: the doubling and the reversal. It is a narrative entitled "Dall' opaco" in the collection *La Strada di San Giovanni*.[14] The narrator observes the "form of the world" from his balcony. Each of us, he says, finds himself at the crossing-point of three dimensions: "pierced by a dimension which enters one through the stomach and exits through the back, by another which passes from one shoulder to the other, and by a third which pierces the cranium and exits through the feet; this is an idea which one will accept only after much resistance and rejection; but one will act afterwards as if one had always known it. . . ." These three dimensions thus become six: "in front behind above below right left"—obviously a "doubling."

And here is the end of the narrative, where a play of doubling-reversal is inscribed, which Sallis would not deny:

> and even considering that the observer is immobile, his situation with regard to the opaque and to what is in the sunlight will always be controversial because this I which is turned towards what is in the sunlight sees the opaque side of each bridge, tree, roof while the wall or the slope to which my back is turned is in full sunlight. . . . This is why it is right to say that this I which is turned towards what is in the sunlight is also an I which retreats into the opaque. . . . And it is useless for me to try to remember at what moment I entered the shade, for I was there from the beginning. . . . I shall know from now on that the only world which exists is opaque and that what is in sunlight is the reversal of this. . . . It is from the abyss of opacity that I write. . . .

CHAPTER SEVEN

TWISTING FREE OF METAPHYSICS

ECSTATIC PHILOSOPHY

Walter Brogan

> Imagine then a spacing of closure that would exceed
> closure, that would perforate its covering, rending
> and riddling its sphere, opening it ever so minutely
> towards beginnings that would exceed the end, that would
> pluralize and defer it, endings. (S 132)

The telling of the story of this μῦθος, this mythical beginning that John Sallis asks us to imagine, is, in one way or another at the heart of all of his work. It is a story that needs to be told in our times, indeed is perhaps fated to be told; for it is the rethinking and reenactment at the end of metaphysics of μοῖρα, which, in Heidegger's words, is "the beginning that has dispensed the destiny of being."[1] I believe μοῖρα to be one of the words for this event that Sallis's philosophy never ceases to question.

But already in *Being and Logos: The Way of Platonic Dialogue,* first published almost two decades ago, Sallis found in the Platonic dialogues a key facet of his own philosophical task. What Sallis traces in that work is the way the Platonic dialogues effect the separation of the dimensions of μῦθος, λόγος, and ἔργον—myth, speech and deed—and thereby initiate metaphysics by repressing myth in favor of λόγος. At the same time, Sallis demonstrates that Plato is operating out of a space in which these dimensions belong together. What interests Sallis in Plato's work is the character of the originary movement by which the earthly opaqueness of myth and the superior light of *logos* are divided and pitted against one another. Sallis carefully shows the previously unnoticed or unappreciated complexity of Plato's thought, which always involves a movement that allows this division to bend back on itself, thereby enacting a displacing of the apparent stability of these divisions.

But what Sallis discovers in his effort to mark the origin of Plato's thought and to mark the re-turn of his thinking to the origin is that the originary movement that is the point of departure of Plato's thought is imagination. Sallis shows this most profoundly in his discussion of the dyadic character of the good. When Socrates acknowledges to Glaucon that he cannot show the good directly but only through its offspring, Sallis suggests that this refusal and inability, this withdrawal at the highpoint of the *Republic* in the face of the good, is not due to an inadequacy on Socrates's part to accomplish a vision that could in principle be accomplished; nor is it an indication that each individual has to have this direct vision of the good for himself or herself. Rather it is because the good is not itself a presence but is this very activity of imaging that it is impossible to approach the good except through images. To quote Sallis:

> Hence Socrates is saying that it belongs to the good not to show itself as one. . . . The good [that is beyond being and presumably beyond the separation of the intelligible and the visible] *shows itself only through images.* (BL 412)

To Sallis, this infiltration of imaging into the self-showing of the good, that the story of the good needs to be shown through the drawing in an image of the divided line, etc. is what is most thoughtworthy in Plato's philosophy. "To know," Sallis says, "is not only to imitate the good but also to assist in the birth of the children of the good. This is the fundamental sense of Socratic midwifery" (BL 412). Later, I would like to address more specifically the metaphorics in Sallis's writing through which he attempts to be the midwife at the end of the history of metaphysics that Plato's philosophy helped to generate. But before turning to that task, I want to draw upon another related aspect of Sallis's reading of Plato in *Being and Logos.* It involves a question that Sallis raises there but, as far as I can tell, postpones. This is the question of procreation, the question of father and mother. After pointing out the male imagery which Socrates uses in speaking of the fathering of the good and its offspring, Sallis raises but then drops a very provocative question:

> The erotic imagery leads us to wonder whether there is not also a mother who gives birth to these images of the good that are fathered by the good. But the identity of the mother is left completely *concealed.* (BL 404)

In a manuscript on Plato's *Timaeus* that is being prepared for publication, Sallis repays the debt on this postponed question.[2] It is, I believe, this question of the concealed imaging of the mother that Sallis is addressing in his discussion of the χώρα in the *Timaeus.* This is particularly interesting in that Plato sets the dramatic chronology of the *Timaeus* so that the discussion is said to take place the day after the discourse on the city and to be for the purpose of setting the city (the male republic that imitates the good) in motion. The first city was founded on the division between the intelligible and the sensible. Sallis shows how this division, which is the basis of a meta-physics of presence, is founded upon a repression of imagination, a repression necessary in order to secure a realm in which the "original" is protected from the dyadic play between image and original. This division is held together and apart by the good that is beyond but fathers being. Now the description of the second city in the *Timaeus* is announced as having the intent of destabilizing this division. But this task is apparently postponed in favor of Critias's description of the genesis of the cosmos.

Sallis points out that there are actually three discourses on the origin of the cosmos given by Timaeus. I want here very briefly to frame out each of these, because each, in Sallis's careful analysis, differentiates very different and increasingly complex aspects of imagination as it functions in Plato's work. In turn, I believe that one of Sallis's most important and original philosophical contributions is the identification of these complex and intertwining levels in the operation of imagination, along with his ability, his stylistic genius, in reopening within the text the play of imagination, setting back in motion the activity of imagination and thereby releasing the repressed imagination from its bondage within the confinements of metaphysical limits.

Very briefly, the first discourse that Timaeus presents on the origin of the cosmos is the story of how the divine craftsman fabricated the cosmos, including time, out of the elements. It is a story of molding and stamping things with the image of the intelligible paradigm, a story of the production of images. This first discourse operates within the dyadic structure of generated image and the self-same, original εἶδος. The second story, the one that is taken up by Sallis in a detailed study, is the discourse on the χώρα, the chorology. For this discourse, not only the twofold of intelligible εἶδος and visible image is necessary but yet a third, namely this chora. The chora is the name of the place before cosmic time, which houses the primordial elements out of which the demiourgos fabricates the cosmos. This third kind, the chora or receptable, Plato calls mother. The chorology is the discourse of the mother, a more original story, one that is excluded from the founded order of time and the stable division between intelligible and sensible that is fathered by the demiourgos in the first discourse. Sallis points out, with great subtlety, the irony of this exclusion, in that the metaphysical ordering of the cosmos according to intelligible εἶδος and visible image is both founded on this exclusion and yet dependent on what is excluded. Virtually all of the work of John Sallis of which I am aware is involved in recovering this lost city, this repressed story of the mother, or else in discovering places where, even if only in fragmented and fleeting ways, this other, repressed discourse shines through the cracks in the systems that attempt to close themselves off from exposure to it. It goes without saying that Sallis's work often involves not only reflecting glimmers of this fragmented light but also participating in the philosophical task of enlarging those rifts to the point where the closure of the system comes into question and is once again destabilized, threatened and set into motion.

Timaeus calls this χώρα the receptacle and nurse of all generation. What is received, supported, held, and granted an abode by the chora is the irrepressibly multiple proto-elemental flux at "a time before the elements come to be formed in the image of self-same being." In Sallis's analysis, what is shown is that the claim that the intelligible εἴδη are able to be wholly self-same and at the same time able to be duplicated in images, the integrity and duplicity of being, is able to be sustained because, as Timaeus says, the chora comes to the aid of images and holds them in being in a certain way. To quote Sallis here:

> The chora is that by which the image, from which being as such is withheld, holds nonetheless to being; the chora is that *other* (that something different) that *secures* the image in its being in a certain way, that secures it so that, though remote from being, the image is still not nothing.[3]

So there are two stories that involve imagination and imaging in Sallis's interpretation of Plato. The first is the story of the good that fathers images as imitations of the intelligible εἴδη. This duplication of the intelligibles in images produces the division between the intelligible and the sensible and thereby the cosmos. The imaging activity produces beings that can only be as phantom shadows of what is as such. The second discourse is the story of another relationship to imaging, one that preserves and sustains the image as image, the being of the image as such, not φαντασία but εικασία. In such a place, the image is released from the repression of its being, untethered from its definition in terms of the singular oneness of εἴδος.

But there is yet a third story about the origin of the cosmos that Timaeus tells, namely the story of the being of those sensible images that are released from bondage to true being. It is the story of these image-beings, these sensible beings that belong to a primordial time and a realm before or after the collapse of metaphysical dualism, visible, sensible beings outside of the confinement to a contrasting and opposing order of intelligible real being. It is this story, a chorology that has not yet been told, and in a way cannot be told, that finds a voice for itself, a respect, even a reverential resonance in Sallis's work. It is a story of proto-elementary indeterminancy, of a play of difference that is not yet a matter of difference between things.

There is a hint at the very end of Sallis's essay on the χώρα of how one might draw from the resources of λόγος an echo of this new sensibility. The difficulty here is twofold. Not only is it unsayable because it belongs to a realm that is prelinguistic, which is in a sense true; but also λόγος itself is only possible through the suppression of this voice. So the λόγος that one must employ must disrupt and violate the rules of λόγος. Sallis names this kind of speaking "ventriloquy." Timaeus calls it bastard saying. Ventriloquy is a kind of double saying, an echoed saying, a saying that is also a hearing, a voice of oneself that comes as other.

Sallis practices this ventriloquy in his work by spawning a metaphorics that speaks about this twisting free of the sensible in a way that at the same time (hamology) shows both the integrity and selfsameness of being and the duplicity of being—together. This metaphorics, through which Sallis would show the sensibilization of reason, can be found scattered throughout his works in such words as: hoverings, tunnelings, crossings, enroutings, tremorings, thresholds, turnings, echoing and, most importantly, soundings. For to the stilled voice of the unspoken, repressed, fluctuating origin, Sallis the musician brings an ear that is attuned to the almost but not completely silenced tremoring of the spacings that open up with the doubling of the notes in a composition. I have been struck over and over by the quiet but forceful attention that Sallis brings to the need to listen to the sounds of being. I will try to show later that it is this attitude of attunement, of listening to a musical symphony with the ear of a composer, being able to hear what Heidegger calls "the concealed, ecstatic, lyrical echo of an unspeakable saying"[4] that permits us to say of John Sallis that he is the artist-philosopher, the practitioner of ecstatic, Dionysian philosophy.

There is in Sallis's work a recurrent story, one that he tells in almost every major work he has written. I am not sure if he is aware of how often he has made this story the focus of his attention or the starting point of his considerations. It is not his story but Nietzsche's, told in *Twilight of the Idols* about "How the 'True World' Finally Became a Fable." It is a story told in bold strokes that begins with Plato and ends with Zarathustra. Though Sallis has contributed revolutionary interpretations and analyses of many of the major thinkers in the history of philosophy (notably of course Kant and the German idealists) and though I acknowledge the great affinity of his philosophy to that of his contemporaries (notably Heidegger and Derrida), nevertheless, I would suggest that the thought of John Sallis remains always in a special way intricately linked to that of Plato and Nietzsche. Both of their writings frame for Sallis a *Sache* for thought.

In the case of Plato, I believe it was the difficult task of following after the ἐπέκεινα τῆς οὐσίας, that which, beyond being, initiates, comes before and is excluded from the realm of what is, while nevertheless infiltrating, endangering and contaminating that realm of being that it surpasses. To think beyond being, Sallis shows, does not mean to abandon being but to transgress and disrupt the pretense to self-enclosure that would shield it from being contaminated by the sensible. To think beyond being, about which Plato speaks to Glaucon only in hushed tones and indirectly, is to think beyond the separation of being from the sensible. This means not only to think of the multiple sensible image "as such," that is, in a singular way, but also it is to allow the twofold, double character of the intelligible self-same being to become manifest by exposing the movement of imaging, repetition, and return that belongs to the oneness of intelligible being. In a sense, Sallis's work on the imagination is a report on what he heard Socrates and Glaucon whispering to each other in their conversation about the good.

One of Sallis's attempts to render Nietzsche's story of "How the 'True World' Finally became a Fable" is found at the end of *Echoes*. There he attempts to situate Heidegger's thinking in terms of the "rethinking of the sensible that is required once it has been, as with Nietzsche, twisted free from its opposition to the intelligible" (E 193). Heidegger is shown to have a trace of this turn towards the freed sensibles in "The Origin of the Work of Art." Sallis describes this movement as "the necessity of a doubling return from the truth of being back to beings" (E 174). It is a movement that reinscribes the phenomenological project of caring for the appearance and the apparent world after the "true world" has become a fable.

I believe that this is an important link between the work of Heidegger and that of Sallis. What Sallis often engages in is also a phenomenological investigation of the sensible reconstituted outside the framework of the "true world." For Sallis, this takes the form of a phenomenological recovery of the sensible image and imagination outside the privilege of presence, which always bans the unstable and pluralizing activity of imagination from the realm of being. By taking up the task of an attunement to the sensible image that assists it in twisting free of its determination in opposition to the intelligible, Sallis is able to advance phenomenology beyond the contours of Heidegger's thinking. This is especially evident in his analysis of what Heidegger considers to be the unutterable domain of tautological thinking.

For Sallis, if I am not mistaken, Heidegger's decision to leave as inviolable the simple saying of this primordially other place (*die Sprache spricht, Welt weltet*, etc.) and his willingness to run the risk of being dumbfounded in the face of the saying of the same, so that his thinking stops short at tautology, marks the limit of Heidegger's thought. For Heidegger, that which is beyond being is unsayable and thinkable only as tautology precisely because it is withdrawn from the realm of metaphysical language and thought. For Sallis, this realm is nevertheless open to phenomenological investigation, not through questioning but through listening and hearing the resonances of that in the face of which Heidegger could only be silent. Sallis has found a way to uncover, without reducing its inherent obscurity, this apparently ineffable realm that Heidegger was pointing towards in his studies on language and poetry. The possibility for this lies within the tautological moment itself, within the space that is opened up in tautology. For what Sallis demonstrates is that mimetic repetition—and what he calls a doubling—comes into play in tautology in such a way as to allow a disruption in the self-securing, self-delimiting sphere of well-rounded tautological truth.

Heidegger thinks the withdrawing of truth and its being held in reserve as other than that which appears in the metaphysical schema of the beingness of beings. He thinks at the limits of metaphysics but holds back his thinking from transgressing the well-formed circle in which truth moves. Sallis, in contrast, does not withdraw from the task of allowing to be redrawn the Parmenidean circle in a way that would reflect the collapse of the "true world" and the twisting free of the sensible that Nietzsche announced. The Sallisian circle is bent, out-of center, more of a circling than a completed circle, an open enclosure that would delimit the closure of being while opening it to its disfigurement and displacement. It is an "eccentric" circling not drawn by reason in its sameness with being but through the doubling, circling activity of a recovered originary imagination. One of the metaphors that Sallis uses to describe (in the context of a discussion of Fichte) this circling around is "hovering":

> The circle(s) of reason would, then, have been redrawn as the displaced circling of imagination, withdrawn from being and ground, drawn into the spacing of oppositions. Philosophy would end—or be denied an end—with imagination hovering ἐπέκεινα τῆς οὐσίας, hovering between heaven and earth, a dove. (S 66)

In his various versions of Nietzsche's story of the collapse of the "true" world, Sallis never hints at any nostalgia towards this old world of unity, permanence, and completion. Sallis has already set sail again and become engrossed in the new explorations that are needed of the philosopher today. But he is keenly interested in what would remain at the end of metaphysics, namely appearances. Sallis's thought, it seems to me, is haunted by the following declaration by Nietzsche:

> The true world—we have abolished. What world has remained? The apparent one perhaps? But no! *With the true world we have also abolished the apparent one.*[5]

It is this event, its occurrence and recurrence, that is allowed to be shown and mirrored in the work of John Sallis. He follows this event not so much to capture it in his reflections or to fix its meaning as much as to keep it in play, to celebrate with his philosophical art the sublime character of this terrifying event. When Sallis retells this story, even when he follows Nietzsche back through the history of philosophy to Hegel and Fichte and Kant and Plato, it is a story about spacings. It is an account of the spacing that opens up with the closing up of the space between the intelligible and the sensible within which metaphysics has operated. It is the story of the previously repressed space where the mixing of opposites that metaphysics forbade and devalued can be supported and once again set in motion. Sallis calls this spacing "occlusion":

> Occlusion is, then, the spacing that sets the "true world" adrift, that lets it drift so utterly out of sight that there remains only the "apparent" world. But the latter is then displaced. . . . Occlusion is the spacing that occurs at the end of metaphysics, the final spacing of metaphysics. (S xiii)

But, most appealing to Sallis, it is the story of the twisting free of the sensible multiplicity from its determination in opposition to oneness. It is this story that is most appealing to Sallis, the thinker of the artwork who discovers in Monet a painter who, contemporaneous with Nietzsche, makes visible by painting the shining of the sensible that threatens to overflow at the end of metaphysics.

We are accustomed to insisting on the separation of the philosophical work of a philosopher and the person of the philosopher. Such a separation had a certain merit within the framework of a world view that divided subjective and objective considerations. Such a division is, however, untenable and thoroughly surpassed by one who would be engaged in a philosophical project such as that of John Sallis. What kind of philosopher would be able to engage in this sort of philosophical project? What is required of an author whose texts would engage the μίμησις of things. In the final pages of his discussion of Heidegger in his text: *Echoes: After Heidegger,* Sallis names, I believe, the primary characteristic of such a philosopher: *ecstacy.*

> In ecstacy, in being outside oneself, one is not simply present either inside or outside, but rather the operation of the simple limit that would separate inside from outside, presence from absence, is disrupted. (E 193)

Sallis's book *Crossings: Nietzsche and the Space of Tragedy* calls this ecstacy "Dionysian." In a caution that I believe Sallis would apply to our attempts to comment on and ground his texts and works, Sallis states:

> Dionysian excess revealed itself not even as a *fundamental* truth, not even as *the* fundamental truth, the truth by which all others would be grounded. For one could take Dionysian excess to be such a ground, to underlie all truths or things as their ground, as the origin from which they would arise in their determination, only at the cost of ignoring the way in which the would-be ground disrupts the very ordering that belongs to the concept of ground and dissolves the very determinateness that ground would produce. (C 58)

But, to write such excessive texts, which cannot be owned or authored and which echo in the work of those who read them, one must oneself be Dionysian:

> In reference to the self, the Dionysian is the exceeding of the limit by which one's individuality would be delimited, by which the self would be defined and constituted as an interior space of self-possession. Such exceeding is thus a disruption of determinate selfhood, a certain loss of self. (C 56)

CHAPTER EIGHT

ECHOES AT THE EDGE

SHIMMERING IMAGINGS IN *DELIMITATIONS*

Kenneth Maly

> Shimmering lightly in the breeze,
> Profusions of delicate mirrors,
> Raised by earth to give
> To sunlight
> Its dancing shadows,
> Its play.
>
> Tinkling softly in the breeze,
> Profusion of tiny bells,
> Cast above to give
> To wind
> Its gentle voice,
> Its song.
>
> —John Sallis, "Leaves in
> Late Summer," unpublished

The last sentence in the essay "Image and Phenomenon" (Chapter V of *Delimitations: Phenomenology and the End of Metaphysics*) ends with the words: ". . . the play of imaging in the things themselves" (D 75). This ending of the essay follows several other phrases dealing with imaging:

... the release of image into imaging.

... *imaging belongs to showing:* That showing in which an object comes to show itself ... *comes to pass as imaging.*

... *showing as imaging* comes to pass *from* the objects themselves.

Then, finally, the phrase: " ... the play of imaging in the things themselves."

My first question is: What is the relation of imaging to the things themselves (here also called: "objects")? What is the relation of image to original? In what sense, if any, is there an object-thing at all? And in what sense, if any, can an object-thing be called an original?

Earlier in the same essay Sallis says that a painting is initially seen as an image—an image that, in its turn, reveals "an original which it itself is not" (D 71). One always already looks through (or beyond) the image at the thing itself. One sees an image *of* the thing, i.e., one looks at the thing through the image. Sallis writes: "One apprehends the image *as* already linked up with the original of which it is an image, as opening onto the original, as letting the original show itself" (D 71).

But how does the original show itself? What is this play of imaging in the things themselves? If we think the showing/imaging as such and let it unfold, what happens to the things, to the original? When imaging as such becomes the focus for thinking's attention, what happens to the image-original distinction?

I offer this thought: The root-character of imaging takes its shape, not from the character of image—how an image images/announces—but rather from its connection with self-showing, or with imaging as such. Thus the image-original dichotomy collapses completely, in favor of disclosing/revealing/showing as such—in favor of imaging as such.[1] I want here to take up the question of showing/imaging as such and to weave it together with the question of the ends(s) (end of metaphysics) that is at the heart of *Delimitations.* For hidden within the collapse of the image-original distinction, in favor of imaging/self-showing as such, is the collapse of the end of metaphysics, in favor of ... ? That is the question.

Delimitations offers a hint as to how to proceed, in the epigram by which the book begins. It is a quotation from Heidegger's *Parmenides*:[2]

> When thought as the Greeks would think, boundary (*Grenze,* πέρας) is not that whereby something stops; but rather that into which something emerges, in that it stands within that which "shapes" what has emerged, i.e., lets it take shape and lets what has come to stand emerge.

And then in his introduction to the book, entitled "ὁρισμός," Sallis quotes Heidegger again:

> Boundary (*Grenze,* πέρας) is not that at which something ceases; but, as the Greeks recognized, boundary is that from which something begins its root-unfolding [*sein Wesen beginnt*]. Therefore, the concept is ὁρισμός, horizon, boundary. (D ix)[3]

Usually the word *boundary* implies a demarcated line, a marked boundary, a place or line "somewhere" which we in our thinking (*a*) can cross (transgressing the boundary, crossing the line)—a distinguishable "zone" to be crossed (ζώνη: belt; ζώννυμαι: gird)—or (*b*) cannot cross (this is all there is, the end and nothing beyond—not even the "no-thing" that enables), where our thinking comes up against the *utterly* limited, because there is nowhere and nothing there. Given the long-standing tradition of substance-metaphysics, in which our thinking is situated and necessarily moves, this tendency is hard to ignore, hard or impossible to avoid—even though it is itself very limiting.

If we think boundary as defined—as a line that demarcates—then either we cross over that line "to the opposite"; or we stay on this side of the line entirely. This is the usual context for thinking the end of metaphysics—and with that the beginning of metaphysics. In chronological terms we think it as before metaphysics and after metaphysics, as the not-yet-metaphysical and the no-longer-metaphysical. If we think boundary or end as a demarcated line that can be crossed, then the question becomes: How do we cross over the boundary *into* this "opposite side" without leaving behind finitude or limitedness as such? How do we avoid thinking in absolute terms, in terms of substance or presence—how do we avoid thinking merely metaphysically? If we think boundary as limitedness as such, as end beyond which nothing goes/is, then the question emerges: How does our thinking circle back on itself—i.e., inherently in its metaphysical structure—without leaving its own beginnings behind? How do we keep possibility alive? How do we avoid getting *trapped* in the metaphysical thought in which our thinking is situated?

Being sensitive to the dangers at the end of metaphysics and in an attempt to think truthfully, honestly, i.e., phenomenologically, much of "contemporary continental thought" thinks this notion of boundary/end very cautiously. Boundary implies some "place," line, encirclement, which genuine thinking ("postmodernist") goes up to and turns back from—staying within the circle that the boundary line demarcates. For such circling back seems to be the only "honest" way to go—anything else would be conjecture and ungrounded. If the boundary marks the end (endpoint?) of metaphysics, then this circling back from the boundary to the within is a marking of staying within metaphysics—and leads to the surmise that all thinking is and has always been metaphysical: Parmenides and Heraclitus are *within* metaphysics; and Heidegger, too, here at the end is ultimately within metaphysics. This way of thinking fits if the line/boundary itself is taken as something substantial and has a "place" in very much the same way as substances inhabit place.

However, the step that the thinking of Heidegger takes regarding boundary/ *Grenze*/πέρας—and where Sallis's work takes its first step, at the beginning of *Delimitations*—is to shake up the import of substantiality by letting the movement and enabling character of end/boundary/πέρας be manifest. Boundary takes its measure from how it enables and *not* from its place (or its being placed by metaphysics) as end-point or limit as such. This loosens up the "where" of the boundary in the traditional metaphysics of substance (especially and including the discussion of presence and trace/absence). Thinking which takes its measure from the open-ended enabling of the boundary is a move to think precisely that which is *not* present but is carried along within presence/substance as precisely what presence/substance is *not*. But because it is more af-finity than de-fined, there are no clear lines to be drawn. Rather this thinking attends to what is *not* there, what is no where. Thus it gathers the light and the dark, the manifest and the hidden, the disclosure and closure.

We might say that what happens at this shape of boundary is a *shimmering*. (Following Nietzsche's *durchschimmern*, Sallis calls this shimmering a "tremulous gleaming"—D 71.) When the notion of boundary is opened up in this way, then it shimmers in that within itself it crosses over from light to dark and dark to light without leaving either one behind. It crosses over from letting be seen to what in its core remains hidden—without leaving either point. It shimmers in that it shines with a certain unsteadiness—namely: whereas it is always at something like a boundary, it can never cross that boundary, even as it is always moving "across" the boundary. It is a flickering shining. Rather than there being a "shimmering of the truth," truth *is as* shimmering.

What takes place at the boundary is a shimmering: (*a*) an af-finitive, non-defined, open-ended (*b*) changing, unfolding movement. Seen thus, boundary does not show two sides (where one might cross over from one to the other) nor end limited as such, but rather shows itself as an issue of expanding/openness, in contrast with contracting, frozen, rigid structure.

The finest example of how boundary points not only to line of demarcation and limitedness as such, but also to a shimmering (open-ended, non-steady shining) is how the word *bound* is related to the word *bourn* or *bourne* (from the Late Latin *bodina, bonna:* boundary, limit), meaning brook or stream—and then the Scottish word *burn,* meaning little stream or spring (akin to the German *brunnen*). Bound-bourn-burn-spring: place where something begins, but is "itself" nowhere, not definable; border with no demarcation, a shimmering; movement emerging, but from no "where."

Boundary, as in bourn, burn, spring, is source, origin, beginnings, replenishing. It is wholeness, gatheredness, fullness—converging in and out, where several "layers" of manifesting/non-manifesting come over one another, go in and out of one another. To think boundary in its convergings is to think it in more than one place, in a way that it comes back upon itself from a place other than from where it went out.

Delimitations. A striking word. A new word from the voices of philosophy. A new name in philosophy's texts. The book *Delimitations* opens within the context and undercurrent of boundary, limit, and "a series of transgressive delimitations" (D x). Intertwined therein is *end,* as in: end of metaphysics (brought to center stage in the subtitle: *Phenomenology and the End of Metaphysics*). It is at this limit that thinking today is situated. The question—I might say: the whole question—is how to think at that limit which is the end of metaphysics. Sallis names the thinking that properly unfolds at the end of metaphysics *displacement* and *transgression*—among perhaps others. How is that thinking situated but not imprisoned within metaphysics? Or is it? Is it somehow indeed trapped?

Is phenomenology within the limit of metaphysics, enclosed within metaphysics? Can phenomenology go no further, "turning back" from the boundary line that marks the "end of metaphysics"? Or does phenomenology take place precisely in the stretch of the transgressions? Is phenomenology transgressive? Is the work of transgression what phenomenology at root is?

What kind of thinking appropriately transgresses the limit of metaphysics, while always situated within it? How does one appropriately name the region of the transgressions—granting that it is not de-termined or de-fined by human thinking, but that human thinking is in response to it?

One requirement for the thinking that is called for is *reticence* (D 75). Another requirement for this thinking is *engagement (ibid.)*. With the showing of showing as imaging, the self-showing that thinking lets take place by its reticence (for the sake of imaging from the things themselves) and by its engagement (in showing-imaging as such) transgresses the limit—not by going beyond or behind it, but by carrying itself out in a way that collapses the distinction between "staying within" and "going behind/beyond." Any legitimacy to a stabilized circle/limit is undermined as thinking thinks, not beyond, but other than within that framework.

Sallis's book is an opening onto this dimension for thinking. And it is indeed where thinking thrives (only where it can thrive?) at the end of metaphysics—whose beginnings are then disclosable as the turn away from the very movement of self-showing.

Sallis writes: " . . . to mark the limit is to broach a transgression of it," thus "venturing . . . transgressive delimitations" (D ix, x). These transgressive delimitations take place in the expanding/opening thinking that is imaged in the root-sense of boundary. Transgressions take place at the edge, where the unseen shimmers along with—and the seen shimmers away from presence.

As boundary, the limit encloses metaphysics. But it also enables a thinking that metaphysics cannot hold, even as that thinking is situated *within* metaphysics.

Delimitations thinks the discord within metaphysics, "by beginning to puncture the enclosure from within" (D x), as well as an opening beyond metaphysics, "redetermining *die Sache des Denkens* as clearing" (D x). In pursuing the "transgressive question" in this way, Sallis lets be seen the difference between the limit of metaphysics and the limit as such, or "limitedness as such"—or better yet, the open-ended, unfolding boundary: the shimmering.

Limit of metaphysics is the metaphysical withdrawal, awareness of which prepares thinking for the transgression of that limit. It takes its shape from metaphysics—as "decisive discord." Limit as such (shimmering) is the withdrawal that belongs at root to the self-showing of being (or non-being). It does not take its shape from metaphysics, but rather from somewhere in the shimmering, "the horizon within which the self-showing . . . can take place."

The very edge where these two limits converge is the shimmering boundary between what is (metaphysics and its end) and what is not (void, non-being)— gathered together: the self-same shimmering.

Sallis's book is an echo-thinking—echoing this shimmering of the boundary. In this book the point of the boundary becomes in its central core the point of thinking itself. In its unfolding this book invites the work of shimmering imagings.

Gathering the way taken here, there is a certain distrust in letting the word *boundary* loose from its rigidly formed circle/line, in reading the word *boundary* beyond its definitions. But I find in thinking's attentiveness an overwhelming attraction to this opening of what has been closed in metaphysical thinking. To follow this attraction is to respond to a claim that is placed on thinking. There is also a certain risk involved, namely that one may not be able to say at all. I prefer this risk to the caution of security, which somehow always is sure about what it does not know—but is also contractive and closed off.

But it is not a matter of "choosing" one way or the other. For to thinking's attentiveness boundary reveals itself as an intermingling, a shimmering, with *no* marked "boundary." Thus rather than line or demarcation, boundary images a shimmering openness.

At this jointure it becomes paramount for thinking not to leave behind metaphysics or its end, nor to turn sullenly back from the boundary/end. It becomes paramount for thinking to move *into* the end of metaphysics *with the same attachment* to the shimmering of open-ended and unfolding boundary as it would have if it had turned away from metaphysics (would have if it could have). Rather than turning away from metaphysics, it is time now to confront those metaphysical attachments in their deep unfolding, as they are embodied, in blood and marrow. Thinking must go in and attend to those metaphysical attachments, let them be seen for what they are, and then—as an attentive witness—let them be transformed through the shimmering of open-ended and unfolding boundary.

In his writings Sallis turns again and again to this opening boundary, the beginnings which preserves and sustains thinking, while itself remaining unthought and unthinkable. He does this by returning again and again to the "shimmering" dimension that emerges within the tension in philosophy's elemental words.

It is useful at this point to make explicit just how Sallis's work opens up and permeates this shimmering imaging. What follows is a series of examples which demonstrate how Sallis's thought gets directed, in various ways, *away from* things or objects and what lies behind them, away from images and the originals behind them, away from the boundary/end that demarcates two distinguishable sides— *toward and into* shimmering imaging, self-showing, imaging as such.

(1) In "Imagination and Metaphysics" (Chapter 1 of *Delimitations*) Sallis writes:

> Or, on the contrary, does the closure of metaphysics perhaps serve precisely to free imagination and to open fully its field? Is it perhaps even on the wings of imagination that one can effectively transgress metaphysics and station oneself at the limit, hovering there without security?
> (D 4)

"Wings" and "hovering" are images referring to the dove. The dove is the bird of embodiment, the earthy-flyer. The dove is the one who does not soar away from earth (like the eagle), but rather who *hovers*. This hovering is a shimmering.

In *Spacings—of Reason and Imagination* there is the simple sentence that opens Chapter 2, "Hoverings—Imagination and the Spacing of Truth": "Reason is also a dove" (S 23). Then, several paragraphs later:

> What is required is not that the dove desist from flight but only that it be disciplined not to soar off—or to try to soar off—into the beyond. What is required is that it remain in that space between earth and heaven, that instead of soaring into the beyond it learn to hover above the earth.
> (S 25)

This hovering images shimmering.

(2) At the end of "Image and Phenomenon" (Chapter 5 of *Delimitations*) Sallis speaks of "the imaging within things themselves," how the showing of objects "*comes to pass as imaging*" (D 74). Thus this showing is not de-finable—by the very nature of imaging. Somehow it is between sense and understanding, between thing and concept, between the sensible and the intelligible—but not delimitable. That is, this showing, as imaging, is shimmering.

(3) In discussing the relation of author to text (in reference to his own book *The Gathering of Reason*) Sallis says that "there is no uniform relation of author to text but rather a dispersion of the relation, a splitting and scattering of the textual I" (D 30). Given that *The Gathering of Reason* is a text by Sallis that is grafted onto the Kantian text, and given that there is necessarily no uniform relation of author to text, thus there is a dispersion within the author-text relation. In this dispersion there is a double distancing: (*a*) the distancing whereby Sallis speaks in his own name and away from Kant and (*b*) the distancing whereby Kant's text is shown to work against Kant's explicit intention, to say what his text says, but to say it "better than" he could say it. As text, it is at a distance from the author in that it takes on a life of its own. Text and author become involved in a deeply rooted complexity. Sallis writes:

> This complexity lies in the capacity of language to outstrip the intentions of the author, so that what is said diverges from, perhaps exceeds, what the author intends to say. (D 31)

It is within this excess that shimmering takes place. The excess in its core keeps shimmering imaging agoing. The excess is the boundary, shimmering.

(This excess that shimmers is not to be mistaken as something merely textual, i.e., of the text—but rather as harboring within it and in its very core the *Sache* into which every text must always already break open. Herein lie the questions: Is deconstruction also phenomenology? Does deconstruction want to say that phenomonology is dead? Does phenomonology, in any of its various shapes, have anything to say *back* to deconstruction? These are some of the issues that I have taken up in the Introduction to this volume.)

(4) In that same essay Sallis shows how *reason* in the *Critique of Pure Reason* has an "open but unmarked ambiguity" (D 36), one that Kant himself intended to eliminate, with "trial, practice, and instruction" (Kant's own words). Kant himself held the assurance that, with diligent thinking, reason would show itself in self-presence, that whatever self-concealment had plagued reason was not essential, and that he would eventually "reach shore." But Kant's assurance in this regard is not born out in the unfolding of the *Critique of Pure Reason,* especially resistant in the notions of inner sense, apperception, and freedom. Sallis writes: "What is astounding is how much these developments seem instead to withdraw that self-presence that reason would require in order, even retrospectively, to be assured of its critical distance" (D 37). The "withdrawing of self-presence that reason would require" is precisely to be on the verge, to be at or within the boundary that shimmers and does not come to rest (to shore).

(5) At the end of the essay "Imagination and Metaphysics" Sallis quotes Emerson's essay "Circles":

> Our life is an apprenticeship to the truth, that around every circle another can be drawn; that there is no end in nature, but every end is a beginning; that there is always another dawn risen on mid-noon, and under every deep a lower deep opens. (D 15)

Emerson in *his* way loosens up the sharp boundary lines, in the image of another and another and another—until the head starts to swim. That is what shimmering does: swim.

(6) In the essay "The End of Metaphysics" Sallis suggests three "transgressive strategies" for thinking at the end of metaphysics: (*a*) Derrida's opening up and transgressing the limits of the Husserlian understanding of presence, (*b*) Heidegger's strategy of questioning beyond being to the open, the clearing, and (*c*) Sallis's strategy of radicalizing the opening power of imagination. In this context Sallis quotes Heidegger on clearing:

> Light can stream into the clearing, into its openness, and let brightness play with darkness in it. But light never first creates the clearing. Rather, light presupposes the clearing. (D 27)[4]

If we read this in terms of boundary, we can read: Light never first creates boundary. Rather, light presupposes boundary. The clearing, this open space, is the shimmering boundary.

In describing the third "transgressive strategy," Sallis writes:

> Opening up, extending, the bounds of the possible, imagination awakens desire within us, sets astir that eros capable in the most profound sense of opening us beyond ourselves and beyond what can ever be, even ideally, present. (D 28)

Imagination would open and expand the bounds of the possible. Thus imagination-thinking becomes crucial for boundary-thinking.

This dimension of the shimmering boundary, of the opening of the bounds of the possible, transforms the character of the end of metaphysics, as revealed in the shimmering in the tension in image-original. The root-character of imaging moves away from the character of image, does not found itself there. Imaging in its core does not take its queue from how an image is in actuality. Rather, the core-character of imaging is in self-showing. Thus imaging is freed from the substantive character that inheres in image, even the announcing image. Therefore, imaging of imaging is not the shimmering of an image that "betrays" that image, showing it to be "mere image" and *not* the original; but rather it is the self-showing/revealing/imaging, from within which the image-original dichotomy collapses completely.

Behind images are imagings, in the sway of the twilight of shimmering. If an image seems to appear *as* image, it shows only the movement away from imaging—an attempt to find the shore—whereas thinking's attentiveness is called away from shore, to imaging as such.

There is the dimension of the difference between image and original, which is held open in a kind of continual displacement—as it images the end of metaphysics. And there is the dimension of the gatheredness in showing/imaging/self-showing, which cannot be characterized. At the boundary which is the shimmering, these two dimensions are one. However, to think the gatheredness of imaging as such ("in and of itself") is to enter where we already are, in the delimiting of the stretch of image-original, but now to enter in a transformed way.

Boldly stated: The metaphysical is always there as a necessary hesitation, but the issue of imaging/boundary/shimmering does not take its name *from* the metaphysical—but rather from that "wonder that one could never aspire to surpass" (S 157).

Gathering up the way gone here, I might suggest that a certain "wildness" is in play. Part of that "wildness" is my attempt here to let two dimensions mirror each other: the dimension of the stretch between image and original, which is continually shaken up in Sallis's thinking of displacement, *and* the dimension of the gathering in the shimmering. What I want to suggest is that there is a significant difference between these two—in terms of thinking itself—and that part of this significance comes from out of the language of difference that is named by image-original, even as they get shaken up—and then from out of the language of the gathering-conjoining everywhere and nowhere at the same time. The gathering in the shimmering is the same dimension in which "post-modernist" thought operates. But here thinking enters that dimension in a transformed way, simply because it is not taking its queue from the limit at the end of metaphysics, in which thinking always circles back from the end into metaphysics. In this context I take Nietzsche's notion of "excess," not as going beyond somewhere, but as simply the explosion of this where one is. (Note: Herein, in the interplay of these two dimensions—of displacement and of gathering—lies the *Sache* that is at stake in deconstruction and phenomenology. Sallis's various texts show a delicate balancing between the two. The question is: Where, finally, does his thinking "dwell"?)

There is no beyond metaphysics. To think the gathering in the shimmering is to think at the end of metaphysics, but in terms of the possibility that opens itself to us at the end of metaphysics—such possibility is not simply "metaphysics." I wanted here to open up that boundary. I wanted to show the permeation in the image-original in terms of the end of metaphysics, because the act—the transgressive strategy, the transgression from within metaphysics or from within the situation of metaphysics—is one which breaks the seams; it opens up the seams of the line of demarcation that we know as the end of metaphysics. Another way to say it, perhaps, is that the end of metaphysics is this boundary, but it is not the ending of anything!

At that point I think that Heidegger needs to be rethought when he says that thinking reaches its most extreme shape at the end of metaphysics. There is a certain sense in which *äußerst* indeed names an extremity, that place beyond which one cannot go, in a kind of "stop" sense. But one can also think this as an opening. Opening up the issue of boundary: to rethink the end of metaphysics, not as extremity as such, but as that *shimmering,* which is also named in *äußerst.*

If we attend with full attention to the *phenomenon* that gets said when Heidegger's thinking deals explicitly with boundary-thinking, our thinking marks the working of boundary in a deeper sense. It is a question of letting the full attention of one's thinking into the *dynamic movement* in this way of imaging boundary. Boundary is the edge where the unmanifest borders on, thus giving shape, holding, and preserving. Thus boundary-thinking is thinking on the border—bordering bounding enclosing which *allows* everything its unfolding. Boundary is opening. In this context we listen to Heidegger:

> Boundary (πέρας) in its Greek sense does not block off (cut off). Rather, being itself brought forth, it (in turn) first brings what emerges (unfolds) to shine. Boundary releases (opens up, frees) unto the dis-

closed. By its outline within Greek lighting, the mountain stands in its towering and repose. The boundary that fixes firmly is this reposing— in the fullness of movement. All of this holds for *work* in the Greek sense of ἔργον: Its "being" is ἐνέργεια, which gathers infinitely more movement within it than modern "energies."[5]

It is easy to delimit within a kind of metaphysical thinking. It is easy to delimit when one can establish somehow a separation between oneself as thinker and the boundary, or between thinking and the boundary. I think that what happens when thinking this in its "nearness"—what happens at the end of Heidegger's "conversations on a fieldroad": *in die Nähe gehen*—is that nearness collapses the separation that has been established. And part of that collapse is the transformation of boundary as line, the transformation of the end of metaphysics as a stopping point or something up against which one comes to a stop. Rather it is a shimmering, a regioning that shimmers. As a regioning that shimmers, it is not out there; nor is it a line. It belongs right "here," the nearness of the near. The nearness of the near actually breaks down the separation whereby we can think in terms of subjectivity and objectivity, breaks down the separation whereby we can think boundary as something that is other than us, other than thinking—or boundary that is *in any way* distinct.

It is clear that it is not a matter of some beyond or some kind of new beginning that would not remain at the boundary and think the shimmering edge of the boundary. But how does one fill out the blood and the marrow? How does one think so as to embody this boundary?

The final lines of "Imagination and Metaphysics" read:

Just as the emptiness above is an absolute absence which precisely as such is the promise of full presence grown silent, so the ground below is equally compromised by those endlessly opening caverns in which, as in Hades, there are only shades and only images. What the dove must learn is to hover between heaven and earth, drifting a bit with the currents, resisting the lure of the emptiness above and the illusion of fullness below." (D 15–16)

From out of that, how does the dove hover, resisting the lure of the emptiness above and the illusion of fullness below? It seems to me that the dove does that precisely by letting itself into the blood and marrow. The blood and marrow becomes the imaging whereby this tension comes together in a gathering that remains a hovering, that stays away from "the emptiness above" and "the illusion of fullness below." But this hovering is within the opening unfolding emerging—in its gathering.

> Verging at the threshold
> Bound bourn, in the burn, the spring

Thinking's attention
Embodied.

Shimmering.

Boundary opening
A pregnant chaos
Yielding and Enabling.

Standing attentively
Within the chaos
One with the self-same:
Ecstasy.

PART TWO

SALLIS: READER OF TEXTS

CHAPTER NINE

VOICES

Adriaan Peperzak

El ojo que ves no es
ojo porque tú lo veas;
es ojo porque te ve.

—Antonio Machado, *Proverbios y Cantares* I

La philosophie et la sociologie contemporaines nous ont habitués à sous-estimer le rapport social direct des personnes qui parlent, à lui préférer le silence ou les rapports complexes déterminés par les cadres de la civilisation—les moeurs, le droit, la culture. Mépris du mot qui tient certes aux déchéances qui guettent le langage—à ses possibilités de devenir bavardage et gêne. Mais mépris qui ne saurait avoir raison de la situation dont le privilège se révèle à Robinson quand, dans la splendeur du paysage tropical, n'ayant rompu ni par ses ustensiles, ni par sa morale, ni par son calendrier, aucun lien avec la civilisation, il connaît dans la rencontre avec Vendredi le plus grand événement de sa vie insulaire; où enfin un homme qui parle remplace la tristesse inexprimable de l'écho.

—Emmanuel Levinas in *Hors Sujet,* p. 220

"Je crois de moins en moins qu'il y ait *la* métaphysique. Il y a une certaine multiplicité dans ce que nous recevons comme unité de la métaphysique. La déconstruction, c'est la lecture de cette multiplicité."

—Jacques Derrida in *Les Fins de l'homme,* p. 602

According to the letter of invitation to which I am responding in writing this text, I must "devote an essay to an encounter with the writings of John Sallis." It should "deal seriously," that is, "directly and critically, with some part of Sallis's opus." The "in-depth reading and appropriation of the texts of John Sallis" allow for something other than praise, celebration and confirmation: I am invited "above all" to participate in "a philosophical *Auseinandersetzung*" or "confrontation."

Since the question of signature has lost its simplicity, it is difficult to determine the extent to which my encounter with "the texts of John Sallis" entails an encounter with the colleague, the friend, the person, John Sallis. However, a certain bond between John Sallis himself and his writings is forged in the promise that he will write a "contribution that will in some sense be a 'response.'" I am not sure that a "direct encounter with a text" is possible, but if I succeed in relating (more or less directly) to certain texts authorized by John Sallis, he will take up the responsibility for them, lend them assistance, perhaps interpret or reinterpret them, and so—"in some sense," "directly?", "indirectly?", "critically?"—respond to me who am writing this. In my text he will recognize some echoes of earlier texts written neither for nor to me, but for and to everyone who would hear or read them.

Can one encounter a text, or does it belong to the essence of a text that it refers its reader to someone who wrote it for and to some other(s)? If the latter is the case, then its being addressed and directed, its direction, belongs to the meaning of the text (it is meant for . . .), and any encounter with a text is *ipso facto* (essentially and necessarily) a response—albeit a purely receptive one. A text reveals itself as authorized, addressed, originated, spoken and coming from a past which might be anonymous but cannot be wholly impersonal. (I know, I know: the word "person" is dangerous. It can be used and/or destructed as typically "metaphysical" etc., etc.; but so can most other words and devices, such as a preference for single words, substantives, preceded by neutral forms of the article—*das Seiende, das Sein, das Ereignis, die Sprache, la différance, la dissémination* etc.—and all forms of privileging certain concepts, denials, phrases or images.)

Would I prefer to encounter Sallis himself rather than have an encounter with his texts? Is my "encounter" with his writings a pre-text for reaching him in a sort of letter writing or dia-logue? Did I, in accepting the invitation, grasp an opportunity to actualize some sort of φιλία? Is φιλία more important, farther reaching, more decisive, more promising than textuality? Or perhaps even than philosophy? Does the point, the meaning, the directedness of philosophy lie rather in its laying the ground for wise friendship than in its desire for a certain wisdom?—But what would Sallis be without his words? Could one be sufficiently interesting, friendly, "friend," "wise" or even "human" without texts?

It would certainly make a difference if we could hear Plato's teaching, at least if we believe—as the seventh letter affirms—that he never inscribed his own thinking through any form of writing. The texts through which he has survived put into the center an idealized Socrates, who—in the *Politeia*—condemns the non-simple διήγησις by which Plato brings him to life. Can we appropriate these "dialogues"? We can neither encounter them, nor Socrates, nor Plato, who, as author, withdraws from the scene at which the readers are invited to attend. And yet, we receive his texts as elements of a παιδεία granted by Plato, and as urging us to integrate them into a παιδεία of our own time.

Even Hegel, who claimed that the entirety of the life of the Spirit can be adequately translated within the dimension of conceptuality, remains different from, and "more" than, an element in his own or any other system. To engage in appropriation of his texts, we cannot separate them from their author's voice. If we read them as his—albeit posthumous—teaching, we relate to him as a speaker (either as a rather ghostly one who speaks from the beyond, or, more realistically, as a professor of the past whose contemporaries we become by historical reconstruction and imagination). A denial of the ties between Hegel the man and Hegel's work does not make his texts self-sufficient. Even as scripture they need the support of someone mortal—a teacher, commentator, or presenter—who offers them to the reader. The fact that a reader can simultaneously be the presenter who addresses the text to this same reader contradicts neither the necessary plurality of persons involved nor the impossibility of a textual *causa sui*. Of course one can make a case for a certain independence of scripture: It can survive the death of its author(s) or even that of a whole civilization; it can accompany and inspire other generations long after the writers have been forgotten, etc. Through interpretations and reinterpretations, quotations and translations, a classic is multiplied, historicized, and disseminated. Not even the most anonymous, archaic, mythical, sacred or God-given text says anything however, unless it is represented—sent, urged, handed out, or prescribed—by someone who appeals to his own or another authority, such as "the State," "the Church," "the people," a god or God.

Sallis does not want to deny his own authoritative presence in his texts. On the contrary, he underlines it repeatedly with the characteristic formula "Let me . . ." or "Let me then . . ." (turn, mention, narrow, venture, return, concentrate, etc.), with which he begins many paragraphs (for example in *Spacings* pages 93, 135, 139, 144, 152, 155; and *Echoes* pages 63, 64, 65, 68, 70, 118, 123, 124, 126, 127, 132). At the same time this formula affirms the unbreakable bond between the author's voice and the reader's willingness to listen. Once in a while this tie is also expressed through the pronoun of solidarity: "Let us, then, regard . . ." (S 60). The reader must decide whether he or she will grant the space and time that are necessary for a sounding and resounding of the author's thought. Writing seems to entail the prescription "Read me!" and/or "Listen!" "Grant me the opportunity, permit me or recognize my right to speak!" What or who possesses the authority which is presupposed in such a command?

* * *

Of Plato, Hegel, Nietzsche, Heidegger, we have echoes only. The "encounter" with Sallis's texts captures echoes of a thought, speech, teaching, which he himself modestly calls "echoes." Since I have heard and seen Sallis presenting and addressing papers to an audience, my memory and imagination can, to a certain extent, recall the intonations, the melody, the accents, the movement, the spacing, the gestures, etc. which are lost in the inscriptions of Sallis's thought called "his texts." It is my task as reader to lend intonation, melody, accentuation, spacing, etc., to these same texts. This already changes them from what they were when Sallis delivered them (and if he presented them more than once, in different circumstances and for a different public, those representations have already multiplied and differentiated the initial text in an authoritative way). If I had never heard of the author John Sallis, my repetition of his text would change it even more. Or perhaps I should say rather that his text is a score which permits many readings, just as a musical score is no more than the possibility of real music, while real music exists in a variety of performances only.

The voice which speaks in Sallis's texts affords similarities to other voices known to me, as well as differences, echoes, and contrasts which de-limit the originality of his thought. By promising that he will take the responsibility for his writings in giving—at least "in some sense"—a "response" to those who deal seriously with the texts he has signed, Sallis has executed a right to consider these texts "his." But the possibility of responsiveness and responsibility presupposes also that the author does not coincide with his opus. He is "more" than his written thought, "more" (or "other") than his gift, "more" and other than what he will ever be able to give in spoken or written thought.

The distance between Sallis and his texts guarantees that "more." Although they disclose his thoughtful voice, his texts also protect and hide the life and the roots from which that voice emerges. Non-coincidence reserves a "space" for what he, himself and originally, "is." The texts refer me to John Sallis himself in a protective way: they disclose and protect the "*Ansich*" or the "καθ'αὔτο" of John Sallis, the "in itself" that would—at least partially—survive if his writings were burnt and sent to Hades. Sallis is "more" than his work: a thinker, a friend, a man who has a distance from philosophy. Are we talking now about Sallis's "truth"—a truth that would not coincide with the truth of his writings? Are we, those who are encountering him in responding to his texts, trying to clear a space for his coming to the fore? Is this an attempt to create a clearing that grants him a certain past, a present, and a future?

Or must we state that Sallis, as distant and distinct from his work, does not fit into any space, context, world, or clearing? Must we agree that nobody, in the end and originally, can be treated or understood as a phenomenon or figure within the horizon of a world, a history, a culture or civilization, a context, or a space?

Would there be "anything" in Sallis that escapes the all-pervasive referentiality of
the "in" of "being-in-the-world"?

Is this an attempt to reintroduce "metaphysics," concealed behind the mask
of a "more" or a "rest" that cannot be integrated into the context of any "world"?
Does the denial of contextuality hint at the old "metaphysical" desire for infinity,
eternity, and immortality? Is it a belated attempt to save "the soul" or the human
essence as an "end-in-itself," to free it, as an "absolute," from the referential network that ties all experiences and phenomena together as moments or functions of
"the world"?

But *when* and *how* did we "refute," "abolish," "overcome," or transcend
"metaphysics"? I know: we did not overcome it, since we are still steeped in it and
perhaps we will never be able to free ourselves from its horizons. But we can, to
a certain extent at least, de-limit its limits and, thus, broach the dimension shut off
by those limits.

This is not the place to discuss at length and in depth the question(s) of metaphysics as formulated by Kant, Hegel, Nietzsche, and Heidegger. However, since
the Heideggerian echoes in Sallis's opus are clear, I cannot respond "directly and
critically" to his opus without at least stating succinctly—and without sufficient
argumentation—some doubts and disagreements about certain presuppositions
which Sallis seems to share with the thinker whom I, too, gratefully consider the
most powerful philosopher of our century.

* * *

Echoes (10–14 and 206–209) seems to characterize our situation as a "Now, *after
Heidegger,*" but how exactly must we interpret the historical place of Heidegger
to which this expression refers? Is Heidegger a guardian at the gate of Truth? A
threshold that one must pass to be saved for authentic thought? Is thinking still
possible in forms other than that of an echoing? Is any other way of writing either
nonsensical or trivial, or else "metaphysical"? Has Heidegger's work in fact said
the last word on the nature and the meaning of "metaphysics"?

If "metaphysics" is the name of a certain pattern of thought which Heidegger, in *Identität und Differenz* and elsewhere, characterized as an onto-theo-logy,
then indeed the main task of thinking is the delimitation of its limits in a turn to
ἀλήθεια and spacing. From the perspective of the great classics of Western
thought, however, such a characteristic is a caricature. The overcoming of such a
caricature can neither terminate nor "delimit" the history of that thinking; it might
even blind us for the most thoughtful part of it.

I cannot enter here into a thorough debate about the historical truth of Heidegger's interpretations, but for the sake of clarity I must give at least some indication of the non-orthodox appreciation of Heidegger's hermeneutics which I
would like to defend. To begin with, I would stress that Heidegger's understand-

ing of Plato and Platonism is far from adequate, and that his neglect of the 1600 years of remarkable thinking between Aristotle and Descartes weakens the claim that he was able to characterize (and to "destroy") European philosophy as a whole (if such a whole is possible at all—this seems to me to be a Hegelian preconception which denies the historicity of thinking as responsible praxis of vital, sensible, emotional, concerned, and communicative individuals). The main question is, of course, not merely a historical one, yet the meaning of Heidegger's position cannot be determined without a judgment on the relation between his critique of "metaphysics" and the real thought of his predecessors. Is Heidegger a threshold? An end and a new beginning? Is his work an authoritative scripture that must only be quoted or echoed?

In Heidegger's own interpretation, the main question was formulated by opposing the ontological difference between "being itself" and the totality of beings to the onto-theo-logical structuring of the ontic universe, typical for Western metaphysics. Much can be said about Heidegger's rather hasty sketch of classical metaphysics. Its most amazing feature is not the identification of ϑεός or *Deus* with a *causa sui*. (Before Descartes and Spinoza the idea that God could be understood as a *causa sui* was forcefully denied). It is rather his ignoring or repressing the fact that all the great thinkers from Plato, Plotinus, and Pseudo-Dionysius to Thomas and Bonaventure, Cusanus and Hegel have concentrated their thinking on the truth that "God" (or "the One," "the Spirit," "the Absolute" etc.) can neither be a being nor beingness as such, neither a highest entity, nor a "Chaos" before any being. A careful analysis of their struggles would reveal many similarities between their paradoxes and those which emerge from Heidegger's endeavor to think the ontological difference. His attempt to evoke "being itself" by using impersonal substantives in the singular (*das Sein, das Ereigniss, (die)* ἀλήϑεια, *die Sprache,* etc.) can be compared with classical attempts to use such expressions as *the good, the one,* ὑπέρουσία, *summum ens, esse subsistens,* etc., in combination with very explicit denials of the ontic character these words suggested. Heidegger's mature work does not show any serious *Auseinandersetzung* with that long onto-theo-logical meditation on the different meanings of finite and infinite, relative and absolute being. One who is familiar with that tradition however, is necessarily struck by the echoes of the Platonic, the Plotinian, the Dionysian, the Bonaventurian, and even the Spinozian onto-theo-logy in Heidegger's naming "being itself" through predicates which in premodern times belonged to a treatise called *De divinis nominibus.*

If my suspicion is correct, Heidegger's work does not demonstrate any historical "closure" of metaphysics and so there is no necessity for any "destruction." There is rather all the more need for an *Auseinandersetzung* or a critical dialogue with the classics, which—and this is Heidegger's great merit—appear in a new light since his transformation of phenomenology. Instead of being a decisive farewell to the tradition, his work prepares us for a more radical retrieval of the classics, and especially of certain premodern texts which treat the onto-theo-logical differences with more care than most texts of modernity.

If it is not possible to circumscribe the entire history of pre-Heideggerian phi-losophy within the horizon of "metaphysics" in Heidegger's sense, we can still try to delimit its dangers and its reality within the texts of pre- and post-Heideggerian thought. This is what Sallis has done for texts of Plato, Kant, Fichte, Hegel, and Heidegger himself, and rightly so. I am not sure that the words *transgression, darkness,* and *Hades* (D ix-xi) indicate the orientation of a truth-desiring thought more clearly than the blinding light of Plato's ἀγαθόν or the Pseudo-Dionysian beingless and nameless ὑπέρουσία. Still, I do agree that hermeneutics "after Hei-degger" has other possibilities than before.

*   *   *

Can we summarize the rules of hermeneutics in the word (or name or title) "Echo"? Sallis takes care to distinguish a hermeneutical echo from simple mirroring or repetition (E 3–6). The resounding of such an echoing is—at least to a certain extent—an *original* sound and a multiplication of possible sounds that are not heard as such in the voice from which the echoes stem (E 4–5). "Here monologue and its interiority are unthinkable" (E 5). But how can an echo have an original fecundity? And what sort of non-monological discourses does it make possible?

A first rule of hermeneutics is formulated by the repetition of the imperative "Listen!" (twice on p. 190, three times on p. 191, once on p. 192, where we also read "let us listen", as on p. 199—all from *Echoes*). To whom, to what must we listen? To "what is said" (190, 194), to "what sounds in it" (the text, 190–191), to "the spoken" (201), "the text itself" (11, cf. 191). However, the right way of lis-tening discovers something more original *in* the text: language itself, "its way of saying" (199), "the speaking of language," different from "human speech" (201). At the same time, Sallis asks that we heed the guidance of one who presents the text and who attends Heidegger's, his own, and our listening to it: "Let me then [redouble] Heidegger's listening" (202), "Let me say, then . . ." (203), "Let me say, simply . . ." (203), "Let me translate . . ." (204 and 205). Through listening, our thinking discourse must "be governed not by the questioning drive to ground [the metaphysical temptation] but by listening. Let it be a responsive discourse, tracing the shape of what is heard in listening, translating it" (192).

A responsive discourse is not necessarily an expression of responsibility. Sal-lis's insistence that he be present in saying, redoubling and translating "what is said and sounds in" the text, however, does show that he takes a certain responsi-bility for the text and its echoing. He lends his voice to the text, which, without that echoing responsibility, could not call us to listening, echoing, or translating. His voice invites us to displace the responsibility of our listening from the "human speech" of his imperative (*Listen!*) to "the speaking of language." His imperative opens the possibility of ecstasy. Since language does not speak in any "ordinary" or "normal" sense of the word, but can perhaps be evoked by saying that it "tolls silently" (E 208), the ecstasy trans-fers and trans-lates us into an abyss of "stillness" which echoes or resounds in (some of) our discourses.

How should we relate the responsibility of the presenter and his order (*Listen!*) to the speechless, non-responsible language which answers our questions by the echoes of human speech (such as Sallis's "Listen" and "Let me say")? How could responsibility emerge from language? From an abyss? If it can, is it, then, a pre-face, a for-word that reveals itself in scripture? How, then, is it different from the divine Word of sacred Scripture? Is Hades itself the abyss, to which only mortality grants access (E 207–209)? How can a for-word be heard if it is not addressed? And how can I respond to it? How can I become obedient to an order (Listen!) if it is not preceded by a more primordial and more original—silent but already demanding—voice or word or demand?

Fortunately Sallis's voice is in the text to direct my focus and, perhaps, to answer—now or in a later response—(some of) my questions. His responsibility seems to lie in his teaching me, through his writings, a certain way of hearing, reading, unfolding. Is this not the traditional model of philosophical writing from the Sophists on, and which is prevalent in modern philosophy? In one of his early writings, Augustine declared that he was interested only in the dialogue between God and his soul—although he wrote this with a view to discussion with his companions in Cassiciacum. The structure of such writing seems to have survived the replacement of "God" by Substance, Spirit, History, Life, ἀλήθεια, Language, or Destiny, except that the latter instances hardly permit a dialogue.

The bonds that tie Echo to Narcissus might bother us. We can shake off our anxiety by considering Ovidius's quasi-myths decadent and frivolous, but an allegorical explanation focusing on the double figure of reflection fits too well with a certain conception of hermeneutics. Narcissus's mirroring imprisoned him in an exact but vulnerable repetition of the same. Echo's phrases differ from Narcissus's sentences by the shortness of their reproductive memory. The endless repetition of the same killed both figures of tautology: the egoistic and the altruistic.

In his preface to *Echoes* (4–5) Sallis carefully explains that "echoing" is different from a tautological fading away. There is a way—through imagination, twisting, and spacing—to free yet unheard, unthought, unsaid fecundities of "what is said" or "what sounds" in the texts of our past. We should thus be led away from Narcissus's neither loving anyone nor wanting to be loved. In reducing all otherness to the exact doubling of his own appearance, Narcissus rejects φιλία and creates a Hades of his own. In embracing himself he loses himself; because there is no other than he and his mirror, his riches empty him: *inopem me copia fecit!* (Metamorphoses III, 466). The only way to escape from the solitude of his self-reflection seems to lie in the separation from his uni-dual existence: a tragedy from which only flowers can emerge. *O utinam a nostro secedere corpore possem*! (v. 467). Only another's face or voice can free him from his *enfer*. This presupposes a *looking* and *listening* that permits the other to appear as such, to "let" the other "be" another—*not* as a figure or function in a context, but as looking at me, speaking to me, judging me, telling me what I am by the silent call which awakens me to my responsibility, and not by some echo or addition to my words.

In being addressed by a voice, a letter, a text, I am constituted as "you" for the one who addresses words to me. This makes it understandable that I hear an imperative: Listen! Let me speak, call, awaken you; let me give you guidance! Such a call makes me responsive: I cannot simply ignore words that are meant for me. If I do, I presume or decide that these words, those texts, are not addressed to me. I presume or decide then that the speaker does not want to be (a) you for me. If, however, I let myself be involved in reading or listening, I confirm the "*Jedeinigkeit*" of all speaking, writing, reading, and echoing. Is it not a matter of amazement that the address and the double "you-ness" of all texts have hardly been thematized in the twentieth century selection of treatises which constitute the traditional corpus of philosophy?

Here, perhaps, begins the question that should be asked before I can answer my own question as to whether I want to encounter Sallis himself rather than his texts. This, my text, has not spoken "directly" to him. If I had really desired to address him directly, I could have written: "Dear John, I admire your work because . . . , but . . ." and signed my name. The publication of a personal letter is however, embarrassing, and may even border on exhibitionism. But it is also embarrassing to *write about* you, John, in the third person, in a paper that is meant for anybody who decides to read it. When you read it, you might feel excluded or objectified or reduced to an instance, a role, a mask. To speak about a person in his presence, but without addressing the saying and the said to him, is not only impolite, but seems to border on the unethical. Perhaps it is better to enact the other-directedness of saying rather than to thematize it; but if thinking cannot stop at any limit, it cannot shrink away from a consideration of the "you-ness" which is involved in all writing. Let me, then, try, to redeem my speaking about you by assuring you that the former words were also said *to you* and *meant for you*.

> Despertad cantores
> acaben los ecos
> empiecen las voces.
> Antonio Machado, Proverbios y Cantares XXIX

CHAPTER TEN

SOULS SMELL IN HADES

ARCHAIC THINKING AND
THE RETURN TO EMBODIMENT

Peg Birmingham

Very early in Sallis's first work, *Phenomenology and the Return to Beginnings,* Diotima is mentioned. Obliquely referred to in the context of gods and the ignorant (both of whom do not concern themselves with the question of finitude and, therefore, are not wise), an implicit confrontation with Diotima begins. Indeed, the very language of return marks the locus of such a confrontation. A third journey is about to begin which turns away from the ascent, back towards "the indissoluble inscription in the world, an inscription for which perception is to be exhibited as the irrefutable testimony" (PR 22). The name of Diotima accompanies Sallis throughout his writings—writings which radically question the very site of thinking itself through a continuous reflection on Eros, imagination, and "the mystery of human embodiment."

THE RETURN TO BEGINNINGS: PHILOSOPHY AND THE BODY

Sallis's reading of Merleau-Ponty is marked by questions. These questions, involving the primacy of perception, are critical insofar as they mark those places where Sallis begins to go beyond Merleau-Ponty's understanding of embodiment. The questions focus on three issues: the originality, the autonomy, and the founding character of perception.

The issue of *originality* asks of the originality of perceptual experience in its relation to thinking. According to Merleau-Ponty reflective thinking must be understood in terms of a body which already possesses the world. The body has an original directionality. At the same time, Merleau-Ponty argues that this originality cannot be grasped (PR 31). There is no non-spatial subject and object; therefore, no originary constitution of space or directionality can come to light. Sallis, however, raises an important consideration: "But does the failure of a reflection with regard to a certain matter establish that that matter is intrinsically impenetrable to every attempt at reflection?" (PR 32). This question points to a way of return other than perception.

Furthermore, Merleau-Ponty argues that there is no need to invoke a founding act of thought in order to give an account of perceptual experience (*ibid.*). All the properties of the thing form a phenomenal field. Thus, perceptual experience is autonomous. Yet, Sallis points out, the object is always "for-me":

> Merleau-Ponty's entire consideration of the issue of synthesis serves, therefore, to point back to a primordial stratum that consists of the always already established anchorage of the bodily perceptual subject in the world. . . .What is the character of this reflective "pointing back" to a stratum which is radically antecedent to reflection itself? (PR 40)

Here Sallis is asking whether there can be any account of reflection if the body is always already bound up in a totally interconnected system.

This leads to the third issue, concerning the foundational character of perceptual experience. According to Merleau-Ponty, perception founds thought. Thus, there is no possibility of complete thematization, and, hence, the return to beginnings is also incomplete:

> The consequence is that the very activity of thought by which Merleau-Ponty will seek to establish the dependence of thought is itself dependent and, hence its result—namely, that thought is dependent—is itself dependent. The entire project recoils upon itself. (PR 41)

This recoil, Sallis suggests, leads to the necessity of a new project that seeks to articulate the relation of expression and thinking to perceptual experience.

This new project, Sallis argues, is taken up in *The Visible and the Invisible,* which attempts to address the problem of this relation by interrogating the logos of the invisible (PR 56). The task is to descend into the invisible and "bring what is inherently silent to expression" (PR 64). To accomplish this task, Merleau-Ponty rejects the notion of an inner, tacit *cogito.* Instead, subjectivity is understood as an intertwining with the world. I am of the visible. There is a pre-established harmony between the seer and the seen. Sallis uses the example of the hand, and asks: "Since only a very particular kind of movement of my hand over a surface can reveal the texture of that surface, how is it that I exercise the appropriate movement?" (PR 78) Sallis shows that this harmony is possible because my hand "knows" its way around tangible things. The body brings us to the things themselves. He further points out that things are more than surfaces and, hence, that it is not a matter of seeing from the perspective of the ascent unobstructed by the body. Things have latency, dimensionality, flesh—we must stay in touch.

The body, therefore, is no longer an impediment to our access to things. The flesh of the body is the site of a crossing, a chiasm (PR 80–81). It is that realm which lies neither inside nor outside a subject; rather, it is that place at which seer and seen come into being. This leads Sallis to ask a further question: "How is this fundamental chiasm to be brought to expression?" (PR 84) In pursuit of this question, Sallis takes as his guide a passage from *The Visible and the Invisible* which claims that the body is a sensible for-itself. As a sensible for-itself, the body is self-reflexive. Indeed, Merleau-Ponty argues that it is bodily reflection which originates self-consciousness. Moreover, this origination involves speech. Body and world are in a dialogue. They articulate themselves, express and define themselves. The body is the bearer of signification.

Sallis, however, notes the problem in the movement from perception to reflection and expression via the body: It is a question of "the assurance that there is continuity, if not complete identity, between prereflective experience and the thematization of that experience in reflection" (PR 89). While Merleau-Ponty argues that the continuity is given in the very experience of perception, Sallis cautions against such identity and coincidence. He points out that insofar as bodily reflection is now in the position traditionally occupied by self-consciousness, bodily reflection is the ground of experience (PR 90). At the same time, the incorporation of things by the body communicates difference, a divergence between the within and the without. Sallis argues that there is no sheer coincidence: "My left hand is always on the verge of touching my right hand touching the thing, but I never reach coincidence" (PR 92). Furthermore, bodily reflection itself fails: "To say that the reflection fails is to say that as soon as the hand is touched, the same hand withdraws, recedes into a depth beneath the touched surface" (PR 93). This is particularly true with the advent of the Other who reveals the limits of bodily reflection insofar as the Other shows that reflection is always perspectival, incomplete, partial.

To overcome this partiality, Sallis argues that Merleau-Ponty must go further, articulating a new flesh: the flesh of language. Merleau-Ponty calls this new flesh, "a less heavy, more transparent body," and makes an analogy between the reversibility of the body and that which it senses *and* the relationship between language and the other dimensions of being. Just as there is a reflexivity of touching and seeing, so too, there is a reflexivity of speaking and hearing. This new reflexivity and the emergence of flesh as expression are the points wherein speaking and thinking are inserted into the primordial stratum of silence.

Sallis argues, however, that this relation between language and flesh is problematic. Merleau-Ponty calls for an act of speaking that marks a transformation throughout the mute dimensions of Being (Wild Logos); and yet, at the same time, he will not break the mute dimension of Being. Sallis points out the tension in this understanding of flesh as language. On the one hand, there is an understanding of being which has always already been transposed into language, while, on the other, there is still evoked a silent stratum of being present to itself and prior to the productivity of language. Sallis asks: "Is it possible, in the end, to vindicate a philosophical reflection that begins with an ontological interrogation of wild being that is presumed to be pre-linguistic?" (PR 113)

Sallis suggests that such a demand for a speech that is ultimately self-effacing in the presence of the silence of wild logos is impossible. Philosophical thought is always already bound to expression. Thus, he asks further, "Is it possible to take up the question of being in advance of the question of logos in its full sense?" (PR 113). Furthermore, Sallis's analysis suggests that Merleau-Ponty has misunderstood embodiment: "Merleau-Ponty, casting the subject out of interiority, anchoring it in the world of perceptual experience, ends up abolishing the distance between thought and beginnings" (PR 115). At the same time, Sallis's critique of this naive abolition of distance and noncoincidence should in no way be taken to imply that he is suggesting a return to interiority. Instead, he raises the question as to whether the body as the locus of the chiasm must be understood differently, that is, as the locus of difference and differentiation rather than identity and coincidence. Indeed, Sallis has been showing this all along in his reading of Merleau-Ponty. All attempts at formulating an understanding of bodily reflection in terms of coincidence fail. A new mediation is always posited.

At this point, Sallis makes an unexpected contrast between Fichte's and Merleau-Ponty's understanding of the finite I. While Merleau-Ponty's understanding of finitude, via the chiasm and transcendence, abolishes the difference and distance between thinking (understood as bodily reflection) and its beginning, Fichte understands the finite I in terms of the imagination. This allows him to retain the tension between thinking and its beginnings. According to Fichte there is always something that draws forth thought and at the same time withdraws from the beginning to be thought (PR 115). Sallis thinks this withdrawal in terms of the body, making the fascinating suggestion that the imagination might allow us to think the distance between the body and "that which draws forth erotic progress of bodily reflection toward the completion of its circuit." (ibid.)

This possibility leads Sallis to raise the final question at the end of *Phenomenology and the Return to Beginnings:* "Whether there can be a philosophy of imagination which is not also a philosophy of the cogito?" (PR 116) This final question not only calls into radical question the possibility of a return to beginnings, but at the same time raises the possibility of an understanding of the imagination that is tied to a new understanding of embodiment. It is a question that calls into question the speech of Diotima and her understanding of Eros as the will toward the invisible and the intelligible.

THE COMEDY OF THE BODY

At the beginning of Book Five of *The Republic*, Socrates, having arrived at a place where he is beginning to see clearly, is arrested for the second time by Polymarchus:

> But Polymarchus . . . took hold of his cloak from above by the shoulder, began to draw him toward him and as he stretched himself forward, said some things in his ear. . . "Shall we let it go or what shall we do?"
>
> "Not in the least", said Adeimantus, now speaking aloud.
>
> And I said, "What in particular won't you let go?" "You", he said.
>
> "Because of what in particular?" I said. (449b)

The particular that stops Socrates's journey upwards towards the truth is the body. A comedy ensues. In *Being and Logos: The Way of Platonic Dialogue,* Sallis argues: "The comedy has to do with Eros. This changes the entire direction of *The Republic"* (BL 378). Again, Sallis invokes an implicit confrontation with Diotima and her suggestion that Eros can move upward in an unimpeded way. Important for our discussion is how Sallis's refusal to dismiss this comedy allows for his radical reading of the subsequent discussion of the Good. Sallis's reading shows that *The Republic* is not moved by the τέλος of pure presence, but instead, moves via the imagination and embodiment, a movement without beginning or end.

The comedy, Sallis argues, actually begins in the prior discussion of the three types of human beings: those who are in a state of sleep among the many beautiful things; those who are in state of wakefulness, who see both the many beautiful things and the beautiful itself; and, finally those rare beings who transcend both states (which are bodily) and see the εἴδη themselves. The rare is comic, and Socrates's "forgetfulness of the body ensures in laughter" (BL 378). Sallis is interested in this comedy and its laughter. Why is there a comedy surrounding the body, and why is there a comedy at this particular point in the dialogue? Here it is helpful to consider briefly Plessner's description of the comic:

> To deal with the comic by not taking it seriously is not to be unrelated to it. The only possible relation to the comic is not to take it seriously. But the necessity of this attitude can be understood only with reference to its unmanageability by any other means, in accordance with the con-

trariety inherent in the structure of comic situations. To this extent "comic" means: falling outside the frame of reference, shocking, contradictory, ambiguous—something one can't get hold of and can't set to rights.[1]

The body refuses to be managed or dismissed. The group at the table cannot get hold of it; it cannot be set to rights in the orderly schema of the upward way.

Hence, there is the hilarious discussion of sexual difference as being no different from the difference between men with hair and those who are bald. There is the comic image of naked men and women at the bath, no more erotically interested in each other than male and female dogs raised in the same doghouse. Laughter bursts out. Indeed, laughter is the body's response to the attempted forgetfulness. (One is reminded of that other dialogue where the comedian's uncontrollable bodily hiccups disrupt and force a reordering of the speeches about Eros.) Through laughter, the body itself erupts on the scene, forcing the dialogue to stop. Sallis points out, "The comedy reveals that the ascent is impossible given the body." He cautions us to pay attention to Glaucon, who sees that the direction of the upward way has been irrevocably altered due to the comedy of the body.

Yet, Sallis also points out that the journey is not stopped in its tracks. Instead, there is a new beginning, a longer way, that will lead to the question of whether there is any end to the journey, any haven from the road (D 14). He calls our attention to the new beginning of the ascent wherein Socrates requests *images*: "At all events, listen to the image so that you may see more how greedy I am for images" (*Republic*, 488a). The desire for images governs the journey towards the Good.

Moreover, Sallis's reading shows that the Good is itself the producer of images; it is the father who makes offspring who are the images of itself. (He also asks the all important question: "Where is the Mother? Why is she completely concealed?" [BL 405]) He points out that if the Good is the One, then, "when something shows itself as a one, it shows itself as the image of the one" (BL 441). Sallis, therefore, argues that the Good does not show itself as one. It shows itself as what it is not; it shows itself only through images. Yet, he also argues that there is never an absolute difference between image and original: "When I see the image, I see it as revealing the original. There is a tension—an instability: a kind of 'double seeing' " (BL 422). This double seeing is the beginning of philosophy:

> The transition from the visible to the intelligible involves the *very drawing of the distinction* between the visible and intelligible, the very opening up of this difference . . . the opening up of this difference coincides with the *beginning of philosophy*. (BL 424)

Two points must be emphasized. First, Sallis points out that the movement from the sensible to the intelligible proceeds via the imagination. Socrates is greedy for images. He wants the truth, at least as it appears to him:

It would be a matter of seeing the truth itself instead of an image, a matter of seeing the original truth, the true original—at least Socrates says, as it looks to me, that is, in that appearance that it offers to me, the image that it casts in my direction. (D 14)

Socrates's greediness is made possible by the imagination which "opens up" and extends the boundary of the possible. The beginning of philosophy's ascent proceeds by way of the play of the imagination. Yet, that which initially draws thinking beyond itself is also that which resists any return to an absolute ἀρχή or τέλος:

Hovering between presence and absence, resistant by its very nature to being governed by the ideal of presence, imagination does not accord with the figure of closure that this ideal generates. Over against metaphysical closure, imagination is discordant, disruptive, transgressive. (D 28)

This leads to the second point that must be emphasized in Sallis's reading of the second beginning: the ascent towards the Good goes by way of the play between the body and the imagination. Recall that the comedy disclosed the disruptiveness of the body which bursts on the scene through its laughter, refusing to be dismissed; it is disorderly and disruptive. Imagination's play of presence and absence is also disorderly and disruptive; indeed, it is this disorderly play that allows for the movement out of the cave. On the one hand, the body and the imagination appear to share similar features. On the other hand, Sallis reminds us that the upward ascent appears impossible precisely because the body refuses to be dismissed. The body's downward pull, therefore, would appear to be radically at odds with the upward movement of the imagination.

I suggest, however, that Sallis offers a third possibility for understanding the relation between the body and imagination. The play of the imagination, the play of original and image, proceeds by way of embodiment. In other words, the movement of the imagination, which always includes absence and concealment, proceeds through the *place* of negativity and concealment, that is, the place of embodiment: "Thus, the body is the locus of the negativity that adheres to the human condition—which, however, is *not* to say that the body is identical with that negativity or the cause of it. It is to say only that the body gives that negativity a place" (BL 450). The question of the mother is answered: it is this place of embodiment, the place of negativity, (understood as the play of concealment and revealment, presence and absence). Sallis agrees with Diotima that the Eros of the imagination is a daemon that pulls us beyond. At the same time, he takes issue with Diotima's insistence that the pull of Eros is from the visible and bodily to the invisible and intelligible. The pull of the imagination is towards that which withdraws rather than to that which illuminates; furthermore, it is a pull that never leaves the place of embodiment. Instead, the body gives imagination its place to play.

Finally, at the end of the comedy of the body, Sallis implicitly answers the question asked at the end of *Phenomenology and the Return to Beginnings:* "Whether there can be a philosophy of the imagination which is not also a philosophy of the *cogito.*" At the conclusion of his reading of the comedy, Sallis answers by suggesting that the possibility of a philosophy of imagination is tied to the place of the body. And, moreover, he suggests that a philosophy of imagination tied to embodiment forces a rethinking of the very task of philosophy itself. Philosophy has a new task: the vigilant task of never forgetting the negativity of embodiment. It is the task of beginning by *going down* to Piraeus.

DELIMITATIONS: THE VOICE AND THE HAND

While the question of embodiment continues to occupy every essay in *Delimitations,* I suggest that it is the essay "Heidegger/Derrida—Presence" that is remarkable in thinking further the place of embodiment.

In this essay, Sallis's analysis of Derrida's critique of the Husserlian voice, as well as his analysis of Heidegger's understanding of the operation of signification, answers a question raised in *Phenomenology and the Return to Beginnings:* "Can there be a pre-linguistic sphere of Being?" These analyses show the impossibility of such a sphere. Briefly, Sallis's reading of Derrida shows how Husserl's privileging of intuition and self-presence is most precarious at the level of language. Husserl attempts to respond to this precariousness by privileging the voice. The voice, Husserl argues, recreates at the level of pure expression the self-presence found at the more primordial level of sense. Sallis stresses, however, that Derrida's reading of Husserl's understanding of internal time consciousness reveals that Husserl's own understanding of temporality delimits such presence. Derrida shows how difference is already operative in the very production of self-presence. The voice, therefore, must contain difference. Sallis points out the profound consequence of this disruption and limitation of self-presence. Because difference is already present in the voice, the presence of the signified (found at the more primordial level of sense) would not be immediate. Therefore, the signifier (the voice) does not merely reflect, at the level of pure expression, a pre-predicative experience. At the level of the pre-predicative, there is always already an operation of signification. There is no simple presence, no purely perceptual consciousness. In answer to the question posed above, Sallis replies that *nothing escapes language.*

Following this analysis, the epigram of the essay becomes most important. An ingenious turn occurs. Sallis follows a clue that has everything to do with the task of keeping a vigilance over embodiment. The clue is found in the text of Heidegger's lecture course of 1942–1943 entitled *Parmenides:* "The hand is, along with the word, the essential mark of man. Only a being which, like man "has" words (μύθος) (λόγος) also can and must 'have' hands." (D 147) Singling out this reference, Sallis suggests that the body is not only the place of negativity, but also that place which is extended, ek-sisting, "in such a way that it can handle things as they come and go." (*ibid.*) Having shown the impossibility of the Husserlian voice of presence (through his analysis of Derrida's *Speech and Phenomena*), Sallis argues that it is the body which plays the important role in the operation of signification. He suggests that Derrida's critique of the voice does not go far enough—there is the further task of taking up embodiment.

To reiterate: Because humans have logos, they must have hands. Sallis asks: "And yet, what is the character of the connection such that it is one of necessity?" (*ibid.*) His subsequent analysis suggests an answer: "The word provides, grants, sustains that space, that open expanse, within which the hand can be operative in its appropriate way." (*ibid.*) The domain, Sallis argues, is the *Da* of *Dasein,* the open expanse, the place of unconcealment and concealment: "In the very briefest formula, it is that open expanse in which things present themselves and out into which Dasein is extended, standing out (ek-sisting) in such a way that it can handle things as they come and go." (*ibid.*) Again, Sallis implicitly takes issue with Merleau-Ponty. Just as there is no pre-linguistic stratum of wild flesh, so too, there is no possibility of self-presence through bodily reflection. The I, using its hands, is never mirrored back to itself: "[It is] always extended beyond itself into the referential totality by which it is determined, its presence limited and yet rendered possible by its insertion in that totality" (D 149). Paradoxically, the embodied I, which is always radically individuated, is also that place of dispersion, difference, and loss of self-presence. The embodied I is always drawn along beyond itself in the deed of accomplishing this clearing.

In this analysis of ek-sistence, Sallis clarifies Diotima's teaching concerning Eros as a daemon being pulled beyond itself. He points out that, while the body never allows us to leave completely the cave, it does allow the possibility of going beyond the "all too human":

> Such is, then, the last stretch of the way that I proposed to outline. It is
> a matter of exceeding the separation installed in man as rational animal,
> a matter of regathering the human body to reason, but to a reason that is
> itself regathered to its element, reason become ek-sistence. The human
> body, too, would be stretched beyond the all-too-human, beyond (to)
> Being. (D 159)

The embodied I, through its handling of things, is always decentered and stretched beyond to Being. Thus, the embodied I is engaged in the realm of concealment and unconcealment. At the same time, Sallis, continuing to think the relation of embodiment and imagination, argues that the body, as the place of this strife of concealment and unconcealment, is also the place where images play (D 193).

Here I can only point very briefly to Sallis's work in *Spacings* on this relation of embodiment and imagination. In this later text, specifically in his analysis of Kant's understanding of the sublime, Sallis elaborates upon this site of the play of images, offering a non-humanist understanding of the sublime by showing that the site of the sublime cannot be understood as a state within the subject, but instead, as the kinetic different of the "sublime body" set tremoring by the imagination:

> In the judgment of the sublime the self comes to be disclosed in that its essential space is disclosed, its proper field and the orientation within that field. That space, that field, is just the expanse delimited by the difference between the supersensible and sensible, and the orientation is simply prescribed by the sense of that opposition. (S 125)

The site of the self is the site of embodiment. The body is the site of the difference between the sensible and the supersensible, limit and limitlessness. Volatilized and set tremoring by the imagination, the body is always beyond itself, losing itself. It is a site, therefore, that is always eccentric, open, and adrift. It is the site of the presentable and the unpresentable. Hence, it is the site of the sublime.

SOULS SMELL IN HADES

In conclusion, I would like to return to the confrontation with Diotima, suggesting that, throughout Sallis's work, it is Alcibiades who has "burst suddenly" upon the scene. All along, Sallis has been reminding us that it is Alcibiades, not Diotima, who tells the truth of Socrates. And he tells the truth through images. Indeed, all along and in various ways, Sallis has been reminding us that Socrates not only allows Alcibiades's speech, but sees its necessity:

> Here I say, protested Socrates. What are you up to now? Do you want to make me look like a fool with this eulogy or what?
>
> I'm simply going to tell the truth—you won't mind that, will you?
>
> Oh, of course, said Socrates, you may tell the truth, in fact I'll go so far as to say you must. (*Symposium* 214)

Furthermore, if Socrates is arrested by Polymarchus for forgetting the body, it is Alcibiades who brings this indictment to trial. This time it is Alcibiades who is the prosecutor and addresses the "gentlemen of the jury":

> After that he had the insolence, the infernal arrogance to laugh at my youthful beauty and jeer at the one thing I was proud of, gentlemen of the jury—I say "jury" because that's what you are here for, to try the man Socrates on the charge of arrogance. (*Symposium* 219c)

Is Socrates guilty of a certain type of ὕβρις? Is he guilty of an ascent which forgets the body? Sallis hears the evidence and renders a verdict.

The trial is conducted through images. The truth of Socrates can only be apprehended through the imagination. The dominant image in the apprehension of the truth of Socrates is that of "opening": "I don't know whether anybody else has ever opened him up when he's been serious, and seen the little images inside, but I saw them once, and they look so godlike, so golden, so beautiful" (*Symposium* 217a). Sallis and Alcibiades agree: the Socratic engagement with concealment is opened up, made possible, through the imagination. Yet, the opening up of the imagination leads only to other images: "What he reminds me of more than anything is one of those little sileni that you see on the statuaries' stall; you know the ones I mean—they're modeled with pipes or flutes in their hands, and when you open them down the middle there are little figures of the gods inside" (*Symposium* 215b). The desire to apprehend the truth of Socrates leads only to further images; it does not lead to an ἀρχή or τέλος. Agreeing with Alcibiades, Sallis points to this "drawing" power of the imagination: "Opening up, extending the bounds of the possible, imagination awakens desire within us, sets astir that Eros capable in the most profound sense of opening us beyond ourselves and beyond what can ever be, even ideally, present" (D 28). Leading neither to beginnings nor to an end, Alcibiades's speech reveals that the truth of Socrates is given in what Sallis calls "concentric circles."

Sallis's judgment at the trial might well be to argue that Socrates can be charged with arrogance. After all, he recited the speech of Diotima. Since then, philosophy has been guilty of repressing the play of imagination and of forgetting its place, its body. Sallis, however, has been cautioning us all along to see the ambiguity of Socrates's truth. Socrates is also greedy for images. Unlike at the later trial, during this particular evening Socrates cannot be found guilty; for, while he recites the speech of Diotima, he allows Alcibiades to have the last word. In the end, he listens to Alcibiades telling the truth about himself, of bodily Eros, of the imagination, and of truth as a strife of images, that is, a strife between unconcealment and concealment. Sallis reminds us: "But it is also a strife which is reflected, duplicated from afar, in the structure of every image, even the simplest—in that dual character by which revealment and concealment are conjoined in every play of images." (*ibid.*)

I suggest, therefore, that Sallis's thinking, from its very beginnings in his work on Merleau-Ponty, is guided by that final speech of the *Symposium*. He constantly reminds us that the truth about ourselves and the world must take seriously the site of the body, a site that makes it impossible for thinking to return to an ἀρχή, but instead demands that thinking *go down* to Piraeus, that is, that thinking remain at this site of embodiment where the imagination plays.

CHAPTER ELEVEN

COMEDY AND MEASURE IN SALLIS

Bernard D. Freydberg

> Everyone is charmed by song.
> —Archilochus, Fr. 262[1]

The final words of John Sallis's *Crossings* are: "a song of holy laughter" (C 150). These words recall the words of Hegel: "the blessed laughter of the Olympian gods."[2] And these latter words speak of the music of Aristophanes. Those final words of *Crossings,* a meditation on Nietzsche's *Birth of Tragedy,* suggest at least a call for a crossing from tragedy into comedy. But as I will show, this crossing has already occurred in Sallis's thought, a thought which reaches back to the prior Dionysian spirit of music as the fundament of both. This tragedy-to-comedy via Dionysian fundament may be entitled *Gathering Spacing Crossing,* after the titles of three central works of Sallis which enact this transition; and I will attempt to expose this movement in terms of these texts. I will also attempt to locate the movement within these texts as shadowed and measured by two Dionysian artists who remain almost entirely nameless in Sallis's texts: Aristophanes and Archilochus.

I will begin by examining "spacing" in terms of an image which plays a large role both in Aristophanes's poem of Socrates (*Clouds*) and in the second of the three Sallis works under consideration here, by showing how its comic razing prepares a comic rehousing. (This preparation requires, among other things, significant contact with moles and pigs.) In other words, I will call attention to the old poetry undergirding and supplying the analyses of Kant explicitly (and Fichte and Hegel by extension). Then I will show how the comedy extends backward into the gathering of reason (and into the spirit of the tragedy at its heart) and forward into that crossing through tragedy which culminates in a song of holy laughter.

In *Spacings—of Reason and Imagination in Texts of Kant, Fichte and Hegel* Sallis calls attention to "that metaphorics that haunts the text and that generates the very concept of architectonic. The metaphorics is of course architectural, and it governs the orientation and the most general articulation of the *Critique of Pure Reason*" (S 4). He calls spacing "a 'movement' that is such as to open the very space in which it occurs" (S xiv). This brief discussion can be seen as an early enactment of that movement by which his text is named. For the metaphorics determines the concept for Sallis. The concept is a consequence, an outgrowth of a μεταφέρειν, a certain transporting across realms. The concept, here "architectonic," is a secondary phenomenon: the metaphor "architecture," the first art but most fundamentally the art of erecting edifices, is primary. The erection of edifices, then, carries across into philosophizing. Accordingly, the assembling of materials begets a doctrine of elements in Kant, the projecting of a plan begets a doctrine of method, and the preparing of the ground begets critique. The edifice in question is "a system of pure reason, that is, the edifice of metaphysics proper" (S 4) and the task is to replace the "wild metaphysics" arising from natural disposition with one "produced not by nature but by art, by an art akin to those of the architect and the builder" (S 5).

The architectural metaphor opens up (spaces) the Kantian text for Sallis by *haunting* it, and I argue for a *comic* haunting in which the perpetual self-undermining of the architectural task as disclosed by Sallis results not merely in a building in ruin but in a restoration of proper measure and a rebirth of play. This task is at least implicitly haunted by the most famous philosophical edifice constructed by art, the φροντιστήριον presided over by a Socrates who walks on air "looking down upon (περιφρονῶ) the sun"[3] in Aristophanes' *Clouds*. Using Sallis's own threefold structure[4] as a guide, λόγος in the φροντιστήριον is a mere means to the winning of law suits; μύθος is mere ignorance of abstruse mechanical principles and of the non-existence of the gods; and ἔργον consists of acts of folly, distortion, and outrage.

> That is the φροντιστήριον for wise souls
> In that house live men who can persuasively argue
>   that heaven is a coal oven
> and it exists all around us, and we are pieces
>   of coal.
> They teach you, if you give them some silver,
> To win lawsuits both just and unjust.[5]

The architectural flaw in this house shines through the ridiculous activities housed therein: the collapsing into a unity of the ethereal heavens and the coal pit residing in the deepest depths; the ascription of speech to lumps of coal; the treatment of speech as though it were a thing to be turned indifferently toward truth and falsehood, justice and injustice; the ascription of wisdom to all of the above. These give an image of comic absence of measure, a forgetfulness of the distinctions in terms of which humans orient themselves. The flaw in the ἀρχή concerns the relation of λόγος to what is said. The house is primarily a house of λόγοι; and despite the appearance of coherence which would give philosophy completely over to sophistry, this disparity of λόγος with respect to itself will prove its undoing.

I'm told they have two λόγοι,
The stronger, whatever that is, and the weaker.
And of the two different λόγοι one of them, the
weaker, wins always using most unjust means . . . [6]

Here, the thoroughgoing nonsense of the relation of the two *logoi* allows the division of the house against itself to show through—weaker and stronger λόγος are so thoroughly intertwined as to be indistinguishable, despite the absolute distinctness granted by their names. The measure-giving measure-attending shape of the comedy arises out of what is forgotten when in the hold of the drama: the λόγος of the comic poet which spends itself in the imagery.

The missing measure is present in the music of the poetical image; laughter is the acknowledging response. The philosophical writing of Sallis calls for the analogue of laughter in thought. He interprets the seminal texts of our philosophical tradition in ways which show both how they enact that measure in philosophical reflection, and how from within themselves they turn themselves out of themselves. Nowhere is this clearer than in his treatment of Kant, in whom he exposes both how Kant undermined the metaphysics of his tradition in order to establish a more well-grounded one, and how this critical project, precisely through its strength, silently contained the means of its own undoing. The Kantian text exposed as comic, given over to play—this is one of Sallis's outcomes.

The architectural metaphorics haunts the text of Kant in two ways. First, it refers all of the Kantian reflections back to the image of a house, thereby enclosing the discourse within a structure which proves unable to contain it. But secondly, the metaphorics itself is haunted by what it would represent: reason, which serves as both edifice and ground. To restructure the edifice of the overgrown wild metaphysics generated by natural disposition, the ground must be prepared and firmed. But this ground has been weakened by "all kinds of mole-tunnels [*allerlei Maulwurfsgänge*] that reason has dug in its futile but confident search for treasures . . ." (S 5–6).

This word "mole-tunnels" occurs only once in the *Critique of Pure Reason;* for Sallis it is a fateful occurrence. The giving over of reason to the image of a blindly burrowing insect serves both as a particular metaphorics and as an enactment of μεταφέρειν and spacing itself. The distance between reason and mole is at once opened explicitly and bridged. For reason, which would be pure knower of pure being, is given over to what might seem to be its direct antithesis: blind, crawling corporeality. Reason cannot at first recognize the tunnels it has made as its own. It does not see that, in order to fortify and firm these underground tunnels, it must descend. And in burrowing under, it must make new mole-tunnels which deform the ground of the edifice before it can even be reformed. This ongoing deforming of the ground makes the idea of arriving at a firm bedrock hopeless.

Further, this self-undermining of reason as ground-reformer is mirrored in the self-undermining of the edifice itself that the critical project would erect. As Sallis points out from unambiguous references to the Kantian text, reason is both essentially one and can be divided against itself; reason is both self-enclosed, yet infringed upon by sensibility; reason is self-present, yet divided from and deceived about itself (S 11–12). Thus reason seems to be capable of all things, of holding all positions and presenting itself in all guises—all the while giving itself away as a sort of fraud. It can do all things except present the science of itself, metaphysics, which would establish just what, if anything, it can do at all. The one little mention of the burrowing mole which itself tunnels as it would close all tunnels resonates through the Kantian text in the thought of Sallis.

Reason/mole; mole/reason—what is Sallis up to? For one thing, he is allowing the imagery of the Kantian text to work in juxtaposition with itself and to do so firmly within the "doctrine" of the text: only in connection with sensation can reason find its appropriate home in experience, and only so can reason establish a modified metaphysics of the first part under "the modest title of an analytic of the understanding"[7] in which the bond to imagery alone saves it from self-division. The extremity and the doctrinal appropriateness of the reason/mole metaphorics and the ridiculous sobriety issuing from it foreshadow an outcome of an architectural project which is at once profoundly successful and hopelessly misbegotten.

In *Clouds,* airborne Socrates fashions accounts for the flatulence of gnats, arguing that a narrow hollow in the backside of the gnat (identified as a "war trumpet" by Strepsiades) allows the blast to resound.[8] Again, the comic juxtaposition of greatest and smallest in a ridiculous manner presents a tension which foreshadows the undoing of the house where λόγοι without measure are for sale. After Pheidippides uses a φροντιστηρίον-inspired argument to rationally justify beating his father Strepsiades, Strepsiades burns down the φροντιστηρίον and chases Socrates with a torch.[9] The φροντιστηρίον, a house for *logoi* without measure and built by the silver fruits of λόγος without measure and built by the silver fruits of λόγοι without measure, is undone as a result of a λόγος without measure: the one by which Pheidippides explains his right to beat both his father and his mother from their chastisement of him as a youth. The poetic images of a Socrates in the clouds far above the earth discussing the unseen architecture of unheard insect flatulence and of a Strepsiades initially looking only to escape his debts coming to restore order by torching a house of *logoi* are originary intensifications of issues which will come forth in poetry at a different pace, but not in a different spirit, than in thought. This is why Sallis, who stands in the power of the imagery which drives philosophy as well as poetry, can write of the mole-tunnel-driven Kantian text "that [it] requires not only a hermeneutics but also a poetics" (S 21).

Sallis's mole/reason image, together with the ground-undermining ground-preparation of an edifice certain to totter if not crumble from within, must be seen as both comedy and thought. They leap over the abyss separating pure ahistorical reason from "empirical" and time-bound moles, joining them in the tunnels which bear witness to their preposterous juxtaposition. But the comic image is a serious image as well, disclosing the fateful tension in the assumptions of an architecture which would erect a building intended to be free of the finitude and decay attending all real buildings. Sallis suggests a playful architecture "that would require no ground, no final bedrock, an architecture not of rigid edifices but of moving, self-developing forms—a metaphorics that would be more musical than architectural, a hymn to pure reason" (S 23).

But he has already begun the enactment of such an architecture with the reintroduction of the spirit of Aristophanic music. The collapse of the house through the very principle which gives rise to it is at least as much comic as it is tragic. The Kantian text is neither refuted nor overcome, but released from its metaphysical moorings. The movement from reason to imagination is hardly superimposed but already present in the Kantian text. What Heidegger showed in his first Kantbook in terms of the problematic of *Being and Time,* Sallis presents as built into the already flowing forms of the ever enigmatic *Critique of Pure Reason,* an apparently rigid edifice transformed by a mole into song.

But what sort of song? Sallis writes: ". . . a hymn to pure reason" (!) (S 22). But ὕμνος sings praise to gods and heroes. Is pure reason a god or a hero? Perhaps its entomological guise allows a showing of the shattering against the limit belonging to the nature of its architectural/metaphysical task. Thus another kind of hymn is called for, celebrating (among other things) gnats and moles.

II

Pigs will serve to transport *Spacings* back to *Gathering.* "Mole-tunnel" is the first major spacing of reason and imagination in Sallis's book, and it is a spacing in the sense that it enacts "a self-relation that is eccentric" (S xiv): it is an image which provocatively challenges and releases the relation of reason and imagination in the *Critique of Pure Reason* such that neither can stand firmly at the center. In "Enroutings," the second major spacing, the route back to imagination as the unknown root can be undergone by a reason given over to the nature of swine. Among the senses of "route" and "rout" given by Sallis is one which describes the activity of pigs with snouts in the soil searching for food. "Reason would take up its utmost, its ownmost duty only at the risk of also being cast in(to) the state of swine routing in the soil, turning it up, deforming it perhaps even more than those blind, sub-terranean creatures who, in Kant's word, fill it with their *Maulwurfsgänge"* (S 22).

Why would the deformity be greater? Perhaps because reason as pig has more to do than reason as mole, and must do it in a more disordered fashion: it must not merely make small tunnels which subtly weaken the ground, but it must tear up the ground with its snout in order to forage for the means of its survival. In any case, this is how the ground looks through Sallis's imagery: beset from below by treasure-hunting moles burrowing tunnels blindly, beset from above by hungry swine purposefully tearing it up for its sustenance. And as the ground is supposed to be reason, it is reason besetting itself with an animality that is supposed to be alien to it.

Reason as pig is ground-deformer, but it is also *gatherer,* a possibility of rea-son as gathering. In *The Gathering of Reason* Sallis presents this gathering in its shattering against the limits of the enterprise: "in each of the gatherings of reason, critique exhibits a radical non-correspondence between the two moments that be-long to the structure of the gathering, between the unity posited by reason and the actual gathering of the manifold into that unity" (GR 153). A similar incongruity obtains when the movement of gathering is viewed from the side of imagination. Thus, one can well understand Sallis's earlier note, that the aspiration of the gath-ering ascent is threatened "with tragedy" and in danger of "diverting philosophy into sophistry" (GR 29). The danger on the level of tragedy of ὕβρις in the ascent of reason to the unconditioned is mirrored appropriately on the level of comedy in the routing of pig-snouts in the dirt for nourishment. And the ascent which begets the diversion of philosophy into sophistry is food for laughter in Sallis's ancestor Aristophanes's image of Socrates in *Clouds*. The comic image gathers playfully; its profound seriousness is always in service to play.

Sallis writes: "The determination is that the gathering of reason fails, that it cannot be fulfilled" (GR 152). But this "failure" is as far as possible from an er-ror; even the word "determination" belongs within the language of that unful-filled/unfulfillable gathering toward unity. This failure and lack of fulfillment have their ultimate source not in any desire to transgress the limits of the possible but, as Sallis suggests in a question, in imagination's ecstasy and madness which have "always already encroached upon the very origin of reason and its gathering, of metaphysics . . ." (GR 163). The seriousness of the metaphysical ascent, which makes itself manifest in its lawfulness in the first two critiques and in the free con-formity to law in the third, issues from a lawless origin, from a certain chaos. So the very seriousness itself may be comic at its heart.

Immediately following the determination of the failure of gathering comes: "The fragmentation which it would repair thus proves irreparable" (GR 152). But this fragmentation may not be a flaw, may have nothing to do with flaw or repair at all. For Sallis, the fragments are essential to the image-play which dwells as an ever-lurking possibility within and beneath the gathering of reason. "[The play of imagination] is the undeveloped possibility that I want to retrieve from the Kantian beginning and bring to bear upon the issue of utter occlusion, the crisis of meta-physics" (GR 174). The "I want" occurs from within that crisis and is directed toward the releasement of the play-antecedent-to-gathering lurking within it. In their undermining of the ground in advance of its preparation for edifice-building with its many gatherings, Sallis's moles and pigs bear eloquent (if inelegant) witness to this possibility.

After two cursory mentions at the beginning of the final chapter of *The Gathering of Reason,* the word "gathering" does not occur; gathering gives way to the mad, ecstatic play of imaging which Sallis at one point calls "the play of occlusion itself, of absolute occlusion" (GR 76), i.e., the play of the ever-closing-even-as-it-opens distinction of sensible and intelligible. In terms of this chaos of sensible and intelligible, images come forth seeming to incorporate both; in a traditional sense images are a union of sensible and intelligible and indicate a relation to an original. But there are no originals of which these images are images. There is no gathering, except insofar as gathering itself belongs to the image play.

But just as in *Clouds,* the comedy is itself always in service to measure. Only here the measuring occurs in terms of the playfulness belonging to poetry (in its most general sense as issuing from ποίησις) rather than the seriousness of reason (which now occurs as a moment of the former). *The Gathering of Reason* concludes with the passage from Plato's *Laws,* recalled not as an argument but as a "gesture" by Sallis, in which the best part of man is said to be a plaything of the gods and that of "sacrificing, singing, and dancing" we will win their favor and vanquish our foes in battle" (GR 177). All three arts require submission to certain standards governed in significant ways both by traditional practice and by the recognition that one is not the source of the measure of these arts. Sacrificing, singing, and dancing require both a discipline and an innocence for their gestures of the body to be enacted in a properly playful way; but reason is not their measure. In a comic sense, the foe is vanquished on the battlefield by these gestures. But the foe is excess—here the excess of reason—and play returns rational humanity within its proper measure. Sallis's radicalism always returns to a Greek root, and always to play.

III

In *Crossings—Nietzsche and the Space of Tragedy* Sallis's treatment of comedy is sparse, but it is direct and quite literally crucial. He twice cites a passage from Nietzsche which sets comedy side by side with tragedy, proclaiming the two ways that art turns

> "these disgusting thoughts about the horror and absurdity of existence into representations with which one can live. These are the *sublime* as the artistic taming of the horrible and the *comic* as the artistic discharge

of the disgust of the absurd. The satyr chorus of the dithyramb is the sav-
ing deed of Greek art." (C 74, 109–10)

This discussion takes place within the framework of the interpretation of
Dionysos, who for Sallis "is an excessive figure, a figure in excess of (the) metaphysics (of presence), echoing, resounding from beyond being" (C 75). Excess is
thought not primarily as superfluity or even transgression in a moral sense but as
"the truth that is, at once, the dissolution of truth. Let it be called: abysmal truth"
(C 59).

This side-by-sideness is imaged in the co-presence of tragedy and comedy at
the festival bearing Dionysos's name. Both are born from Dionysos as dark, as
holding sway beneath thought and being. Tragedy seems to move to the center,
however. The higher truth of tragedy—"the abyss as sublime," ecstasy even in the
face of woe (C 99)—marks it out as preeminent complement to nature born full
in art.

Almost as an afterthought (in both Nietzsche and Sallis) but an afterthought
which stretches through Sallis's work, he writes:

> Comedy, too, would be a supplement to nature, doubling it in such a way
> as to overcome it. As in tragedy, the doubling would effect an over-
> coming by disclosing a certain unity of opposites in their opposition, a
> play of unity and duality. By means of caricature and inversion, comedy
> would open a certain vision of the play of crazy confusion, a play in
> which nonsense is shown to belong to sense and impossibility to reality.
> (C 110)

How, then, can we think comedy into the heart of Sallis's thought, given what
seems to be comedy's secondary nature, its location at the extremities rather than
at the heart? But since Sallis's task here is the recovery of unthought (pre-
metaphysical) possibilities in Nietzsche's *The Birth of Tragedy,* our question is
also: How can we think comedy into the heart of Nietzsche out of Sallis's dialogue
with the seminal texts of our tradition? To put the question in more technical terms:
how can we locate comedy within that "logic" of poetic inspiration antecedent to
the overlay of reason which Sallis calls "ecstatic logic"? (C 55)

I suggest that this question, which always remains a question of specific
artists as well as of art itself, receives its answer in terms of the one called the truly
Dionysian artist by Nietzsche and alluded to but strangely not named by Sallis; his
art allows for a glimpse of the original unity of comedy and tragedy and of the
abysmal, ecstatically excessive self which this unity suggests: *Archilochus.*

> When Archilochus, the first Greek lyrist, proclaims to the daughters of
> Lycambes both his mad love and his contempt, it is not his passion alone
> that dances before us in orgiastic frenzy; but we see Dionysos and the
> Maenads. . . . And now Apollo approaches and touches him with the

laurel. [The poems then] in their highest development are called tragedies and dramatic dithyrambs.[10]

For Nietzsche, only the intoxicated reveler is Archilochus the poet; the everyday subjectively willing and thinking man cannot create. The lyrics are the song not of the individual singer but of the ground of being itself; the "I" sounded in the song is the "I" of the world soul and not Archilochus as everyday man. Sallis speaks of Dionysian ecstasy as "an *exceeding* of the limit that would delimit the self, an exceeding in the dual sense of transgression and disruption. Thus is expressed in the logic of the Dionysian the dual nature of the god: reunion and dismemberment, transgression and disruption" (C 55). This ecstatic logic names the movement actuated by the outside-standing ever-creative-disruptive image of a not-quite-god who enacts his destiny within the rhythms of birth-death-rebirth. It is a movement within the nature of imagery rather than formal thought, which is why Sallis says that "lyric poetry, commencing as Dionysian art, begins with a certain death of the author, such death is to be thought ecstatically and not metaphysically" (C 71). This is Nietzsche's Archilochus, whose name traces a certain transport to a pre-subjective state.

It is crucial to remember that the folk song of the Dionysian artist is not yet tragedy; it is not yet touched by Apollo, whose touch enables its imageless, melodic music to take the form of images on the stage and to break up the unity of the song and singer into characters and chorus. But the Archilochean lyric is tragedy's subsoil, the properly Dionysian element in tragedy, the place of original ecstasy from which the tragic edifice grew. Yet it is the place from which the *comic* edifice grew as well.

> . . . beneath the arch and through the portal there,
> and you, my dear, be not ungenerous
> for I will stop   23
>
> within your grassy garden plot. And learn this well:
> Neobule another man may take!
> She's [doubly] ripe . . .   26
>
> the bloom is off her maidenhood,
> the charms she had are gone, for she
> can never get her fill . . .   29
>
> but, frenzied, shows the measure of her shame.
> Crows take her! and
> may [Zeus ensure]   32
>
> that I shall never be the butt of neighbors' jokes
> for having one like her!
> It's you I want   35

for you don't deal in lies or treachery,
where she is sharp and takes
a hundred [friends]

indeed I fear she'll bear litters premature
and blind, for she's as eager as
the fabled Bitch.[11]

This passage of Archilochus belongs to the kind mentioned by Nietzsche in which the poet vilifies one of the daughters of Lycambes. It evoked the legend that the three daughters and Lycambes hung themselves, so badly wounded and disgraced by the poems of Archilochus were they. One might say that the (wholly unverifiable and empirically unlikely) legend itself belongs to the spirit of the poem, as a justice or injustice born of the blood-passion out of which it arises—transgression and disruption, to use Sallis's language. In this sense the song of transgression and disruption itself transgresses and disrupts.

But without change of melodic or metrical pattern the lyric reintroduces measure within the circle of sexual passion. The seduction of Amphimedo's child, which the song celebrates, culminates in an embrace of love without violation of her παρθενήιον:

and then my fingers learnt her lovely body well
before I let the white sperm go,
touching golden hair.[12]

In what sense is this lyric the music of the world-soul, and not of an individual man distressed by love matters? The coursing cries of outrage, lust, mockery, and tenderness all occur within the framework of a certain measure. Sexual desire in the poem occurs not for the sake of individual conquest but for a passionate, sacred completion. The lustful sexual act with the daughter of Amphimedeo occurs in the song for the sake of a union which leaves the other intact even as it is at its most irrational height. The "I" of the poem distances itself from the once beloved Neobule; its trashing of her is not merely from a wound of jealous pain but also of the transgression of the bounds proper to sacred union. The poet sings the divinity of lust by letting it show itself in the closest accord with chastity, its apparent opposite—and thus in Archilochus we hear the playful, painful contradiction of the Dionysian and not just some mere personal complaint.

This theme of transgression and disruption, and more particularly the way transgression and disruption hold within measure, is clearly the province of comedy as well as tragedy. And this lyric of Archilochus, while it surely can be encountered on its own terms as a distinct and distinctive poetic form, can be seen as a musical precursor to comedy as well as tragedy. Γείτοσι χάρμ᾽ ἔσομαι (line 34) is itself something of a joke, given the break-up with Neobule and the consequent bashing of her character. So also is this strange presentation of a supposedly human ἔρος which stops short of its fulfillment when at its height, transforming it poetically into pure play by lifting it out of the conditions of embodiment which bind it in the everyday human arena.

"Holy laughter"—these words, and the song which would beget both dance and this sacred mirth, do not merely conclude Sallis's *Crossings* but trace the contours of that final crossing which crosses back both to Nietzsche and to Archilochus/Dionysos, to the ecstasy of transgression-disruption measured not by a concept of any kind but by a playful, playing image which contains its measure within itself. To be sure, the laughter to which Sallis most likely refers in Nietzsche—the laughter of Zarathustra which has overcome the need for metaphysical comfort—is not restricted to comedy as such. But Nietzsche's famous remark in *The Birth of Tragedy* to the comedy of art, in which our justification consists entirely of our role as player in this comedy, suggests that at bottom any tragic vision involves a comic vision. In this light, the laughter of Zarathustra occurs as belated recognition of this.

In Sallis this work of transformation is undertaken by the likes of moles and pigs and nameless poets and other beings which are discovered to disrupt the very texts in which they occur, sounding old songs which come toward us out of our future.

CHAPTER TWELVE

REASON'S ENTANGLEMENT

James Risser

I

Let us think for a moment about entanglement. It is a condition of being caught up in something in a complicated and, in some cases, confusing way. It is to be caught up in something whereby a twisting free becomes almost impossible, for what is entangled is knotted together in such a manner that a separating out proceeds unevenly, if at all. An element of perplexity appears in what has been brought together. Someone entangled in lies, for example, cannot immediately retrace the steps—the network is too interwoven, the origin is lost.

Let us ask, then, with what is reason entangled? What is the ensnarement that has captured reason and from which it cannot be extricated? Provisionally, it appears that this very question is one peculiar to modern rational metaphysics and that Kant seemingly knew best about this matter, about reason and its science, metaphysics. Kant saw that reason, in its extension beyond the limits of experience, becomes entangled with itself. In reason's production of metaphysical knowledge an unavoidable and quite natural illusion occurs where the subjective necessity of a connection of our concepts is taken for an objective necessity in the determination of things in themselves. In trying to meet its own demand for unity, reason becomes self-entangled; reason gets caught up in the web of its own dialectic, twisting and turning, complicating its production. In the *Critique of Pure Reason* Kant writes:

> There exists, then, a natural and unavoidable dialectic of pure reason—not one in which a bungler might entangle himself through lack of knowledge, or one which some sophist has artificially invented to confuse thinking people, but one inseparable from human reason, and which, even after its deceptiveness has been exposed, will not cease to play tricks with reason and continually entrap it into momentary aberrations ever and again calling for correction.[1]

The *Critique of Pure Reason* is itself the attempt of reason to free itself from its complication. Using the metaphor of law, Kant wants to set reason before a tribunal which will extricate reason from its muddled condition, from the perplexity into which it has fallen. This tribunal is a project of reason circling back upon itself; it must legitimize reason's claims with respect to human knowing by reason itself. But, as the passage from the *Critique* indicates, reason's entanglement is inescapable. What the tribunal declares is that if reason cannot un-knot itself, it can at least—for the sake of a solution to its initial muddled condition, for the sake of a science of pure reason—recoil, draw back, and install itself on the other side of the border of metaphysics. The tribunal would have us draw a distinction between a science of metaphysics, which with respect to theoretical reason is impossible as a science, and a science of nature, in which reason finds its legitimation with respect to science. Reason thus avoids its own entanglement when it is employed simply as a faculty of rules (*Verstand*).

But reason's entanglement is inescapable. Ironically, in the process of disentangling itself, reason comes to recognize that it must, for the sake of science, become entangled with something other than itself, namely, the image. Reason, in the form of understanding, requires images (*der Bilder bedürftigen*): The discursive understanding is in service to receptivity, to sensible intuition. Reason's entanglement here is not, strictly speaking, merely the connection between reason and sense as a condition for knowledge of objects of experience. Since whatever is given by sense cannot have its own principle of organization, Kant assigns to the imagination the role of synthesis; and thus strictly speaking reason's entanglement happens with this act of synthesizing. The proceedings of the tribunal indicate just how elaborate this activity of the imagination as an act of synthesizing is. On an empirical level, the imagination functions reproductively. The imagination forms a unified image and can recall in memory past images so as to form a unified experience. On a transcendental level, the imagination functions constructively. The imagination pertains to the power of synthesis in general, which constitutes the ultimate condition under which we are able to experience any object whatsoever. The productive imagination answers the question of how the subsumption of intuitions under pure concepts is possible. The schematizing activity of the imagination, which is itself "an art concealed in the depths of the human soul," mediates between image and concept. Reason's entanglement is with the image and its production by the imagination.

The question before us pertains to the scope of reason's entanglement. Is it not the case that the Kantian problematic, in standing within the history of western metaphysics, is the problematic of western metaphysics as such? Is it not the case, in other words, that reason's entanglement is the question of metaphysics as such? And, *mutatis mutandis,* that the question of the end of metaphysics, which is broached in a peculiar way by Kant, presents us with the task of redrawing the configuration of reason's entanglement?

II

This entanglement of reason and image has been traced out for us in its broader context in the essay "Imagination and Metaphysics." This text, signed by John Sallis, investigates the dynamics of the relation between reason and imagination within metaphysics.[2] It traces the double gesture by which metaphysics both appropriates and yet excludes imagination. Initially and perhaps most decisively, the relationship gets expressed in Socrates's account of philosophy in the *Phaedo.* Recounting his own dissatisfaction with a natural philosophy as a way of explaining the causes of things, Socrates speaks of the movement into philosophy whereby one proceeds to investigate things indirectly. The indirect investigation is at once a recourse to images and a recourse to discourse (reason) which seeks those things (εἴδη) that stand under the sensible present things. The indirect investigation opens the distinction between the image and the original, in this case, the sensible present thing (image) and that which stands under the present thing (original). The indirect investigation, however, does not want to open up the distinction between image and original in order to leave the image behind. On the contrary, the turn to metaphysics—that turn to the beautiful itself, the good itself—shifts away from the fragmented presence of the immediate and sensible "in order to prepare a reappropriation of those things in their originary presence" (D 6). Metaphysics is founded as a drive towards presence structured by the dyadic relation between image and original. Even beyond sensible things, as we see imaged in the ascent out of the cave, the prisoner gazes on things as they are imaged. But this implies that the opening of metaphysics is an opening of a metaphysics of imagination, provided that imagination can be distinguished from mere fancy (φαντασία). Metaphysics proceeds by an eikastic imagination, of apprehending images "in such a way that one sees through them to the originals which they image."

And yet, metaphysics wants to set imagination at a distance. "Imagination and Metaphysics" also recalls for us Socrates's remarks in the *Republic* where the poet is distinguished from the philosopher, where image-maker is made to stand at the extreme opposite of the philosopher's apprehension of things. The poet makes use of images that are quite removed from an originary presence. In the discussion with Glaucon, Socrates concludes:

> Then must not we infer that all poets, beginning with Homer, are only imitators; they copy images of virtue and the like, but the truth they never reach? The poet is like a painter, who, as already has been observed, will make a likeness of a cobbler though he understands nothing of cobbling.[3]

Leaving aside the question of subtlety and irony in Socrates's remarks, the double gesture of taking distance from imagination and the appropriation of imagination remains in effect in the Platonic project: On the one hand, the drive to presence is oriented by the schema of image-original; on the other hand, the image-original schema diverts the drive to presence into a play of presence and absence (D 7).

When the issue of metaphysics and the imagination reappears in the work of Kant, not only does the very idea of metaphysics undergo a transformation—there occurs here a first movement towards a certain closure of metaphysics—but the conception of imagination has shifted from εἰκασία to φαντασία. Kant inaugurates a shift in metaphysics by holding the claim of knowledge through pure concepts under the restraint of human sensibility: The pure concepts are at work in the very constituting of the sensible object. Accordingly, "the difference originally opened up by the Socratic turn, the difference between sensible and intelligible, is now, in Kantian critique, opened within the sensible itself—or, if you will, confined within the sensible" (D 10). The Kantian imagination, in its shift from εἰκασία to φαντασία, plays the role of mediator in its power of synthesis. It functions as a retainer of impressions in the constituting of the sensible object, no longer moving eikastically through image to original. And yet, within this, one can detect a trace of the Platonic conception of the imagination. In its power of synthesis, the imagination "is the faculty of representing in intuition an object that is *not itself* present."[4] In the Kantian project, the imagination is no longer set against metaphysics precisely because imagination is installed within a "field which has itself been displaced, a field which is no longer simply governed by the drive to presence" (D 11).

But the relationship between metaphysics and imagination is complicated all over again when we move beyond Kant's First Critique. The appropriation of imagination to metaphysics is decisively limited by the division within reason itself, the division between theoretical and practical reason. Reason in its practical employment rigorously excludes imagination; it is a matter of a self-determination unmediated by imagination. However much imagination is appropriated to theoretical reason as a metaphysics of nature, it remains excluded from a metaphysics of morals.

And yet, the question posed in "Imagination and Metaphysics" is whether the dynamic relation between imagination and metaphysics can ultimately be repressed, whether a refuge could be found beyond the play of imagination in which reason could be self-determining. The text of Plato is recalled once again. In the *Republic* the repression of the imagination seemingly occurs at the highest level of the soul's ascent, the level of dialectic. The ascent at this highest level proceeds without images towards an ἀρχή that would no longer be susceptible to the "dispersive play of the imagination." But when we pay close attention to the text of Plato, the subtlety and irony are unmistakable. At the end of the journey it would be a matter of seeing truth itself instead of an image—at least, Socrates says, "as it looks to me,"[5] that is, in the *image* truth casts in Socrates's direction.

III

Let me break off my summary reading of "Imagination and Metaphysics" at this point—and thus temporarily hold in abeyance the question about the end of metaphysics that is subsequently posed in the text—to insert a continuation of the tracing of reason's entanglement from the perspective opened up in that text. I am thinking here of a sense of eikastic imagination that is at work in the text of Kant.

We should recall the analysis in Kant's Third Critique in which an eikastic image is introduced to account for the necessary appearance of the intelligible order—the moral order—in the sensible. This mediation is accomplished by expanding the way in which intuition and concept are related:

> All intuitions which we supply to concepts *a priori* are . . . either schemata or symbols, of which the former contain direct, the latter indirect, presentations of the concept. The former do this demonstratively; the latter by means of an analogy (for which we avail ourselves even of empirical intuitions) in which the judgment exercises a double function, first applying the concept to the object of a sensible intuition, and then applying the mere rule of the reflection made upon that intuition to a quite different object of which the first is only a symbol.[6]

A symbol, unlike a schemata (*Schemate*) which functions in the constitution of experience, is an object of sensible intuition which refers beyond the limits of experience; it serves to render the intelligible present in its absence. Now the beautiful, we are told, is this kind of sensible appearance. The beautiful is the one image which is capable of a shining forth of the intelligible in the sensible. The beautiful is the one image which images self-determining reason. The beautiful is a symbol of the moral realm.

But Kant's analysis merely serves to pose the appropriate question for us. If metaphysics cannot ultimately distinguish itself from a metaphysics of imagination, what would a metaphysics of the beautiful, a metaphysics of that one image that mirrors reason's entanglement, say to us about image and reason? In a somewhat different context, a response to this question is found in *Wahrheit und Meth-*

ode.[7] Here Gadamer wants to elicit the function of the beautiful within Greek metaphysics as a way of expressing the opening onto intelligibility and truth that occurs in hermeneutic experience. For our purposes, what is decisive in this analysis is the way in which the "double gesture" by which metaphysics both appropriates and yet excludes imagination gets reinscribed.

In order to see what is distinctive of the beautiful, Gadamer points to the close connection that Plato makes between the beautiful and the good. The beautiful, like the good, is chosen for its own sake. Both go beyond everything that is conditional and multiple. When, in the *Symposium,* Plato describes the beautiful itself as that which lies at the end of the journey through many beautiful beings, we should immediately compare this claim, Gadamer insists, with his remark in the *Republic* where the good is described as that which lies beyond that which is good in certain respects. But this common feature does not by itself indicate the intrinsic connection between the beautiful and the good. In the *Philebus* Plato tells us that in the attempt to grasp the good itself, the good takes flight in the beautiful; that is to say, the good is conceived here according to the ideal of mixture and thus inseparable from other aspects: "the power of the good has taken refuge in the nature of the beautiful; for measure and proportion [μετριότης γὰρ καὶ συμμετρία] are everywhere identified with beauty and virtue."[8] Plato then adds truth to this "mixture" so that beauty, proportion and truth are named as the three aspects of the good which appear as the beautiful. In this context, the good (which is at the same time the beautiful), contrary to the description found in the *Republic,* does not merely exist beyond being, but exists as well in those things that we recognize as a beautiful mixture.[9]

And yet, for Gadamer, this close connection between the beautiful and the good points at the same time to one respect in which the beautiful is different from the good. Insofar as the good takes flight in the beautiful, the beautiful appears to have a specific advantage over the good. The beautiful has the advantage of presenting itself; it is part of its nature to be that which appears (*Erscheinendes*). As such the beautiful, unlike models of human virtue, which have no light of their own—and thus "often succumb to impure imitations and appearances of virtue"[10]—has its own radiance. Accordingly, to say that the good is displayed in the beautiful simply means that the good is visibly manifest.

This feature of the beautiful—to be visibly manifest—is also found in the *Phaedrus.* In the myth of human destiny presented there, Plato describes the procession to the vault of the heavens where true being is revealed. In this procession the human soul is drawn back by the unruly steed, and thus is a soul whose vision is clouded and has, at best, a fleeting memory of true being. There is one experience, however, that allows the "wings to grow" and thus rejoin the ascent, namely, the love of the beautiful. Beauty, we are told, is the one εἶδος that is most brilliant, that preserves something of the former lustrousness of an idea, and shines forth in the visible stimulating love in us: "For the beautiful alone this has been ordained, to be most manifest [ἐκφανέστατον] to sense and most lovely to the all."[11] For Plato, the example of the beautiful illustrates the controversial relation of participation in the εἶδος without attending to any of the logical difficulties inherent in the problem. The function of the beautiful is precisely one of mediating between the intelligible and appearance. The beautiful itself, as an εἶδος, rises above the flux of appearances; and yet, it is itself that shines forth (*herausscheinen*) in the appearance (*erscheinen*).

For Gadamer, what is most significant here is the link that Plato establishes between the beautiful and the structure of being. Plato's metaphysics of the beautiful describes a self-presentational character of presence. Radiance, shining-forth, constitutes the being of the beautiful such that being present belongs decisively to the being of the beautiful. As that which is most radiant (ἐκφανέστατον) the beautiful is the appearance itself.[12] In Gadamer's eyes, though, Plato has not gone far enough; for the metaphysical conception of the beautiful only serves to raise the problem of the ontological status of appearance. This further problem is taken up by Gadamer in his attempt to construct an analogy between the classical conception of the beautiful and the event structure of hermeneutic understanding. The question, now, is the extent to which the metaphor of light, which characterizes the beautiful, is an analogue for genuine experience, for an encounter with something that asserts its own truth. To what extent, in other words, is the metaphor of light an analogue for the self-presentational character of being? Of course, the answer to this question, posed here at the end of metaphysics, must avoid the metaphysical tradition that makes use of this metaphor in the framework of a substance metaphysics as in Plotinus and Augustine.

According to Gadamer, the beautiful, in connection with the comprehensibility of the intelligible, is *einleuchtend*. Literally, a "shining in," its meaning is conveyed in the expression "an enlightening experience." The enlightening refers to the fact that something has come to light in the sense that something becomes *clear*. Such clarity is never the result of a methodological procedure, and thus stands in contrast to Cartesian certainty (which marks the outcome of methodological procedure). The clarity of *einleuchtend*, in a sense, comes upon us, perhaps even surprises us. Gadamer thinks that one finds this notion of clarity in rhetoric. The art of rhetoric, which ties itself to the immediacy of its effect, advocates a claim to truth that defends the probable, the εἰκός, and that which is convincing to ordinary reason.[13] The true has the mark of "true shining" (*wahrscheinlich*), asserting itself of its own merit, as we find in argumentation where an argument may have something true about it even though we may argue against it. In such situations, the way in which what is true is compatible with the whole of what we consider correct is left open.[14] Similarly, the beautiful engages us, charms us, without being immediately integrated into the whole of our orientations.

In becoming clear, in "true shining," there is, at least in some fashion, a shining-forth (ἀλήθεια). From what we have seen, all too briefly in Plato, the peculiar character of this shining-forth of the beautiful is such that it collapses the differentiation between illuminating and illuminated: the beautiful, as the way in which the good appears, makes itself manifest in its being. It is the condition of the εἶδος itself to shine, to present itself. Thus, for the beautiful, it makes no difference whether it itself or its image (*Abbild*) appears. For Gadamer, this being of the beautiful, this self-presentational shining-forth must always be understood ontologically as image (*Bild*).[15] The whole issue of the self-presentational character of being turns on Gadamer's understanding of image (*Bild*). Clearly, in this context, image is no longer the distorted copy that appears as semblance, an image with something behind or beneath it. One has to turn to his analysis of the image/picture (*Bild*) in the experience of art in order to see the significance of this notion.

In discussing the ontological value of the picture, Gadamer is quick to point out that the problematic character of a picture is derived, as it is for Plato, from the problem of the original picture (*Urbild*). The concept of a picture, linked to the concept of (re)presentation (*Darstellung*), is a form of imitation. What Gadamer wants to show is that the presentation of the picture, as in a framed painting, is related to the original in a different way than the relation of the copy to the original. Gadamer has already been able to show that for the performing arts at least the imitative presentation is not a mere copy. In drama "the world which appears in the play of presentation does not stand like a copy next to the real world," but is the real in the heightened truth of its being.[16] The presentation of Achilles by Homer, for example, is superior to the "original" Achilles. A transformation occurs in dramatic play: What is meant is intrinsic to the presentation, and only in a secondary, critical stance do we ask about the identity of the player or the quality of the production (those comparative questions that force a distinction between copy and original).

What is ontologically true of the performing arts is true of the work of art in general: Every production is a self-presentation; its being has its τέλος within itself. Such a claim is hardly striking at all if one recognizes, as Gadamer does, that this presentational character of art is what is expressed by the original concept of μίμησις. Originally, the concept of μίμησις has little to do with the imitation of something that is already familiar to us. Rather, it pertains to the way in which something is presented such that it is actually present in sensuous abundance. The imitation, the "copying" character of the presentation, is simply "the appearance (*Erscheinung*) of what is presented." Without the imitation of the work, the world is not there as it is there in the work.[17] Consequently, we can say that the work of art does not refer to something, because the presence of what is presented stands in its own right as a completed whole in the presentation. It is in this context that we would want to claim that the Platonic image-original structure collapses in the presentational character of art.

The question, though, is whether the same analysis can also be applied to the picture (*Bild*). It would appear that with respect to a picture, copy (*Abbild*) and original (*Urbild*) are quite distinct, since the original picture, unlike dramatic play which has its real being in being performed and thus produced, resists production as self-presentation. But here too we can see that the image-original structure collapses. Notice what being a copy entails. Its function is to announce the original by resembling it. The measure of its success is that one recognizes the original in the copy. That is, although a copy exists in its own right, by pointing beyond itself, its nature is to cancel out its independent existence. An ideal copy, then, would be the mirror image, "for its being can effectively disappear; it exists only for someone who looks into the mirror, and is nothing beyond its pure appearance."[18] But in truth it is no picture or copy at all, for it has no existence for itself. And yet, the fact that we speak here of a mirror *image* and not a copy is by no means insignificant. "For in the mirror image the being itself appears in the image so that we have the thing itself in the mirror image," whereas a copy requires in addition "to be seen in relation to what is meant by it."[19] A picture is not itself a copy since it is not intended to be canceled out. Similar to the mode of being of performance, the picture itself is what is meant; and thus one is not directed away from it to some anterior or posterior presentation. This feature of presentation is the positive distinction of being a picture as opposed to being a mere reflected image.

And yet, as presentation, the picture is not the same as what is presented. According to Gadamer, "even the mechanical technically-produced pictures of today can be used artistically in that they can get something out of what is portrayed that is not found in simply looking at it [*Anblick*]."[20] Of course such a picture remains limited by the original, but the relation to the original here is quite different from a copy-original relation. In the case of the picture, the relation is no longer one-sided. Since the picture has its own reality, one can say that the original presents itself in the presentation, whereas the original is inferred in the copy; the original has its semblance in the copy. Such presenting is no incidental occurrence, but belongs to its actual being. Through the presentation the original experiences, as it were, an increase in being. In a sense the picture is the original's emanation.

This conception of presentation, in which the picture stands in a unique relation to the original, is not that novel. Gadamer thinks we find this same mode of being in the concept of representation (*Repräsentation*) in canon law. *Repraesentare* means to make present. But, "the important thing about the legal concept of representation is that the *persona repraesentata* is put forward and presented [*Vor- und Dargestellte*], and yet the *Repräsentant,* who is exercising the former's rights, is *dependent* upon him."[21] This concept of representation suggests something even more about the relation of image and original. Now we can say that the picture has an independence that effects the original, for strictly speaking it is only through the picture that the original actually becomes original (*Ur-bilde*).[22] The religious picture is a good illustration of what is meant here. The appearance of the divine acquires its picturalness (*Bildhaftigkeit*) only through the word and the picture. The religious picture is not a copy of a copied being, "but is in ontological communion with what is copied." The pictorial image is thus not an imitative illustration, but allows what it presents to be for the first time what it is.

If we take this analysis of the pictorial image as indicative of what Gadamer means by the self-presentational character of being, as an event by which the world comes into being, then self-presentation can be described as a play of image. Gadamer admits as much when he speaks about language, which is the particular expression for what he means by tradition. The word is not simply a sign, but more like an image (*Bild*). This means that the structure of being, the intelligible, is not simply copied in language; rather in language the intelligible forms itself.[23] In the word, as in the beautiful in its shining-forth, there is a showing forth. Such an image play—since it is not something produced by a subject—is that in which we find ourselves entangled. Gadamer writes:

> When we understand a text, what is meaningful engages [*einnimmt*] us, just as the beautiful engages us. It has asserted itself and engaged us before we come to ourselves and be in position to test the claim to meaning that it makes. What we encounter in the experience of the beautiful and in understanding the meaning of tradition has effectively something about it of the truth of play. In understanding we are drawn into an event of truth and arrive, as it were, too late, if we want to know what we ought to believe.[24]

IV

As a way of marking the end of this further tracing of reason's entanglement, let us rejoin the movement of the text "Imagination and Metaphysics." In the face of Socrates's subtlety and irony, it can be asked whether pure intelligibility can ultimately be protected from the threat of imagination. The closure of metaphysics can be said to mark this "emptying of every refuge in which pure intelligibility might find protection from the threat of imagination" (D 14).

Now, a philosophical hermeneutics appears to be one such expression of the closure of metaphysics. It appears to be an image play that no longer subordinates the drive to presence, to a τέλος of pure presence, to a place "undivided by any casting of images." For philosophical hermeneutics it is not a matter of seeing truth itself instead of an image, but precisely the inverse: of getting entangled in the image which entangles us with truth. With neither τέλος nor ἀρχή in the image play we are left with thick images, whose depths reveal the profound entanglement of λόγος and εἰκασία.

But there is another expression of the closure of metaphysics, where intelligibility can no longer be protected from the threat of imagination, that deserves mentioning here, if only briefly. What if the intelligible is found out to be itself an image? What if reason's entanglement is not an entanglement *with* image, in which the intelligible remains somehow encased, but is itself an entanglement *of* image whereby the intelligible vanishes? This is the question that Nietzsche asks of metaphysics.

In "Truth and Lies in a Nonmoral Sense" Nietzsche describes for us precisely how it is that the intelligible is nothing other than image.

> Anyone who has felt [the] cool breath [of logic] will hardly believe that even the concept—which is as bony, foursquare, and transposable as a die—is nevertheless merely the **residue of a metaphor,** and that the illusion which is involved in the artistic transference of a nerve stimulus into images is, if not the mother, then the grandmother of every single concept.[25]

We encounter the world as creators of images and metaphors, which are themselves transformations of their objects; but through time, these metaphors become sedimented—they become concepts. We philosophers become, according to Nietzsche, ingenious architects building a complicated "cathedral of concepts" (*Begriffsdom*) on a foundation of "running water." The ingenuity consists in the delicate entanglement of the construction. Nietzsche continues:

> As a genius of construction man raises himself far above the bee in the following way: Whereas the bee builds with wax that he gathers from nature, man builds with far more delicate conceptual material which he first has to manufacture from himself. In this he is greatly to be admired, but not on account of his drive for truth or for pure knowledge of things. When someone hides something behind a bush and finds it there as well, there is not much to praise in such seeking and finding. Yet this is how matters stand regarding seeking and finding "truth" within the realm of reason.[26]

Later on Nietzsche describes this truth as "fictive."[27] Life can only be what it is: a self-mockery that makes us feel that all is appearance, a dance of spirits. One is maintained in life only by images. The task is thus to maintain the image, to see how the image is an *Heilmittel*,[28] a φάρμακον, which opens up the world in such a way that it can be lived.

And yet, it can be said that neither of these two expressions of the closure of metaphysics releases the play of image into the entire field. For the field here essentially remains the same, even if—in the one case—all hell has broken loose in reason's entanglement. The release of the imagination into the entire field, it is said in "Imagination and Metaphysics," would inaugurate a movement beyond the closure of metaphysics. It would be a matter

> of taking the directional, oriented character and the reiterably dyadic character of the field as traces or residues of what metaphysics began by calling λόγος and εἰκασία and ended by calling reason and imagina-

tion. It would be a matter of venturing, beyond the closure of metaphysics, to reassemble these moments which metaphysics from its beginning has set apart. Writing under erasure, attending to the subtlety and risk of the move, one might then broach the demands of a logic of imagination. (D 15)

Beyond the scope of both Gadamer's and Nietzsche's projects, it would be a matter of a further play, the play of a detective, who, without a suspect, must in Kafka-like fashion follow the traces of reason and imagination. It would be (to state the matter quite provisionally in the context of the Kantian project, for example) a matter of reinscribing imagination by determining it "as the primary sense of *image* prior to its assimilation to the problem of transcendental schematism—viz., image as the manifest look of something which at the same time shows how such things look in general" (E 116). It would be, in other words, a matter of attending, under the demands of a *logic* of imagination, to another *shining,* one no longer reducible to presence, one no longer joined to reason that would bring the shining under the determination of presence.[29]

CHAPTER THIRTEEN

TRAGIC JOY

Michel Haar

Translated by Peg Birmingham and Elizabeth Birmingham

> "The Dionysian, with its primordial
> joy experienced even in pain, is
> the common source of music and
> tragic myth."
> *The Birth of Tragedy,* Ch. 24.

> "I am the first to have discovered
> the tragic. . . ."
> "Tragedy is a tonic."
> *Will to Power,* 1029, 851.

> "Tragedy both reveals and conceals
> the Dionysian abyss."
> "Tragedy is a disclosing of the
> abyss as sublime."
> John Sallis, *Crossings, Nietzsche and the Space of Tragedy,* chap. 3.

Nietzsche is not the first (far from it) to have extended the concept of tragedy to such a point that he could apply it well beyond tragedy as a theatrical genre—the staging of a myth of destiny—to a fundamental determination of human existence, even of being as such, taken in part or in its totality. Already for Plato, the "tragic" characterizes all of "life" (βίος) or this world, or everything down below.

He has Socrates state this in the *Cratylus* (408c) at the moment that he affirms (something he rarely does) that "logos conveys everything" (ὁ λόγος τὸ πᾶν σημαίνει):

> That which is true (ἀληθές) is free and divine (λεῖον καί θεῖον) and dwells with the gods on high; but the false resides below with the throng of people and it is uncouth and tragic; because it is here below that myths and lies are most numerous regarding tragic life (περὶ τὸν τραγικὸν βίον).

And immediately following this, Socrates insists upon this redoubling of being in the redoubling of λόγος: "threads to the double nature of Hermes: on the one hand polished on high, on the other uncouth and tragic below." Plato plays therefore upon a subtle difference between two adjectives: τραγικόν and τραγοειδής, both derived from τραγός, the goat, the animal of immemorial sacrifice—prior to the institution of the religion of two Olympians—in order to indicate on the one hand that which is literally, empirically, or of itself tragic (τραγικόν), and that which appears through the logos, the "idea" of the tragic (τραγοειδής from τραγός-εῖδος).

In the Nietzschean reversal of Platonism, the tragic becomes not only ἀληθές, but also divine, as well as that which characterizes totality, or that which can be affirmed from a non-totalizable whole. It remains, simply and exclusively, "tragic life": illusory and even more non-illusory, to consecrate and not turn away, to love it as it is and not to stray. But why then "tragic"? For Plato, tragic is the incarnation, the separation of what is above from what is below, the quasi-abandonment of the here-below, ambiguous, mortal, blind penumbra, difficult to preserve. For Nietzsche tragic is the inseparability of the above and the below, of the true and the false, of good and evil, because Nietzsche accepts this dichotomy in order to better refuse the antinomy. Tragic would be the infinite melange, forever woven, flawless. Why does this non-division, the unity of being (which the youthful works call the originary One), remain "tragic"? What can still signify the terms of "tragic knowledge (or) wisdom," which seem to imply a final *elucidation,* a non-illusion as to the falseness of all the antitheses? As Jean Hyppolite said regarding Hegel, does such a *pantragism* not necessarily contain a new *panlogicism?*

Nietzschean thought was ushered in around 1869 and was cut short rather than concluded in 1888 by a reflection on the meaning of the tragic phenomena: "I am within my rights to consider myself as the first *tragic philosopher,*" he wrote in *Ecce Homo*. First, the reversal of Platonism with the unlimited fragmentation of being in non-mimetic appearances, and later, the divided unity intrinsic to all the great ultimate "concepts" (the will to active/reactive power, Overman/last man, infinite, linear lost time/cyclic time of the eternal return): such are the first and last words of a continual and unique tragic philosophy. But before and after the double "turning" that for Nietzsche (around 1875–1879) constituted the passage through positivism in *Human, All Too Human,* and simultaneously the rupture with Wagnerian music, is the *same* intuition of the essence of the tragic which endures and which constitutes the most abiding thread of his thought, his ultimate fidelity to himself. This intuition, present from the outset of his itinerary in *The Birth of Tragedy,* assures him that the tragic, even considered in the "sublime and the terrifying"[1] spectacle of tragedy, is not a synonym of resignation, of pessimism, not the overpowering or defeat of humans by fate, but a symptom of strength, indeed of an "excess of strength," he will say in 1880, a phenomenon of the pure affirmation or of a *redoubled* affirmation of existence. This paradoxical approbation rests on a fundamental, affective disposition: joy, a joy other than any ordinary joy, a *religious* joy.

But we will see that this "religious" phenomenon—for which tragedy was the official liturgy (representations were financed by rich, successful citizens) did not proceed from that public, dogmatic, codified religion, the religion of the temple, but from a secret, mystical religion, without articles of faith, from a religion that is momentary, discontinuous and magical, astonishing for its involuntary followers seized by the divine transmutation of sadness into joy, the paroxysmal religion of the theatrical moment, that of the death of heroes. How can we conceptually account for such a phenomenon whose ultimate meaning is "musical"?

On the "objective," exterior plane of the drama (but for Nietzsche the tragic has its essence neither in myth nor in drama), the death of the hero or his fall or destitution is, we could say, his triumph. "The most universal form of tragic destiny is [. . .] victory winning in defeat."[2] Prometheus, Oedipus, or Antigone (of whom Nietzsche does not speak) triumph their "cause" through their destruction. Oedipus's "cause" would be the will to know everything about himself, the excess of the *libido sciendi,* the "eye that sees too much," as Hölderlin writes, and his symbolic "death": his eyes that he pierces, his ostracism. On this level—more profound for the philosopher—of the spectator, there is a jubilation which surpasses itself into a superior, aesthetic dimension: the vision, distressing in itself, of the collapse and destruction of the hero. The tragic is aesthetically sublime. *Sublime* in Kant's very precise sense (or rather according to *one* of Kant's definitions): "a feeling of life . . . a pleasure . . . produced by the feeling of an arrest of vital forces lasting a brief moment, followed immediately by an *outpouring* of them that is all the stronger. . . ."[3] Tragic joy is linked to the sublime taken in this sense and not according to other definitions such as, for example, "the presentation of the supersensitive," or the inadequate symbolization of freedom, or even "negative pleasure." Tragic joy is not a simple oxymoron. It accompanies and perhaps makes possible the apprehension and the approbation of a power which goes beyond all finite form. There is in the Nietzschean sentiment of the sublime a play with the infinite, a play which, while "serious" and effective, is not weighty or recuperative and—turning away from moral seriousness—is not edifying.

In *Crossings: Nietzsche and the Space of Tragedy,* a study remarkable for its accuracy and penetration on many other points as well (the best and most inspired that I know of on *The Birth of Tragedy*), John Sallis has shown that the relationship with Kant is very close, even including the word *Erschütterung* (tremoring) (C 95). Indeed, in chapter 27 of the *Critique of Judgment,* Kant describes the sublime in opposition to the restful and limited contemplation of the beautiful, as "an agitation which can be compared to a tremoring" of all limits which makes them vibrate and which produces a rapid acceleration of repulsion and attraction. Likewise Nietzsche, in regard to the Dionysian sublime wrote, "Dionysian man seeks to attain his model (i.e., the instinctive poet—singer—dancer, and not the actor conscious of himself) in the *shock* of the sublime. . . ."[4] Sallis also underscores the close presence of a "frightening abyss" in Kant, and, of course, in Nietzsche (*Kluft der Vergessenheit,* "the abyss of forgetting").[5]

If it is entirely a question of a sublime effect in the "joy taken from the tragic"[6] (*die Lust am Tragischen*), it will be important not to confuse the sublime that gives birth to the tragic with the moral sublime, which has been the tradition since Aristotle.[7] Every finite loss (such beauty, such pillaged grandeur) is compensated, without being repaired on another level, by an infinite gain or renewal . . . *of life:* tragedy is for the Greeks a force of healing (*Heilskraft*) or a "prophylactic" instrument, and yet nothing of what is destroyed is recovered or restored, nor dialectically conserved, but *returns,* only perhaps for the sole joy of the One—and not for the rational self-satisfaction of pure practical universal subjectivity or the omniscient historico-world Subject. How do we grasp this conjunction of the vital and the sublime, this odd tie, this sublime vitality which is called *tragic?*

JOY—SERENITY OF THE HERO AND JOY
OF THE "SPECTATOR-ARTIST"

But before answering this question, once again, why joy? How do we justify this rupture with every tradition, which is tied up with an apparently irrefutable reference to the experience of the spectator, the tragic effect on the feelings of φόβος (extreme fear, distress) and ἔλεος (pity, compassion), which is to say on the effects (that Nietzsche will qualify "reactive" and "distorted") of intense fear on the one hand, for the hero or for one's self through projection and identification, and intense sadness on the other, of poignant sorrow (in German *Trauerspiel* [mourning play] is a doublet of tragedy) before the lucid and frantic precipitation, the ineluctable slide into the abyss of a grand, admirable, and superb being? How shall we not suffer in the face of the cruel and disastrous demise and the never entirely merited demise of this "hero" (is the sex important?) who was beautiful, happy, glorious, powerful, respected, sometimes good, always noble, gifted with a magnanimous soul, in any case never seeking—at least in Aeschylus and Sophocles[8]—

only his own interest, his own vengeance or the satisfying of an egotistical or vile passion? How shall we not recognize here with Hegel the atrocious reading of the universal?

From an Hegelian point of view, joy could originate from the intimate, solitary conviction (*Meinung*, "opinion," means literally *mineness*) of "being right," of possessing the universal in oneself. A fatal illusion. "I wanted it, I predicted it," Prometheus often repeats. "I commit this act voluntarily. . . ." "I know the future completely and in advance. Nothing bad will happen to me that I have not already predicted. . . ." (*Prometheus*, v. 101–103, v. 265–266) The rupture with Schopenhauer's thought on art as the negation of the will-to-live and of tragedy in particular as the school of "resignation, renunciation, and even abdication of the will to live"[9] is not sufficient to explain the reversal of melancholy—certainly isolated, distanced by beauty, having become other and like a stranger ("the effect of estrangement, "*Verfremdungseffekt*," Brecht wrote)—in an exaltation, in a paroxysm of pleasure and above all in an unlimited approbation of existence and totality which "permits" this evil. "The [tragic] hero is gay" [*heiter,* serene],[10] saturated with this "serenity" [*Heiterkeit*] that Nietzsche finds in Homer and that he considers as the most fundamental *Stimmung* of the ancient Greeks. Their gaze "plunged into the deepest depths of nature"; but as our wounded eyes have looked at the sun full face and seen dark spots dancing under our eyelids, they knew to draw from the unbearable vision of the night the luminous images that are the heroes of myth: "luminous spots to cure eyes damaged by gruesome night."[11]

The joyous serenity of heroes is not as paradoxical as it appears. The exemplary serenity of Oedipus, a refugee at Colonus, exiled, blind, symbolically already dead—the Christian tradition is wise to be tempted to understand him as a saint—as well as the serenity of Prometheus, both evoked in chapter nine, belong to the Apollinian principle of the separation of individuals and abstract universality. Elsewhere, the tragic dimension is singularly curtailed. Oedipus attaining a "mysterious serenity" in a supraterrestrial transfiguration, and Prometheus moved by a rational desire for a universal justice who in some sense introduces or invents by the sacrilegious kidnapping of fire the advance of a new deity that we today call "the rights of man"—having lost the original tie with the sphere of φύσις— Dionysian. No longer autochthonous or vital, they remain, however, the "masks" of Dionysos, fabulously complete projections or the mirrors of the One, originally divided into pleasure/pain, one/many, good/evil.

Oedipus at Colonus, groping along like a living corpse, a prophetic old man broken by the monstrosities of his crime and his archetypal destiny, entering through the supreme passivity of pure endurance, of pure suffering, into a supranatural dimension, "agrees to this ultimate activity which far surpasses the end of his life," gains a "supraterrestial serenity,"[12] by leaving Dionysian vitality. Prometheus, stealer of divine fire and through this the founder of every human hearth, originary founder of every πόλις and every culture, symbolizes in relation

to the "glory of passivity" of the first Oedipus the "active sin," the affirmative moment of the transgression of human limits that he believes to have been arbitrarily
established by the "jealousy" of the Gods. His ὕβρις, unbounded pride, places him
not only above the present gods, but above divine generations: He knows that Zeus
has castrated his father Kronos, he predicts that Zeus, in his turn, will be dethroned
by his own son, the child of a mortal. "Knowing in advance" (Prometheus comes
from πρo-μανϑάνω) the twilight and death of olympian gods, he places his ti-
tanic, archaic force (he is a son of the earth) and his pro-mathesis in the service of
future universal justice. He draws upon the revolutionary Dionysian energy to pro-
mote a pure Apollinism, an egalitarian universality. He has no goodness, no sen-
timentality, but marvels and boasts of having *reason* to be above everyone and
everything, against all his enemies: all the gods. *His solitude* exalts him. "In order
to will the unique essence of the world,"[13] in order to be equal to the One, which
implies an offense to the truth of the original internal discord of the One, he must
"perish" as much as a god or titan can "perish," which is to say to remain enchained
(until, according to other myths, Zeus reassured, releases him, or until he is delivered by Hercules). His mad serenity comes from the absolute, but irresponsible,
will to knowledge, because he does not risk death (because he is immortal, Zeus
can only torture him, not exterminate him). His generosity is deprived of discrim-
ination, his justice is not in proportion to the image of an infinite cosmos. His in-
dignation at the sufferings inflicted upon mortals by Zeus is a rhetorical game,
even a bit sophistic. His mad joy lies in the insane affirmation that all the gods will
die. The later Nietzsche will say that his joy is mitigated by the spirit of vengeance,
by the malevolent prescience of the dethronement of Zeus and his fall into obliv-
ion. "Me, I know, how Zeus will perish . . ." (*Prometheus,* v. 915) He does not *announce* the accession of a new god, son of the Earth, he does not *affirm* this, even
though he *knows* it. Son of the Earth, prophet par excellence, he badly serves his
prophetic gift, because he uses his knowledge only to raise himself in imagination
above the god and, especially, above his times, therefore losing the Dionysiac
foundation.

The serene joy of heroes (even if it is more Dionysian than that of Antigone,
which touches the obscure connection of bloodlines) is, however, not true "tragic
joy." Nietzsche, through his relative adherence to the metaphysics of subjectivity,
attaches himself to the "aesthetic" in the Kantian sense, that is to say, in the sense
that aesthetic pleasure is "pleasure of reflection", pleasure (*jouissance*) in the creative subject or the spectator. For him the creator or spectator are the same insofar as the goal of art is for the creator to communicate to the "spectator," (who
ceases to be passive in order to become "listener-artist") the high tonality of intoxication which drives him to create. The content, the message is of little importance; it is the *aesthetic creative state* which one is concerned with transmitting,
somewhat like the "inspiration" that the poet receives in Plato's *Ion.* However, that
subjectivity is neither an individual subjectivity nor an abstract, transcendental

subject: That which delights in the tragic play, as that which sings in the lyrical poem, is not the paltry individual subject; it is "the only truly existing and eternal self, the elusive "subject" whose foundation is the abysmal ground of things, "the genius of the world itself."[14]

If tragic joy appears at a higher dimension, it is because it is the metaphysical joy of the One celebrating itself in ecstasy over its superabundant plenitude and its perfection in spite of its suffering.

> From the nature of art as it is usually conceived according to the single category of appearance and beauty, the tragic cannot honestly be deduced at all; it is only through the spirit of music that we can understand the joy involved in the annihilation of the individual.[15]

The Kantian category of the beautiful is insufficient for understanding tragic joy. One must appeal to two dimensions: (*a*) a fresh thought of the sublime, beyond the hold of practical reason and moral infinity; (*b*) the difficult notion of *Geist der Musik*, wherein *Geist* is neither Hegelian nor spiritual, but signifies *Grundstimmung*, the preobjective rhythm which "inspires" any production of forms—a notion difficult to elucidate because it points toward the very root of the "musical."[16]

In the second third of the work, Nietzsche strenuously insists on placing the accent on this theme of "metaphysical joy." Let us read two of the most striking passages. They are still somewhat enigmatic, because the phenomenological explication of the irruption of joy in the spectator only comes in Chapter 22.

> Metaphysical joy which is born of tragedy is the translation, into the language of image, of Dionysian instinctive and unconscious wisdom: the hero, this ultimate manifestation (*Erscheinung*) of will, is denied for our pleasure because he is only a manifestation—and his destruction in no way affects the eternal life of the will.

> For brief moments, we are actually the original being himself, we experience his unconstrained desire, and his pleasure in existing; the struggles and the torments, the destruction of phenomena, all seem suddenly necessary to us given the *superabundance* (*Übermass,* excess, profusion) of the innumerable forms of existence, which hurry and rush us toward life, the overflowing fecundity of universal will: the furious goading of these torments transport us into the very time where we are so to speak no longer anything but one with the incommensurate and original pleasure of existing and where, ravished in Dionysian ecstasy, we foreshadow the indestructible eternity of this pleasure;—where, notwithstanding terror and pity, we recognize the blissfulness of living, not as individuals, but in this unique aliveness which engenders and procreates, and in the orgasm (*Zeugungslust*) in which we meld together.

Note that the words "joy" and "pleasure" go back to the single German word *Lust*. The idea that "every true tragedy" is permeated with "the thought that life is at the bottom of things, despite all the changes of appearances, full of joy in its indestructible power . . ."[17] has been introduced without elaboration in Chapter Seven. Having explained "how it is possible that this irresistible disposition redirects man to *unity* with himself and with the cosmos, beyond the social and outside of the individual," it is necessary to inquire into the complementary difficulty of the Apollinian and the Dionysian. Nietzsche continues to return to this, except during his years of "intellectualist" critique (from 1874 to 1879), in order to show more and more clearly that there is truly no duality. The two "principles" are indissolubly "physiological" (dream and intoxication), proto-artistic (two kinds of *rhythmos:* the stabilized form and the mobile, unstable form) and "theological" (Olympian divinity and the more archaic divinity). As fundamental as the differences of the sexes (the first phase of the *Birth of Tragedy*), they are only able to communicate, to be communicative with one another, one in the other, to correspond, to exchange indefinitely their attributes. The symbolic richness of the Apollo/Dionysos couple is inexhaustible. Their eternal conflict can only give rise to ephemeral reconciliations which are not syntheses, but moments: the moment of the myth when Apollo heals Dionysos of his wounds (we will return to this), the moment of tragedy where the exchange becomes a "fraternal alliance between two divinities: Dionysos speaking Apollo's language" (there is no other because the language of Dionysos is music), "but Apollo, *finally* the language of Dionysos,"[18] which would mean Apollo metamorphosed by the all-powerful appeal of the Dionysian sublime.

At an exterior level, not at all superficial, but full of innumerable nuances, Apollo and Dionysos—as the masculine and the feminine in the unity of a single body and in sexual life—oppose and penetrate one in the other, forming a series of non-antinomic antitheses, or a vast nondualistic system of complementarities. These opposites can be outlined in a succinct and simplified table (necessarily incomplete, because unattainable), as follows, without "logical" or deductive order:

> Apollo/Dionysos
> day/night
> stasis/dynamism
> limit/unlimited, "panic" principle
> principle of contraction/principle of expansion
> forms/forces
> stopping/gushing
> beautiful/sublime
> surface/depth
> "dream" (as the vision of forms)/rapture (as the production of forms by rhythm)
> regular rhythm/syncopated rhythm

consciousness/collective unconscious
individuation/fusion
principle of reality/"dissolution of self", orgiastic
occident/orient
culture/savagery,[19] barbarism, natural chaos
work/festivities
language/music
melody/harmony
law and order/nondelimitation of boundaries
State/nomadism
wisdom/folly
proportion/disproportion
healing/sickness
appearance/undetermined ground
identity and εἶδος/disindividuation—mask—interior chaos
memory/forgetfulness
space as distance and separation/time as
                    principle of simultaneity, ecstatic
                    artistic moment where forms
                    disappear (later the Eternal
                    Return)
time as chronological or successive/space as the
                    unifying and dispersing principle,
                    as originary spatiality
                    anterior to time
visible divinity/hidden, masked divinity

Is this "system" metaphysical? Yes and no. Yes, insofar as it has an appearance of the "total" explication of the world. No, given that it is not a closed system, given that it is not by definition a system in the Hegelian sense, given that the duality is ceaselessly articulated and not articulated, and given that the opposites continually exchange their roles and entangle themselves in an infinite play of equilibriums and disequilibriums.

The originality and the difficulty of the thought in the *Birth of Tragedy* emerge because Nietzsche, from the beginning, thinks the One as Dionysos or Dionysos as the One while, however, exposing two principles and their *history*. Because Apollo only becomes who he is when faced with the intrusion of the barbarian god who came from Asia in a storm and when doing battle with that barbarian god. He ignores that he is his own brother; he does not recognize his sublime parents in the unsettling stranger who is both host and enemy (*hostis*). At first, Apollo is only beautiful. Dionysos, as we will see, will be rendered sublime. But above all *if there is no system,* it is because the Dionysian One is itself originally divided and already contains the solar principle of appearance (*Scheinen*); it is hermaphroditic, split and shared—as we will see in a moment—in an irreducible duplicity, and it is in no way pure withdrawal or pure Night; it would only be this because it is the first principle of ecstasy, of being-outside-of-self (*Ausser-sich-sein*).[20] But the Apollinian is not originary, it is only the visual projection of the ground of the Dionysian abyss, in virtue of the One, of an "originary desire for appearance,"[21] the elucidation of the Dionysian staged or reflected.

"What we name the 'tragic' is exactly this Apollinian elucidation of the Dionysian. . . ."[22] Beginning with the fragments of 1870–1871, these are solely the sufferings of Dionysos (torn apart according to different myths by the Menades or by Prometheus himself, or by the revolting Titans; Promethean Man, the 'enlightened' civilizer who rips apart, dismantles, denies Dionysos, cf. *Fragment* 7 [83]), and their proper transfiguration which are at the center, the Dionysian as the single and unique 'subject': a Dionysian 'chorus', under the effect of an Apollinian action, discloses itself in a *vision of its own state.*"[23] The vision in its turn is regarded as action; it is personified in living images which struggle throughout the dialogue. All of this which is exteriorized is intended to veil the terrifying base which appears as a very harmful, "grotesque and brutal power"[24] against which it is extremely necessary to protect and heal oneself. Apollo is a physician, the Apollinian is a φάρμακον, a remedy which "poisons" because it dissociates the surface from its roots.

Masking the base, the Apollinian above all conceals the ambivalence which is constitutive of this base, of its double nature which it can only despise, deny or be tempted to reduce. Because the Dionysian harbors an essential and intolerable ambivalence: "sweetness" (voluptuous fusion with nature)[25] and "cruelty" (the mythical dismembering of the god and, for human subjectivity, the abysmal loss of identity), or even *joy and suffering,* contradictory unity for the Apollinian logic of affects of pleasure and pain, or even the unity of a crucifying fury and a calming ecstasy (what Hegel called the "Bacchanal delirium" identical with "translucent and simple repose").

Nietzsche again takes up this double nature of Dionysos, life affirming and carrier of death, attested to by fragment 15 of Heraclitus that he partially cites in the Posthumous of the *Birth of Tragedy,* (3 [82]): "Hades and Dionysos are the same (ὁῦτος), who strike them with delirium (μαίνονται) and with enthusiasm from the divine wine press." Citing the choruses of Euripedes' *Bacchae,* he recalls that Dionysos has the epithet *Zagreus* (a contraction of *Zeus* and *agreus,* the ancient hunter who kills animals and devours them live, eating their raw flesh). And Dionysos is simultaneously called ἀγριόνιος the Hunter (an allusion to the archaic, pre-Hellenic rites of the hunt where the animal killed was ceremoniously and fraternally eaten in a propitiatory rite);[26] and ὀμηστής, he who eats raw flesh; and μειλίχιος, gentle as honey. This sweetness, which symbolizes the reunion with nature, is evoked in a posthumous text[27] permeated with an extremely sensual pantheistic magic, with an "eroticism," with a "musical intoxication of transfiguration" as Nietzsche wrote, which is all the more surprising in that he remains completely silent on the violent scene which in the *Bacchae* immediately follows this Eden-like scene. (Here the Menades pillage the plain of Thebes, cutting to pieces the herds which peacefully graze, slicing the bulls, "tearing the young heifers to shreds," they cover the firs with blood, "flames flickered in their curls and did not burn them." They wound and frighten the poor shepherds who cover them with arrows which draw no blood, the god immediately healing them (*Bacchae*, v. 669 to 780). But here is the idyllic and magical scene which precedes this:

> A messenger tells how in that hour when the sun lets loose its light to warm the earth, our grazing herds of cows had just begun to climb the path along the mountain ridge. Suddenly I saw three companies of dancing women who lay in the deep sleep of exhaustion, some resting on boughs of fir, others sleeping where they fell, here and there among the oak leaves—but all modestly and soberly. Suddenly the mother of Pentheus began the celebration, gave a great cry to waken them from sleep. And they too, rubbing the bloom of soft sleep from their eyes, rose up lightly and straight—a noble sight to see: all as one, the old women and the young and the unmarried girls. First they let their hair fall loose, down over their shoulders, and those whose straps had slipped fastened their skins of fawn with writhing snakes that licked their cheeks. Breasts swollen with milk, new mothers who had left their babies behind at home nestled gazelles and young wolves in their arms, suckling them. Then they crowned their hair with leaves, ivy and oak and flowering bryony. One woman struck her thyrsus against a rock and a fountain of cool water came bubbling up. Another drove her fennel in the ground, and where it struck the earth, at the touch of god, a spring of wine poured out. Those who wanted milk scratched at the soil with bare fingers and the white milk came welling up.—This is an enchanted world, nature celebrates its reconciliation with man.

For the young Nietzsche, the benevolent and cruel Dionysos is not far from designating the essence of the world, "the co-mingling of suffering and pleasure in the essence of the world,"[28] but upon the ground of joy, that is to say in an ecstatic movement of becoming-one and not-one in a stable essence which is already there. An ambivalence which only exists in act, in the exaltation of the festival, under the convulsions of music, in the magic of the dithyramb, in the "artistic jubilation" of the archaic, not yet ritualized and pre-ceremonial celebration: heart-rendering delight, pleasure born of the same sorrow, double conditions, inverse but similar φάρμακα ("the remedies [of Dionysos] recalling mortal poisons," chapter two), through which the duplicity of a god is incarnated in the dance of the possessed, of the "Dionysian madness": "the curious blending and duality in the emotions of the Dionysian revelers remind us—as medicines remind us of deadly poisons—of the phenomenon that pain begets joy, that ecstasy may wring sounds of agony from us. At the very climax of joy there sounds a cry of horror or a yearning lamentation for an irretrievable loss."[29]

This archaic prefiguration of the spectator of tragedy's strange joy foreshadows the essence: the eclipse of the Apollinian surface, the collapse of the visible on the one hand; the identification with the double nature of the Dionysian and the victory of the "spirit of music" on the other.

In passing, we must emphasize the profound continuity between the positions of 1872 and those of 1888 regarding the double polarity of the Dionysian and the Apollinian, and this despite the preponderance of Dionysos. First and foremost, for this is the romantic idea of an art directly dictated by nature, (which proves that his self-critique of 1886 is not to be taken literally):

> *Apollinian-Dionysian.*—There are two conditions in which art appears in man like a force of nature and disposes of him whether he will or no: as the compulsion to have visions (*Zwang zur Vision*), and as a compulsion to an orgiastic state (*Zwang zum Orgiasmus*). Both conditions are rehearsed in ordinary life, too, but weaker: in dream and intoxication.[30]

Elsewhere, the two conditions are described as two degrees of "intoxication," which is to say of receptivity, creativity and of extreme lucidity, but only with a "difference in tempo" (*Tempo-Verschiedenheit*).[31] We will return to this. Then the idea of Apollinism as the "will to measure, to simplicity, to submission to rule or concept"[32] is imposed on the Greeks who ought to have been *conquered* by them, to have been elevated to a loftier struggle, "in the struggle against their own Asiaticism," against "the terrible, multifarious, the uncertain, the frightful."[33] The Apollinian was constructed from "a Dionysian substratum" which was the spontaneous nature of the Greeks. Thus the later Nietzsche joins Hölderlin, for whom the characteristic of the Greeks was first and foremost panicked ecstasy, the Asiatic unity with nature, whereas "the sobriety of the Occident and Juno" would only come to them through a kind of expatriation.[34] This change of position—insofar as for the young Nietzsche, an Apollo unconscious of his own essence, preceded the arrival of Dionysos, who, we will see, is going to metamorphose him—does not change the relation of dependence and the derivation between the two principles. The later Nietzsche maintains that the legislating, regulatory, unifying, simplifying power that the Greeks call Apollo is only a figure of the Will to power, Dionysian in its essence because it is capable of provoking the largest horizon of the forces in dissension—chaos: "The Dionysian, an overflowing (*Überströmung*) and a unity of many things, in part terrifying excitations. . . ."[35]

The joy of the spectator-artist is evidently transindividual, *metaphysical*. On the most elementary level, it links the artistic self-affirmation of life: "joy (*Lust*) is more originary than suffering; the latter is itself only the consequence of the will to joy (—to create, to mold, to devote oneself to loss, to destroy) and, in the highest form, a kind of joy. . . ."[36] In the situation of the spectator, it results in a scenic event which comes to break the fragile equilibrium between the musical Dionysian of the chorus and the singular heroic figures. It is a fragile equilibrium between Dionysos and Apollo, because it is in no way a "reconciliation" in the Hegelian manner that some have prematurely interpreted,[37] but a halt of hostilities, a cease-fire, a point of suspension in a perpetual battle. In this battle, Dionysos will eventually come out on top: "*in order to end,* Apollo says the language of Dionysos."[38] What is "the language" of Dionysos? It is the original "music," the infinite rhythm of the oscillations of the will—of joy to suffering, and of suffering to joy. An audible language certainly, but unintelligible to logical and chronological thought. Speech which is always clear and serene, bereft of stammerings and ambiguity, nevertheless, the Apollinian hero, speaks the abyss of the relativity of any figure, that the ground is on the verge of being absorbed into itself. And at the culminating point of action, when the hero is on the verge of foundering, it is the manifestation of the pit, the yawning of forces which produces an extraordinary effusion of joy in the spectator, a joy which is inexplicable in Apollinian terms. All the appearances, the "images," the beautiful sculptural figures of the myth collapse under the unfurling of a "sacred," numinous (in Rudolph Otto's sense)[39] discharge of energy, an ambivalent mystical revelation, not of pure and simple joy, but of terror (the spectator "trembles with terror")[40] and tangled voluptuous ecstasy (he quickens an infinitely more intense and powerful enjoyment), a joy all the more intense in that it envelops and surpasses suffering. The *mysterium tremendum et fascensorum* is seen in the evidence of a blinding joy: in this vision that grows ever darker of the catastrophe of the spectator who "hopes no more than to be blind." (Ibid.) Such is the truly religious moment of tragedy, when the "clear night" of Dionysos eclipses the illusory ray of representation. Or further, in physiological terms, this is to say φύσις: "the drives of visualization and transfiguration" pushed to their highest degree of intensity, suddenly perceive their essential "object," the hero, until then unexceptional and closed, almost ludicrous, precarious, infinitely weak. Under the force of an immense, "e-normous" (*ungeheure*) Dionysian "musical" drive, the veil of the phenomenon expands, and the "listener who is truly an artist" participates in an active, affirmative destruction. He no longer identifies with the suffering of the hero, with the process of the act coming to its fatal end, but with the process of creation/destruction of the tragic artist himself; and through this, he again unites with the originary One to which this "moment" returns him. This single *metaphysically* tragic "moment," the *enchanted* moment of the "Dionysian" (Dionysian *Zauber*) where nothing remains except the One, Nietzsche calls the "fracture of the Apollinian at its extreme." We cite part of this description that must be quoted in its entirely:

> Here he [the spectator] beholds the transfigured world of the stage and
> nevertheless denies it. He sees the tragic hero before him in epic clear-

ness and beauty, and nevertheless *takes pleasure in his annihilation.* He comprehends the action deep down, and yet likes to flee into the *incomprehensible.* He feels the actions of the hero to be justified, and is nevertheless still more elated when these actions annihilate their agent. He shudders at the sufferings which will befall the hero, and yet anticipates in them a *higher, much more overpowering joy.* He sees more extensively and profoundly than ever, and yet wishes he were *blind.* How must we derive this curious internal *bifurcating,* this *blunting of the Apollinian point,* if not from the *Dionysian* magic that, though apparently exciting the Apollinian emotions to their highest pitch, still retains the power to force into its service *his excess of Apollinian force?* The *tragic myth* is to be understood only as a symbolization of Dionysian wisdom through Apollinian artifices. This myth leads the world of phenomena to its limits *where it denies itself* and seeks to flee back again into the womb of the true and only reality.[41]

The vast (*ungeheure*) Dionysian impulse then devours his entire world of phenomena, in order to let us sense beyond it, and through its destruction, the highest artistic primal joy, in the bosom of the primordially One.[42]

At the paroxysm of the Apollinian force, a howl of poignant joy submerges and drowns under the successive waves of pleasure (*jouissance*) the long sequence of images which have preceded this moment. Nietzsche cites here the death of Isolde in Wagner's opera:

In the rapture ocean's
billowing roll,
in the fragrance waves'
ringing sound,
in the world breath's
wafting whole—
to drown, to sink—
wafting whole—
to drown, to sink—
unconscious—highest joy.[43]

The Wagnerian heroine would no longer embody the serene joy of the ancient hero, but the joy of the listener-artist himself in a confusion of subject and object. The surpassing of the visual by the musical would only be fundamentally a self-overcoming which outlines in advance the ontological structure of the Will to Power: the epic order of dramatic development, the self-sufficiency of sculptural figures, their plastic deployment giving rise to pity by the effect of human, all too human compassion—all of these Apollinian passions are eclipsed and give way to a euphoria which is higher than the outdistanced joy-sorrow. This superior euphoria—a strange and unjustifiable happiness—is, finally, a complete stranger in its essence to the thematic unfolding of the action, indifferent to the lot of the protagonists and to the cruelty of their overwhelming destiny. This euphoria shockingly erases the horror of the fatal crisis, unraveling and setting loose the "spectacle" other than by the logical mortal denouement of the tragic situation. And the spectator perceives in a flash that the true theme of tragedy does not reside in the myth and that the curious happiness that he or she experiences plunges or impels him or her into a depth where a musical resolution has always reigned, a perhaps dissonant accord, without speech, outside of every signification reducible to the principle of reason. "Music has nothing to do with beauty."[44] "Sound emerges from the night."[45]

"It is in the annihilation (*Vernichtung*) of even the most beautiful appearance (*Schein*) that Dionysian happiness (*Dionysisches Glück*) attains its fullness."[46] Many times previously in this same fragment, Nietzsche proposed a difference between two "happinesses" or perfections or ultimate joys: on the one hand, the "happiness of existence" (*Glück am Dasein*), connected, he says, to the "happiness of appearance," and the "happiness of becoming" (*Glück am Werden*) which arises from "destruction" (*Zerstörung*) of the "beautiful semblance" (*schönen Anschein*) or from all actuality when it disintegrates as illusionary. Tragic joy is this happiness of becoming, put to the test in the collapse of "being," taken in the sense of the eidetic "form," eternally illusory. This provides the way for a new, superior, and decisive precision. That which is destroyed is "the most beautiful appearance" itself; the superlative indicates the overcoming of the beautiful. It is a beauty already sublime, which darkens before the eyes of the spectator under the irresistible unfurling of the Dionysian sublime. The tragic effect results from the entwined exchange leading to the mortal collision—mortal for the more fragile—of two sublimities, of which the second encompasses, supports, and elevates the first. For Nietzsche—as for Schopenhauer before him—("in its principal determination the sentiment of the beautiful is the same as the sentiment of the sublime[47]")—and for Schelling ("the sublime in its absoluteness contains [*begreift*] the beautiful, just as the beautiful in its absoluteness contains the sublime[48]"), and later for Rilke ("the beautiful is nothing but the first stage of the terrible[49]")—the beautiful is sublime insofar as it is the tamer and master of a shapeless or multiform diversity. But how can Apollo, the divinity of the "principle of individuation," god of limit, measure and determined beauty, elevate himself to the sublime, which in one way or another implies a movement toward the infinite, the unlimited and the excessive? How is this Apollinian sublime distinguished from the Kantian edifying moral sublime that Nietzsche held in horror?[50] What text supports the idea of a double antagonistic sublime, which would unite in a single moment to form the tragic work of art?

No better than John Sallis—and he was the first, the only person to my knowledge to do this—has shown this Nietzschean problematic of the sublime in the

Birth of Tragedy and has shown the line of continuity and of rupture with the celebrated Kantian problematic. Chapter Two of *Crossings: Nietzsche and the Space of Tragedy*, "Dionysus—Resounding Excess" (how does one translate this in French? Perhaps: "vibrante surabondance[51]") and Chapter Three, "Tragedy—Sublime Ecstasy," relegate to the ranks of obsolete propositions the theses that B. Pautrat once advanced in *Versions du Soleil*[52] on an assumed "melocentrism" that was hastily supported by the early G. Deleuze on the "Hegelianism" in Nietzsche's first work.[53] Thanks to a sustained attention to the text from beginning to end, relying upon the decisive work of J. P. Vernant and P. Vidal-Naquet, and above all upon an admirable knowledge of the Presocratics and Greek Tragedies (which he cites)—as well as on the penetrating Hölderlin "commentaries" (ignored, it seems, by our hexagonal interpreters)—Sallis gives a subtle and for first time *historical* reading of the *Birth of Tragedy*. Rather than concerning himself solely with the connection with Schopenhauer, or with Hegel and Plato, Sallis textually analyzes the connection with Kant in the passage of *Crossings* cited earlier. The sublime is a movement of *Erschütterung* which exceeds the capacity of that which thinks it while confronting nature or which contemplates it on the stage. It is this "excessive" intuition (Sallis's translation of the Kantian word *das Überschwengliche,* Third Critique, section 27) for the imagination of a grandeur or of a force, a "mathematic" or "dynamic" sublime which attracts and repulses at the same time, the "intuition of an abyss (*Abgrund*), so to speak, where the imagination fears to lose itself." This study appears immediately as a classic in the best sense of the word, in the Nietzschean sense, which is to say, in the sense of the "grand style," because without affection it imposes itself while scorning the need to please, "in a logical, simple, categorical, mathematical way,"[54] in an exemplary way, with a light touch, beyond all fashion and without jargon. It shows that the logic which governs the Nietzschean text is not that of the dialectic of the *Aufhebung,* according to which the Apollinian and Dionysian would be *sublimated* in the work of tragic art, reconnected in a higher unity, reduced to a synthesis, but rather "a logic of excess, of resounding excess, excess of shining" (C 57). The ex-cess on both sides is exorbitant, transgressive, passage to the limit, boundlessness towards the abysmal: the double ecstasy of "music" and appearance, the ecstasy of the hidden and the ecstasy of the open, the ecstasy of darkness and the dazzling ecstasy, the ecstasy of rhythm and the ecstasy of order.

This excess of ecstasy, which foils or would foil every attempt to conceive it, but which—contrary to the Hegelian Absolute—does not want its own Parousia, how does it merit being called "tragic"? Joyous in itself, it is not content to rejoice in its play, indefinitely constructing and destroying worlds, always young and regenerative, never weary or sad. And, indeed, Nietzsche firmly maintains that the "Gay Science" is a tragic science. *Incipit tragoedia.*[55] Tragedy (re)commences. The curtain rises on a new tragedy, which is no longer that of the Greeks nor that of Wagner, but that of Western nihilism.

One can interpret the recommencement of tragedy as the failure of *Zarathustra* to communicate his doctrine, departing alone with his animals, who remain a bit stupid, because this doctrine does not concern them, and who dies alone in accordance with an end which remains posthumous. But in the larger sense, tragedy would not designate the destiny of a man, of any hero of history, or even of the fictitious Zarathustra, who returns to announce the end of resentment, the end of the thought of time conceived as vengence against time. In the larger sense, tragedy is the being of Nature thought as chaos, and of our relation to it; but even more, tragedy is the funereal moment of the twilight of our world, which rushes toward the night and where History seems to hesitate in the face of a possible recommencement, warily groping along, suspended, because it is as blind as Oedipus, and shares the same excessive will to know.

But Rhythm and Chaos, is there not here yet another one of these contradictions that one is happy to raise in order to disqualify Nietzschean philosophy? If the being of Nature is Rhythm, then it is Order, even if this is complex and hidden. If it is Chaos, it is "of all eternity," if not disordered, then at least lacking finality, "not the lack of necessity but of a lack of order, arrangement, form, beauty, wisdom, and whatever other names there are for our aesthetic anthropomorphisms."[56] Now, in this text there is the idea that chaos, insofar as it is a gaping, abysmal opening, a primordial fault or fissure, is *necessary*. The necessity of the world does not permit reducing to categories our human faculty to judge. Therefore, in the end, it would be neither beautiful nor sublime, neither wise nor mad, neither formal nor informed. It escapes to our finality, to our perspectivism, however multiple that may be. The counter-concept of chaos springs, as Heidegger well saw, from a *negative theology*: The world insofar as it is divine escapes it. Its divinity slips away from "human, all too human" attributes that we are tempted to confer upon it. It becomes worldly, it plays the game-of-the-world, it opens itself. Rhythm is the indescribable, everywhere imitated and inimitable "schema" of its opening. As the intelligible character in Kant is the schema of the empirical character, Rhythm is—contrary to the apparent "laws of nature," a fiction which the sciences utilize—the secret and unformulable principle which commands them. Thus the concept of chaos is not contradictory with the notion of an immanent order of things. It is a preventive concept which functions as the guardrail, destined to ward off the risk of a romantic delirium, a *Schwärmerei,* a delirious exaltation of an intuition which would give the Absolute. Nietzsche is close to Kant on this point. Everything is "phenomena," which is to say, interpretation; the thing in itself is not representable. But it remains that it can be schematized, indirectly through symbols: inverse symbolism, because "all that is imperishable is only symbol." "To see chaos," this initial necessity of artistic creation, does not mean to have an intuition of it, but to strongly experience the impulse to project new schemas in order to unify the diversity of forces. The existence of rhythm, to which joy attests, and its originary productivity cannot mean, as Heidegger thought, that there would be latent pre-existing forms in chaos. There is—and this is "every-thing"—the formative power of φύσις, *die gestaltende Kraft,* not pregiven *Gestalten* but *Gestaltung,* the ordering, shaping force which intoxicates us with joy when we approach it at close range.

Our relation with this power that supports us is, however, tragic. Caught by it, carried away by it, as though perched on the back of a tiger or a dragon, we must renounce knowledge other than through art, which is to say through analogue and impenetrable symbols, or better, by a rare and instantaneous fusion which deprives us of the instrument and representations of knowledge. "Tragic knowledge" as it is defined in Chapter 15 of the *Birth of Tragedy* remains the first and last word on the value of science. Science is spurred on by a "sublime illusion" (hyper-Apollinian), a "delirious hallucination" which comes into the world with Socrates, the belief that scientific thought is able, thanks to the principle of causality, to un-cover every mystery, to pierce the secret of nature, "to penetrate to the foundation of things."[57] But *tragic* knowledge knows that the more science advances as an endless spiral, the more the enigma grows, the more shadows and the unknowable spread.

The tragic joy of modern man, long after the death of tragedy, belongs to a classicism, equally distant from both extremes, the explicative delirium of science and the intuitive delirium of the romantic worshipers of nature. Today this alter-native provides a place for the opposition between, on the one hand, the crazy road to instrumentalization, the endless spiral of technology, and, on the other, the eco-logical dream, which even if it is realistic, cannot restrain the irresistible devasta-tion of the earth. To know without the least bit of melancholy that only artistic symbolization can allow for life, "that we have only art in order to avoid dying from (scientific) truth," this is tragic.

Tragic is the sorrow of the Greek scientific illusion. Everything has not yet been proven. Tragic is the everlasting loss of the Dionysian festivals of reunifica-tion with the One; tragic is the forgetting of the primitive Dionysian state of the transfiguration of the world. Today's artist can only touch the recesses and rarely illuminate them. Tragic is the loss of "the long, tremendous light and color scale"[58] which among the Greeks made the summits of divine joy and the gaiety of the more humble forms of nature come together through human happiness. Tragic is the irreparable loss of secret religions. Dionysos will no longer be reborn as an epochal god. Some can still have a "god of the heart," which is to say: a god ac-cording to their heart. But tragic is waiting for a god to appear, in the middle of the desert which grows in the relentless darkening of the world and in the scarcity of celestial premonitions. Tragic is the twilight of the idols.

And yet joy remains because it is not epochal, but in all times it is the angel of those who work in silence, the initiating grace of steadfastly sustaining the view of the gaping opening. Joy remains as a calm force, close to anguish, the gift of loving, not the completed work, but the work in progress, without being able to recognize the Model in it. Joy, in its unquiet calm, remains out of reach of the "sound and fury" of the age, because it is already—without believing it—halfway to the impending clearing; it is a "power which no longer has need of proofs, which does not care about being pleasant, which does not have an easy response . . . which rests *in itself*"[58] in a smiling fatalism, joy which continues to operate soberly, addressing its continual *da capo* of existence, forgetting in its extreme happiness that it is so cruelly bereft of any proof of the future.

CHAPTER FOURTEEN

DECONSTRUCTIVE REINSCRIPTION OF FUNDAMENTAL ONTOLOGY

THE TASK OF THINKING AFTER HEIDEGGER

Parvis Emad

> What is needed is specifically to let
> ourselves into (*Sicheinlassen*) the mode
> of being that we always already are. . . .
> What distinguishes this method is just
> this *specifically letting-ourselves-into*
> *our relationship to what encounters us.* . . .
> The act of will required in order not to
> close ourselves off from this letting-
> ourselves-into—this act belongs in a
> certain sense to phenomenology. Thus
> we must get on the path that leads us to
> ourselves. But this path is no longer
> the one that leads to an isolated ego,
> which appears at first to be the only
> one given.
>
> —Martin Heidegger,
> *Zollikoner Seminare*

Considering that sixty-five years have passed since *Being and Time* first appeared and that Heidegger's *Gesamtausgabe* has been available for more than a

201

decade and a half, it might appear that the work of thinking which is Heidegger's legacy belongs now to the domain in which historical figures are preserved. Given our present access to Heidegger's work, we might regard him as a classical figure who terminates one period and heralds the beginning of another. In this vein we might look for what comes after Heidegger and goes beyond him. The expression "after Heidegger" then might indicate termination of one period in philosophy and the beginning of another.

However, it is also possible to hear something altogether different in the expression "after Heidegger." These words may be heard as an invitation to thinking that "now, after Heidegger," it let itself into (*Sicheinlassen*) a relation to being (*Bezug zum Sein*). Heard in this way, the expression "after Heidegger" does not indicate termination of an historical period in philosophy; rather, "after Heidegger" articulates a task that faces thinking today and consists in thinking's getting into a relation to being. Since all of Heidegger's texts bespeak this relation to being and since the expression "after Heidegger" must be understood in terms of this relation, I want to say a few words about thinking's relation to being as articulated in Heidegger's texts.

First I want to say that in Heidegger's texts the relation to being is not proffered to thinking as something thought through to completion (*Fertig-gedachtes*). Heidegger's texts are not a blueprint for setting up an edifice according to thinking's relation to being, nor do these texts contain instructions for grasping that relation wholesale. For these texts articulate a relation to being that is proffered to thinking and that thinking always already has, but is not always willing to admit and to let itself into, i.e., to become engaged in. This means that it is incumbent upon thinking, after Heidegger, to take this relation seriously—by opening up this relation, disclosing it, and so keeping it open. This is, secondly, to suggest that in the context of the relation to being, the willingness of thinking to let itself into and become engaged in the relation to being is of such importance that, as Heidegger points out in the *Zollikoner Seminare*, this act is inseparable from phenomenology. And herein lies the mark that distinguishes Heidegger's endeavors from other efforts in philosophy. He is concerned with the correlation between the relation that being proffers to thinking *and* thinking's *deliberate* and *decided* preparedness for letting itself into and becoming engaged in that relation. In view of this correlation we can say that for Heidegger thinking is never a process that is complete, static, and already at its destination, but rather one which is underway, awaits engagement, needs to be enacted—is, in short, *vollzugshaft*. Thinking is unceasingly exposed to the relation proffered by being. But only to the extent that thinking responds to this exposure by deliberately consenting to let itself be engaged in that relation—only to that extent is thinking *vollzugshaft*. It is the willingness of thinking to respond through engagement to that exposure that is the prerequisite for grasping what goes on in Heidegger's texts.

Thirdly, I would like to point out that, as far as the incomplete character of thinking is concerned—to which the relation to being is proffered—this incomplete character of thinking is nowhere in Heidegger's texts the topic of a specific discussion. In order to understand that in Heidegger's texts the relation to being is not proffered to thinking as something thought through to completion, we must *at the very least* consider the following themes in the following texts: (1) the theme of the "analysis of Dasein" versus the "analytic of Dasein" in *Being and Time*, (2) the reference to thinking as acting/*handeln* and to the "active/doing character of thinking"[1] in the *Letter on Humanism*, (3) the theme of "thrown projection" in *The Origin of the Work of Art* and in *Beiträge zur Philosophie (Vom Ereignis)*, and (4) the theme of "pathways of thinking" and "mere works" (*Wege nicht Werke*), which serves as the motto for Heidegger's *Gesamtausgabe*. If we consider *all* these themes and extract from them a number of significant distinctions, then we realize that the characterization of Heidegger's thinking as a thinking that awaits enactment/engagement—is *vollzugshaft*—is a characterization that originates from within Heidegger's thinking and is not brought to bear upon it from the outside. Consequently, we realize that "after Heidegger" pertains to the engagement with/in the relation to being—an engagement which still needs to take place—and does not merely indicate termination of an historical period in philosophy. The term *after* preserves a call for thinking to get engaged in the relation to being, by enacting that relation as it is proffered to thinking.

I

John Sallis is one of the first to take up the issue of thinking after Heidegger. In his recent study *Echoes: After Heidegger* he engages in the question of what it means to think "after Heidegger." This takes him into many turns and twists throughout Heidegger's works. At the end he arrives at the conclusion that thinking "after Heidegger" amounts to hearing echoes that come from Heidegger's texts. ("Is there really anything wrong with speaking of the echoes of a text?" he asks [E 12].) These texts are so peculiar as to repel criteria of coherence and consistency. According to Sallis, from the beginning in fundamental ontology Heidegger's texts manifest unavoidable internal instabilities that are not lost to Heidegger himself. As he becomes increasingly aware of those internal instabilities, Heidegger regularly and steadily abandons the provisional achievements of his thinking, in search of a more stable form of utterance for his views on metaphysics. But he fails to find such a form. For Sallis, then, "after Heidegger" means hearing the echoes that still come from the "ruins" otherwise known as Heidegger's "texts."

I put the word *texts* in quotation marks, because I want to draw attention to Sallis's central concern. He states with remarkable clarity what guides his thinking throughout the book *Echoes: After Heidegger* and is a key for understanding it. At the beginning of this work Sallis writes:

> My concern will be then to reinscribe several of Heidegger's texts so as to draw them toward the limit, to mobilize the figure of echo in order to free those texts to say what they can say, now, after Heidegger. (E 13)

By carefully attending to this programmatical announcement, and simultaneously bearing in mind what I said about engagement of thinking in the relation that being proffers to thinking, I find that this passage from *Echoes* contains in nucleus form Sallis's response to the issue of engagement and reveals his understanding of the task of thinking after Heidegger.

I propose to move through this passage slowly and carefully, isolating and identifying what it says about Heidegger's texts. Accordingly, I shall begin with the following question: Would there be a need on Sallis's part to *reinscribe* Heidegger's texts, if these texts would "*say* what they can say, now, after Heidegger"? This programmatical announcement in *Echoes* already anticipates the response, which can be formulated as follows: As far as the thinking in *Echoes* is concerned, Heidegger's texts as they lie before that thinking *do not* "say what they can say, now, after Heidegger." Were these texts capable of saying what they can say, obviously there would be no need for the thinking of *Echoes* to *reinscribe* them. This means that, in order to understand the texts of Heideggerian phenomenology, the thinking in *Echoes* must seek recourse in the philosophy of deconstruction for assistance and guidance. In other words, the language and thinking of *Echoes* adopts and employs the deconstructive reinscription, in order to make Heidegger's "mute" texts articulate and comprehensible.

But is it actually the case that Heidegger's texts are so "mute" and incomprehensible as to need the "liberating intervention" of the philosophy of deconstruction? What if Heidegger's texts are not "mute" and incomprehensible? What if reinscription of these texts, far from "freeing them to say what they can say," creates misunderstandings and confusions? To pursue this "What if?" I shall attend to the portions of Heidegger's texts that Sallis exposes to the full force of his reinscription. As might be expected, Sallis begins with *Being and Time*; and he begins by targeting for reinscription mainly those segments of this work that deal with the formal structure of the question of being.

What is the "formal structure of the question of being" all about? It is well known that the analysis of this structure distinguishes three moments that Heidegger calls *das Gefragte*, *das Befragte*, and *das Erfragte*—each of which is derived from the verb *fragen* (questioning). With the word *Gefragte* Heidegger points at what in the question of being directly and specifically asks about being (*Sein*). With the second word *Befragte* Heidegger draws attention to a being (Dasein) who is the locus for eliciting, evoking from being (*Sein*) an appropriate response. And the third word, *Erfragte*, designates what is to be found out by questioning being, namely its "meaning" (*Sinn*).

However, of equal importance to the analysis of questioning and these distinctions is what Heidegger says in the last paragraph of section 2 of *Being and Time*, which concludes the entire analysis of the threefold structure of the question of being. Gathering the outcome of the analysis of the three moments of *Gefragte*, *Befragte*, and *Erfragte*, he adds:

> There belongs to the innermost meaning of the question of being the essential concern of questioning with what it asks.
>
> *Die wesenhafte Betroffenheit des Fragens von seinem Gefragten gehört zum eigensten Sinn der Seinsfrage.*[2]

Since what is asked (*Gefragte*) in this question is being (*Sein*), this concluding remark means that the question of being cannot be asked without an essential concern with and "being taken" by being. This means, not only that a discussion of the formal structure of the question of being must attend to the three-fold structure of this question, but that this discussion must also be generated, affected, and directly concerned with—literally, "taken" (*betroffen*)—by what this question asks, namely being. As far as I can see, this *Betroffenheit vom Sein*,[3] the manner in which being itself "affects" the question of being, has at least two implications.

First, this *Betroffenheit vom Sein* gives a special status to being/*Sein*, although being as *das Gefragte* is co-original with the other two structural moments, called *Befragte* (Dasein) and *Erfragte* (the meaning of being). In view of this special status we must say that, when asked according to this *Betroffenheit*, the question of being is essentially affected by and concerned with being—which concern extends to the other two co-original structural moments—and that the special status accorded to *Gefragte* (being) in the question of being is a status that is also extended to Dasein (*das Befragte*). Dasein *is* Dasein because of its being concerned with, affected by, or "taken" by being. The first implication of *Betroffenheit vom Sein* concerns Dasein. It is Dasein's radical, total, complete involvement and engagement with being that this *Betroffenheit* conveys. Dasein in Heidegger is not the name for a rational person and a conscious subject, who in addition to playing tennis and attending lectures has the occasional propensity to relate to being and to be concerned with it. In Heidegger, Dasein expresses first and foremost this *Betroffenheit vom Sein*, this being concerned with and affected or taken by being. Thus asking the question of being is what Dasein does and *not* what the rational person or conscious subject does. Does this mean that a rational person or conscious subject cannot ask the question of being? No; a rational person and a conscious subject, too, can ask the question of being. But because the rational persons and conscious subjects are not concerned with and taken by being, the thinking of

these subjects operates from a distance that separates them from the "living" relation to the question of being. Such thinking may use the word *Dasein*, but what is
actually meant is not Dasein but the rational person and conscious subject. The rational person and conscious subject is not exposed to what Heidegger calls *Betroffenheit vom Sein*; thus the so-called subject must be differentiated from Dasein.

What we learn from this *Betroffenheit von Sein* that Heidegger mentions at
the conclusion of the analysis of the question of being is that this *Betroffenheit* extends to the entirety of fundamental ontology, which is not concerned with the rational, conscious person qua "subject," but with Dasein as concerned with being.
This means that the question of being does not occur on the "subjective" plane that
is peculiar to the rational subject. For, whatever *Being and Time* and we, in its
wake, do with the question of being—given the priority of *Betroffenheit vom
Sein*—it is elicited and evoked from being itself.

The second implication concerns thinking. It means that to elicit and to evoke
a response from being, thinking must let itself into and become engaged with the
relation that being proffers to thinking-questioning. It is through this relation that
being affects the question of being. The term *Betroffenheit* at the conclusion of
section 2 of *Being and Time* is intended to show that the question of being comes
from being itself—and is not a question that a "rational conscious subject" may or
may not ask. If we overlook the significance of *Betroffenheit vom Sein*—of being
"taken" by being—and if we continue on talking only about the three moments of
the question of being, we think about a "subject," even if we use the word *Dasein*.
For it is in the "subject's" discretion to attend to the question of being, to attend to
the structure of this question or not to attend to it, to get engaged with being or not
to get engaged with it. What is fundamental in Heidegger is that *Dasein does not
have such a discretion*. To be Dasein means to be "taken" by being (*betroffen vom
Sein*) and to think according to this *Betroffenheit*.

But Heidegger's thinking does not allow us to take Dasein as a "subject" who
may or may not instigate the question of being. By explicitly pointing out that what
is at stake in the question of being is the *Betroffenheit* or questioning's concern
with being, he eliminates with one stroke the possibility of taking the subject as
the initiator in the raising of the question of being. The question of being will be
raised, not because this question is at the discretion of a subject, but because being proffers a relation to thinking which changes the nature of what *was* the subject, thus bringing forth Dasein and eliciting and evoking an appropriate response
from Dasein/thinking. This is no longer a "subjective" thinking.

Now let us turn to the reinscription of the formal structure of the question of
being as it takes place in *Echoes: After Heidegger*. This reinscription thoroughly
obfuscates the *Betroffenheit vom Sein* and consequently the relation that being
proffers to thinking—a relation that gives rise to Dasein and sustains the question
of being. In order to see the full extent of this obfuscation, we must consider what
Sallis approvingly takes over from Derrida. Speaking of the formal structure of the

question of being, Sallis says that "the structure is such that the questioner is to take up the question by interrogating a being (Dasein) with which it coincides" (E 19). What does this mean? Simply put, this means that "the questioner" is an "outsider," is not Dasein itself. How else could a coming together, as coincidence of the two, be necessary? The coincidence of "questioner" and Dasein means for *Echoes* that the formal structure of the question of being is completely and thoroughly cut off from *Betroffenheit vom Sein*, from being's affecting the question of being, from being's concern with and being "taken" by the question of being and its structural moments. Taking the formal structural moments of the question of being in such a way as to deliberately exclude the questioner from the impact of *Betroffenheit vom Sein*—an impact which puts forth Dasein and reiterates the "questioner" as Dasein, i.e., as the one who no longer stands outside this question—does this exclusion not amount to offering this whole matter of the "formal structure of the question of being" to a "subject" for its consideration? Does this exclusion not amount to excluding Dasein, even if one goes on using this word? When we take the formal structure of the question of being without the *Betroffenheit vom Sein*, are we not taking questioning itself as a structure unaffected by being and thus accessible (or inaccessible) to examination? Do we not thereby betray our distance from this question and its structure? Only when such a distance becomes operative can we view the structure "objectively" and say: "He who takes up the question of being and interrogates a being (Dasein), he, as such a questioner, must first coincide with Dasein."

Phenomenologically—that is, according to what shows itself by itself from out of itself—there is nothing in the structure of the question of being with which the "questioner" coincides, because the questioner is *das Befragte*, is Dasein.[4] The characterization of the formal structure of the question of being as a structure in which "the questioner is to take up the question by interrogating a being (Dasein) with which it coincides" (E 19) is a characterization that deadens the "living" moment of a phenomenological description. This deadening is achieved by excluding the *Betroffenheit vom Sein*. But this *Betroffenheit* or being taken by being, which happens to Dasein, is the event which once and for all eliminates the possibility of any separation of Dasein from being. If Dasein *is distinct but not separate* from being, then no separation—such as the one that Sallis assumes to exist between "questioner" and Dasein—operates in Dasein's being. This means that it is never the case that the questioner is at first separated from Dasein, only later to coincide with it. In the context of *Betroffenheit vom Sein* the questioner *is* always already Dasein and need not coincide, i.e., come together with it. The very concept of "coincidence" is a separative concept and introduces nothing but a comprehensive and thoroughgoing separative force into the work that *Echoes* does with fundamental ontology.

The comprehensive and thoroughgoing separative force that runs through Sallis's entire study finds its first decisive expression in the way in which Sallis characterizes more closely "the coincidence of questioner with questioned." He specifies this "coincidence" as

> what guarantees the possibility of the analysis of Dasein that opens onto the question of Being, the possibility of carrying that analysis through in a rigorous manner, phenomenologically. (E 19)

The fact that the term "phenomenologically" appears in this characterization must not mislead us into believing that what "guarantees the possibility of the analysis of Dasein that opens onto the question of being" is obtained phenomenologically. As in the case of "Dasein" and "subject"—where the mere use of the word *Dasein* is no guarantee that Dasein is not actually a substitute for "subject"—so also here the mere use of the word *phenomenology* is no guarantee that the thinking presented here is actually phenomenological. In order to respect what words like *Dasein* and *phenomenological* mean—as distinguished from their mere usage—I will begin by asking what sort of an analysis this is, if the first condition of its possibility is "the coincidence of questioner with Dasein"? The answer is at hand: The analysis that is guaranteed by this "coincidence" is an analysis that is *not* carried out by Dasein as a being who is *betroffen vom Sein*, taken or affected by and concerned with being. If the analysis of Dasein were to be carried out by Dasein, *as affected and taken by and concerned with being*, this analysis would not need this coincidence, which is a coincidence of Dasein (the questioner) with Dasein. To make the coincidence of "questioner" with Dasein—coincidence of Dasein with Dasein—the guarantee for the possibility of the analysis of Dasein is a misreading of *Being and Time*. This means that the analysis of Dasein that *Echoes* undertakes, and which presupposes the "coincidence of questioner with Dasein," is an analysis that presupposes and is carried out by a "subject." This is to say that in Sallis's *Echoes: After Heidegger* the distinction between "subject" and "Dasein" is not maintained.

But Sallis not only says that that "coincidence" guarantees the possibility of the analysis of Dasein; he also says that the analysis of Dasein, so guaranteed, "opens onto the question of being." This means that Sallis is concerned here with a sequence: First, the analysis of Dasein must be prepared in that "questioner coincides with Dasein"; *then, after* this "coincidence" happens, the "analysis opens onto the question of being." Of utmost importance for me is the connective that Sallis uses when he mentions that the analysis of Dasein "opens onto the question of being." I consider the phrase "opens onto" to be important and to reveal what deconstructive reinscription does to Heidegger's text, because this phrase suggests that "what guarantees the possibility of the analysis of Dasein" precedes "the opening of this analysis into the question of being." And this means that before this connection is established, the analysis of Dasein, taken by itself, *is not yet open onto the question of being*. Is Sallis here repeating, albeit in a new language, the old and refuted misunderstanding of the preparatory fundamental analysis of Dasein according to which in the phase of his "Dasein-oriented" thinking Heidegger first presents an analysis of human existence and then in the phase of his "being-oriented" thinking he proceeds to lay out his philosophy of being/*Sein*?[5] If the "questioner's coincidence with Dasein" is "what guarantees the possibility of the analysis of Dasein" and if this analysis is that which "opens onto the question of being," then Sallis would seem to subscribe here to the "Heidegger I and Heidegger II" view. If so, does he perhaps misunderstand the analysis of Dasein from the ground up?

But the analysis of Dasein does not need the guarantee of a "coincidence of the questioner with Dasein." If one needs a guarantee, one need not look any further than what Heidegger calls *Betroffenheit vom Sein*, which I already discussed as the manner in which questioning is concerned with, affected by, and "taken" by being. But Heidegger's concluding remarks on this *Betroffenheit* are not the only statement he makes about being's direct involvement in the structure and raising of the question of being. Raising the question of being is a comportment/*verhalten*, and the preliminary structural analysis of this question lays out the directives that the analysis of Dasein has to take. Heidegger tells us in section 2 of *Being and Time* that both that comportment and this preliminary structural analysis occur under the direct experience of being. He refers to this experience with two key phenomenological phrases: *Hinsehen auf Sein* and *Hinblicknahme auf das Sein*. If the experience to which these key phrases refer is properly understood and enacted, then we shall see that the analysis of Dasein is carried out in such a way as not to need "opening onto the question of being," since this analysis always already occurs within that question.

I call the phrases *Hinsehen auf Sein* and *Hinblicknahme auf das Sein* key phenomenological phrases, because both make use of words like *sehen*/seeing and *blicken*/looking-at, which are deeply rooted in the phenomenological tradition and indicate a comportment/*verhalten*. *Hinsehen auf Sein* does not mean looking at being in the way in which one looks at a stop sign. *Hinsehen auf Sein* means taking into consideration the relation that being (not *a* being) proffers to thinking. Likewise *Hinblicknahme auf das Sein* does not mean taking being into consideration as one takes into consideration a business letter in view of which one undertakes some action. *Hinblicknahme auf das Sein* means making the effort of directing our thinking to the relation that being (not *a* being) proffers to thinking. Both key terms express the ongoing and perduring character of the ontological difference.

Heidegger links the raising of the question of being to a number of comportments, all of which occur under the experience of being. The key phrase *Hinsehen auf Sein* (directly regarding being) is the first phrase that refers to this experience. It is this experience that guides all those comportments/*Verhaltungen* which are involved in the questioning and aim at:

rendering lucid and clear a being—the questioner—in its being.

Durchsichtigmachen eines Seienden—des fragenden—in seinem Sein.[6]

This means that the experience of being named in the comportment *Hinsehen auf Sein* is what guides the process of rendering a being lucid and clear, i.e., the analysis of Dasein. Since this analysis is guided by the comportment toward and experience of being, this analysis occurs in the domain of being: It need not "open onto the question of being," as Sallis suggests.

With the second key phrase, *Hinblcknahme auf das Sein*, Heidegger brings more light into the first key phrase, in that he tells us more specifically what is involved in the enactment of the comportment of *Hinsehn auf Sein*. He says that this enactment

> has the character of an antecedent look taken at being in such a way that this look provisionally articulates the being, already given, in its being.
>
> *hat den Charakter der vorgängigen Hinblicknahme auf das Sein, so zwar, daß aus dem Hinblick darauf das vorgegebene Seiende in seinem Sein vorläufig artikuliert wird.*[7]

Now the being already given in its being is Dasein as *Befragte*. Seen in light of this characterization of *Hinsehen auf Sein*, we can say that Dasein and its analysis are articulated in the light of an antecedent "look" taken at *Sein*/being. The thrust of the second key phrase is to name a comportment toward being named in the experience of a *vorgängige Hinblicknahme auf das Sein*, "antecedent look taken at being." It is this experience which articulates a being (Dasein) in its being, thus making possible the analysis of Dasein. Accordingly, this analysis follows the comportment named in the experience of being, *vorgängige Hinblicknahme auf das Sein*. This means that the analysis of Dasein does not "open onto the question of being," as Sallis suggests, because this analysis always already follows the comportment toward and experience of being. Thus Sallis's statement, according to which the analysis of Dasein "opens onto the question of being" *after* having gained ground in the coincidence of questioner with Dasein, does not take into account what happens phenomenologically.

Considering the experience of being which is to guide the analysis of Dasein, I do not wish to underestimate the difficulty of the task of this analysis. Already in 1974 F.-W. von Herrmann pointed out how difficult the task is, when he said that the analysis of Dasein is an analysis in which the

> constitution of human beings [in *Being and Time*] . . . is viewed in its ontological, essential interrelatedness to being. . . . To clearly take being into consideration throughout an interpretive passage through *Being and Time* is one of the most difficult but indispensible tasks of interpretation.[8]

This is to suggest that, when we go through *Being and Time*, consideration given to the aforementioned comportments toward being named in the experience of being is difficult and indispensable, but not impossible. The possibility foreshadows the effort of our thinking to think through the relation that being proffers to thinking.

As far as I can see, the thinking of *Echoes: After Heidegger* does not take into account the aforementioned comportments toward being when it enters into the analysis of Dasein; and by *not* taking these into account, it creates a formidable obstacle for enacting this analysis by not seeing that the comportments toward being named in experiences such as *Betroffenheit vom Sein, Hinsehen auf Sein*, and *vorgängige Hinblicknahme auf des Sein* belong to Heidegger's discourse. The moment that one asserts that the questioner must coincide with Dasein, in that very moment one excludes the aforementioned comportments toward being from Heidegger's discourse. The separative force in *Echoes* that obfuscates Dasein and puts forth the "subject" determines the entirety of Sallis's treatment of fundamental ontology.

What does this approach indicate? My response is that the discourse of fundamental ontology in *Echoes* is totally determined by a misguided and exclusionary approach to Heidegger's texts. This approach is misguided because the separative force which obfuscates Dasein in *Echoes* compels the discussion to aim at the "subject." This approach is exclusionary in that it leaves out—cuts off from Heidegger's discourse—the rootedness of Dasein and *its* analysis in the experience of being named in *Betroffenheit vom Sein, Hinsehen auf Sein*, and *vorgängige Hinblicknahme auf das Sein*. (I repeat these terms advisedly to avoid the unspecificity that the phrase "experience of being" conveys.)

I must forego examining at close range other deconstructive reinscriptions that obfuscate the stages of Heidegger's explicit articulation of the analysis of Dasein, including the discovery of ecstatic temporality, the meaning of the being of Dasein, and finally the meaning of being. To identify obfuscations that Sallis's deconstructive reinscription lays over these themes requires at the very least an analysis similar to the one that I carried out in regard to section 2 of *Being and Time*, but this time drawing upon large portions of *Zur Bestimmung der Philosophie* (written in 1919, GA 56/57), *Phänomenologische Interpretationen zu Aristoteles: Einführung in die phänomenologische Forschung* (written in 1921/22, GA 61), the 1924 lecture text "The Concept of Time," *History of the Concept of Time* (written in 1925), *Logik: Die Frage nach der Wahrheit* (written in 1925/26, GA 21), *Being and Time* (published in 1927), *The Basic Problems of Phenomenology* (written in 1927), *The Metaphysical Foundations of Logic* (written in 1928), and *Phänomenologische Interpretation von Kants Kritik der reinen Vernunft* written in 1927/28, GA 25). This list must include *Kant und das Problem der Metaphysik* of 1929 and *Die Grundbegriffe der Metaphysik: Welt—Endlichkeit—Einsamkeit* of 1929/30, among others. This is simply impossible to do here. Instead I shall limit my discussion to what constitutes Sallis's deconstructive and reinscriptive springboard into fundamental ontology, namely the 1924 lecture text "The Concept of Time," which Gadamer calls the *"Urform von Sein und Zeit."*[9]

Sallis's springboard into the fundamental ontology of *Being and Time* is the 1924 lecture text "The Concept of Time," which according to its editor has been inappropriately called the *originäre Form* of *Being and Time*. (When Gadamer refers to this text as *Urform von Sein und Zeit*, he presumably means the *originäre Form*.) This labeling of the 1924 lecture text seems inappropriate because a treatise called *Der Begriff der Zeit* (*The Concept of Time*), also written in 1924, appears to have been the basis from which Heidegger put together (in July 1924) the lecture text "The Concept of Time." The treatise *Der Begriff der Zeit*, which is scheduled to appear as volume 64 of the *Gesamtausgabe*, will shed light on the context from which the *lecture text* "The Concept of Time" is taken. Because the question of being is bracketed out of the 1924 *lecture text*, its editor Hartmut Tietjen points out that "the discussion generated by this lecture under the rubric of the original form of *Being and Time* remains without appropriate basis and ground in the lecture text."[10] Tietjen says this because he has access to the text of *Der Begriff der Zeit* (GA 64). Sallis is also aware of this text and of the need for a certain reservation in this regard.[11] What Tietjen means to convey is that, considering the magnitude of the work accomplished in *Being and Time*, it is a simplification to consider the lecture text "The Concept of Time" as the original form of *Being and Time*. But, granting this simplification and the need for reservation and caution, Sallis still works on a deconstructive reinscription of fundamental ontology by first taking up the lecture text "The Concept of Time." One wonders why this text provides Sallis with the needed springboard, rather than the text of volume 61 of the *Gesamtausgabe*, which was written two years earlier. Could it be that the language and terminology of GA 61—close to and sometimes repetitive of the terminology of *Lebensphilosophie*—would confront Sallis with a real philosophical distance that only a non-deconstructive thinking could handle? However we respond to this question, the fact remains that Sallis jumps into the fundamental ontology by using the lecture text "The Concept of Time."

Sallis at first characterizes the lecture text in a general sort of way, which is nevertheless quite telling:

> The 1924 lecture marks, then, the beginning of the Marburg period. Perhaps also something more. Perhaps the text in which Heidegger will have begun to write not only *Being and Time*, but also the texts of those courses that immediately follow, in which the slippage of the project will, even if almost imperceptibly, have begun to operate. (E 47)

Sallis could not have been more clear as to why he begins with this lecture text, rather than with another text that precedes *Being and Time*. He begins with "The Concept of Time" because, in his opinion, this lecture marks the beginning of the Marburg period. This is not correct. *Der Begriff der Zeit* (GA 64) marks the beginning of this period, and Sallis has access to this fact. Still he says: This lecture text marks the beginning of the writing of *Being and Time* as well as those courses that were written right after *Being and Time*. This cannot be shown as long as one has not studied the text *Der Begriff der Zeit* (GA 64). Then why does Sallis begin with the lecture text "The Concept of Time"? The real reason appears to be that in this text Sallis believes to have identified in Heidegger's text the first significant destabilizing element, which, in spite of Heidegger, extends its destabilizing "effect" into all the texts that follow "The Concept of Time," including *Being and Time* and the courses immediately following this work. This element is what "The Concept of Time" calls "future."

Sallis does not deal with this destabilizing element head-on, but at first only alludes to it with a word that he borrows from the work-world of building and construction. He refers to the destabilizing element in Heidegger's text with the word *slippage*. Given the frequency with which he uses this word in the pages of *Echoes: After Heidegger*, and considering that at the very end of what he has to say about Heidegger's texts he alludes to the "demolition of the edifice of fundamental ontology" (E 117), he leaves no doubt in the reader's mind as to how he perceives "Heidegger to be at work" and he (Sallis) himself "doing work after him (Heidegger)." For him Heidegger works across an impassable space. This is the "space" between what Heidegger wants to say and what he actually says. This space is what is called Heidegger's text. The destabilizing element works in that space insofar as this element disrupts the *construction* that is going on in/as Heidegger's texts. Independently of Heidegger, and unbeknownst to him, this element comes forward as unstable, as one of the "slippery" elements.[12] This means: Heidegger's constructions (what he wanted to say) cannot be said (the edifice is unstable). The "activity" that brings enlightenment to this tension—the tension between what Heidegger wants to say (what he wanted to construct) and what he actually says (his texts)—is called déconstruction. It is not the relation that being proffers to thinking that counts. What counts is deconstructing what has been constructed. After all, without a foregoing *construction* a *deconstruction* would not make sense.

At this point I would like to remind the reader that phenomenology has nothing to do with building edifices whose constructive elements may themselves become "slippery" and disrupt the progress of the edifice and doom it to demolition. Furthermore, I would like to remind the reader that the French term "déconstruction" misses the main thrust of Heidegger's *Destruktion*. The German *Destruktion* is more akin to what the French translation of *Being and Time* calls *désobstruction*,[13] i.e., removal of obstructions, obstacles, and blockages. *Désobstruction* as such works at the service of phenomenology and not against it. Having brought forth these reminders, I want to: (1) identify the destabilizing element that Sallis's deconstructive reinscription finds in the text "The Concept of Time" and (2) lay out the full scale of obfuscation that Sallis lays over this text.

How the thinking of *Echoes: After Heidegger* deals with the lecture text "The Concept of Time" is also misguided and exclusionary because this approach is determined and guided by the same separative force that dominates the whole of *Echoes: After Heidegger*. When Sallis sets out to deconstructively reinscribe "The Concept of Time," the separative force makes its initial impact felt in that, without a moment's hesitation, he identifies what Heidegger says about the futural-being (*Zukünftigsein*) of the end/death of Dasein with the concept of future. With the self-assuredness and confidence of one who stands above the text, controls and surveys every move, and observes every tension in it, Sallis characterizes in clear terms the future as presented in the lecture text. Of this future he says: "It *is a future that will never be present*, that will never have been present" [Salis's italics] (E 51). Adding a colon to this sentence, he brings in a quotation from "The Concept of Time," which he uses to support the above-mentioned reinscription of the "future." What follows after the colon reads: "As the authentic future, *das Vorbei* can never become present" (E 51).

The separative force in Sallis is directed at "future" and "*das Vorbei*/goneness/overness/end/death of Dasein." To see the full impact of this force, we must carefully distinguish between "future" and "*das Vorbei*/end or death of Dasein" as expounded in "The Concept of Time." To be sure, the lecture text identifies *das Vorbei* with "the authentic future which can never be present." But the lecture text also speaks of a future which generates present and so *is* present. To see this we must consider a lengthy passage from "The Concept of Time":

> Even in the presence of its concern, Dasein is also the whole of time in such a way that it [Dasein] cannot get rid of the future. Now, the future is not the authentic being-futural of goneness/overness, but that to which care holds itself. This future builds the present out of itself as belonging to itself because goneness/overness [of Dasein] as the authentic future can never be present.

> *Das Dasein ist auch in der Gegenwart seines Besorgens die volle Zeit, so zwar, daß es die Zukunft nicht los wird. Die Zukunft ist jetzt das worin die Sorge hängt, nicht das eigentliche Zukünftigsein des Vorbei, sondern die Zukunft, die sich die Gegenwart selbst als die ihrige ausbildet, weil das Vorbei als die eigentliche Zukunft nie gegenwärtig werden kann.*[14]

What is important in this passage is the characterization of future as one which "builds the present out of itself as belonging to itself." If future builds the present and present belongs to it, then this future must be present.

Heidegger distinguishes this future from *das Vorbei* by saying that "as authentic future *das Vorbei* can never be present." Clearly Sallis overlooks the difference between "the future that builds the present out of itself" and is present *and* the authentic future, i.e., *das Vorbei* which will never be present.

It is quite probable that in "The Concept of Time" Heidegger calls "*das Vor-bei* the authentic future" because the lecture text, like *Der Begriff der Zeit*, is underway toward *Being and Time*. However this may be, the fact is that "The Concept of Time" recognizes a future that generates present and is present.

The obfuscation that Sallis's deconstructive reinscription lays over the concept of future as discussed in "The Concept of Time" consists in eliminating the distinction between future as generative of present and future as the authentic future which is not present. This is no instability or "slippage." This is only an indication of how Heidegger is carefully and painstakingly underway toward the concept of future as ecstasis, which he will expound in *Being and Time*. This expounding will be carried out under the directives of the question of being. Therefore, juxtaposing the two concepts of future, the one from "The Concept of Time" and the other from *Being and Time*, and asking:

> To what extent will Heidegger in the 1924 lecture text already have written the two divisions of *Being and Time* that will be published in 1927? To what extent will [Heidegger] also have begun [in the 1924 lecture text] writing the texts of those courses . . . in which the slippage of the project will begin coming into play. . . . (E 53)

amounts to leveling what is accomplished in 1924, when future is uncovered as being present, and what will be accomplished in 1927, when, under the directives of the question of being, future is uncovered as an ecstasis. The questions that Sallis raises here take the phenomenon of the future, not as something to be disclosed in the light of the question of being, but as an intellectual *fait accompli*, already accomplished in 1924. Only when such a leveling takes place can one assume that one form of the future was already operating, albeit unbeknownst to Heidegger, as a destabilizing element or "slippage" in the 1924 lecture text. But this way of thinking disregards the character of Heidegger's thinking which *occurs* as a pathway (*Denkweg*). If my analyses of the "future" in "The Concept of Time" are correct, then the future of which the 1924 lecture text speaks is also a future that returns and is present. This means that Sallis's deconstructive reinscription of this future as a "future that will never be present"—an instability and "slippage" in this text—does not stand the test of a close textual scrutiny. In that case, what Sallis calls a "slippage" is an obfuscation which he himself lays over the concept of future in the 1924 lecture text. This is to suggest that the "future" according to the 1924 lecture text presents no instability and is no "slippage." Moreover, the 1924 concept of future is underway toward the future as "ecstasis" in *Being and Time*.

The mere claim that future as conceived in "The Concept of Time" is a "slippage" is an indication that Sallis believes to have detected the beginning of a series of "slippages" which sketch "the very plan for demolition of the edifice of fundamental ontology . . ." (E 117). And so, the question upon which our entire estimate of deconstructive reinscription of fundamental ontology *after* Heidegger depends—and the question that confronts us with the task of thinking *after* him— becomes this: Can one justifiably talk about a "demolition of the edifice of fundamental ontology"?

II

There can be no talk of a demolition of the edifice of fundamental ontology, for at least four reasons. First, there is no such thing as an edifice of fundamental ontology, but a work of thinking that awaits co-enactment (*Mitvollzug*). The term *edifice* implies a stability and completeness that is foreign to *any* work of thinking. Secondly, the idea of a demolition does not apply to fundamental ontology because this idea comes from the assumption that there are instabilities and "slippages" in the texts of fundamental ontology that accelerate its demolition. In truth no such "slippage" exists: What Sallis takes for "slippage" is only possible on the basis of an obfuscation of a particular issue of fundamental ontology. Thirdly, there can be no talk of a demolition of fundamental ontology, because this ontology never lost its significance for Heidegger. Had this not been the case, i.e., if Heidegger had wanted to demolish fundamental ontology, he would not try to make it more accessible by offering, more than thirty years after its inception, a series of carefully prepared seminars on this theme (between 1959 and 1969 in Zollikon, Switzerland). Known as the *Zollikoner Seminare*[15] and published in 1987, i.e., three years before *Echoes: After Heidegger*, the texts of these seminars treat fundamental ontology as if this ontology is *the most* immediate concern of Heidegger's thinking during that decade. If, as Sallis suggests, the "slippage" intrinsic to the texts of fundamental ontology would have moved Heidegger to demolish this ontology, why would he then return to fundamental ontology in 1959–1969, i.e., for a whole decade, and why would he elucidate its main issues? The mere existence of the *Zollikoner Seminare* is "living" proof that Heidegger never entertained the possibility of demolishing fundamental ontology.

The fourth and, because of its philosophical significance, most important reason that this talk of a demolition of fundamental ontology does not make sense is given in the basic and crucial character of Heidegger's thinking. I alluded to this character at the outset of this essay, by suggesting that "in Heidegger's texts the relation to being *is not* proffered to thinking as something thought through to completion." The fourth and final reason why there can be no talk of a demolition of fundamental ontology is the actual work of thinking that needs to be done with this ontology. What I am suggesting is foreshadowed in the distinction between "analytic of Dasein" and "analysis of Dasein," which, when properly understood, makes fundamental ontology an unfinished business in philosophy. It is in view of this distinction that the relation to being proffered to thinking as fundamental ontology is not yet thought through to completion. It is this proffering that makes for the lasting significance of fundamental ontology. I think that Heidegger had this significance in mind when, in 1953 in the prefatory note to the seventh edition of *Being and Time*, he states that "its pathway even today remains a necessary one, if our Dasein is to be moved by the question of being—*Deren Weg bleibt indessen auch heute noch ein notwendiger, wenn die Frage nach dem Sein unser Dasein bewegen soll.*"[16]

Generally not much attention is paid to the distinction between "analytic of Dasein" and "analysis of Dasein"; and they are often treated as interchangeable terms, as they are in *Echoes: After Heidegger*. However, in the sessions of the seminars on fundamental ontology held in Zollikon in November, 1965, Heidegger puts a great deal of effort into elucidating the phrases "analytic of Dasein" and "analysis of Dasein."

Heidegger begins by reminding the participants in the seminar that an analytic is primarily concerned with a unity which it presupposes. Analysis and analytic need not always go together. Analysis can happen for the sole purpose of dissolving something into its elements. Here what is analysed is traced back to the elements of which it was initially composed. By contrast, analytic is a process that is concerned with a unity or a gathering; and as such this process does not strive for dissolution of things into their elements. Referring to his own usage of the terms "analytic of Dasein" and "analysis of Dasein" in *Being and Time*, he then says:

> The task of the analytic [of Dasein] is to bring into view the whole of a onefold [gathering] of ontological conditions. As ontological, analytic is not a process of dissolution into elements, but articulation of the [gathered] onefold of a structural jointure.
>
> *Die Analytik hat die Aufgabe, das Ganze einer Einheit ontologischer Bedingungen in den Blick zu bringen. Die Analytik ist als ontologische kein Auflösen in Elemente, sondern die Artikulation der Einheit eines Strukturgefüges.*[17]

But where does the gathering onefold come from with which the analytic of Dasein is concerned? This gathering onefold is already indicated in the question "What is *the being* of a human being?" which is essential to fundamental ontology. The onefold that the analytic of Dasein strives for is already alluded to with the word *being* in the phrase "the being of a human being." What *Being and Time* calls "analysis of Dasein" is a way of disclosing and opening up this pre-given gathering or onefold. Thus analysis of Dasein implies a certain "active" or "doing" character that thinking must achieve. Heidegger points directly to this "doing" character of the analysis of Dasein when he says:

In the course of the analytic of Dasein in *Being and Time* I speak also of an analysis of Dasein, by which in each case I mean the enactment of the analytic [of Dasein].

Im Verlaufe dieser Daseinsanalytik in "Sein und Zeit" spreche ich auch von Daseinsanalyse, womit ich jeweils den Vollzug der Analytik meine.[18]

Let me try to illustrate the "doing" or "active" character as the most distinctive mark of the thinking which Heidegger puts forth as the analysis of Dasein. I shall try to do this by working with the word *where* as it prompts a question like: "Where are you?"

One way of responding to this question—the one most often given—is to say: "I am here," meaning "near the tree," "next to the desk," "in the workshop," etc. This response merely indicates a location and says almost nothing about the term *am* in "I am." As indicative of a location, this response is restrictive, because it does not reveal what "being there" (near the tree, etc.) means. But when transposed into the domain of the analytic of Dasein, this response demands an analysis which is strictly ontological and is called analysis of Dasein. When taken up into this analytic, the response "I am here, near the desk, etc." is a response that implicates "Dasein's relation to being." Considering this relation, the response "I am near . . . next . . . in . . ." not only indicates a location, but also

names the openness within which beings can emerge for human beings and become present, including beings like the human being itself.

sondern soll die Offenheit nennen, in der für den Menschen Seiendes anwesend sein kann, auch er selbst für sich selbst.[19]

Now what is important about this "openness" is that it must be thought through and analyzed. When this thinking occurs as the analysis of Dasein, it turns out that this "openness" is not a characteristic or quality or attribute of an individual—as the way, for example, in which the existence of hydrochloric acid in one's stomach is a characteristic of that individual. What is important about this "openness" is that *it needs to be disclosed, opened up, and kept open.* And this is where the "active" or "doing" character of the thinking comes in. For example, as analysis of Dasein, this thinking faces the task of elucidating what the term *am* means in the response: "I am here near the tree, etc." The ontological sense of expressions such as "where" and "am" is the openness which needs to be disclosed and opened up. Heidegger sums up all of this when he says:

Here the analysis of Dasein means nothing other than enacting the demonstration of those determinations of Dasein which are the themes of the analytic of Dasein. . . .

Dabei besagt hier Daseinsanalyse nichts anderes als Vollzug des Aufweisens der in der Daseinsanalytik zum Thema gemachten Bestimmungen des Daseins. . . . [20]

The main determination of Dasein is the "openness." This means that we must not only *state* that such openness occurs as Dasein, but we must also analyze this openness/Dasein. This occurs as the analysis of Dasein, which requires the "active" or "doing" character of thinking.

Considering the "active" or "doing" character of the thinking which is called analysis of Dasein, I can say, finally, that there can be no talk of a demolition of fundamental ontology because it is up to each and every human being to enact the ontological determinations of Dasein which as such are not thought through to completion. (Were they thought through to completion, there would be no need for the analysis of Dasein.) These determinations are not thought through to completion because the relation that being proffers to thinking—and which sustains these determinations—is not thought through to completion. How can fundamental ontology be demolished if it continuously demands to be taken up by thinking and to be thought through?

CHAPTER FIFTEEN

MARGINAL NOTES ON SALLIS'S PECULIAR INTERPRETATION OF HEIDEGGER'S "VOM WESEN DER WAHRHEIT"*

Walter Biemel

Translated by Parvis Emad

My intention in this essay is not to offer an interpretation of Heidegger's essay "Vom Wesen der Wahrheit." The reader will find such an interpretation of the train of thought in Heidegger's essay in the introduction to the French translation by De Waelhens and myself (Paris-Louvain, 1948) and, following Heidegger's wish, in

---

*The title of Heidegger's text *Vom Wesen der Wahrheit* appears in the original German, because no single English word can say what the German *Wesen* wants to say here. The closest we can get to translating this title is perhaps to render it as "On the Essence and Being of Truth, its Root-Unfolding." As Biemel points out near the end of his essay, the term *Wesen* in Heidegger's formulation *das Wesen der Wahrheit ist die Wahrheit des Wesens* does not have the same meaning in each instance. Thus to render this formulation in the usual way as "the essence of truth is the truth of essence" is inappropriate and drastically curtails the range of meanings that Heidegger intends.   (*continued*)

the introduction to the German version of the essay that appeared in Volume III of the yearbook Symposion.[1] Thus here I will simply offer some marginal comments on Sallis's lecture "Deformatives: Essentially Other Than Truth," which he presented at the Heidegger Conference held in September, 1989, at Loyola University in Chicago.[2] My purpose is to elucidate how Sallis could arrive at his interpretation—an interpretation which fails to grasp what is actually being thought in Heidegger's text. Because of this failure, Sallis's charge of "monstrosity" as a "deformation of what is natural" (39) applies to Sallis himself. I do not mean to suggest that Heidegger's text is easy to understand or that no critical comments can be brought forward regarding the text. This is a difficult but central text of Heidegger's thinking. Sallis struggles with its difficulties, but he does not lead the reader into the text, nor does he enable the reader to see the difficulties and to overcome them. Rather, in my opinion, Sallis misleads the reader. The following observations are intended to show how this happens.

At the beginning of his lecture Sallis surprises us with some provocative questions. He adopts Heidegger's approach of beginning with a series of questions. In asking these, Sallis subjects the theme of truth in Heidegger to questions which let this central thought of Heidegger's appear in an entirely new and almost terrifying light. His questions are:

> What if truth were monstrous? What if it were even monstrosity itself, the very conditions, the very form, of everything monstrous, everything deformed? But, first of all, itself essentially deformed, monstrous in its very essence? What if there were within the very essence of truth something essentially other than truth, a divergence from nature within nature, true monstrosity? (29)

Also reminiscent of Heidegger's approach, these questions show a progression, an intensification. First, Sallis asks whether truth is monstrous. Then he proceeds to

---

How does one translate the word *Wesen*? Considering Heidegger's thinking in general and the text *Vom Wesen der Wahrheit* in particular, we can say that the term *Wesen* sometimes refers to *what* something is and sometimes to the peculiar way in which something comes forth, abides, emerges, unfolds. In the first instance, where "whatness" of something is intended by Heidegger, *Wesen* can be translated as "essence," bringing to mind the rich philosophical tradition of *essentia*. In the second instance, where Heidegger intends to convey a special way in which something comes forth, emerges, abides, and unfolds in its core, the word *Wesen* could be translated as "root-unfolding." I shall follow this approach throughout this translation.

Given the unfamiliarity with this rendition that some people will have and given the subtlety of the thinking that inheres in this word, I shall quite often include the German words *Wesen* and *Un-wesen* in parentheses in the text. For more on the question of translating *Wesen*, see my introduction to Heinrich Wiegand Petzet's *Encounters and Dialogues with Martin Heidegger, 1929–1976* (The University of Chicago Press, 1993), p. XVII ff.

ask whether truth is not just monstrous but monstrosity itself, i.e., the very pre-supposition for everything that is monstrous and filled in by the decadent, the de-formed. In this way Sallis wants to convey truth deformed in its essence (*Wesen*). Because of this "deformation," truth is directed to what is other than truth—noth-ing short of a decadence that contradicts the nature of truth and is thus the true monstrosity, i.e., something contrary to nature.

But how can we discuss truth and how can we talk about truth—or even about the root-unfolding of truth (its *Wesen*)—if truth itself is such a monstrous thing? Must not such a way of talking be itself deformed and monstrous, if we are con-cerned with truth? Does not this presuppose a deformed discourse? For, precisely in its mode of inquiry a discussion of truth is bound to truth. And when we inquire into the root-unfolding of truth, truth itself is the subject of discussion in a twofold way. The inquiry into truth is in an exemplary fashion bound to what this inquiry inquires into.

Sallis refers to a passage in *Beiträge zur Philosophie (Vom Ereignis)*,[3] but without taking up the thirteen points about truth that are offered there. His only concern is that we always already have an answer to the question of *Wesen*, i.e., that this answer is already presupposed. In other words, he assumes that, inquir-ing into the core of truth's unfolding, we are always already within truth. Accord-ingly, Sallis then asks the following question: If we are already within the domain where truth unfolds, can we inquire at all into something that is "essentially other than truth"? He draws upon a passage from *Beiträge zur Philosophie (Vom Ereig-nis)*:

> Grasped in its originary sense—as the fundamental character of φύσις—and according to its own root-unfolding, ἀλήθεια blocks ac-cess to any question concerning the relation to something else, like a re-lation to thinking.

> *Die ἀλήθεια, anfänglich begriffen als Grundcharakter der φύσις, ver-wehrt ihrem Wesen nach jede Frage nach dem Bezug auf Anderes, etwa auf das Denken.*[4]

This means that in the question concerning "something other than" truth is not an original question; rather such a question emerges in a decadent phase, in which thinking is removed from the original issue. But Heidegger does not inquire into "something other than" truth. What appears to Sallis to be the "other" in truth is for Heidegger precisely the *Wesen* (root-unfolding) of truth.

Presumably this other in truth is error. Sallis adds: Can this other be so pre-cisely fixed—as error? Can its ambiguity be examined and, so to speak, held in check? Heidegger says, ironically, that metaphysics and common sense seem to agree that the "other" in truth is error. But error does not lie outside truth. Sallis does not follow through Heidegger's new effort at thinking through the relation of truth and un-truth in *Beiträge zur Philosophie (Vom Ereignis).*[5] For Sallis is content with referring to what is strange (*das Befremdliche*) in the theme of truth for Heidegger: "the *clearing for concealing*, i.e., as what unfolds in *Ereignis*" (*die Lichtung für die Verbergung und dieses als Wesung im Ereignis*)[6] and the transformation which Heidegger wants to take up by no longer thinking the connection between truth and error in terms of metaphysics.

So much for the introduction of Sallis's lecture. Subsequently he begins with a careful reading of the text *Vom Wesen der Wahrheit*, in order to show that when Heidegger eliminates the opposition between truth and un-truth, truth itself gets "deformed."

Sallis announces the crucial character of his novel reading as a reading "that would focus on the moment in which the text twists free, one that would trace the displacement in which the mere opposite would become a proper untruth and would come to deform truth itself." (30). If I understand this correctly, Sallis wants to show the transformation through which the opposition within truth gets changed in such a way as to become the actual un-truth and so to distort and deform truth itself. Therein lies Sallis's main charge: According to Sallis, instead of speaking *of* and *about* truth, the text *Vom Wesen der Wahrheit* experiences a rupture. The new, second theme of Heidegger's text is untruth—and with that the thematic of truth gets deformed and distorted.

But everything depends on determining whether in fact un-truth drives truth out or, rather, whether with his remarks on un-truth Heidegger penetrates into the ground of the question of truth, i.e., penetrates not into something that is a stranger to truth, but into the proper domain and root-unfolding of truth (*zu ihrem eigentlichen Wesen*). To see this presupposes, of course, that we do not proceed with the ordinary meaning of the term *un-truth*, but pay special attention to what Heidegger *thinks* as un-truth. And this also means that we are prepared to abandon the realm of common sense.

For Sallis the task is to work out what is strange in Heidegger's text. That is, of course, a critique that would not bother Heidegger, for he is not overly concerned with what is self-evident. His interpretation of truth—of the root-unfolding of truth—is indeed unusual. What is strange in Heidegger's treatment of the question of truth needs to be brought to light in the original text of 1930, as well as in its first published version of 1943; and all of this needs to be supplemented by taking into account references to the issue of truth that appear in *Beiträge zur Philosophie (Vom Ereignis)*. It should be noted right away that alterations in the text of 1930 are minimal. It is indeed impressive how little Heidegger changed in the original text. This text is woven so tightly that it could withstand—and in fact does withstand—the passage of decades.

Sallis quotes from section 213 of *Beiträge zur Philosphie (Vom Ereignis)*, which is entitled "*Worum es sich bei der Wahrheitsfrage handelt*: What the Question of Truth Is All About," by mentioning the first four out of six statements that comprise this section. The fourth statement reads:

> And accordingly [the question of truth is] about a transformation of humans in the sense of a *Ver-rückung* of their place among beings.
>
> *Und demzufolge um eine Verwandlung des Menschsein im Sinne einer Ver-rückung seiner Stellung im Seienden.*[7]

Sallis translates the word *Ver-rückung* as "derangement," which means a disorder in the sense of madness. That is why he can immediately add: "What is the question of truth all about? Human derangement, madness!" (31) But this violates the meaning of the word *Ver-rückung* and does not correspond to Heidegger's intention. *Ver-rückung* means a transformation of the place of humans in the midst of beings and has nothing to do with a pathological derangement. Nevertheless, Sallis bases his interpretation on this violently distorted translation. If Sallis had considered statements 5 and 6 of section 213 of *Beiträge zur Philosophie*, his interpretation would have been not only improbable but also impossible. These two statements read as follows:

> 5. [The question of truth] therefore [is] about a more originary appreciation and empowering of beon itself as *Ereignis*.
>
>   *Und deshalb zuerst um eine ursprüngliche Würdigung und Ermächtigung des Seyns selbst als Ereignis.*
>
> 6. [The question of truth] therefore [is] above all about founding humans in *Da-sein* as the ground that beon needs to set up for its truth.
>
>   *Und daher allem zuvor um die Gründung des Menschsein im Da-sein als dem vom Seyn selbst ernötigten Grunde seiner Wahrheit.*[8]

I understand why Sallis does not want to discuss the intimate connection between truth and *Ereignis* before we know how to think truth. Nevertheless, statements 5 and 6, which follow from the preceding four, would have protected him from mistranslating *Ver-rückung* with "madness"/*Verrücktheit*. It is unfortunate—that is, not helpful to the reader—that Sallis begins by referring to common sense, but then jumps to the conclusion which is unintelligible, i.e., is a seeming tautology: "*the essence of truth is the truth of essence.*"[9] By speaking of common sense and then jumping to this conclusion, Sallis seems to want to create the impression that, to put it cautiously, we are here actually dealing with a strange or peculiar text. This impression is given especially when Sallis points out that this formulation is not to be understood as a proposition, but rather as "*die Sage einer Kehre innerhalb der Geschichte des Seyns*/the saying of a turning within the history of beon."[10]

It would have made more sense to have discussed this text at the end, in conjunction with section 9.

After referring to the formal structure of the text (31)—i.e., how the text is put together, something that is very important and constructive in Heidegger, in contrast to Husserl—Sallis immediately presents this structure as questionable: "In the movement of the text, however, there is a certain eccentricity that finally transforms—or rather, deforms—this formal structure" (31).

How is this "deformation" supposed to happen? According to Sallis this deformation takes place when un-truth suddenly pops up and doubles the center in the text dealing with truth's essence and its root-unfolding—producing "a doubling of the center." The result of this doubling is a "de-centering" of the entire discourse, i.e., a loss of the center, which Sallis calls "monstrous," emphasizing his initial thesis, namely "a monstrous decentering." At this point Sallis begins to read the text by taking up the question of the essence of truth and its "essential unfolding" and the altercation with common sense.

I want to say something about Sallis's critical remarks aimed at the marginal notes to *Vom Wesen der Wahrheit*. (These notes appear in the text of the *Gesamtausgabe* as footnotes.) Whenever Heidegger re-reads his texts/after some time has passed, he is wont to make marginal notes to them. Most of these marginal notes (of which only a small number has so far been published) must be taken as a kind of monologue, i.e., not primarily intended for the reader. As the editor of *Wegmarken*, von Herrmann, points out in his epilogue, it is not easy to date these notes. To determine their dates, we would need to compare samples of Heidegger's handwriting, which have not yet been prepared. These marginal notes are important to us insofar as we can use them to highlight the pathway which Heidegger has traveled. Moreover, some marginal notes might assist the reader in understanding a difficult passage. In a first reading one can skip the marginal notes that I characterized as monologues, because they are usually too difficult to understand for a reader who is unable to recognize the "pathway" on which these notes are commenting. Furthermore, we must refrain from viewing these notes as evidence that Heidegger had already anticipated his future thinking. Heidegger never goes over the paths that he has already traversed. Rather, all his life he opens up new pathways. Very few marginal notes were published during Heidegger's lifetime; therefore we must welcome the fact that more and more marginal notes are included in the editions of Heidegger's works. However, it is not right to blame Heidegger for the difficulty of understanding his marginal notes—nor ought these notes be criticized when we study the structure of the text *Vom Wesen der Wahrheit*. We are to learn this structure from the original text itself—in this case from the 1943 edition as well as later separate editions and in *Wegmarken*. The fact is that the marginal notes are not incorporated into the text of *Vom Wesen der Wahrheit*.

Sallis's critique is unfounded when he writes: "Thus is the text 'On the Essence of Truth' oriented from the beginning to that non-proposition to which it will finally lead: the essence of truth is the truth of essence" (33). At first the reader of Sallis is not at all able to understand the proclamation "the essence of truth is the truth of essence" (*das Wesen der Wahrheit ist die Wahrheit des Wesens*) because it comes at the end of a development which Sallis does not elucidate at all. This development includes, for example, a discussion of various meanings of the word *Wesen*. If the various meanings of the word *Wesen* are not elucidated, what is the point of mentioning them? It is difficult to resist the impression that Sallis mentions these meanings without explaining them in order to set up a mood in which the reader will react negatively to the text *Vom Wesen der Wahrheit*. Sallis begins (33) to interpret the first four sections of the text and initially stays close to the text, as Heidegger unfolds with precision the train of thought here. But Sallis fails to work out clearly the moves that Heidegger makes in discussing truth as correctness as well as what makes correctness possible, namely manifestness and its ground. Sallis does not work out what Heidegger means when he says:

> Giving itself free for a binding measure is only possible as *being free* unto what becomes manifest within an opening.

> *Das Sich-freigeben für eine bindende Richte ist nur möglich als Freisein zum Offenbaren eines Offenen.*[11]

and concludes that

> Openness of comportment as the inner possibility of correctness is grounded in freedom. *The being of truth . . . is freedom.*

> *Die Offenständigkeit des Verhaltens als innere Ermöglichung der Richtigkeit gründet in der Freiheit. Das Wesen der Wahrheit . . . ist Freiheit.*[12]

Sallis does not take up the theme of openness of the open (the *da* of Da-sein) at that place where Heidegger determines freedom "as being exposed to the uncon-cealment of beings/*als die Aussetzung in die Entborgenheit des Seienden.*"[13] Moreover, he does not discuss and elucidate Heidegger's statement:

> For humans Dasein keeps open the long un-unfolded ground of unfolding from out of which humans are able to ek-sist.

> *Im Da-sein wird dem Menschen der langehin ungegründete Wesensgrund aufbehalten, aus dem er zu ek-sistieren vermag.*[14]

Likewise Sallis disregards Heidegger's statement that

> The ek-sistence of the historical human begins in that moment when— still not grasped and not even deemed to be in need of a grounding-unfolding—the first thinker exposes himself through questioning to the unconcealment/disclosure of beings by asking what a being is.

Noch unbegriffen, ja nicht einmal einer Wesensgründung bedürftig,
fängt die Ek-sistenz des geschichtlichen Menschen in jenem Augenblick
an, da der erste Denker fragend sich der Unverborgenheit des Seienden
stellt mit der Frage, was das Seiende sei.[15]

Disregarding these statements, Sallis jumps directly to the passage where Heidegger says:

> Humans do not "possess" freedom as a property. At best the reverse is
> the case: Freedom, i.e., the ek-sisting and disclosing Da-sein possesses
> humans. . . .
>
> *Der Mensch "besitzt" die Freiheit nicht als Eigenschaft, sondern höch-*
> *stens gilt das Umgekehrte: Die Freiheit, das ek-sistente, entbergende*
> *Da-sein besitzt den Menschen. . . .* [16]

At this point Sallis asks what sense could be attributed to the word *Wesen* as it applies to freedom. But this question is already answered in the discussions that Sallis disregards—discussions that are intended to show how *Wesen* is to be
understood. The passages from Heidegger's text that I have just quoted show that
the "*Wesen*" of freedom should be understood as the essential or root-unfolding of
freedom. Through discussions that run throughout these pages, Heidegger provides a directive as to how we are to grasp the root-unfolding of freedom, what
happens in that unfolding, and what its fundamental significance is. Sallis simply
says: "the essence of freedom is freedom—that is, freedom itself, freedom proper"
(37). Without entering into this discussion, Sallis starts to play with words such as
"itself" and "proper" and tries to show that the ecstatic character of freedom de-
stroys the root-unfolding of freedom. A certain traditional meaning of "proper" is
at play here, a meaning which Heidegger's analysis has already left behind. I might
say that Sallis identifies freedom with a certain category of consciousness whose
being-outside-itself contradicts the character of consciousness. Given Sallis's failure to grasp the uniqueness of Heidegger's analysis of freedom, the conclusion that
he reaches is quite consistent: "freedom, as ek-sistence, is the very *disproportion*
of the essence of man" (38). Such an assertion can only be made when one refuses
to engage in discussing what Da-sein means for Heidegger.[17] Only then can one
claim that at the center of *Vom Wesen der Wahrheit* little is said of truth. But what
Heidegger says in this essay about truth is more than enough and remarkably
plenty, in order for us to persist in it and to enact it in thinking.

Sallis is also silent about the crucial relation to history that Heidegger discusses in the fourth section of the essay (with the title "*Das Wesen der Freiheit*").
Instead of taking up this section, he proceeds with his discussion of un-truth. At
the end of this section Heidegger says quite clearly:

> Un-truth must rather come from the core of truth's unfolding. Only be-
> cause at the center of their unfolding truth and un-truth are not indiffer-

ent to each other but belong together—only thus can a true proposition become the acute opposite of a correspondingly untrue proposition.

Die Unwahrheit muß vielmehr aus dem Wesen der Wahrheit kommen. Nur weil Wahrheit und Unwahrheit im Wesen sich nicht gleichgültig sind, sondern zusammengehören, kann überhaupt ein wahrer Satz in die Schärfe des Gegenteils zum entsprechend unwahren Satz treten.[18]

Right after this Heidegger says:

A discussion of the dis-unfolding (i.e., that it does *not* unfold in its core) does not mean that we are adding something to fill a gap. Rather, to discuss the not-unfolding of truth is the crucial step in adequately raising the question concerning the root-unfolding of truth.

Die Erörterung des Unwesens der Wahrheit ist nicht nachträgliche Ausfüllung einer Lücke, sondern der entscheidende Schritt in die zureichende Ansetzung der Frage nach dem Wesen der Wahrheit.[19]

Only if we bracket out un-truth, as common sense is apt to do, can we estimate the extent to which a "de-centering" is supposed to go on at the center of the essay *Vom Wesen der Wahrheit*. Sallis does not want to admit that here we face that retrieval process of questioning (*Rückfragen*) which is found in Heidegger's writings again and again.

That Sallis considers questioning's return to Da-sein to be a process whereby the human dimension is abandoned, impoverished, and plainly and simply a deprivation, shows how difficult it is to enter into Heidegger's questions. If we adopt Sallis's perspective and speak of an "alienation" here, then we can say that he sets a second "de-centering" alongside this "alienation," the de-centering of the theme of truth, which now focuses on un-truth. First he quotes the sentence with which the fifth section ends, without saying much about this section:

Letting-be is in itself and at the same time a concealing. In the ek-sisting freedom of Da-sein there occurs the concealing of beings in the whole—there *is* concealment.

Das Seinlassen ist in sich zugleich ein Verbergen. In der ek-sistenten Freiheit des Daseins ereignet sich die Verbergung des Seienden im Ganzen, ist Verbergung.[20]

But Sallis does not quote this sentence in its entirety. He omits the phrase "the concealing of beings in the whole" as discussed in this section, so that his quotation reads as follows: "In the ek-sistent freedom of Dasein . . . there is concealment." (39) The result of this omission is that naming "concealment/*Verborgenheit*" seems strange, even arbitrary.

To continue with the questioning that goes back to un-truth appears to Sallis as a "monstrous decentering," i.e., a monstrous and enormous destruction at the center of the text. Thus Sallis returns to his initial criticism and tries to justify it by intimating that Heidegger does not arrive at a conclusion about the question of truth, but rather introduces a new phase in questioning, namely un-truth. This is especially shocking to common sense. I do not wish to identify Sallis with that standpoint, although sometimes he reacts according to that understanding.

We encounter something of this shock in his text when we read:

> From this point on it will become ever more monstrous—beginning with the passage from the would-be center to the remaining sections of the text, a monstrous transition that is thus not a passage or transition at all but a leap. (39)

In the marginal note to the text of 1943 Heidegger uses the word *Sprung*, i.e., leap in the sense of "a leap into the turning/*Sprung in die Kehre*." This means that the discussion here no longer sets out from humans in order to move toward being (*Sein*), but that thinking begins with being. This marginal note is evidently not readily understandable by the reader who is not well versed in the way in which Heidegger's thinking unfolds. In Sallis's view such a monstrous transition takes place here that one cannot speak any longer of a transition but must speak of a leap. The sixth section of the essay *Vom Wesen der Wahrheit* (entitled "*Die Wahrheit als die Verbergung*/Un-truth as Concealment") provides Sallis with special difficulties, because from his perspective he must understand this section as a monstrous violation of the perspective of truth. He cannot see the meaningfulness of a sentence such as this:

> Thought through from the place of truth as unconcealment, concealment then is non-unconcealment and is thus the genuine untruth most proper to the essential and root-unfolding of truth.
>
> *Die Verborgenheit ist dann, von der Wahrheit als Entborgenheit her gedacht, die Un-entborgenheit und somit die dem Wahrheitswesen eigenste und eigentliche Un-wahrheit.*[21]

He is satisfied with saying that un-truth in the most genuine sense belongs to the essence of truth. But if truth is thought as unconcealing and unconcealment, it is not at all odd or even monstrous to claim that concealment as non-unconcealment belongs to truth and that this non-unconcealment in this sense can be named untruth. Heidegger puts a hyphen between *un* and *Wahrheit* (*Un-wahrheit*/un-truth) to show that he is not dealing here with what one usually means by untruth as opposed to truth and as such gets devalued, even to the point of needing to be avoided at all costs. Sallis's charge reads as follows:

> Now untruth belongs most properly to the essence of truth, belongs to what would have been the proper of truth, had that very proper not been disrupted by the submission of freedom to ἀλήθεια. (39)

I do not understand this sentence. How are we to understand the statement that what genuinely belongs to truth is "disrupted"—disturbed or destroyed—when freedom is submitted to ἀλήθεια? In the essay Heidegger has just shown that in ἀλήθεια an opening takes place. A domain of openness breaks through, such that what is manifest becomes accessible to humans and humans let what is "be" manifest. Sallis dealt with this already. However, now what genuinely belongs to truth is to be viewed as *disturbed*, simply because freedom in the sense of letting-be submits itself to the domain of openness—so that manifest beings become accessible to a being to which letting-be can hold firm. Instead of continuing to read the text carefully, Sallis jumps to the following passage:

> Here the dis-unfolding (not unfolding in its core) does not yet mean reduced to *essentia*, i.e., the universal (κοινόν, γένος), its *possibilitas* understood as possibilization, and its ground. The dis-unfolding or non-root-unfolding here is the fore-unfolding-root-unfolding. However, initially and for the most part, the dis-unfolding speaks the disfiguration of *essentia*, i.e., what already has fallen away from root-unfolding. But in each of these senses the non-root-unfolding unfolds, each in its own way, *as* root-unfolding (essentially tied *to* the root-unfolding) and never becomes non-essential (*not* tied to root-unfolding) in the sense of "indifferent."

> *Un-wesen bedeutet hier noch nicht abgefallen zum Wesen im Sinne des Allgemeinen (κοινόν, γένος), seiner possibilitas (Ermöglichung) und ihres Grundes. Un-wesen ist hier das in solchem Sinne vor-wesende Wesen. "Un-wesen" besagt aber zunächst und zumeist die Verunstaltung jenes bereits abgefallenen Wesens. Das Un-wesen bleibt allerdings in jeder dieser Bedeutungen je in seiner Weise dem Wesen wesentlich und wird niemals unwesentlich im Sinne des Gleichgültigen.* [22]

But it would have been more appropriate for Sallis first to have taken up this dynamic: While beings are unconcealed in letting-be, beings in the whole remain concealed. This is what Heidegger means when he says that "concealing appears in the first place as concealed/*die Verbergung als das erstlich Verborgene erscheint.*" In this connection let me draw upon what I say in the introduction to the Symposion-edition of Heidegger's text:

> The second paragraph of this section begins with a sentence which is unintelligible to traditional thinking: "*Im entbergenden und zugleich verbergenden Seinlassen des Seienden im Ganzen geschieht es, daß die Verbergung als das erstlich Verborgene erscheint/*In the unconcealing and simultaneous concealing that the letting-be of beings in the whole undergoes, there takes place a concealing which appears as what is at first concealed." It is the second part of this sentence that is especially

offensive. How can something that is concealed appear? Does it not belong essentially to what is concealed not to come forth in appearing? What is the point then of still talking about "appearing"?

Here "appearing" indicates that concealing occurs and as such is experiencible by Dasein. But along with this occurrence and its experiencibility, it is by no means a given that what is experienced as concealed is accessible in its root-unfolding and is uncovered in its being. It is possible to experience something that, though experienced, remains mysterious. When concealing occurs, i.e., "appears," this does not necessarily mean that concealment must be something un-concealed. Were this the case, then concealment would not appear *as* concealment. Concealment is older in the sense that concealment is the basic presupposition for unconcealing. Dasein "shelters" the first and broadest un-unconcealment, the genuine un-truth, in that it is only with Dasein that concealment as such can come forth and appear. This also means that concealment is the "sheltered" and kept, rather than transformed into its opposite.

Accordingly, un-truth is not the opposite of truth but, as concealment, its original presupposition. Heidegger says, "The genuine non-root-unfolding of truth is mystery/*Das eigentliche Un-wesen der Wahrheit ist das Geheimnis.*"[23]

Now let us take a look at Sallis's interpretation. According to him truth becomes monstrous, a distortion of what truth actually is. What does he mean by this? Does he mean the usual understanding of truth? The following sentence seems to me to be without meaning:

Truth becomes monstrous: a deformation of what is natural (i.e., of the essential); a divergence from nature, something unnatural, within nature (non-essence within essence). Here the sense of essence is disrupted so decisively that it erases its very designation as a disruption of *sense*, namely, by disrupting the very operation of the concept of sense as well as the sense of concept. (39)

At this point it is impossible not to hear and perceive Sallis's misunderstanding of *Vom Wesen der Wahrheit.* What does he mean by "nature"? To what extent is Heidegger's interpretation of truth opposed to nature? To what extent does a "disruption" of sense take place here? As I explained, it is because Heidegger assigns a special meaning to the prefix *un-* (in *Un-wahrheit/*un-truth) and because with this prefix he points to something original, that in Sallis's view Heidegger initiates a "deformative writing," i.e., a disruptive language. Sallis expresses his dismay by equating un-truth (*Un-wahrheit*) with dis-unfolding (*Un-wesen*) and saying that essence now has to include non-essence. But according to Sallis this unbelievable transformation must draw in words like "such," "within," and "itself." And when

Heidegger says that the issue under discussion in *Vom Wesen der Wahrheit* is not about propositions, but rather about freeing the matter for thinking, Sallis wants to find a contradiction, in that he says that the response to the question concerning the essence, essential unfolding, or root-unfolding of truth is still a propositional assertion.

From this point on Sallis presents, in three steps, a criticism of Heidegger's discourse on un-truth. As far as Sallis is concerned, the destructive move is intensified when Heidegger introduces errancy (*die Irre*). Let me now try to show (*a*) how for Heidegger errancy (*Irre*) is different from mystery (*Geheimnis*) and (*b*) how, whereas Sallis sees something of this difference, he still mixes up the distinction. The concealment that Heidegger shows in section 6 to be the genuine un-truth, turns out to be mystery (*Geheimnis*). Accordingly, the concealing of what is concealed in the whole, beings in the whole, is mystery. As Heidegger puts it,

> The concealment of beings in the whole, the genuine un-truth, is older than any manifestness of this or that being. This concealment is also older than letting-be itself—the letting-be which as it unconceals always still keeps concealed and comports itself toward concealment. What is it that "letting-be" preserves in this relation to concealment? Nothing less than the concealing of what is concealed, a being as such in the whole, i.e., nothing less than mystery.

> *Die Unverborgenheit des Seienden im Ganzen, die eigentliche Unwahrheit, ist älter als jede Offenbarkeit von diesem und jenem Seienden. Sie ist älter auch als das Seinlassen selbst, das entbergend schon verborgen hält und zur Verbergung sich verhält. Was verwahrt das Seinlassen in diesem Bezug zur Verbergung? Nichts Geringeres als die Verbergung des Verborgenen im Ganzen, des Seienden als eines solchen, d.h. das Geheimnis.*[24]

Sallis fails to understand this; for him mystery is another deformation of un-truth that belongs to the "essence" of truth. By stating that "The genuine non-root-unfolding (*Un-wesen*) of truth is mystery," Heidegger is not bringing a new element into play, but rather is determining more precisely the non-root-unfolding. Heidegger's text states this clearly: "Here non-root-unfolding in this sense indicates the fore-unfolding-root-unfolding/*Un-wesen ist hier das in solchem Sinne vor-wesende Wesen.*"[25] Thus it is not correct to speak of "another deformation of un-truth." To see this, it is necessary to recall briefly this particular context in Heidegger's presentation. I quote again from my earlier introduction to the Symposion-text:

> Thus section 6 makes the crucial move from truth as unconcealment (ἀλήθεια) to un-truth as concealment, a move by which un-truth is understood as the ground upon which each and every unconcealing can be-

gin to unfold. But as such this ground remains concealed and, as mystery, determines Dasein. Truth and un-truth belong together; they make up the onefold discordant being of the original truth. The consequence of forgetting the mystery is that ek-sisting Dasein is at the same time an in-sisting Dasein, i.e., one which clings to what is unconcealed and forgets what does not let itself be unconcealed in unconcealing, i.e., the truth of being. " . . . this concealing of being's root-unfolding and of originary unfolding is the move in and through which being originarily lights up, such that thinking does not directly follow being."

In section 6 Heidegger shows how mystery is forgotten and indicates the consequences of that forgetting. Section 7 explicitly deals with the manner in which un-truth is distinguished by the lost relation to mystery. At the same time this section discusses the being of Dasein which corresponds to that lost relation, namely the in-sisting Dasein.[26]

(1) Sallis's first point of criticism concerns the introduction of errancy. For Heidegger, "Errancy is the counter-root-unfolding of originary root-unfolding of truth/*Die Irre ist das wesentliche Gegenwesen zum anfänglichen Wesen der Wahrheit.*"[27] This means that errancy is the originary counter-root-unfolding of truth and not, as Sallis claims, the same as mystery. In order to elucidate the difficulty that Sallis has with this section of Heidegger's text, I must quote from a passage from Sallis's text and then comment on it:

> The first is the extension that the deformative move undergoes through the introduction of *errancy.* Thus would Heidegger name—alongside the concealment already introduced into the essence of truth as its proper non-essence (*eigentliche Un-wahrheit*), what he now calls *the mystery (das Geheimnis)*—another form"or rather, deform—of untruth belonging to the essence of truth, belonging to it as its essential counter-essence (*das wesentliche Gegenwesen*). (40)

According to Sallis, by introducing errancy, Heidegger continues and intensifies the distorting presentation of the theme of truth. But, regrettably, Sallis ignores the passage in which Heidegger presents errancy as both the ek-sisting and the in-sisting mode of comportment of humans, i.e., as the mode of comportment in which mystery is forgotten.[28] Sallis acts as if Heidegger simply and arbitrarily introduces errancy as another disruption of truth, in addition to mystery. He omits or skims over the passage where Heidegger sees the errancy as a consequence of in-sisting Dasein. Sallis overlooks how ek-sisting Dasein can always cling to what is in its proximity and take that as genuine—in which case the ek-sisting Dasein is at the same time in-sisting. This is carefully shown at the beginning of section 7. It is regrettable that Sallis chooses not to read this passage. Instead, he wants to show that Heidegger posits a doubling of un-truth: " . . . there is a doubling of untruth, into non-essence and counter-essence." (40)

Heidegger actually demonstrates mystery as "the genuine non-root-unfolding of truth/*eigentliche Un-wesen der Wahrheit.*"[29] But non-root-unfolding here must be understood in Heidegger's sense, i.e., as original root-unfolding. And Heidegger juxtaposes this original root-unfolding over against the "counter-unfolding that unfolds." What transpires in the counter-unfolding-unfolding is "forgetfulness of concealing/*Vergessenheit der Verbergung.*" In order to elucidate the matter at hand, let me quote a passage from my introduction to the Symposion-text:

> . . . "Errancy is the counter-unfolding that unfolds as originary root-unfolding of truth/*Die Irre ist das wesentliche Gegenwesen zum anfäng-lichen Wesen der Wahrheit.*"[30] When we judge this statement according to the rules of ordinary logic, this statement obviously presents a contradiction. We are told that errancy is the counter-unfolding of the unfolding of originary truth. It would seem that counter-unfolding is something that unfolds in opposition to root-unfolding, i.e., counter-unfolding is the opposite of root-unfolding. The opposite of root-unfolding is what does not unfold, fails to connect to unfolding, is *unwesentlich* in the ordinary sense of this word. But Heidegger addresses this counter-unfolding precisely as *the unfolding*-counter-unfolding. This seems to cancel what I just said. Either errancy is the counter-unfolding of originary truth—and thus it is necessarily unconnected to unfolding, is *unwesentlich*—or errancy belongs to originary truth as the way it unfolds. However, in this case errancy is not the counter-unfolding to root-unfolding.
>
> The only thing to which we need to take exception is the presupposition that the rules of logic determine what truth and what un-truth is. But for Heidegger root-unfolding of truth and untruth determine thinking (λόγος in the significant sense). We cannot decide in advance whether there is or there is not a counter-unfolding that unfolds, i.e., is connected to *Wesen* and is in this sense *wesentlich*. The path that thinking takes must decide this question. The pathway of thinking leads us to the juncture where we uncover the discordant root-unfolding of truth—an unfolding which is unconcealing and concealing, truth and un-truth at the same time. Now we can see how the relation to concealment is in itself twofold, namely as the experience of mystery and as forgetting of mystery. The experience of mystery is the originary root-unfolding of truth—understanding *Wesen*/root-unfolding here as a verb. The forgetting of mystery is the counter-root-unfolding of the originary truth. Through this forgetting, concealment withdraws so radically that this withdrawal is not at all uncovered. Because this forgetting actually begins with the originary root-unfolding, this forgetting is the counter-root-unfolding of originary truth that unfolds, is *wesentlich*. This counter-root-unfolding is not just *a* counter-root-unfolding that unfolds, but *the* counter-root-unfolding.

The expression *Gegen-wesen*/counter-root-unfolding does not mean something cut off, detached and isolated from root-unfolding/ *Wesen*. Rather the word *gegen* is relational and expresses a tension within *Wesen*, within root-unfolding. This tension excludes indifference. The tension within *gegen* (counter) articulates the distance from root-unfolding. But this distance is as such always connected to and born up by root-unfolding—as articulated in the adjective *wesentlich*, which defines counter-root-unfolding. Counter-root-unfolding as the counterpart is the part that necessarily belongs to root-unfolding as its counterpart. Were we to think of *Gegen-wesen* (counter-root-unfolding) as something simply discarded from *Wesen*/root-unfolding, then we would fail to think the tension within the relation to *Wesen*. Then the connection to root-unfolding would still determine counter-root-unfolding, even as discarded form *Wesen, but* the "power of the tension" would no longer be there—and counter-root-unfolding would be merely privation. As privation the counter-root-unfolding loses the force of the "counter/*gegen*." And one could call it a non-essential counter-root-unfolding—or a counter-root-unfolding that does not unfold, is not "essential."[31]

I present this passage as a rejoinder to Sallis's interpretation, i.e., as an example of another possibility of understanding Heidegger's text.

Indeed Sallis sees the difference between mystery and errancy. However, I cannot understand what he means when he claims that in addition to a doubling of un-truth by means of mystery and errancy, another doubling takes place as the doubling of errancy. When he says, "On the one hand, it is concealing of concealment, that is, a covering up the mystery," he understands this in Heidegger's sense. But when he says, "On the other hand, it is a turning toward readily available beings" (40), this can only be the consequence of forgetting the mystery. Because mystery is not experienced, Heidegger says, "humans turn to the most proximate accessibility of beings/*ist der Mensch der je nächsten Gangbarkeit des Seienden zugewendet.*"[32]

This "turn" distinguishes the in-sisting comportment of humans that is exposed to errancy. This means that there can be no talk of a doubling of errancy—a charge Sallis unjustly makes against Heidegger—in order to account for his (Sallis's) criticism of "disruption." According to Heidegger, errancy appears as the "counter-root-unfolding" that unfolds as the root-unfolding of truth. This means that errancy does not appear as an accidental counter-root-unfolding.

The being of humans is determined by the comportment toward mystery (toward the concealing of concealment) and by staying within errancy. It is therefore wrong to speak here of a "proliferation of deformatives" and to charge Heidegger with destroying the unity. It is thus wrong to arrive at the conclusion, as Sallis does, that "as truth becomes essentially duplicitous, it becomes also ever more monstrous" (40). Instead, such things happen in Sallis's "duplicitous lecture," which fails to do justice to the text, which deforms it. Sallis's lecture is duplicitous even if we assume that his transformation of Heidegger's text is not done with any destructive intent, but because of a desire to make Heidegger's text accessible to the reader, to protect the reader from being enchanted by this text. Following Sallis's interpretation, truth (*Wahrheit*) becomes duplicitous because essence (*Wesen*) is duplicitous.

(2) The second step in Sallis's criticism is the impression that speaking of disunfolding and un-truth leaves: the paradoxical character—a way of speaking that Heidegger avoids. But Sallis fails to show what "*un-*" means. To elucidate this, let me quote one final time from my introduction to the Symposion-text:

> What needs to be done first is to elucidate the prefix *un-* which marks basic words of this section, such as *un-truth, un-concealment, un-/non-root-unfolding*. Usually the *un-* indicates a negation in the sense of the not. Thus when we say *unendlich* (infinite), we mean what is not finite/*endlich*; *un-schön* (not beautiful), what is not beautiful; *Un-glück* (misfortune), what is not fortunate. In Heidegger *un-* never has a negative meaning in the ordinary sense. Rather, the prefix *un-* in his text undertakes the function of intensification. In ordinary usage of language we find this intensification in words like *un-tief* (shallow, not deep). The German word *Un-tiefe* does not negate the depth but underlines it. But the intensification and emphasis that Heidegger wants to achieve should not be confused with wanting to quantitatively puff something up. Rather, in each case where Heidegger uses the prefix *un-*, he wants to point at something original. In Heidegger *un-* indicates the relation to the origin and corresponds to the real *ur-*. The origin as such or what is original precedes everything that is ordinary and familiar but not recognized and seen as such. In this sense *un-* retains the meaning of the not, not as disparaging and negative, but rather as the not that breaks through the domain of the ordinary. This breaking through/open is unavoidable because the original is always what gets buried first and becomes inaccessible.[33]

Sallis fails to see what sense the prefix *un-* has in Heidegger, namely as indicative of the dimension of being. Instead, proceeding from the principle of contradiction which must be recognized in any reasonable discourse, he attacks Heidegger, charging that Heidegger fails to respect this principle and that as a result Heidegger's discussion must be viewed as an example of monstrosity of speaking.

(3) The third point concerns especially the formulation *das Wesen der Wahrheit ist die Wahrheit des Wesens*. Sallis tries to determine the significance of this formulation, which is not just a play on words. For, root-unfolding of truth

(*Wesen der Wahrheit*) says what makes truth what it is, while the truth of root-unfolding (*Wahrheit des Wesens*) indicates how the clearing of being occurs, how being unfolds. Sallis's criticism of Heidegger amounts to this: If the non-root-unfolding (*Un-wesen*) of philosophy belongs to philosophy, then this non-root-unfolding must lead to a decadence of philosophy—must lead to its "dispropriation," its alienation. But this is not at all the sense to be drawn from Heidegger's characterization of the root-unfolding of truth. On the contrary, Heidegger wants to draw attention to the danger which, historically speaking, happened with the emergence of sophism. Moreover, Sallis leaves open the question of whether for Heidegger there is a way of thinking other than the metaphysical one.

Sallis is wrong in claiming that the original title of the lecture-text *Vom Wesen der Wahrheit* was *Philosophieren und Glauben* (Philosophizing and Faith). Heidegger chose this title for the lecture in Marburg. In the original text, which Heidegger gave to me as a gift, this title appears only in parentheses as a subtitle. Sallis's remarks regarding *der Glaube und die Wahrheit* (faith and truth) in *Beiträge zur Philosphie (Vom Ereignis)* are good supplements. But the conclusion of his presentation is misleading when he says: "If one takes 'knowing' in the prevailing sense of representing and possession of representations, then essential knowing is indeed not a 'knowing' but a 'believing' " (43). Taken out of context, such a conclusion may create the impression that ultimately Heidegger gives up knowing in favor of faith and so enacts a reversal. But this is not the case at all. For, Heidegger is concerned with a knowing that is not

> merely holding something for true—be it simply something or something outstanding. Rather, this knowing is original insofar as it is *staying within the root-unfolding of truth*.
>
> *Dieses Wissen ist dann kein blosses Für-wahr-halten irgend eines oder eines ausgezeichneten Wahren, sondern unsprünglich: das Sichhalten im Wesen der Wahrheit.*[34]

To make clear that knowing is not to be replaced by faith, I want to draw upon another passage from *Beiträge zur Philosophie (Vom Ereignis)* where Heidegger says:

> Essential knowing (knowing that unfolds in its core) is staying within the domain of root-unfolding. This is to say that this knowing is not merely representing an encounter, but is carrying out a breakthrough of a projection which by opening up gets to know the abyss that sustains it.
>
> *Das wesentliche Wissen ist ein Sichhalten im Wesen. Damit soll ausgedrückt sein: Es ist kein blosses Vorstellen eines Begegnens, sondern das Aushalten innerhalb des Aufbruchs eines Entwerfens, das in der Eröffnung selbst den es tragenden Abgrund zu wissen bekommt.*[35]

What can be criticized in Sallis's text is that he fails to differentiate adequately the word *Wesen*. When Heidegger says *das Wesen der Wahrheit ist die Wahrheit des Wesens*, the word *Wesen* has two different meanings. In its first meaning the word *Wesen* means "what determines truth as truth." In this sense *Wesen* is usually translated as "essence." On the other hand, in its second meaning the word *Wesen* means "being" (*Sein*).

Sallis's lecture ends with the question concerning what is other than truth. This is an attempt to place this "other" outside truth in such a way that it has nothing to do with truth. Here Sallis returns to the beginning of his theme, where he said that, in dealing with the question of the essence of truth, what is ultimately "other" than truth is to such an extent "other" that we must speak of a kind of madness, a disease to which we are exposed. Without a doubt this is how the question of truth's root-unfolding appears to common sense. To the extent that we are delivered over to this understanding, Sallis's conclusion is correct.

In the end I must be grateful to my friend Sallis for having forced me to do a thorough reading of Heidegger's text. Every interpretation runs the risk of deforming the text, not only the interpretation that aims at unmasking the text itself as a deformation. Perhaps my own interpretation of deformation is a deformation, even though my interpretation is meant to remove the deformation.

The question remains: Can Heidegger's text *Vom Wesen der Wahrheit* really be interpreted as an expression of derangement, or is such an interpretation itself the result of a deranged interpretation?

PART THREE

RESPONSE

CHAPTER SIXTEEN

"... A WONDER THAT ONE COULD NEVER ASPIRE TO SURPASS."

John Sallis

Before I begin—
    Nearly everything will already have been written. Primarily, of course, the series of texts that Kenneth Maly has generously gathered and introduced. It goes without saying that I cannot begin without first of all thanking him for this veritable feast of discourses. Let me add that never have I wondered quite so intensely about reading as I did in reading these texts; and as, during a period of several weeks, I continued reading and rereading them, the effect was to undo virtually all the certainties that might initially have tempted me, presumed certainties as to what reading calls for and what calls for reading in the case of texts such as these that confound beyond recovery the distinctions between own and other, proximity and remoteness, anteriority and posteriority.
    Not only these texts, to which I promised something like a response, but also in another sense the response too will already have been written. For each of the short discourses that follow will be preceded by an epigraph, a few words gathering in advance what the discourse is to say, words already written, now redoubled, given voice again. In response. Recalling a way and marking a site.
    Nearly everything will already have been written. Indeed in these very words: *before I begin.*

1.

". . . a peculiar *return to beginnings,* a turning toward what already determines it."
Phenomenology and the Return to Beginnings

How is one to recall a way gone? How summon again that thinking, those times, that nothing less than time itself—threatening every *itself,* even that of thinking itself—has withdrawn? How revive from mere traces all the distress of perplexity, the passion of questioning, the attentiveness of reading, the cautious ecstasy of writing, the patience of waiting for what was hoped would come, for the words that might both open and seal a certain way.

Is there a tense—or can one be invented—in which it becomes possible to tell of another time without depriving it of its intensity and reducing it to a vague shadow of the present?

How is one, then, to retrace a way coming from another time? Only by remembrance. Only by thinking back along the way toward its beginning. Such rememorative thinking has nothing to do with representation: It does not aim at reproducing the way, at producing a duplicate, a present double of a past original (which could never simply be withheld and protected from the duplicity of reproduction). Rather, in remembrance one sets out to think what determined the way and extended its fortune. In remembrance one turns back to the beginning that will always have sustained thinking in its fortune, even rememorative thinking itself.

One will want, perhaps first of all, to remember thoughtfully what was bespoken in the word by which the beginning of philosophy was named in the beginning of philosophy, the word by which, even if always with a certain reference back to the Greek beginning, it has never ceased to be named. Both Plato and Aristotle call the beginning of philosophy: θαυμάζειν. Both Hegel and Heidegger repeat the name, even if in order to mark a certain distance from the Greek beginning.

Remembrance will trace more openly an exceeding of philosophy that philosophy itself already broached in its beginning: the return to the beginning, the move back from philosophy to the ἀρχή that precedes it and first makes it possible, the regression across the limit of philosophy to the ἀρχή from which it would first be delimited. Remembrance cannot but unfold as archaic thinking; and in archaic thinking remembrance will always already have commenced. In turning toward the ἀρχή, remembrance will always have been determined also by it. When one comes to pose a question of the beginning, that beginning will already, long since, have been in play, depriving the question of its privilege. One will not have been able to begin without being engaged in the beginning, engaged by it; and when one comes to question it, one only returns differently to it, interrogatively, turning toward what already determines the question.

Remembrance will translate the beginning. Into the stable, well-established English translation of θαυμάζειν it will undertake to translate what is bespoken in the decisive discourses on θαυμάζειν, in those discourses that at the limit of philosophy turn back to name its ἀρχή. The structure of such translation is quite different from that in which a Greek word is merely transliterated or reinscribed in English; it is different, too, from that in which an English cognate of a Latin translation is activated. For *wonder* offers a certain resistance to the translation, that is, it brings its own semantic force into play in a kind of oblique resistance that skews the translation, yet in such a way as to promise a translation in which those ancient discourses may be opened beyond themselves. It is a matter of bringing the semantic force of *wonder* to supplement what is sounded in those discourses, echoing them in another tongue, making them resound in the sounding of *wonder.*

What are some of the things that sound in *wonder?*

There sounds amazement in the face of extraordinary occurrences, the rapture into which one is drawn in beholding mysterious or magical events that appear to bespeak the unknown or to portend what is to come. As in the case of Macbeth, whose letter to his wife tells of his wondrous encounter with the three witches. Hailed by them not only as Thane of Cawdor but also as king to be, he burned with desire to question them further about their more than mortal knowledge. Yet, charged by him to reveal the origin and intent of their prophecy, the witches vanish:

> When I burned in desire to question them further,
> They made themselves air, into which they vanished.
> Whiles I stood rapt in the wonder of it, . . .
>
> *(Macbeth* I, v, 4–6)

Its sound is not very different from that of its Anglo-Saxon ancestor *wundor:* a wondrous thing, a portent, something outside the usual course of nature, like the tracks of the dragon pursued in *Beowulf,* like the dragon itself or the strange creatures (*wundra*) that assaulted Beowulf in the deep (*Beowulf* 840, 1509). Transliterating the Latin, opening *wonder* to its history, one says: monster.

There sounds too the wonder of a vision in which one comes to see the world anew, in which it opens as if for the first time so as to disclose something wondrous. As when Miranda exclaims:

> O, wonder!
> How many goodly creatures are there here!
> How beauteous mankind is! O brave new world
> That has such people in't!
>
> *(The Tempest* V, i, 181–184)

Wonder, as in the face of a young child suddenly beholding something for the first time.

2.

"... putting an end to wonder"
Spacings—of Reason and Imagination

The Aristotelian discourse on wonder occurs within a discussion of the knowledge (ἐπιστήμη) that is most archontic (ἀρχικωτάτη), that is, most royal, most suited to rule. Both the knowledge thus determined and the treatise to which the discussion belongs will later be designated by the word *metaphysics*. Such knowledge is said to consist in speculation (θεωρητική) regarding first beginnings and causes (τῶν πρώτων ἀρχῶν καὶ αἰτιῶν). Aristotle's concern is to show that such speculation is not a matter of production (ποιητική), that philosophy is not pursued in order to produce something. This is shown by consideration of the first philosophers, by turning to the beginning of philosophy, to that beginning from which philosophy proceeded in its beginning. In the turn Aristotle thus doubles the beginning: "It is through wonder that men now begin and first began to philosophize" (*Mtp.* I, 982b12–13).[1] Hence, wonder is identified as the beginning of philosophy both in the beginning and now. All begin from wonder (ἀπὸ τοῦ θαυμάζειν) (*Mtp.* I, 983a12–13) both in the past and in the present. Only as regards the operation of this beginning in the future does Aristotle remain—initially—silent.

Aristotle outlines a progression through which wonder moves: from perplexities regarding things close at hand to perplexities about the genesis of all that is. Thus, wonder would function as beginning not only in the beginning of speculation but throughout its entire course up to the point at which it would finally open upon the whole of what is.

How does wonder function as a beginning throughout the course of speculation? It functions by bringing about an awareness of ignorance: "Now he who wonders and is perplexed considers himself ignorant" (*Mtp.* I, 982b12–13). Wonder is like the sting of the gadfly, driving men out of their pretense to know, setting them adrift in their ignorance, as if paralyzed by a stingray. It is in order to escape the ignorance made manifest through wonder that men pursue philosophy, the aim of which is thus simply knowledge and not production. Thus, it is by making ignorance manifest, by bringing about perplexity, that wonder incites the pursuit of knowledge and functions as the beginning of philosophy.

Aristotle adds that myth, too, can incite the pursuit of knowledge, that the lover of myth (ὁ φιλόμυθος) is in a sense a philosopher. But this is only because myth is composed of wonders (ἐκ θαυμασίων). Philosophy can begin from μῦθος only because the wonders in the μῦθος incite one to pursue knowledge. And yet—one cannot but notice—the wonders within μῦθος (for instance, the wonder of Er's return from the underworld, the wonder of his (re)embodiment) are not quite the same as that kind to which Aristotle's text seems otherwise to refer, a wonder in alliance with perplexity (ἀπορία), a wonder linked more to λόγος than to μῦθος.

Yet, wonder is only the beginning, inciting men in the beginning and now. Wonder does not belong to the future toward which the pursuit of knowledge moves. Rather, that pursuit, Aristotle insists, must lead to the opposite (εἰς τοὐναντίον) of that with which inquiry began (983a12). He repeats that all begin by wondering that things are as they are. But now—most remarkably—he presents wonder not only as making ignorance manifest but also as essentially linked to, even constituted by ignorance: the incommensurability of the diagonal of a square seems wonderful (θαυμαστόν . . . δοκεῖ) to everyone who has not beheld the cause thereof. One ends, he says, with the opposite and the better: the opposite not only of ignorance but also of wonder. Thus, in the end knowledge is opposed, as the better, to wonder. Though it is through wonder that one comes to pursue knowledge, that pursuit has the effect finally of dissolving wonder. In the end there would be no place for wonder in knowledge, no place for a knowledge to which wonder would be essential and not merely an incitement. In the end there would be only knowledge, beyond the wonder of perplexity, beyond the wonders that compose μῦθος. Philosophy would achieve its end by putting an end to wonder.

Hegel renews the Aristotelian discourse on wonder. One such renewal occurs in the philosophy of subjective spirit, specifically, in that part of the psychology devoted to intuition (*Anschauung*). In displacing wonder from metaphysics to psychology Hegel only carries out the displacement that Aristotle has fully prepared by linking wonder to ignorance and opposing it in the end to the knowledge in which it would finally have been dissolved. Hegel puts an end to wonder still more decisively by assimilating wonder to intuition. Thus, it is in a discussion in which Hegel is concerned to explain how intuition is only the beginning of knowledge (*der Beginn des Erkennens*) that he recalls and confirms the Aristotelian discourse:

> *Aristotle* refers to its [intuition's] place when he says that all knowledge begins from *wonder* [*Verwunderung*]. Initially, the object is still loaded with the form of the irrational, and it is because it is within this that subjective reason as intuition has the certainty, though only the *indeterminate certainty,* of finding itself again, that its subject matter inspires it with wonder and awe. *Philosophical* thought, however, has to raise itself above the standpoint of wonder.[2]

With Hegel it is a matter of putting an end to wonder as soon as knowledge progresses beyond intuition. That end, that aim, that function, that Aristotle granted to wonder as the beginning of philosophy is now virtually withdrawn from it, even in confirming the Aristotelian statement that all knowledge has its beginning in wonder. For it is no longer wonder but the power of negativity that drives the advance of knowledge. Wonder belongs neither to the future nor to the present of philosophy but only to its past. And even if, like every past, it is retained in the depth of the present and the future, it is not retained *as wonder.*

Another discussion of wonder is found in the *Aesthetics.*[3] Referring again to Aristotle, Hegel broadens the context by declaring wonder to be the beginning from which art, religion, and philosophy arise; all the forms of absolute knowledge are thus said to have begun from wonder, even though their determination as absolute prescribes that they will—now, in the future perfect—have surpassed wonder. In the case of art, in particular, wonder is said to come into play in the origination of the symbolic form of art, the least developed form of art, a form that, strictly speaking, constitutes only preart (*Vorkunst*) and not yet art as such. Hegel locates wonder in the interval between a *not yet* and a *no longer.* One who does not yet wonder lives still in obtuseness and stupidity, bound to the immediate individual existence of objects, not yet free. On the other hand, one who no longer wonders has broken with such externality and has become clear about it, transforming the objects and their existence into a spiritual and self-conscious insight into them. Wonder occurs in the interval where one has already separated oneself from the most immediate, purely practical relation to nature, that of desire, where one thus stands back and seeks in things something universal, implicit (*Ansichseiendes*), and permanent. At this stage things remain other, an other in which one strives to find oneself again. One is conscious of them as external, natural things, and yet one has a certain awareness, a presentiment (*Ahnung*), of something higher, something spiritual. The contradiction between nature and spirit thus embodied in natural things renders them both attractive and repulsive. It is this feeling of the contradiction along with the urge to resolve it that generates wonder. Within this interval of wonder art has the form of symbol. When developed independently and in its proper form, it has also the character of sublimity.[4]

But only within the interval. When the classical form of art, art proper, comes upon the scene, then the symbol, the sublime, and wonder itself will have been surpassed. In the presence of Greek sculpture there will no longer have been any wonder in play.

In the future perfect of philosophy and of art hardly a trace of wonder is still to be found. And yet, even a trace may make one hesitate to join in putting an end to wonder. Or rather, it may prompt a reversal in which one would submit the end to wonder, bringing wonder to bear upon that very end that would have alleged to bring it to an end. Now, opening wonder to the future.

3.

> "... provoked by the mixing-up
> of opposites ..."
>
> *Being and Logos*

The Platonic discourse on wonder occurs in the *Theaetetus*. This is the only Platonic dialogue that is doubly written: it is authored not only by Plato but also, except for the introductory conversation, by Euclides of Megara. One function of the introductory conversation is to betray the double authorship: Euclides relates to Terpsion that he had once gone to Athens and heard from Socrates himself an account of the latter's conversation with Theaetetus; Euclides goes on to tell that, upon returning to Megara, he wrote down some reminders of the conversation and that subsequently as he recalled things he wrote them down, checking with Socrates on subsequent visits to Athens so as to fill out what he could not remember. He concludes: "So nearly the whole discourse has been written by me" (*Theaet.* 142d). Euclides shows Terpsion the resulting book (βιβλίον) and explains how he composed it, transforming it from a dialogue narrated by Socrates into one directly presented. That transformation will not only, as Euclides says, have eliminated the tedious repetition of such phrases as "and I said"; it will also have eliminated whatever Socrates may have reported about the conversation other than the actual speeches. Thus, Euclides's book, doubling the Socratic narrative, is different from it (and not only by virtue of the difference between speech and writing). Euclides's book is also different from Plato's, though only by virtue of the addition of the introductory conversation. As for the conversation between Socrates and Theaetetus, its inscription is one and the same in both books. In the dialogue the inscription is framed as doubly authored.

The entire dialogue can be read as a discourse on wonder, gathered around a single passage in which wonder is identified as the beginning of philosophy. The entire dialogue is framed by occurrences of forms of the word, both in the final speech by Socrates and at the outset, in the response to Euclides's opening question about Terpsion's arrival from the country: Terpsion explains that he arrived some time ago and that he has been wondering (ἐθαύμαζον) that he could not find Euclides in the marketplace. A brief report on his recent whereabouts leads up to Euclides's account of his authorship of the book from which will be read the conversation between Socrates and Theaetetus. Euclides tells of going down to the harbor (εἰς λιμένα καταβαίνων); as in the opening speech of the *Republic* Socrates had told of going down to Piraeus (κατέβην ... εἰς Πειραιᾶ), the harbor of Athens; as Odysseus had told of how he "went down [κατέβην] to Hades to inquire about the return of myself and my friends" (*Odyssey* XXIII.252–253). There Euclides met Theaetetus, wounded and suffering from dysentery, being carried from the army camp at Corinth to Athens. A little later Euclides will tell of how he accompanied Theaetetus part of the way from Megara to Athens, as far as Erineos, situated on the Cephisus river, also said to have been the place where Persephone was snatched away by Hades.[5]

When Euclides reports that Theaetetus has been praised for his conduct in the battle, Terpsion responds that it would have been more to be wondered (θαυμαστότερον) had he not so conducted himself. Euclides reports his own wonder: as he was returning from Erineos, having accompanied Theaetetus, he recalled and wondered (ἐθαύμασα) at Socrates, at how prophetically (μαντικῶς) the latter had spoken of Theaetetus. Socrates, says Euclides, had met Theaetetus a little before his own death and on the basis of conversation with the young Theaetetus had expressed great admiration for the lad. The conversation is the one that Euclides goes on to report having written down in the book, which is now to be read to Euclides and Terpsion by another, unnamed boy.

Theaetetus proves to be a double of Socrates, closely resembling him in appearance (with his snub nose and protruding eyes), just as the young Socrates (mentioned at 147c–d), who remains silent throughout, is his double in λόγος. Telling Socrates of Theaetetus just before the lad arrives on the scene, Theodorus praises him as being wonderfully fine (θαυμαστῶς εὖ), as one who advances in learning as a stream of olive oil flows without a sound; one wonders (θαυμάσαι) that someone of his age conducts himself in such fashion. Thus is wonder gathered around Theaetetus. Before he ever appears in the dialogue, one knows that he is wondrous.

And yet, as the book in which the conversation is inscribed is being read, Theaetetus is dying. The inscribed conversation takes place not only under the shadow of the impending death of Theaetetus but also under that of the death of Socrates. Euclides has reported that the conversation took place a little before Socrates's death; indeed the conversation ends with Socrates's telling that he must go to the porch of the king to meet the indictment drawn up by Meletus. Thus, as regards its dramatic date, the *Theaetetus*—or, more precisely, the conversation inscribed in it between Socrates and Theaetetus—is the first in that series of dialogues that lead up to the death of Socrates.

Nonetheless, these shadows of death serve to accentuate the opposite, the expectancy of birth and the flowering of youth that inform the conversation between Socrates and Theaetetus. The conversation brings back the dying Theaetetus, brings him back in the vigor of his youth. It also brings on the scene a young Socrates, who silently doubles a Socrates brought back from his death. In the conversation as read to Euclides and Terpsion, both Socrates and Theaetetus, thus brought back from death, are reborn in a conversation devoted largely to birth, especially to the birth of philosophy.

For the question that Socrates asks Theaetetus, "What is knowledge (ἐπιστήμη)?" it suffices neither merely to number (ἀριθμῆσαι) the various forms, to collect them in an enumeration of types, nor to divide, as Theodorus and Theaetetus had divided the numbers into square and oblong. He must, rather, says Socrates, try to address the many knowledges with one discourse (λόγος). Or rather, Theaetetus must try to give birth to such a discourse; for, as Socrates tells him in response to his plea of incapacity, "you're suffering labor pains, on account of your not being empty but pregnant" (148e). Socrates, the midwife ready to assist him, thus launches on his own discourse describing his peculiar art. It is a wonderful art that this son of a midwife practices, also an art over which the Socratic daimon exercises a certain authority. The greatest thing (μέγιστον) in this art is that it can test whether the thought of a young man is giving birth to an image and a lie (εἴδωλον καὶ ψεῦδος) or to something fruitful and true (γόνιμόν τε καὶ ἀληθές). Socrates declares that those who associate with him and receive the benefits of his art make wonderful (θαυμαστόν) progress. Many of these, he observes, thinking they alone are responsible and even despising him, have departed earlier than they should have, only to suffer abortion or to rear badly what Socrates had midwifed. Recognizing their foolishness, they have often returned to Socrates, begging for renewed association and doing wondrous (θαυμαστά) things; whereupon, says Socrates, "the daimon that comes to me checks me from associating with some and allows me to associate with some" (151a).

Theaetetus is quickly delivered: he declares that knowledge is nothing else than perception or sensing (αἴσθησις).

Socrates sets to work determining whether the declaration is fruitful or only a wind-egg. He refers indeed to the wind, applying to it the maxim of Protagoras that man is the measure of all things, observing thus that the same wind may be cold to one person and not cold to another. He continues: sensing is always the sensing of something that is (τοῦ ὄντος), of something existent that appears (φαίνεται) to sensing. Because, according to Theaetetus, sensing is knowledge, it cannot be false. The consequence can be foreseen: such sensing as knowledge, such sense-knowledge, must be knowledge of things that truly are, knowledge of them in their truth. Yet—most remarkably—Socrates foregoes saying that the wind is in truth both cold and not cold, invoking the Graces instead of declaring openly such mixing of opposites, invoking the Graces and then charging Protagoras with having put forth enigmas while reserving the truth for his pupils.

Theaetetus's response is most telling: "How, then, are you saying this, Socrates?" (152d). The response may of course be taken as a request that Socrates explain what his reference to Protagoras's esoteric teaching only suggests. Yet, it may also be taken to refer back to the consequence that Socrates left unsaid; for what Socrates goes on to say in the uncommon discourse that immediately follows is precisely how one says the mixing (κρᾶσις) of opposites. Again it is a matter of birth, of a birth attested to by a great line of philosophers and poets (including Protagoras, Heraclitus, Empedocles, Epicharmus, Homer and excluding only one philosopher, Parmenides): the birth of all things from flow and motion. Thus it is that nothing is one itself by itself (ἓν . . . αὐτὸ καθ᾽ αὑτό). Socrates continues: "But if you address it as large, it will also appear small, and if heavy, light . . ." (152d). It is not as though the opposites simply appear mixed with one another such that something is then said, for example, to be both large and small. Such is precisely the kind of saying that Socrates has left unsaid. Rather, the mixing of opposites comes to light precisely in and through discourse: if you *address* it as large, it will also appear small. Even its appearing small cannot, given the flow of all things, be independent of discourse and of the determinacy (the being one itself by itself) that discourse puts into effect. It is in discourse that the determinate opposition is constituted, and thus it is only in relation to discourse that the mixing of opposites can become manifest as such.

Extending the discussion, Socrates remarks finally to Theaetetus: "We're being compelled somehow to say recklessly some wondrous and laughable things [θαυμαστά τε καὶ γελοῖα], as Protagoras would say and everyone who tries to say the same as he does" (154b). What is wondrous and laughable is (to say) that one cannot say the same, that there is no same to be said, or rather, that sameness (being one itself by itself) belongs only to saying. And yet, for that reason the mixing-up of opposites in discourse is even more wondrous. As in the paradigm that Socrates offers in response to Theaetetus's query: the six dice that are more than four and less than twelve—that, therefore, not only are both more and less but also can become more without being increased. Theaetutus's response is now itself mixed, both affirming and denying the mixing that Socrates has posed. When Socrates goes on to elaborate the conflict, Theaetetus finally responds by confessing his wonder: "Yes indeed, by the gods, Socrates, I wonder exceedingly [ὑπερφυῶς . . . θαυμάζω] as to what these things are, and sometimes in looking at them I get truly dizzy" (155c). Thus is Theaetetus wonderstruck by what must and yet cannot be said in reference to the mixing-up of opposites. Thus is his wonder provoked by the mixing-up of opposites. One can imagine even the look of wonder on his Socratic face; one can imagine even that in the account that Euclides heard Socrates give of the conversation there may well have been reference to the appearance of wonder in the protruding eyes of Theaetetus; but Euclides's manner of composing his book (double-authored with Plato) subordinates everything to discourse, lets things appear only in relation to discourse, thus enacting precisely what it says.

Socrates remarks that Theodorus's guess about Theaetetus's nature—that it is philosophic—is not a bad one, since the pathos of wonder (τὸ πάθος, τὸ θαυμάζειν) is very much that of a philosopher: "for nothing else is the beginning [ἀρχή] of philosophy than this, and, seemingly, whoever said that Iris was the offspring of Thaumas made a not bad genealogy" (155d). One who said this was of course Hesiod: according to his genealogy Thaumas married Electra, and among their offspring was Iris (*Theogony* 265–266). If one takes the names for what they say, then one may say: The rainbow (Iris) is the offspring of wonder (Thaumas) and shining (Electra). Furthermore, both Thaumas and Electra are linked genealogically to Ocean and Tethys;[6] earlier in the conversation, in that uncommon discourse in which Socrates marshalled the great line of philosophers and poets, Homer's saying "Ocean and mother Tethys, the genesis of the gods" is interpreted as saying that everything is the offspring of flowing and motion (152e). Hence, in the beginning there is flowing and motion; and then, born therefrom, if not directly, there is wonder and shining (that is, appearing to sense). There is, as in Theaetetus, the wonder provoked by the appearance of a mixing-up of opposites. The offspring of Thaumas (wonder) is the rainbow and philosophy. Not only this, but also the determination of wonder as the beginning of philosophy is presented as confirmation of the genealogy by which the rainbow is the offspring of wonder.

What does philosophy have to do with the rainbow? Iris is a messenger of the gods to men, and it is this vocation that is evoked in the *Cratylus:* "Iris [Ἶρις] also seems to have received her name from εἴρειν [to speak], because she is a messenger" (*Crat.* 408b). Both philosophy and the rainbow have to do with discourse; for instance, with the discursive distinction between the different colors that blend into one another in the shining rainbow that joins heaven and earth.

Homer speaks of "rainbows that the son of Chronos has set in the clouds, a portent for man" (*Iliad* XI.27–28). A portent (τέρας) is a sign, a marvel, something wonderful that serves as an omen; it may be even some wondrous creature, a monster (Latin: *monstrum*). As in Theaetetus (and perhaps in every philosophic nature) there is a bit of monstrosity: for it is Theaetetus's nature to wonder exceedingly (ὑπερφυῶς); it is his nature to exceed nature.

Yet, the rainbow is not merely a sign sent from heaven to earth but rather is such that in being sent it spans and thus discloses in its openness the very space across which it is sent, that between earth and sky, between the abode of mortals and that reserved for immortal gods. As philosophy, beginning in the discourse of wonder, opens the space between that which appears to sense and that which is said (that is, set forth in and through discourse).

The opening of philosophy is traced perhaps most directly in a discussion between Socrates and Glaucon in Book 7 of the *Republic*.[7] Socrates focuses on those sensings that are such as to provoke thought (νόησις), calling them those that at once (ἅμα) go over to the opposite. Again it is a matter of such mixing-up of opposites as is shown in the *Theaetetus* to provoke wonder and thus the beginning of philosophy. Now the example is that of three fingers: the index finger, which appears large in relation to the smallest finger but which appears small in relation to the middle finger, so that in the index finger there is a mixing-up of large and small. What is required is an opening in which the mixture can be sorted out. Here is the discussion of that sorting:

> "Therefore," I said, "it's likely that in such cases a soul, summoning calculation [λογισμός] and intellection [νόησις], first tries to determine whether each of the things reported to it is one or two."
> "Of course."

"If it appears to be two, won't each of the two appear to be different and to be one?"

"Yes."

"Then, if each is one and both two, the soul will think the two as separate. For it would not think the inseparable as two but as one."

"Right."

"But sight, too, saw large and small, we say, not separated, however, but mixed up together. Isn't that so?"

"Yes."

"In order to clear this up the intellect was compelled to see large and small, too, not mixed up together but distinguished, doing the opposite of what the sight did." (*Rep.* 524b–c)

Thus, it is a matter of a distinguishing that separates the mixture into distinct "ones," taking what *large* says and what *small* says, taking each by itself, taking each as being itself one by itself. And then, it is a matter of posing—or rather, of already having posed and now only enforcing—these "ones" (the large and the small) in their distinctness (each being itself one by itself) over against the mixture; it is a matter of spacing, of letting a space open between these "ones" and the mixing-up of opposites that appears to sense.

Socrates says: "And it was thus that we called the one intelligible (νοητόν] and the other visible [ὁρατόν]" (524c). Thus philosophy opens. Thus it begins in the Platonic beginning. Provoked by the mixing-up of opposites, philosophy begins from wonder.

4.

> "Nothing escapes the play . . . , the
> play of indeterminate dyads."
> *The Gathering of Reason*

Not only in the beginning but also now, in the end, in the future perfect, wonder will have remained the beginning.

Thus one returns to wonder in the end, returns again finally to the beginning, putting the end to wonder, or rather, letting the end be provocative, letting it provoke wonder, or rather—one suspects—reawaken wonder from its metaphysical slumber.

For the end is that which has been called the end of metaphysics. No doubt a great deal of caution is required if this phrase is to be used in a rigorous discourse. One must distinguish the relevant sense of end from others that have been posed for—and by—metaphysics: most notably, that by which the end would consist in a gathering of metaphysics into its fulfillment; and, all too symmetrically opposed to this, the sense that would make of the end of metaphysics its mere termination. In every case one must be attentive also to the slippage to which the sense of end is exposed in the end of metaphysics, since it is within metaphysics that the sense(s) of end (to say nothing of the sense[s] of sense) will have been determined. One must also hold in a certain suspension the assumption of homogeneity that would otherwise be put in play by discourse on the end of metaphysics—that is, one will need to leave the name suspended between singular and plural. Nonetheless, whatever the extent of the pluralizing heterogeneity, the Platonic beginning remains decisive. Metaphysics—whether singular, plural, or both—will always have begun with the opening between intelligible and sensible. Even if this beginning remains largely unrecalled, metaphysics circulates within the space thus opened; and insofar as it assumes that space, taking the opening for granted, it is authorized to put an end to wonder. For wonder, provoked by the mixing-up of opposites, is what first draws one into the opening. It is as such that wonder is the beginning of philosophy.

But what is wonder? The question comes too late. For when one comes to ask the philosophical question "What is . . . ?" ("τί ἐστι . . . ?"), one moves already within the opening; and wonder has already come into play in prompting that opening. The operation of wonder belongs to the very condition of the question "What is wonder?", and one will never be able simply to disengage that question from the wonder about which it would ask. One will never be able to interrogate wonder philosophically except by way of a questioning that the operation of wonder will already have determined. To say nothing of all the means that philosophy would bring into play in response to the question, in declaring wonder to be, for instance, a passion of the soul, in assimilating it, for instance, to intuition.

The end of metaphysics inhibits the question even more. For this end brings, in Nietzsche's formula, the final inversion of Platonism, the inversion which constitutes the final possibility of metaphysics, the possibility which announces the exhaustion of all possibilities of circulating within the space of the Platonic opening. Once—in Nietzsche's phrase—the true world finally becomes a fable, once what was called the intelligible drifts away further and further and finally without limit, rendering the space of metaphysics unlimited, or rather, reducing it again to the plane of sense, then the very resources that would enable the question are themselves put into question, set adrift. And yet, one is then drawn back to the place of wonder, to the place where, in a discourse addressed to the mixing-up within what came to be called the sensible, wonder was in the beginning provoked.

Let it, then, be said: the end of metaphysics brings a return to wonder, prompts a return of wonder.

Yet, the provocation of wonder at the end, of a wonder that would be the beginning of a thinking at the limit of metaphysics, would not be quite the same as in the beginning. One would of course be drawn back toward the discursively articulated mixing-up of sensible opposites. And yet, precisely because the discourse in relation to which the mixing-up would appear to sense is nothing other than the discourse fashioned and empowered by the history of metaphysics, that discourse cannot but effect the double separation, that between opposites and that between the mixed-up sensible opposites and the distinct intelligible opposites. It is a discourse that *means* something, a discourse that in its very operation is taken to mean something, to exceed what appears to sense, to open the difference between meaning and sense, between two different senses of sense. Even if in the end of metaphysics meaning is set utterly adrift, language does not cease to mark the difference that two millenia of shaping and theorizing have taught it to mark. Inasmuch as one continues to speak the language of metaphysics—is there any other?—one continues to exceed the plane of sense, opening the difference that is bespoken by the ambiguity in the word *sense,* the gigantic difference within *sense.*

What now cannot but provoke wonder is the γιγαντομαχία into which one is thus drawn. For the end of metaphysics brings a double effacement of that which would be opposed to the sensible (that is, to what has been called the sensible). On the one hand, the intelligible is effaced as original, as independent of its sensible imagings and as governing such imagings. Now there will be no preventing its becoming in turn an image, if not in a simple reversal then at least in a perhaps unlimited chain of pairs, related as image/original without any final anchoring in an original as such that would be itself immune to the play of imaging. On the other hand, the intelligible is effaced as meaning, or, more precisely, as preestablished meaning such as would antedate discourse, as a transcendental signified that would precede and govern from without the play of signifiers.

However much meaningful discourse drives one beyond sense, the intelligible can no longer be released from the play of discourse and sense and posited over against that play, aloof from it. The dyads cannot be submitted to final determination by reference to a term that would no longer be itself determined by dyadic linkage. Thus would wonder be provoked at the end of metaphysics: wonder at the play of the indeterminately dyadic, wonder at the gigantic opening within the word *sense.*

One could also call it poetic wonder, provided *poetic* is either diverted toward what Jacques Derrida calls *invention* or referred back to the ποίησις that Heidegger sought to preserve in advance of its determination as production (*Herstellung*). It is a matter of wonder at the power of the sense image to bring forth its original and of discourse to bring forth meaning, to bring forth in the double (one would have said, at least, almost contradictory) sense of both first giving place to (letting take place) *and yet* uncovering as already there (not simply produced). It is a matter of wonder at a bringing-forth that is both inaugural and memorial—like remembrance. One could call it a wonder of imagination.

5.

". . . to *hover* between heaven and
earth, . . ."
Delimitations

Can wonder be provoked still more archaically? Can it be provoked by what one might call still—even in the end of metaphysics—the ἀρχή: neither an intelligible nor *the* intelligible nor even the beginning of the intelligible, but rather the opening, the openness, within which sense could be exceeded and dyads brought into play? Such wonder would be in place before one could come to address something *as* something, for instance, to address as large what then would appear small, such that a mixing of opposites would become manifest, provoking the wonder at the beginning of philosophy. Archaic wonder would also be in place before discourse could exceed sense and broach the opening, setting in play the dyads that, even in the end of metaphysics, still would provoke wonder. Such archaic wonder would be, not just the beginning of philosophy (in its beginning or in its end and transmutation), but rather a beginning that would precede philosophy, a turning toward the beginning in which the very space of philosophy would open. The place of such wonder would be the very unfolding of place as such, the spacing of the ἀρχή, archaic spacing.

Heidegger attests to a wonder that, like such archaic wonder, would not simply stand at the beginning of philosophy. Referring to a wonder that, instead, would sustain and in a sense govern philosophy throughout, he writes: "To say that philosophy arises from wonder means [*heisst*]: it *is* essentially something wondrous and becomes more wondrous the more it becomes what it is."[8]

In *Was Ist Das—Die Philosophie?* Heidegger refers to the πάθος of wonder (*Erstaunen*) and translates πάθος as *Stimmung* or *dis-position,* proposing thereby to avoid understanding it in the modern psychological sense. Wonder (θαυμάζειν) he then characterizes as a stepping back in the face of beings ("Wir treten gleichsam zurück vor dem Seienden"), a stepping back that becomes attentive to beings, that they *are* and that they are *so* and not otherwise. Thus to step back is at once to be also transported to and bound by that before which one has stepped back. Wonder is, hence, the "dis-position in which and for which the Being of beings opens up."[9]

In the lecture course of 1937–38 *Grundfragen der Philosophie,* Heidegger discusses wonder at much greater length. Again he regards wonder as *Stimmung,* taking the latter as a displacement (*Versetzung*) by which one is brought into a fundamental relation to beings as such. Wonder (θαυμάζειν—now Heidegger writes it: *das Er-staunen*) is the fundamental attunement (*Grundstimmung*) that—at least for the Greeks—was the origin of philosophy. Heidegger carefully distinguishes wonder from a variety of related forms of attunement: surprise

(*Sichwundern, Verwundern*), in which one is struck by something out of the ordinary; admiration (*Bewundern*), in which one frees oneself, sets oneself over against, the extraordinary thing or event by which one is struck; astonishment (*Staunen, Bestaunen*), in which one is thrown back by the extraordinary. Wonder, Heidegger insists, is essentially different from these forms; for in all three of them there is a determinate individual thing, something extraordinary, that is set off, contrasted, with the things of ordinary experience. In wonder, on the other hand, "the most ordinary becomes itself the most extraordinary" (GA 45: 166). Everything becomes extraordinary (GA 45: 174), and one is displaced into the utter unfamiliarity of the familiar, into an inverted world.[10] Yet, what is most ordinary is simply that which is, beings; and what is extraordinary about them is that they *are*. Wonder, says Heidegger, brings the most ordinary forth in such a way that it announces its extraordinariness, shines forth as extraordinary. Wonder attends to the outbreak of the extraordinariness of the ordinary. Wonder, says Heidegger, opens to what is "uniquely wondrous, namely: the whole as the whole, the whole as being [*als das Seiende*], beings as a whole [*das Seiende im Ganzen*], *that* they *are what* they *are; beings as beings, ens qua ens*, τὸ ὂν ᾗ ὄν." He adds: "What is named here by the *as,* the *qua,* the ᾗ, is the 'between' thrown open in wonder, the open space . . . in which beings as such come into play, namely, as the beings *they* are, into the *play of their Being* [Spiel seines Seins]" (GA 45: 168–169).

In a sense, then, Heidegger ventures to say what wonder is: not, however, by submitting it to the philosophical question of *what* it *is,* but rather by situating it, delimiting its place, with respect to the very shining forth of the *is,* by bringing out its attunement to the very opening of the *as* of beings *as* beings. Thus, in spite of all that he says of wonder, Heidegger can also insist that such wondrous displacement withdraws as such from explanation, from analysis of the sort that would resolve it into various components. If one can in a sense say what wonder is, one can do so only through a *Wiederholung,* only by "a reproject [*Rückentwurf*] of the simplicity [*Einfachheit*] and strangeness *of that displacement* of man into beings as such, which takes place [*sich ereignet*] as wonder, which remains just as incomprehensible as the beginning [*Anfang*] to which it is bound" (GA 45: 171).

One could think archaic wonder only in the return to it, only in a certain doubling back to its place as that of the opening of beings as such. It is a matter, then, of how the opening is to be thought, or, more precisely, a matter of that *from which* the opening is to be thought, a matter of that from which the spacing of the ἀρχή would take place. No doubt it is to be thought, as Heidegger insists, from beings *as* beings. Then one may, extending the project of fundamental ontology, undertake to think the space in which beings come into the play of their Being—that is, to think what would be called *Temporalität, Lichtung,*

Ereignis, to think (the) beyond (of) Being (ἐπέκεινα τῆς οὐσίας), as did also Plato. Or one may insist on pairing such a project with another, with one that would be attentive to the eruption of questioning from out of beings as a whole; a project that in adhering to beings *as* beings would in the end be no project at all but rather a return to thrownness, a *Wiederholung* of the thrownness of the project (as in metontology, to recall the most striking title that Heidegger gave it).

And yet, beings as beings always also—from the beginning, before every beginning—*appear to sense;* the opening is always also an opening within what one can call (twisting it free of the metaphysical opposition): *the sensible.* Is archaic spacing not, then, to be thought from the sensible? Is it not in the opening from and within the sensible that archaic wonder has its place? *From and within the sensible*—a spacing that would trace within the sensible the opening from the sensible, the opening in which the sensible would be exceeded, either in the metaphysical opposition of intelligible to sensible or in the play of indeterminate dyads that commences in the end of metaphysics. From and within the sensible—just as the word *sense,* which comes to be divided from itself (divided into two different senses of sense—an abysmal division, presupposing itself), is nonetheless divided within itself, enclosing the gigantic space in which both imaging and discourse have their place.

One would return, then, to a wonder placed at an opening from and within the sensible, an opening that in a sense—in *sense* itself, if there could be sense *itself*—would precede even the play of beings in their Being, a foreplay, a prelude, as with Wordsworth:

> As if awakened, summoned, roused, constrained,
> I looked for universal things; perused
> The common countenance of earth and sky.
>
> ("The Prelude," 3: 105–107)

One would return, then, to a wonder whose place would be to hover, like a dove, between heaven and earth, open to the wondrous shining of the rainbow that joins earth and sky even while setting them apart. Then one might abandon oneself to the wondrous sights and sounds of earth and sky and, in Emerson's sense, draw a new circle, a circle that would open upon everything that could be said or that could appear to sense:

> The one thing which we seek with insatiable desire, is to forget ourselves, to be surprised out of our propriety, to lose our sempiternal memory, and to do something without knowing how or why; in short, to draw a new circle. Nothing great was ever achieved without enthusiasm. The way of life is wonderful: it is by abandonment.[11]

6.

"'. . . the time when the overturning of
Platonism became for Nietzsche a twisting
free of it . . . .'"

Crossings

At decisive junctures in their texts both Rodolphe Gasché and Kenneth
Maly invoke a "wonder that one could never aspire to surpass," Gasché looking
ahead to the reflection of such wonder in thinking ("a wonder to be reflected in a
new, very new kind of thinking"), Maly linking it to the naming of the issue of
imaging, the very naming that his text ventures in such words as *boundary* and
shimmering. Yet my extended discussion of wonder is not intended only in response to these two texts. The intent is rather to mark the site of a possible response to nearly all the texts. Let me acknowledge right away—without even
proposing to delimit the differences, indeed without even establishing that there
are differences—that this site, this place of wonder, lies on the same terrain as
that on which unfolds the θεῖα μανία bespoken in the *Phaedrus* and the mad
imagination ("imadgination") traced in its derangement in John Llewelyn's text.
It is also the terrain of ecstacy. It is, for instance, the terrain on which François
Dastur places imagination as it becomes ecstatic by opening to something irreducibly absent, something incapable of becoming a *position* outside the play of
imagination, its free play, its delicacy.

This site, this place of wonder, is the opening within which beings come into
play as being, ἦ ὄν—both ὄν and *being* hovering between the nominal and the
verbal in the manner that Jacques Derrida exposes with respect to such words as
spacing(s) (and *hovering* itself). Indeed, the place of wonder is, in more precise
terms, a spacing, an opening from and within the sensible. As such it is not only
the place but equally the time of wonder. It is a time other than that determined by
presence to self, for the latter would be constituted only in the enstatical recoil
from the time to which wonder would extend. Another time, then, a time whose
saying calls for another tense—*un autre temps.*

Wonder, too, if thought *from* this time, would prove to escape determination
by presence, that is, it would be irreducible both to intuition (*Anschauung*) and to
the various powers that come to compensate for the finitude of human intuition.
This otherness of wonder, its anteriority, is indeed bespoken in what was heard
sounding in *wonder:* rapture in the face of extraordinary beings who foretell something of what is to come only then to vanish by their supernatural or monstrous
power (*monstrosity* naming precisely a mode of exceeding nature within nature—
nature as determined by presence); a vision to which the world opens anew, unac-
countably, hence, a vision irreducible to an intuition of something present—such
vision as one can behold in the face of a young child. One could draw a parallel be-

tween such wonder and imagination, since neither can be enclosed within metaphysics: In his reading of "Imagination and Metaphysics" Derrida underlines precisely the way in which imagination (empowering metaphysics yet repressed by it) divides metaphysics from itself, disrupting its propriety; this result is complemented by Gasché's demonstration of the way in which, within the Kantian project, imagination is deprived of (its) itself, of the very propriety that metaphysics would require of it. The question is whether wonder is not even more decisively anterior than imagination (at least as imagination enters metaphysics), something (is it a power at all? is it even, in the end, a *Stimmung*?) that metaphysics would not so much appropriate and repress but rather assume and then dissolve, opening from wonder yet then, at least in the end, putting an end to it. But even if so anterior, wonder would still not be sheltered from the exposure that metaphysical questioning or perhaps other, more dramatic means could bring to bear on it; it would not be a precognitive citadel now transferred outside metaphysics, a πάθος immune to deception and overturning. Later I will come back to this non-immunity of wonder.

But now, having marked the site, I want to address the individual texts and those whose voices I cannot but hear in those texts; I want to address them more individually (and have indeed already begun to do so), though within as continuous and developed a discourse as possible. In doing so I will no doubt augment my own authoritative engagement, letting my own voice sound more distinctly in the discourse, in the manner so aptly described and enacted in Adriaan Peperzak's "Voices." Even if one can only dream of speaking simply in one's own voice; for one's own voice is precisely *not* something *simple,* not something simply one's own, hardly more so than one's signature. Indeed, not even the dream of speaking simply in one's own voice is simply one's own insofar as (here I refer to the beginning of Jacques Derrida's text) oneiric time is other than the time of presence to self. One can only have simulated the dream, and even in feigning it one will already have crossed the boundary into ventriloquy.

Let me begin—again—with a kind of ventriloquy. Walter Brogan has noted how often I have told and retold the story that Nietzsche once told of the history of metaphysics, the story in *Twilight of the Idols* entitled "How the True World Finally Became a Fable." I shall not tell the story again here except to echo what Walter Brogan has said. Let me refer, then, only in the briefest way to the beginning at which is posited the true world—said to be: "the oldest form of the idea, relatively sensible, simple, persuasive"—and then to the various stages in which that world becomes progressively less sensible, less simple, less persuasive, so that as bright day arrives and *bon sens* and cheerfulness return, that world comes to be abolished. At breakfast there is no more truth; the true world—now one writes these words only while also crossing them out—is abolished. But what is perhaps most remarkable about the entire story is that it ends, not in the bright morning hours, but at the moment of the briefest shadow, at noon. Let me cite once more Nietzsche's account of the end:

The true world—we have abolished. What world has remained? The apparent one perhaps? But no! *With the true world we have also abolished the apparent one.*[12]

This is the decisive moment, this moment of the briefest shadow, noon. Compressing into this moment an extended history of interpretation and translation, one can say that this is the moment when Nietzsche's thought twists free of Platonism, of metaphysics. Not only is *die wahre Welt* abolished but also *die scheinbare Welt*—that is, what is abolished is the very schema in which the sensible is regarded as appearance (as *scheinbar*) in opposition to a supersensible, true world. What becomes decisive in this moment is to dislocate the ordering structure that would subordinate the sensible to something higher, not merely to invert but to displace the structure. What remains at this moment of twisting-free is the sensible alone, the sensible released from all determination by opposition to a higher world, hence no longer apparent or semblant (*scheinbar*) but, at most, simply shining (*scheinen*). Under the noonday sun.

In hopes of allaying Charles Scott's very understandable concern about the return of a certain Platonism, let me stress that such shining has nothing to do with the clarity of abstract relations or with a Platonism defined by its orientation solely to such clarity. The turn to shining occurs precisely in the twisting free of Platonism. If in some very recent lectures (such as those mentioned, respectively, by Derrida and Brogan) I return more insistently to a reading of the Platonic texts, it is a turn, not to the solar father, but to the nocturnal mother, or, more precisely, to a mother preceding the very opposition of day and night, more akin to the underworld where that oscillation is forever stalled. Even if one cannot but raise the question that Derrida ponders at the end of his text, that of the connection of the χώρα to the ἐπέκεινα τῆς οὐσίας, that of whether the χώρα is ἐπέκεινα τῆς οὐσίας. I can only underline the difficulty of saying and thinking how the wildness of the χώρα could be ἐπέκεινα τῆς οὐσίας, adding only a sentence from the *Republic* that would seem to make it still more imperative to say and think this connection. The sentence occurs in the discussion of the image of the cave, specifically at the point where Socrates tells of what seems the final stage of the former prisoner's ascent: "Then finally I suppose he would be able to make out the sun—not its appearances in water or in some alien place [ἕδρα], but the sun itself by itself in its own χώρα—and see what it's like" (*Rep.* 516b).

Even in *Being and Logos* there is distance taken from a certain Platonism suspected of covering over the play of the dialogues. There is also severe reservation—which I share entirely with Peperzak—regarding Heidegger's interpretation of Plato, at least the form assumed by that interpretation in *Platons Lehre von der Wahrheit*. In *Being and Logos* I attempted, among other things, to demonstrate a certain solidarity between the Platonic dialogues and the writings of the early Greek thinkers (see *BL* 7f.), and this required, in Peperzak's phrase, "a more radical retrieval" of the dialogues themselves. This retrieval required bringing the distinction between modes of showing to displace and render secondary the distinction that one otherwise takes as utterly governing Platonic thought, that between intelligible and sensible.

But putting these reservations aside for the moment, simplifying a bit more than might ever be suitable in reading the dialogues themselves, let me come back to that decisive moment in which Nietzsche's story culminates, the moment of the briefest shadow. Despite all reservations, it must be said that Heidegger's retelling of the story of "How the 'True World' Finally Became a Fable" has been decisive, and what I have retold of it I have let drift into the language of Heidegger's retelling. First of all, in order to say with Heidegger that what is now called for, now as the sun passes its zenith and noon passes into afternoon, shadows beginning to extend in the other direction—what is now called for is a new interpretation of the sensible. Not even, perhaps, a *new* interpretation, insofar as the sensible has never been *itself* interpreted, but has only been taken as the shadow of something higher, of a true world. What is called for now as afternoon begins is perhaps a *first* interpretation of the sensible.

And yet, despite the decisiveness of his retelling of the Nietzschean story, it seems to me that in the end Heidegger shies away from the most radical result, that he retreats—or at least vacillates—in the face of the most severe consequences of the Nietzschean story as he has retold it. For having told of the twisting free that is now imperative, Heidegger invokes the prospect of "a new hierarchy of the sensuous and nonsensuous." One soon realizes that what is lurking just offstage, ready to make its appearance, is none other than the ghost of spirit, *Geist;* for in the text published as *Nietzsche* in 1961, Heidegger says explicitly what in the original lecture of 1936–37 he still avoided: "With the abolition of Platonism the way first opens for the affirmation of the sensible, and along with it, the nonsensuous world of the spirit [*Geist*] as well."[13] Even as he writes of the necessity of twisting free of metaphysics, Heidegger's text continues to be haunted by a spirit that, one suspects, has not been—and perhaps could not be—itself twisted free.

Let us turn westward, anticipating the afternoon, granting the call for a first interpretation of the sensible. Let us be cautious, however, in speaking of *interpretation,* lest it lead us back to other ghosts of the true world. Let us be cautious not to take the prospect of interpretation as that of detaching a meaning or system of meanings to be set over against the sensible, again subordinating it to an order of truth.[14] As long as meaning is not itself submitted to a redetermination that twists it free of the metaphysical order, one will have to say simply that, from the moment of noon on, the sensible *has no meaning.*

The same will have to be said of the body[15] in its double character as both receptive of the sensible and itself sensible, and this is why the "new understanding of embodiment" for which Peg Birmingham calls is as difficult as it is imperative. How many reservations, how much erasure, would now be required before venturing to say *what* the body *is*? Suppose that the body's *Was-sein* were replaced by *Ek-sistenz* (a consequence I have drawn from Heidegger).[16] Suppose that one were to insist, in Birmingham's words, that "the body is always beyond itself, losing itself." However necessary this move may be (indeed its necessity seems to me quite assured, at least within a very broad context), would such a move of reconfiguring the body as ek-sistent or ekstatic suffice to detach it, to prevent its being again submitted to an order of meaning or to an order of spirit? Can one simply continue to speak of *the* body and of embodiment in general? Or is it perhaps necessary—at least strategically—to cross the ekstatic reconfiguration with a more differentiated analysis, an analysis attuned to "the" body as, in Birmingham's words, "the locus of difference and differentiation"—or rather, not *an* analysis but various analyses focused, for example, on hands, taste, sight, posture, etc. If one were to raise then the question of imagination, one would ask—at least within a certain moment—not so much about its link to the body in general but rather about, for example, the imagination operative (inventively) in the hand of a painter.

If thinking cannot be a matter of interpretation, if thinking the sensible can no longer consist in referring it to an order of meanings or essences in which it would be secured, must one, then, require that thinking become—from this moment on, if not always already—mimetic? Charles Scott repeatedly characterizes my thought as mimetic and describes with rare subtlety the mimetic circulation between the energies animating Greek art, Nietzsche's writing about them in *The Birth of Tragedy,* and my reading of Nietzsche's text. Indeed, I have sought in *Echoes* to identify a mimetic character intrinsic to thinking as nonphilosophy—that is, a certain necessity, attested in the very late texts of Heidegger, for thinking to engage in a mimetic *Wiederholung* of philosophy. This mimetic relation of thinking to philosophy corresponds to the moment of deconstruction in which one marks the structured genealogies within the texts of metaphysics, working from within toward the limit, using the very resources found within.[17] To what extent this movement toward the limit is already, perhaps even with a certain necessity, actualized within metaphysics itself, to what extent it is the very *movement of* philosophy (in distinction from a certain dogmatic inscription)—this question I leave open.

But still, is this to say that thinking is itself mimetic, that it is to be determined as simply—even exclusively—mimetic? Is thinking only a more complex and in the end more narcissistic form of that mimesis that Plato has Socrates describe in Book 10 of the *Republic*? Is it only a compounding of painting, thus understood, of art in general mimetically conceived? Or, on the contrary, has philosophy not always demanded a movement that would exceed mimesis, another moment that would differentiate it once and for all from everything simply mimetic (if indeed anything is *simply* mimetic)? Here I could retell another story, one that I have retold perhaps as often as the Nietzschean story of the end of metaphysics. Indeed, it is the almost perfect counterpart to that story. I refer of course to the *Phaedo,* to Socrates's story of how he came to philosophy, of how he began by beginning again, by way of a second sailing (δεύτερος πλοῦς), in which he turned from what proved—though only afterwards, *après coup*—to be images, how he turned from these back to the ἀρχαί as delineated in advance in and through λόγος. Philosophy has never ceased to unfold as the movement toward the ἀρχή, a movement that would double the sensible with its ἀρχή, opening thus that most gigantic ambiguity, that of the word *sense,* moving to what would be, though in another sense, the sense of sense, moving thus within an ambiguity also abysmal. By moving to the ἀρχή, philosophy reveals that the sensible is mimetic, circling back to it, generating a sequence of circles that one might suspect constitutes the very wheel that drives Platonism on to its end, the dynamics that remains unsaid even when, finally, Nietzsche and Heidegger tell the story.

And now as the sun tilts ever so slightly to the west, making things begin to cast their shadows back in the direction from which the sun has come? Even now, thinking will need to remain archaic, no matter how complex its relation to the ἀρχή may have become and no matter how thoroughly its ἀρχή may be differentiated from the true world and twisted free from the schema by which metaphysics opposed appearance to truth. In order to secure the differentiation and the separation, one may need even to erase the word ἀρχή once the directionality it establishes has been marked. In any case one could speak of a *doubling that would not be a matter of mimesis* in any classical determination thereof. A doubling, for instance, in which one would turn from the sensible to its shining. Or a doubling in which one would turn from the sensible to its spacing, for example, as in its showing itself by way of spaced profiles. Or, at the limit, rewriting ἀρχή as ὁρισμός, one would turn from the sensible to the limits delimiting its very opening. And yet, none of these doublings would turn out of the sensible, away from it, but rather only into its thickness, its spacing, its opening between earth and sky. Openings, spacings, from and within the sensible. Wondrous openings. Limits, doublings, of and within the sensible. Limits for which Kenneth Maly has given a most fitting name: *shimmering.*

These considerations bring into focus the determinateness of the concept of field that figured so prominently in "Imagination and Metaphysics." Though I would insist on the vigilance needed to prevent this field from being reappropriated to the concept, it is something that, as Derrida notes, I do not renounce. Derrida asks—says explicitly that he would have liked to ask me—about this field and about the privileging of gathering that it seems to imply, a privileging of force of gathering over force of dissociation. In response, let me specify, first of all, that in "Imagination and Metaphysics" and elsewhere the word *field* is not to be taken in the abstract or highly indeterminate sense that it often has; it does not merely designate, for instance, a delimitable expanse of beings and/or forces. Rather, the word is determined—hence rendered determinate—by that from which, at the same time, it would be twisted loose, namely, the turn from the sensible to the intelligible, the opening of this difference, as in Socrates's δεύτερος πλοῦς. The determinateness lies, then, in the reference to the sensible and its doubling(s). Whether gathering or dissociation is privileged—construing these, for the moment, as simply opposites, though no doubt it cannot but be eventually a matter of mixing them (see D 34f., cited by Derrida)—will depend on the character of the doubling and will almost certainly be undecidable prior to its specification. Above I have outlined a possible specification at the limit of metaphysics, namely, a determination of the field as that of a dyadic play of images. In this case there would be no definitive priority but rather a mixing: on the one hand, a gathering by virtue of the reiterated linkage of images; on the other hand, dissociation, dispersion, in that the linkage would extend the image beyond itself yet without thereby gathering it in an original as such. It seems to me that what is called for is not simply to resolve the opposition in favor of one term, but to continue to hover between the two and yet beyond them.

Certainly, as Derrida says, imagination will, within this context, be extended beyond the opposition presence/absence and beyond the dyad determined by this opposition. But it would be a matter then—following the lines of my analysis above—precisely of rethinking the dyad(s) outside this opposition, deconstructing the dyadic linkage between image and original and between language and meaning. This is something that, to be sure, I have only broached above and that would have to be extended in a thorough analysis of the specific dyadic configurations. As to the linkage (this word gathers and also masks a host of complications, overlappings, contaminations, supplementations, etc.) between language and meaning, no one has contributed a more rigorous and incisive analysis than Jacques Derrida. To rethink the other dyad will require not only a deconstruction of the opposition between image and original (here I would refer to Risser's demonstration, drawing on Gadamer, of how unstable this opposition is, especially in art); it will also require—and here I refer to work in progress—reopening a certain phenomenological discussion of the image, a discussion that was taken to have been settled once and for all by the introduction of the concept of intentionality. In other words, it will require recognizing to what extent *intentionality* remained the name more of a question than of an answer.

Let me mention one other thing regarding this field of dyadic linkages opening from and within the sensible—namely, that one would need also to analyze carefully the dependence of one linkage on another. This dependence has come to light in the above reading of the *Theaetetus:* The opposition between image and original, indeed oppositionality as such, is related to discourse, in such a way that something comes to show itself as, for example, large and small, as a mixing of opposites, only in and through its being addressed either as one or the other. Correspondingly, at the end(s) of metaphysics (one should let this word hover, as it does, undecidably between singular and plural) the dyadic linkage of images would be drawn (in the sense that Heidegger speaks of the drawing of truth, as in its being drawn, for instance, into the work [*Zug zum Werk*]) or invented (not produced but let come) by discourse, by the play of that other dyad.

Let me return now to the more global considerations of the doublings of and within the sensible—in order to mention that it is from such doubling that I would take up the question of the relation of thinking to art. Both Scott and Brogan introduce phrases that suggest a very close relationship, phrases such as poetic thinker and artistic philosopher. What I have said above about mimesis indicates, on the other hand, that I would insist also on a certain differentiation, even if in the end the concept of mimesis should prove not fully sufficient for the differentiation. One way of proceeding here would be by following up one of Nietzsche's most decisive insights: that art is the countermovement to (what he called) nihilism, that art provides the motive force that can impel rethinking the sensible. For Nietzsche the force of art in this regard lies in its being a yes-saying to the sensible; that is, art both has a distinctive relation to the sensible and, through that relation, affirms the sensible. Because of its privileged relation to the sensible, art can trace in advance those lines along which thinking will set its fold in doubling the sensible. Heidegger writes, in the context of a discussion of Nietzsche's theory of art: "Art induces reality, which is in itself a shining, to shine most profoundly and supremely in scintillating transfiguration."[18] By thus inducing the sensible to shine most profoundly and supremely, in its depths and at its heights (*am tiefsten und höchsten*), art prepares and provokes the doubling that now—as afternoon begins—thinking is to undertake. Thinking can be guided by art, as, in what was once called perception, the lighting and its configuration guide one's vision of a field.

This is the connection that has determined some of my recent texts on art, most notably a long essay on Claude Monet's *Grainstack* paintings.[19] Contrary to what titles such as Impressionism might lead one to expect, Monet does not simply paint things as they appear in the moment; rather he paints the spread of light over things, the very shining of the scene, the shining that ordinarily lets things be visible. On the surface of the paintings there is a doubling that adds to the sensibly present (namely, the grainstacks, the field, the distant houses, trees, hills)— that adds the shining by which these things first become palpable to sense. What is especially remarkable is that the doubling does not involve adding some depth of meaning to the visible surface; rather Monet paints the shining over the things, covers them with it, reversing the ordinary relation in which one sees the things without seeing the shining. Now one sees the shining so brilliantly in some of the *Grainstacks* that most of the other things in the field and beyond sink into virtual invisibility. Elaine Escoubas aptly describes this doubling that is characteristic of such painting (and does so indeed in such a way as to link the text on Monet to my other recent texts on art as well as to certain more theoretical texts): it is a matter of *adumbration,* the double play of the disappearance of the object and the enacting of light as the appearing of what appears.

Before the *Grainstacks,* in the wake of the reversal they effect, here, too, wonder may be evoked, a wonder that one would not aspire to surpass but would only want to nurture and preserve, a wonder to be surrounded with a certain discourse that, instead of dissolving it, might be capable of sheltering and enhancing it.

Let me turn finally—almost finally—to tragedy. There is a certain kind of tragedy that one could call the tragedy of metaphysics and, correspondingly, a metaphysics of tragedy. I refer to those to whom tragedy only proclaims that life is at bottom just a manner of misery and suffering. One could, rather easily I suspect, demonstrate a certain complicity between such pessimism and the metaphysics that comes to theorize tragedy, delimiting thereby (in a way that would supplement *The Birth of Tragedy*) the place of Schopenhauer in the end of metaphysics. But be that as it may, one need not go so far as Schopenhauer to find such pessimism. It is already there among the Greeks, in that so-called wisdom of Silenus, Nietzsche's citation of which in *The Birth of Tragedy* is by now burned into our memories: "What is best of all is utterly beyond your reach: not to be born, not to *be*, to be *nothing;* but the second best for you is—to die soon."[20]

But this is of course not the pathos, the *Stimmung,* that Nietzsche finds to be produced in the disclosure achieved in tragedy. Quite to the contrary, tragedy comes to deliver one from such life-negating pessimism. It does so by disclosing, through its double mimesis, the necessary connection, the yoking together, of suffering and joy.[21] This is the tragic joy to which Michel Haar's extended and incisive analysis is devoted.

In Nietzsche's thinking of tragedy and in my reinscription of Nietzsche's text, Charles Scott locates what he calls the radical moment, the point where tragedy falls apart, collapses, dissolves in and for the thinking of tragedy. Characterizing this moment as one in which metaphysical comfort is disrupted, Scott says that this is brought about "by the disturbing realization that such comfort is provided by images that are themselves ungrounded by anything original beyond image." No doubt there is such realization. The Apollinian images in tragedy do not image an original as such but at most (and only if one aligns *The Birth of Tragedy*—as I would not—along a thoroughly metaphysical axis) only an original so original that it cannot be presented as such. And yet, this realization is not something that is brought to tragedy from without but *belongs* precisely *to the disclosure* brought about in and through tragedy, the disclosure of the Dionysian abyss. The decisive question here is one of limit: In the face of tragedy is thinking exposed to a moment of such incomprehensibility as to bring it finally to submission before the disclosiveness of tragedy, to bring it to listen to what the old Athenian says in the final sentence of *The Birth of Tragedy:* "But now follow me to witness a tragedy, and sacrifice with me in the temple of both gods."[22]

In any case the utmost vigilance needs to be exercised at this radical moment to avoid reverting to metaphysical tragedy, to pessimism and all that Schopenhauerian metaphysics can do to enhance its sting. Indeed, one might suppose that Nietzsche himself came more and more to exercise such vigilance aimed at dispelling the ghost of Schopenhauer—as when in the voice of Zarathustra he says: "Whoever climbs the highest mountains laughs at all tragic plays and tragic seriousness."[23]

What about such songs of holy laughter? What about such comedy as Bernard Freydberg has traced with keen perceptiveness in *Spacings* (beginning to assemble a kind of Kantian beastiary), linking it also to a Kantian tragedy of reason that was the concern of *The Gathering of Reason*? What about such comedy as would establish measure by way of overturning, by showing— in Nietzsche's words—"an inverted world" of "sense and nonsense . . . in crazy confusion,"[24] a world in which nonsense is shown to belong to sense? What might such comedy not overturn? Would even wonder be secure against it? Hardly.

In the *Critique of Judgment* Kant writes of something akin to wonder. The discussion comes as he is dealing with the intellectual interest in the beautiful, specifically, the immediate interest in the beauty of nature.[25] One form that such interest takes is our admiration (*Bewunderung*) for nature. As with all such interest, this wondrous admiration hinges on a natural trace (*Spur*), a trace by which nature shows that it involves some sort of ground for assuming in its products a harmony with our own cognitive powers. Referring to the songs of birds, which, as we interpret them, proclaim joyfulness and contentment with existence, Kant notes that because everything hinges on the natural trace, our interest in, our admiration for, a birdsong would vanish should we discover that we were being deceived and that it was not a bird's song but only an artful imitation that we were hearing. The poet is called forth to listen in rapt, wondrous admiration to the enchantingly beautiful song of a nightingale in a secluded thicket on a quiet summer evening by the soft light of the moon. As he steps on stage listening attentively and admiringly to the very voice of nature, the scene is set for the comedy that overturns his wondrous admiration:

> And yet we have cases where some jovial innkeeper, unable to find such a songster, played a trick—received [initially] with greatest satisfaction—on the guests staying at his inn to enjoy the country air, by hiding in a bush some roguish youngster who (with a reed or rush in his mouth) knew how to copy that song in a way very similar to nature's. But as soon as one realizes that it was all deception, no one will long endure listening to this song that before he had considered so charming; and that is how it is with the song of any other bird.[26]

7.

"Afterword—
After the word of Heidegger."
Echoes: After Heidegger

Another tone is required as I turn now to some of the more sharply critical questions. All of these have to do in one way or another with my reading of Hei-

degger, whether they are presented in the guise of questions about ways of reading, as in Kenneth Maly's Introduction, or are cast more polemically and in direct
reference to certain Heideggerian texts, as in the papers by Parvis Emad and Walter Biemel.

In his Introduction Maly circumscribes several times the description that I
give of a form that reading—specifically, reading Heidegger—may take, namely,
that of locating "certain blind spots" within the text, certain "residues of dogmatic
assertion." Let me note, in advance, that this description of *a* form of reading, one
form among others, occurs in the Introduction (so entitled) to a collection of texts
originally presented at an international conference in Chicago. The context, pre-
scribing that I introduce a variety of very different readings, is not wholly irrele-
vant. But let me focus my remarks now on the connection that Maly draws between
this form that "reading may take" and a certain self-effacement of Heidegger's text
that I mention in this same Introduction. The connection that Maly appears to draw
is that by such a form of reading one would make the texts efface themselves. Yet
clearly this is not the point, and no such connection is suggested by what I write.
One need only note the two examples of such self-effacement that I mention: "One
thinks especially of all the texts that somehow efface themselves: for instance, by
crossing out the word *Being* while still letting it remain legible; or by retracting
something like the propositional character of a text. . . ."[27] The references are un-
mistakably to *Zur Seinsfrage* and *Zeit und Sein,* respectively, in both of which the
self-effacements are explicitly written into the texts themselves. They do not have
to be engendered by any special form of reading such as that to which Maly draws
a connection.

There is an analogous problem of specificity in Maly's discussion of the four
interpretive strategies that I outline in *The Gathering of Reason.* The problem lies
in his taking them as four levels of reading *in general,* in such a way as then to be
in a position (1) to trace a kind of "development" in which I would come to focus
more on certain of the strategies than on others and (2) to pose the question
whether there is not a way of reading that is not accounted for in these four ways.
Yet, if one reads what is written in *The Gathering of Reason* at the point where the
four strategies are introduced, it is clear that these are, at the most, strategies for a
reading *of the Kantian text,* strategies largely determined by *that* text, not at all
strategies for reading in general (the possibility of which I would most seriously
question). Thus, in *The Gathering of Reason* one can read the following: "For the
most part, the relevant structures are materially determined—that is, they are generated from the manifest structure of the text itself, from the matter put at issue in
that text, and from the interplay of reflection, matter, and text. To this degree rigorous predetermination of the hermeneutical space is precluded" (*GR* 11). So then:
very specific strategies. And even as such the sketch that *The Gathering of Reason* goes on to give of them is explicitly characterized—as of course it must be—
as "anticipatory."

Kenneth Maly presents a figure of two roads to characterize the crossroads at which contemporary Continental philosophy is situated, a situation that he suggests may be mirrored in my work. One road seems to be that of a certain deconstruction, which would remain somehow enclosed in the text. It would be, in Maly's description, "closed off to the texture of the text, to the text's 'saying' of and within the ambience of the phenomenon," a matter—as he goes on to say—of "text-enclosedness." The other road would involve remaining open beyond the text, "staying with the phenomenon at the boundary."

If such were the alternatives and these two roads were simply distinct, there would be no choice to be made: the very opposition in terms of which the figure is constructed already privileges the road of openness so thoroughly as virtually to erase the crossroads. I would suggest, on the other hand, modifing the figure slightly by multiplying endlessly the crossroads, so that there are nothing but crossroads, so that at every point one will have to move along both roads, enacting then a kind of double movement. Also, of course, gradually eroding the figure, confounding the opposition with which it began, turning the text inside out so that one could no longer suppose any simple self-enclosedness.

Take the example of reading *The Birth of Tragedy*. To say that this text as a theoretical text crosses itself out, places itself under erasure, is not to describe some purely textual operation that would somehow occur without any relation whatsoever to what *is said* in the text. On the contrary, if the text (as theoretical) comes to be crossed out, it is precisely as a result of the recoil of what is said upon the saying; it is because what proves to be said—that is, shown, that is, enticed to come forth into some manner of manifestation—proves also such as would not be sayable by a purely theoretical text (in this case the Dionysian and the tragic) that there is effected a certain effacement, a certain mutation, of the text. And yet—let me stress—this is not simply to submit the text to an order of the phenomenon that would simply precede and govern it, as if the phenomenon were simply beyond all relation to saying, to textuality, to language. It is Heidegger himself who says that, when one walks through the woods or goes to the spring, one walks through the word *woods* and goes to the word *spring*.[28] Precisely in the wake of Heidegger, nothing seems to me less certain than the supposition that there is something that is *simply* not textual.

Parvis Emad is also concerned about deconstruction, or rather, about what he calls "the philosophy of deconstruction." His interpretation of *Echoes* seems to me quite lacking in precision and in attention to what my text *says*. For example, he, like Maly, questions my proposal to reinscribe Heidegger's texts "in order to free those texts to say what they can say, now, after Heidegger" (E 13). Because I make this proposal, he concludes that I consider Heidegger's texts "mute" and "incomprehensible." That this cannot be deduced from what is written in *Echoes* will be clear even to a cursory reading of that text. Even without my beginning (as I cannot here) to unfold what it would mean to free a text, granted Heidegger's determination of freedom (freeing, letting-be) as the essence of truth.

What I find most astounding in Emad's criticisms is his almost compulsive invocation of the phrase *Betroffenheit vom Sein.* Let me take just one example. Speaking of the formal structure of the question of Being, I say that "the structure is such that the questioner is to take up the question by interrogating a being (Dasein) with which it coincides" (*E* 19). Here is how what I say is then construed: It is said to mean that " 'the questioner' is an 'outsider,' is not Dasein itself." In other words: Because the questioner coincides with Dasein, it is outside Dasein, is not Dasein itself—that is, because the questioner coincides with Dasein, it does not coincide with Dasein! Eventually even it is said: "the questioner is at first separated from Dasein, only later to coincide with it." Even further, then: Because the questioning Dasein does not coincide with the questioned Dasein (*does not* precisely because—such seems to be the "logic"—it *does*), "the formal structure of the question of being is completely and thoroughly cut off from *Betroffenheit vom Sein.*" Let me say only that it would, I believe, have sufficed just to read the very next page of *Echoes,* where the entire complex is outlined: I refer to "the formal determination of Dasein as that being that comports itself to Being," and then continue: "This determination serves to submit Dasein's self-relation to its comportment to (especially) its own Being, which is to say that Dasein's relation to itself could never be a matter of undivided self-presence; Dasein's presence to itself would always already have been breached by its comportment to its own Being" (E 20f.). It is precisely this breach that decisively differentiates Dasein from the subject. Indeed, there is no more direct way back from Dasein to the subject, no more direct way to *reduce* Dasein to the subject, than to require of Dasein—for example, as questioner and questioned—an undivided self-presence.

Walter Biemel's "Marginal Notes" on my reading of "On the Essence of Truth" assumes and continues to repeat throughout that my text "Deformatives" is a critique of Heidegger, that its intent is to make certain objections, certain reproaches (*Vorwurf*) against Heidegger's text, to reproach it, for example, by applying to it such words as *monstrous, deformative,* and *decentered,* by questioning as to its connection with madness, by charging it with contradiction. But nothing could be further from its intent. To be sure, if one takes such words as *deformed* and *monstrous* in a very narrow and popular sense, they may suggest a tone of reproach or critique. But there is absolutely nothing in "Deformatives" to support taking them in such a sense. Still—lest any doubt remain—let me say once and for all that, just as Heidegger situates his own discussion of truth within the most classical framework (truth as *adaequatio rei et intellectus*), likewise the sense and tone of "Deformatives" depends entirely on understanding its perhaps provocative language within a classical framework. When it is read accordingly, one will see that the text attempts to show just how radically Heidegger's analysis of the essence of truth transforms the classical concepts, withdrawing from them their classical form, even that of form itself (μορφή), introducing de-formation. The intent is not at all to reproach Heidegger but to underline, by the provocative formulations, the radicality of his accomplishment in this justly celebrated text. Except for the final paragraph, where I raise what is not yet even a question about a more essentially other of truth, the entirety of "Deformatives" thoroughly celebrates "On the Essence of Truth."

There is, for example, nothing to support construing madness as mental illness or insanity rather than—as one does almost always with Heidegger himself—hearing in it an attempt to say what is heard in a word of Greek thinking—in this case μανία, which, as θεῖα μανία, is so remote from anything like mental illness that it rather characterizes those who see farthest or discern most keenly, the seer, the poet, the philosopher.[29]

Again, to show that Heidegger's text undergoes a certain decentering by virtue of the development of the question of untruth is not at all a matter of "impoverishment [*Verarmung*]" or "deprivation [*Beraubung*]." No more so than is the introduction of the second focal point that allows one to draw an ellipse in place of a circle.

Monstrosity is simply identified in the first paragraph of "Deformatives": It is "a divergence from nature within nature." *Nature* says, first of all, φύσις, and one whose nature is to exceed nature, who from within nature diverges, passes beyond nature (from φύσις to μετα-φύσις), is monstrous—like Theaetetus, like the philosopher who ascends out of the cave even while remaining bodily there. *Nature* can also say *essentia,* as when we speak of the nature of things. Thus it is that Heidegger's installing of the non-essence of truth within its essence introduces a divergence from nature within nature.

In conclusion, two other, specific points. The first concerns the dispute that Biemel introduces as to the title of the 1930 version of "On the Essence of Truth." It is of course not easy to dispute with one who claims to have been given the authoritative text by Heidegger himself. But aside from the fact that the copy in my possession (quite clearly marked as the version presented in Marburg) carries "*Philosophieren und Glauben*" as its main title and "*Das Wesen der Wahrheit*" as a parenthesized subtitle, such entitlement is borne out completely by what Heidegger says in the opening paragraph. I have cited it already in "Deformatives":

> The task of the lecture is stated by the main title. The main title says what is to be dealt with, philosophizing and believing, thus not philosophy and theology. The subtitle states how we are to set about the task . . . , [viz.,] by questioning concerning the essence of truth.

Finally, a note on the curious—though in a sense consistent—reaction to what I say of the marginal notes included with the text of "On the Essence of Truth" in the *Gesamtausgabe*. Again, it is assumed that the stance of "Deformatives" is critical and that a reproach is being brought against either Heidegger or the editors of the edition. Yet, even a cursory reading of these paragraphs of "Deformatives" will show—once this *assumption* is put out of action—that my concern is rather to indicate how complex the relation of these notes to the text really is and to open thus the hermeneutical questions that must be addressed by any reading of the text that would be supplemented by reference to the marginal notes. I would have thought that it went without saying that one can only be grateful that these valuable notes are made available in the *Gesamtausgabe*.

NOTES

NOTES TO INTRODUCTION

1. This text consists of two brief paragraphs and appears in Martin Heidegger, *Aus der Erfahrung des Denkens,* ed. Hermann Heidegger, Gesamtausgabe 13 (Frankfurt: Vittorio Klostermann Verlag, 1983), p. 111.

2. Sallis's translation of this text appears as a frontispiece in Hugh Silverman and Don Ihde (eds.), *Hermeneutics and Deconstruction* (Albany: State University of New York Press, 1985), p. vii, and in John Sallis (ed.), *Reading Heidegger: Commemorations* (Bloomington: Indiana University Press, 1993), p. 2.

3. *Aus der Erfahrung des Denkens,* p. 111.

4. Cf. Martin Heidegger, *Grundbegriffe,* ed. Petra Jaeger, Gesamtausgabe 51 (Frankfurt: Vittorio Klostermann Verlag, 1981), p. 68.

5. The preceding several paragraphs appeared earlier, in a different form, in my essays "From Truth to 'Αλήθεια to Opening and Rapture," *Heidegger Studies,* VI (1990), 31, and "Reading and Thinking: Heidegger and the Hinting Greeks," in John Sallis (ed.), *Reading Heidegger: Commemorations,* p. 237.

For the notion of "sounding the text" and "striking the text," in which the sounding of words by the reader has an intrinsic power to bind the reader as well as open up the gathered, see J. Stephen Lansing, "The Aesthetics of the Sounding of the Text," in J. and D. Rothenburg (eds.), *Symposium of the Whole: A Range of Discourse toward an Ethno-poetics* (Berkeley: University of California Press, 1983), pp. 241ff.

6. Cf. Heidegger's letter to William Richardson, in Richardson's *Heidegger: Through Phenomenology to Thought* (The Hague: Martinus Nijhoff, 1963), p. ix.

7. Sallis (ed.), *Reading Heidegger: Commemorations,* p. 2.

8. Thus gathering gathers—or reading *as* gathering gathers. Note that Heidegger says "Worauf sammelt sie?"— i.e., die Sammlung and *not* das Lesen.

9. *Ibid.,* p. 3.

10. *Ibid.,* p. 2.

11. Martin Heidegger, *Unterwegs zur Sprache,* ed. F.-W. von Herrmann, Gesamtausgabe 12 (Frankfurt: Vittorio Klostermann Verlag, 1985), p. 165.

12. Sallis, *op. cit.,* p. 3.

13. Hermann Paul, *Deutsches Wörterbuch* (Tübingen: Max Niemeyer Verlag, 1966), p. 357.

14. I use here words that Sallis makes central to his essay "Deformatives: Essentially Other Than Truth," in John Sallis (ed.), *Reading Heidegger: Commemorations,* pp. 31, 45.

15. What I have just said here, as well as what I say in this next section, is a reworking of what I have written earlier, in direct response to *Spacings.* Cf. my "The Rooting and Uprooting of Reason: On *Spacings* by John Sallis" and John Sallis's "Response" in *Philosophy Today,* 35:2 (Summer, 1991), 195–211.

16. Jacques Derrida, *Positions,* trans. A. Bass (Chicago: The University of Chicago Press, 1971), p. 3.

17. *Ibid.,* p. 6.

18. Jacques Derrida, *Margins of Philosophy,* trans. A. Bass (Chicago: The University of Chicago Press, 1982), p. 65.

19. *Positions,* p. 96.

20. *Ibid.,* p. 82.

21. Jacques Derrida, *Dissemination,* trans. B. Johnson (Chicago: The University of Chicago Press, 1981), p. 221.

22. *Margins of Philosophy,* p. 65.

23. Sallis, *op. cit.,* p. 3.

24. See Charles Scott's essay in this volume, toward the end.

25. Katie Geneva Cannon, "Moral Wisdom in the Black Women's Literary Tradition, in Judith Plaskow and Carol Christ (eds.), *Weaving the Visions* (New York: Harper and Row, 1989), p. 283.

26. *Ibid.,* p. 291.

27. Sallis, *op. cit.,* p. 3.

28. Martin Heidegger, *Sein und Zeit,* ed. F.-W. von Herrmann (Frankfurt: Vittorio Klostermann Verlag, 1977), p. 118.

29. See p. 000 in this volume.

NOTES TO CHAPTER ONE

1. See Sartre's first publications, *L'imagination* (1936) and *L'imaginaire* (1940), which can be considered as a global interpretation of the phenomenolog-

ical theory of consciousness centered on the difference between perception and imagination.

2. Edmund Husserl, *Ideas Pertaining to a Pure Phenomenology and to a Phenomenological Philosophy,* trans. F. Kersten (The Hague: Nijhoff, 1983), §24, p. 44. Hereafter: *Ideas.*

3. See *Echoes,* p. 98, where this passage from *Ideen II* (§70) is quoted.

4. Edmund Husserl, *Logische Untersuchungen* (Tübingen: Niemeyer Verlag, 1921), II, 2, p. 183. (hereafter: LU): "Es liegt in der Natur der Sache, daß letztlich alles Kategoriale auf sinnlicher Anschauung beruht, ja daß eine kategoriale Anschauung, also eine Verstandeseinsicht, ein Denken im höchsten Sinne, ohne fundierende Sinnlichkeit ein Widersinn ist. *Die Idee eines 'reinen Intellekts,'* interpretiert als ein 'Vermögen' reinen Denkens (hier: kategorialer Aktion) und *völlig abgelöst* von jedem 'Vermögen der Sinnlichkeit,' konnte nur konzipiert werden *vor* einer Elementaranalyse der Erkenntnis nach ihrem evident unaufhebbaren Bestande."

5. See Edmund Husserl, *Grundprobleme der Phänomenologie, 1910/11* (Den Haag: Nijhoff, 1977), §29, p. 71: "Das Hinausgehen über den Bereich absoluter Gegebenheit als notwendige Bedingung der Möglichkeit einer phänomenologischen Wissenschaft." In this section Husserl shows the necessity of "surpassing" the field of the indubitable *cogitationes,* i.e., of going beyond Cartesianism, because the phenomenological field includes not only mental processes which are absolutely given, but also presentations (*Vergegenwärtigungen*) of *absent* objects.

6. LU, II, 2, §46, p. 144: "Phänomenologische Analyse des Unterschiedes zwischen sinnlicher und kategorialer Wahrnehmung."

7. Edmund Husserl, *Erste Philosophie* (Den Haag: Nijhoff, 1959), II, 62ff. In this passage Husserl declares on the one hand that I have an immediate perception of the other human being and not the perception of a body from which I infer that it belongs to a being similar to me, but on the other hand that such meaning of this perception of the other implies a mediation compared to the perception of my own body, so that we should speak in that case of a perception through originary interpretation (*Wahrnehmung durch ursprüngliche Interpretation*).

8. LU, II,1, p. 425: "Man braucht es nur auszusprechen, und jedermann muß es anerkennen: daß der intentionale Gegenstand der Vorstellung *derselbe* ist wie ihr wirklicher und gegebenfalls ihr aüsserer Gegenstand, und daß es *widersinning* ist, zwischen beiden zu unterscheiden." (Cf. D 65.)

9. See *Ideas,* § 43, p. 93. I have modified the translation of the German *Vorstellung* from "objectivation" to "representation."

10. *Ibid.,* p. 92.

11. See the very subtle analysis of the profile given by Sallis in "Image and Phenomenon" (D 74): "A profile not only lets the object show itself but also, in its irreducible difference from what shows itself, compels the object to hold itself

back—that is, guarantees concealment and sets the object at a distance from perceptual apprehension, a distance which serves precisely to free the object from one's grasp of it, to grant it its aloofness from the perceptual apprehension of it."

12. Martin Heidegger, *Phänomenologische Interpretation von Kants Kritik der reinen Vernunft*, GA 25 (Frankfurt am Main: Klostermann Verlag, 1977), p. 99 (my emphasis).

13. Cf. *Kritik der reinen Vernunft*, Vorrede zur zweiten Auflage, B XXVI, where Kant remarks that we can at least think (but not know) the phenomenal objects as things in themselves, that otherwise we would arrive at the absurd proposition that there are appearances (*Erscheinungen*) without anything that appears.

14. This challenge is taken up in Husserl's phenomenological interpretation of Kant—and in a clearer way by Heidegger, who was able to see in Kant's definition of receptivity the theory of a creative intuition.

15. See. M. Merleau-Ponty, *The Visible and the Invisible* (Evanston): Northwestern University Press, 1968), p. 192, where he speaks of "a Self-presence that is an absence *from oneself,* a contact with Self *through* the divergence (*écart*) with regard to Self." On this point see my article "Monde, Chair, Vision," in A.-T. Tymieniecka (ed.), *Maurice Merleau-Ponty, Le psychique et le corporel* (Paris: Aubier, 1988), pp. 115ff.

16. See Derrida's interpretation of this paragraph of the *Ideas* at the end of *The Voice and the Phenomenon*. It is in fact quite possible to say, with Derrida, that "the thing itself always escapes" and that "nothing has ever preceded the situation with which all has started" and which is depicted by Husserl in §100: "A name reminds us, namingly, of the Dresden Gallery and of our last visit there: we walk through the halls and stand before a picture by Teniers which represents a picture gallery. If, let us say, we allow that pictures in the latter would represent again pictures which, for their part, represent legible inscriptions, and so forth, then we can estimate which inclusion of objectivations (*Vorstellungen*) and which mediacies are actually produceable with respect to objectivities which can be seized upon." (*Ideas,* pp. 246–7) But it does not mean that no live perception is ever given, that there are only presentiations of presentiations, as Derrida suggests. And it does not mean either that it is necessary "to supply the shine of presence" (*suppléer l'éclat de la présence*) which cannot enter the necessarily labyrinthian world in which we live. We need not look for substitutes, i.e., images, of presence, because even in presentiations we are still engaged in the sphere of presence, of a presence which is not full presence, but which shows itself always in a reticent manner, as Sallis said. This presence that always involves absence is never full, i.e., already accomplished, but always in becoming. Cf. my article "Husserl et la neutralité de l'art," in *La Part de l'Oeil* (Bruxelles, 1991), pp. 19ff.

17. See *L'imaginaire* (Paris: Gallimard, 1940). In the conclusion of this book Sartre formulates the metaphysical thesis that is behind his phenomenological psychology of imagination: "L'imagination n'est pas un pouvoir empirique

et surajouté de la conscience, c'est la conscience tout entière en tant qu'elle réalise sa liberté."

18. *Ideas*, §99, pp. 244–45.

19. Italics mine. This "performance" can only be attributed to something non-objective. Thus it is attributable, not to the image-object as such, but to the *act* of imaging, as Sallis points out later in this essay.

20. *Ideas*, §111, p. 262.

21. In *Spacings*, where the second chapter is dedicated to Fichte under the title "Hoverings," Sallis quotes this passage of the *Wissenschaftslehre*, in which imagination is defined as "a power that hovers (*schwebt*) in the middle between determination and nondetermination, between finite and infinite." (S 64)

22. D 5: We can say about phenomenology and imagination what Sallis stresses here about metaphysics and imagination.

23. *Ideas*, §109, p. 258.

24. *Ibid.*, §§31 and 32.

25. See E 98.

26. See, for example, J. Beaufret, *Parménide. Le poeme* (Paris: P.U.F., 1955), p. 48, which opposes "Parmenides's foundative transcendence" to "the evasive transcendence which since Plato is metaphysically ours." A little before this passage Beaufret notes that the Parmenidean transcendence is the same as the transcendence which will come back in the *Critique of Pure Reason,* because "the critical transcendence has the effect of reversing the ecstasy, in giving it the empirical object itself as goal." (op. cit., p. 43) Here the (evasive) drive to eternal presence is differentiated from the drive to ground which is understood with the example of the Parmenidean thought as "transcendence *for* the being" (*transcendence* pour *l'étant*) and not "liquidation" of the (sensible) being on behalf of a "transcendent being." (op. cit., p. 46) This last form of transcendence is what constitutes for Beaufret the metaphysical sense of Platonism.

27. *Ideas*, §70, p. 160.

28. See *The Visible and the Invisible*, p. 214: "The sensible is precisely the medium in which there can be *being* without its having to be posited; the sensible appearance of the sensible, the silent persuasion of the sensible is Being's unique way of manifesting itself without becoming positivity, without ceasing to be ambiguous and transcendent."

29. See *Parmenides*, 132a. This argument, whose origin has been attributed to the sophists, shows that if the "participation" of the sensible things to the separate "forms" or "ideas" is understood as a relation of likeness, this will lead to an infinite regress, because a third form will be needed to explain the common character of the original and of its copy, and so on indefinitely. It is quite clear that such a difficulty arises only because there χωρισμός is thought in a spatial manner, as the opposition of two worlds, instead of being thought in a temporal manner, as a differance *in* the sensible itself, which is both image and reality,

multiplicity and identity, and which gives itself all together as presence and absence, or, as Sallis noted, as "the play of imaging in the things *themselves*" (D 75, my emphasis).

30. See Martin Heidegger, *Was ist das, die Philosophie?* (Pfullingen: Verlag Neske, 1956), p. 23.

31. That the philosopher cannot settle himself in the intelligible world, but must go down again into the everyday world, and that this can mean the risk of death for him—this is the true teaching of the Allegory of the Cave.

32. *Ideas,* §22, p. 41.

33. See "Imagination—The Meaning of Being?" in E 97ff.

34. Sallis is here referring to the metontological turn whose outlines are presented in Heidegger's lecture course from 1928 on *The Metaphysical Foundations of Logic;* and he supposes that this overturning into metontology originates in the search for a "site at which transcendence would exceed temporality," because temporality still retains in itself "a trace of internality sufficient to constitute a gap separating it from world, a difference from transcendence." I would rather think that Heidegger's *Kehre* is the attempt to think temporality no longer as the structure of humans alone, but as the structure of being itself, which can be understood in its spatiality and "externality" only from there.

35. See "Mortality and Imagination: The Proper Name of Man" in E 118ff.

NOTES TO CHAPTER TWO

1. Immanuel Kant, *Critique of Pure Reason,* trans. N. Kemp Smith (New York: St. Martin's Press, 1965), pp. 142–43.

2. *Ibid.,* p. 112.

3. Immanuel Kant, *Critique of Judgement,* trans. J. H. Bernard (New York: Hafner Press, 1951), p. 69.

4. Immanuel Kant, *Anthropology from a Pragmatic Point of View,* trans. V. L. Dowdell (Carbondale and Edwardsville: Southern Illinois University Press, 1978), p. 40.

5. After all, all sources of knowledge, to quote the *Critique of Pure Reason,* not only "can be viewed as empirical, namely, in [their] . . . application to given appearances. But all of them are likewise *a priori* elements of foundations, which make the empirical employment itself possible" (141). The chapters on imagination in *Anthropology* stage this parallelism in that the different functions of imagination are first expounded in terms reminiscent of, if not identical to, their definitions in the Critiques before Kant describes their practical significance.

6. All page references that stand alone in parentheses in the text refer to Kant, *Anthropology.*

7. Kant, *Critique of Pure Reason,* p. 183.

8. Hermann Mörchen, *Die Einbildungskraft bei Kant* (Tübingen: Niemeyer Verlag, 1970), p. 16.

9. Aristotle, *The Complete Works,* ed. J. Barnes (Princeton: Princeton University Press, 1985), I, 681–82.

10. Mörchen, *op. cit.,* p. 41.

11. Kant, *Critique of Pure Reason,* p. 144. For everything that is to follow it would have been useful to bring in Kant's developments on association, affinity, and the unity of apperception in the First Critique (pp. 141–49).

12. *Ibid.,* p. 118.

13. Immanuel Kant, *Werke in sechs Bänden,* ed. W. Weischedel (Darmstadt: Wissenschaftliche Buchgesellschaft, 1966), VI, 478.

14. Mörchen, *op. cit.,* p. 37.

NOTES TO CHAPTER THREE

1. On these points I would like to refer readers to "Economimesis," in *Mimesis des Articulations* (Paris: Aubier-Flammarion, 1975), pp. 59 and 62; trans. R. Klein in *Diacritics,* vol. 11, no. 2 (Summer 1981), 3–25; "Le puits et la pyramide, Introduction à la sémiologie de Hegel," in *Marges—de la philosophie* (Paris: Minuit, 1972), pp. 89 and 91; trans. A. Bass in *Margins of Philosophy* (Chicago: University of Chicago Press, 1990), pp. 77 and 79; and "Théologie de la traduction," in *Du droit à la philosophie* (Paris: Galilée, 1990), pp. 371 ff.

2. Martin Heidegger, "Der Spruch des Anaximander," in *Holzwege* (Frankfurt am Main: V. Klostermann, 1950), pp. 317; trans. by D. F. Krell in *Early Greek Thinking* (San Francisco: Harper & Row, 1975), pp. 32–33.

3. I refer here to Llewelyn's admirable *The Middle Voice of Ecological Conscience* (London: Macmillan, 1991), specifically to pp. 229 ff. of the final chapter, pages that seem to me to be particularly rich and lucid on the subject of the "power" of "productive" and "poetic" imagination. This "power" of *Bilden,* this *Einbildungskraft,* is also its contrary, "power for construction and deconstruction," *weltbildend* and *weltabbildend, weltabbauend* (*weltarm, weltlos—* which enables Llewelyn to interweave this immense problem with that of animality in Heidegger). Here it would be necessary to cite the entirety of p. 230, which develops in an altogether convincing fashion this "hybrid or low-bred which is neither purely passive nor purely active but an adynamical or, as Levinas would say, anallergic alternative. . . ." We shall return later to this question of the hybrid, of the "mongrel," or of the bastard.

4. "What becomes of imagination at the end of metaphysics? Is imagination—that is, the word, the concept, perhaps even the thing itself (if I may use, provisionally, this very classical schema)—entangled in the web of metaphysics in such a way that it too cannot but fall prey to a deconstruction that today would dis-

lodge all metaphysical securities? Is the closure of metaphysics also the closure of imagination and of its field of play? Or, on the contrary, does the closure of metaphysics perhaps serve precisely to free imagination and to open fully its field? Is it perhaps even on the wings of imagination that one can effectively transgress metaphysics and station oneself at the limit, hovering there without security?" (D 3–4) Let us follow for an instant the reading of this suspended question, the audacity of this beat of wings. It raises the hypothesis—without leaving matters "up in the air," *en l'air,* as we say in French—that imagination would be the most efficacious of levers for all deconstruction of metaphysics. In short, one must have imagination in order to "think" and to deconstruct metaphysics. Those who do not do this lack imagination; not because they lack a faculty or a power, whether acquired or natural, a gift or a talent, but because imagination is the very thing that metaphysics has either failed to think, in this way determining itself as metaphysics in that very failure, or has succeeded in suppressing, prohibiting, silencing, and marginalizing (we shall return to this in a moment), in this way determining itself as metaphysics in that very success. But then what is imagination? Unless—and this is the doubt that Sallis leaves in suspense by that very same beat of wings—the identity or self-identity of something like THE metaphysical is every bit as imaginary, fantastic, fantasist or phantasmatic in its pretended closure or end as any sort of transgression (whether deconstructive or some other) of said metaphysics. Few deconstructionists, if there are any, are as reserved concerning the *possibility* of deconstruction as Sallis is, it seems to me. And how right he is!

5. The recurrence of the word *shift* poses the entire enigma: does such a "shift" depend on the imagination? does it proceed from the imagination? or does it affect the imagination in its very status? And if these two hypotheses are not contradictory, how do matters then stand with this auto-affection, if we can call it that, of the imagination (of this "power," which as we know Heidegger's "repetition" of Kant allies with the auto-affective power of temporalization)? "The most significant *shift,*" writes Sallis, "occurs in the conception of imagination; it is a *shift* from εἰκασία to φαντασία, from eikastic imagination to phantastic imagination, and it is marked linguistically by the fact that both Latin words *imaginatio* and *phantasia* are translations of the Greek φαντασία. Remarkably, εἰκασία goes virtually untranslated. This *shift* prescribes a whole series of realignments in the relation between imagination and metaphysics. . . ." (D 7, my emphases.) And later: "Pico's text has begun by reenacting the *shift* away from εἰκασία" (D 8). Such a "shift" transpires, in truth, according to Sallis, in a series of "shifts" (are they phases of what I was calling mitosis, turnings, mutations, displacements, epochs?) that taken together would form the very structure of the history in which metaphysics and imagination converge. Thus, after Plato and Pico, Kant: "The primary *shift* is thus a kind of closure, a *shift* of the intelligible into the sensible. . . . The difference originally opened by the Socratic turn, the difference between sen-

sible and intelligible, is now, in Kantian critique, opened within the sensible it-self—or, if you will, confined within the sensible. Such is the *shift* which meta-physics thus undergoes, a *shift,* a relocation, a confinement, of its very field. In the constitution of this field, thus *shifted,* the role played by imagination is no less fun-damental than in the classical instance." (D 10, my emphases.)

6. Heidegger reminds us of this in his 1935 *Einführung in die Metaphysik* (Tübingen: M. Niemeyer, 1953), most precisely in the chapters devoted to the grammar and etymology of the word *being* [Sein]; see esp. pp. 48 and 55. English translation by Ralph Manheim, *An Introduction to Metaphysics* (Garden City, New York: Doubleday-Anchor, 1961), pp. 52 and 59–60.

7. Here and no doubt elsewhere—for if we are holding closely to the open-ing of *Delimitations,* it is for the purpose of risking some sort of preliminary ap-proach to many other philosophical texts, which we can only touch on here. Elsewhere, in effect, Sallis proposes to "displace" this important concept of "gath-ering," which is relayed from λόγος (λέγειν), nothing less, in the direction of a dynamics that once again "empowers." However, the δύναμις or dynasty in ques-tion is, to be sure, neither an act nor even the faculty of a subject, nor *a fortiori* of a subject who possesses objective knowledge. In the course of a reading of the *Cri-tique of Pure Reason,* and more precisely of the Transcendental Dialectic, Sallis suggests that we try "letting the failure of metaphysical gathering serve to displace the very sense of gathering, displace it in the direction of its preclassical origin. It is precisely because I want especially to mark this displacement that I insist on the word *gathering*—that is, λόγος in that preclassical, Heraclitean sense that has been recovered by Heidegger. . . . It is a matter of displacing the sense of gather-ing in such a way as to raise the question of that opening, that space, that field, in which the metaphysical gesture, the turn from the sensible to the intelligible, the classical ascent first becomes possible. Even in the initial sketch it is clear that *gathering* does not name either an act of knowledge or a faculty of the knower but rather the *dynamics* which runs throughout the field of knowledge, *empowering* even the constitution of the objects of knowledge. *Gathering* names the *dynamics* by which the entire field of human knowledge is opened up and structured." ("The Gathering of Reason," D 34–35; I have italicized *dynamics* and *empowering*).

Thus if "gathering" designates a dynamics, a force or power of λέγειν, it is a matter of shielding this preclassical λόγος from everything that one all-too-carelessly calls "deconstruction-of-metaphysics" as "deconstruction-of-logocentrism." And also at the same time, no doubt, shielding it from everything in Heidegger that merits the name assembling or gathering, *Sammlung* or *Ver-sammlung.* And that is not nothing!

8. We know that *The Gathering of Reason* presents itself as the project of a "certain subversion of metaphysics," confirming and developing an ancient subversion renewed by the Kantian critique of metaphysics. One of the two shocks induced by Kant, "the more violent one, has resulted from the installing

of imagination at the origin of reason. Through this encroachment of imagination upon reason, the autonomy of reason is threatened, undermined. . . . The problem is that to *mix* imagination with reason is precisely to subvert reason, to corrupt it, to pervert it. . . . Both intuition and reason are, then, to be contrasted with imagination, which, to speak in Kant's name, is 'the faculty of representing in intuition an object that is not itself present' (B 151). The point is that imagination irreducibly *mixes* presence and absence. . . . What the inversive interpretation of the Transcendental Dialectic shows is that that gathering which should be gathering of reason has instead the structure of a gathering of imagination." (GR 32–33, my emphases.)

9. With regard to the theme of bastardy, I refer the reader to "Plato's Pharmacy," in *La dissémination* (Paris: Seuil, 1972), pp. 69–197; trans. by Barbara Johnson (Chicago: University of Chicago Press, 1981), pp. 61–171; and to "Chora," in *Poikilia: Etudes offertes à Jean-Pierre Vernant* (Paris: Ecole des Hautes Etudes en Sciences Sociales, 1987). See also David Farrell Krell, "Le plus pur des bâtards," in *Revue Philosophique de la France et de l'étranger*, vol. 15, no. 2 (April–June, 1990), 229–238.

10. Consider the following with regard to the Transcendental Dialectic and the fundamentally, genealogically "imaginal" character of the idea: "Even as imaginal, the presentation accomplished in bringing forth the ideas is still illegitimate. An idea is not a legitimate offspring of imagination, even less of reason, but rather—and I take the phrase from Kant—'a bastard of imagination.' Yet even if the idea is not actually akin to that which it would feign resemble, even if it is a deceptive image, it is nonetheless imaginal" (GR 33).

11. For obvious reasons, I must leave these final remarks in the state of a preliminary schema, the potential for a discussion to come or already under way. Allow me to refer to note 9 once again and to "How Not Speak: Denegations," in *Psyché: Inventions de l'autre,* pp. 535–95, but above all to an important essay by John Sallis, "De la Chora," which broaches a discussion of my reading of *Timaeus.* I will cite only the conclusion of his remarks, presented in a recent colloquium at Cerisy-la-Salle ("Passage des frontières"), the papers of which are soon to be published. Sallis's conclusion once again says something about erasure and a certain "may be," a certain "perhaps" ["*peut-être*"], thus once again about the capacity-to-be of a certain possibility, virtuality, capacity, hability or ability. I underline several words in Sallis's conclusion: "Because the χώρα appears [for that is the thesis that orients his essay], discourse *can* be *of* the χώρα. . . . What must be the character of a discourse thus prohibited from bringing determinations to bear on that of which it would speak? Will it not be obliged always also to take back whatever is said, to *cross out* every would-be determination, declaring it finally illegitimate? So, then, as Timaeus himself says, a *bastard* discourse. The fourth one is absent, even in name. . . . *Perhaps* he is the one who would be *capable* of a legitimate discourse of the χώρα. But he is ill. . . ."

12. "Dionysus—Resounding Excess," in *Crossings,* p. 42. Cf. also, on the ἐπέκεινα τῆς οὐσίας, p. 59.

13. "Hoverings," in *Spacings,* p. 49.

14. See note 9.

NOTES TO CHAPTER FOUR

In these notes I will use the following abbreviations for works of Immanuel Kant:

A   *Anthropologie in pragmatischer Hinsicht.* Vol. VII of
        Kants gesammelte Schriften. Berlin:
        Preussische Akademie der Wissenschaften, 1902–.

GMS   *Grundlegung zur Metaphysik der Sitten,* Ak. IV.

HID   *Kant's Inaugural Dissertation and Early Writings on
        Space.* Trans. John Handyside. Chicago: Open Court, 1929.

KrV   *Kritik der reinen Vernunft.* Ak. III.

KU   *Kritik der Urteilskraft.* Ak. V.

I will use the following abbreviations for works of Martin Heidegger:

B   *Beiträge zur Philosophie* (*Vom Ereignis*) (GA 65).

BPP   *The Basic Problems of Phenomenology.* Trans. Albert
        Hofstadter. Bloomington: Indiana University Press,
        1975. *Die Grundprobleme der Phänomenologie* (GA 24).

EHD   *Erläuterungen zu Hölderlins Dichtung* (GA 4).

GA   *Martin Heidegger Gesamtausgabe.* Frankfurt am Main:
        Klostermann Verlag, 1975–.

H   *Holzwege* (GA 5).

HCT   *History of the Concept of Time.* Trans. Theodore Kisiel.
        Bloomington: Indiana University Press, 1985.
        Prolegomena zur Geschichte des Zeitbegriffes (GA 20).

KPM   *Kant and the Problem of Metaphysics.* Trans. Richard
        Taft. Bloomington: Indiana University Press, 1990.
        Kant und das Problem der Metaphysik (GA 3).

MFL   *The Metaphysical Foundations of Logic.* Trans. Michael
        Heim. Bloomington: Indiana University Press, 1984.
        Metaphysische Anfangsgründe der Logik (GA 26).

N   *Nietzsche.* 2 vols. Pfullingen: Verlag Neske, 1961.

PLT   *Poetry, Language, Thought.* Trans. Albert Hofstadter.
        New York: Harper and Row, 1971.

SZ   *Sein und Zeit* (GA 2).

TB *On Time and Being.* Trans. Joan Stambaugh. New York: Harper and Row, 1972.

VA *Vorträge und Aufsätze.* 3 vols. Pfullingen: Verlag Neske, 1954 (3rd edition, 1967).

W   *Wegmarken* (GA 9).

ZSD *Zur Sache des Denkens.* Tübingen: Niemeyer Verlag, 1969.

1. John Sallis, "Monet's Grainstacks: Shades of Time," *Tema Celeste,* 30 (March–April, 1991), 67.

2. In ZSD what Heidegger declares unviable is the attempt to *reduce* (*zurückführen*) Dasein's spatiality to its temporality. He says already in §70 of SZ that the grounding of Dasein's spatiality in its temporality cannot take the form of *deducing* (*deduzieren*) space from time, or dissolving (*auflösen*) space in pure time. It is important to distinguish not only the verbs but also the nouns, *Zeitlichkeit* from *Zeit* and *Räumlichkeit* from *Raum,* if one is to begin to understand the bearing that what is being said here has upon the doctrines of Kant, Hegel (*Enzyklopädie* §257: "*so wird der Raum zur Zeit*"), and Kierkegaard (SZ 338n), all of which Heidegger has in mind.

3. HCT 47 (GA 20, 63).

4. At B 93 Heidegger writes that, in metaphysics and its overcoming, thinking which regresses to presuppositions is indispensable; but a further step back must be made to thinking supposition as such.

5. BPP 170 (GA 24, 241). Compare W 306.

6. MFL 157 (GA 26, 200).

7. PLT 55 (H 43), PLT 63 (H 51), PLT 61 (H 49).

8. PLT 43 (H 32).

9. HID 8.

10. The becausal possibilities of *weilen* and *Verweilen* first occurred to me while reading the gloss on Heidegger's phrase "*sich lichtend-währende Anwesenheit des Je-Weiligen*" proposed in Jeffrey Librett's sublime Introduction to his translation of Jean-Luc Nancy (ed.), *Du sublime* (Paris and Berlin, 1988), forthcoming from SUNY Press under the title *Sublimity and the Question of Presentation.*

11. PLT 154 (VA2, 29).

12. B 380, 384.

13. The relevance of this resonance of *Sprung* sprang to my attention when reading David Krell's remarkable *Daimon Life: Heidegger and Life-Philosophy* (Bloomington: Indiana University Press, 1992). It is confirmed at, for example B 255, when to explain what is meant by "this easily misunderstood word" Heidegger refers to the cleavage of Beyng, *Zerklüftung des Seyns.* The sense of being coiled like a spring is also in play when *Sprung* is described as "the release of a readiness for attentive belonging in appropriation," "*die Er-springung der Bereitschaft zur Zugehörigkeit in das Ereignis.*" *Auf dem Sprunge sein* is to be ready.

14. B 381.
15. E.g. KU §25, cited at S 110 and 111.
16. PLT 65 (H 53).
17. KU §27.
18. E.g. at PLT 226 (VA2, 75).
19. KrV B180, KU §49n.
20. EM 219.
21. B 383 and PLT 55 (H 44).
22. TB 24 (ZSD 24).
23. B 383.
24. B 385–6; EHD 52 (53) ;N1, 226ff.; SZ 338, 339, 401.
25. See also B 235.
26. KU §29, §49n.
27. KU §27.
28. KPM §30; BPP 158, 170 (GA24, 224–5, 242–3); GMS 458, 461.
29. B §44.
30. PLT 43 (H 32).
31. PLT 66 (H 54).
32. B 90.
33. A §15.
34. KU §27, 258.
35. KrV B444.
36. A §32.
37. KU 258.
38. KrV B354.

NOTES TO CHAPTER FIVE

1. Tim O'Brien, *The Things They Carried* (New York: Viking-Penguin, 1991).

2. I am indebted to the recent work of David F. Krell for this strategy.

3. John Sallis, "Monet's Grainstacks: Shades of Time," *Tema Celeste* 30 (March–April, 1991), 56ff.

4. The expositional part of this discussion is taken from *Crossings* and from a series of lectures given by Sallis at the Collegium Phaenomenologicum in Perugia, Italy, in 1991.

5. John Sallis, "Mimesis and the End of Art," a chapter in his *Double Truth* (Albany: Suny Press, 1995).

6. *Ibid.*

7. John Sallis, "The Truth of Imagination," unpublished, p. 17. This text was presented in March, 1991, as the inaugural lecture for the W. Alton Jones Chair of Philosophy at Vanderbilt University.

NOTES TO CHAPTER SIX

1. Before it was published in English, what is now chapter V of *Echoes* had formed the theme of a lecture given in French at the College International de Philosophie on November 12, 1987. The French version is published in the *Cahier du Collège International de Philosophie* (Paris, Editions Osiris, 1989), VIII, 51–57.

2. John Sallis, "Monet's Haystacks: Shades of Time," published in English in *Tema Celeste-International Art Magazine* (Siracusa, Italy), March–April 1991, number 30. This text had previously been published in French under the title "*Ombres de temps: les meules de Monet*" in *La part de l'oeil,* number 7, on *Art et Phénoménologie* (Academie des Beaux-Arts de Bruxelles, 1991). The pagination indicated here is that of the English text.

3. *Ibid.,* p. 59.

4. Cited by Sallis in *ibid.,* p. 64.

5. *Ibid.,* p. 60.

6. *Ibid.,* p. 63.

7. *Ibid.,* p. 66.

8. John Sallis, "Thresholds of Abstract Art," *Tema Celeste—International Art Magazine* (Siracusa, Italy), April–May 1992, number 35.

9. *Ibid.,* p. 44.

10. *Ibid.,* p. 43.

11. *Ibid.,* p. 45.

12. John Sallis, "Recondite Image," preface to Mimmo Paladino, *Amici* (New York: Sperone Westwater, 1991).

13. *Ibid.,* p. 7.

14. Italo Calvino, *La Strada di san Giovanni* (Milan: Arnoldo Mondadori Spa, 1990).

NOTES TO CHAPTER SEVEN

1. Martin Heidegger, "Moira," in *Early Greek Thinking,* trans. by David Krell and Frank Capuzzi, (New York, Harper and Row, 1975), p. 97.

2. In circling back to the question of originary imaging in Platonic dialogue, after having prepared the way in each of his interim texts on imagination, Sallis's return to a second reading of Plato is itself an imitation, in the movement of his work, of the movement of imagination that he addresses.

3. This is a quotation from a yet unpublished manuscript of John Sallis's entitled "Plato's *Timaeus:* The Place of the *Chora.*"

4. Martin Heidegger, *Unterwegs zur Sprache,* (Pfulligen: Günther Neske, 1960), p. 231.

5. Friedrich Nietzsche, *Werke: Kritische Gesamtausgabe,* ed. G. Colli and M. Montinari (Berlin: Walter de Gruyter, 1969), VI 3:75.

NOTES TO CHAPTER EIGHT

1. For an in-depth working out of this move from *image* (and thus the dyadic structure of image-original) to *imaging as such* (a self-showing), see my essay "Imaging Hinting Showing: Placing the Work of Art," in F.-W. von Herrmann and W. Biemel (eds.), *Kunst und Technik: Gedächtnisschrift zum 100. Geburtstag von Martin Heidegger* (Frankfurt: V. Klostermann Verlag, 1989), pp. 189–203.

2. Martin Heidegger, *Parmenides,* ed. M. Frings, GA 54 (Frankfurt: Vittorio Klostermann Verlag, 1982), p. 121. This quotation appears in Sallis's text in German; the translation presented here is mine.

3. Martin Heidegger, *Vortäge und Aufsätze* (Pfullingen: Verlag Günther Neske, 1954), p. 155. I have slightly altered Sallis's translation as it appears in his book.

4. Martin Heidegger, *Zur Sache des Denkens* (Tübingen: Max Niemeyer Verlag, 1960), p. 72.

5. Martin Heidegger, *Holzwege,* ed. F.-W. von Herrmann, GA 5 (Frankfurt: Vittorio Klostermann Verlag, 1977), p. 71. This quotation on "boundary" is not quoted by Sallis in *Delimitations.*

NOTES TO CHAPTER TEN

1. Helmuth Plessnes, *Laughing and Crying,* trans. Churchill and Green (Evanston: Northwestern University Press, 1970), pp. 90–91.

NOTES TO CHAPTER ELEVEN

1. Archilochus, *Archiloque: Fragments,* ed. Lasserre, 2nd edition (Paris: Societe D'Edition "Les Belles Lettres," 1968), p. 72. Translation mine.

2. G. W. F. Hegel, *The Philosophy of Fine Art,* trans. Osmaston (New York: Hacker Art Books, 1975), IV, 330. The German original from Vol. XIV of the Hotho edition (1964) reads: " . . . *die lachende Seligkeit der olympischen Götter*": literally, "the laughing bliss . . ." (p. 561).

3. Aristophanes, *Clouds,* ed. Dover (Oxford: The Clarendon Press, 1968), p. 18 (line 225). Translation mine.

4. See pages 13–22 of BL, where Sallis discusses the mutual mirror-play of the speeches, myths and mythical context, and the deeds within the Platonic

dialogues. As *Clouds* presents a comedy of Socratic practice as presented in the dialogues, Sallis's threefold is similarly illuminating here.

5. Aristophanes, *op. cit.,* p. 11 (lines 94–99).

6. *Ibid.,* p. 12 (lines 112–115).

7. Kant, *Critique of Pure Reason,* trans. N. K. Smith (New York: St. Martin's Press, 1965), A247, B303, p. 264.

8. Aristophanes, *op. cit.,* pp. 14–15 (lines 156–164).

9. *Ibid.,* pp. 77–88 (lines 1321–1511 to the end).

10. F. Nietzsche, *The Birth of Tragedy,* trans. Kaufmann, found in Walter Kaufmann (ed.), *Basic Writings of Nietzsche* (New York: The Modern Library, 1968), p. 51.

11. Found in Ann Pippin Burnett, *Three Archaic Poets: Archilochus, Alcaeus, Sappho* (Cambridge: Harvard University Press, 1983), pp. 84–87 (translation notes on 87–88).

12. *Ibid.,* p. 87.

NOTES TO CHAPTER TWELVE

1. Immanuel Kant, *Kritik der reinen Vernunft,* Band II, *Werke in sechs Bänden* (Darmstadt: Wissenschaftliche Buchgesellschaft, 1975), A 298/B 354. English translation, *Immanuel Kant's Critique of Pure Reason,* trans. Norman Kemp Smith (London: Macmillan & Co., 1958), p. 300.

2. This text was originally presented in December, 1983, as the inaugural lecture for the Arthur J. Schmitt Chair of Philosophy, at Loyola University of Chicago. It appears as the first essay in *Delimitations: Phenomenology and the End of Metaphysics.*

3. *Republic,* Loeb Classical Library, trans. Paul Shorey (Cambridge: Harvard University Press, 1970), 600e.

4. *Kritik der reinen Vernunft,* B151.

5. *Republic,* 510b.

6. Kant, *Kritik der Urteilskraft,* Band V, *Werke,* § 59. English translation, *Critique of Judgment,* trans. J. H. Bernard (New York: Hafner, 1972).

7. Hans-George Gadamer, *Wahrheit und Methode,* 4th ed. (Tübingen: J. C. B. Mohr, 1975). Hereafter WM in the footnotes.

8. *Philebus,* trans. W. R. M. Lamb, Loeb Classical Library (Cambridge: Harvard University Press, 1962), 64e.

9. Gadamer does not think that the text of the *Philebus* represents a change in Plato's doctrine of ideas. Gadamer writes: "It is still true that the good must be separated out of everything that appears good and seen in distinction from it. But it is in everything and is seen in distinction from everything only because it is in everything and shines forth from it." *The Idea of the Good in Platonic-Aristotelian*

Philosophy, trans. P. Christopher Smith (New Haven: Yale University Press, 1986), p. 116.

    10. WM 456.

    11. *Phaedrus,* 250d.

    12. Heidegger makes this connection between the beautiful and appearance in "The Origin of the Work of Art." The beautiful as shining forth, as coming to show itself, does not occur apart from truth as the unconcealment of being: "Appearance—as this being of truth in the work and as work—is beauty." *Poetry Language Thought,* trans. Albert Hofstadter (New York: Harper & Row, 1971), p. 81.

    13. WM 460.

    14. *Ibid.*

    15. WM 462.

    16. WM 131.

    17. *Ibid.*

    18. *Ibid.*

    19. *Ibid.*

    20. WM 133.

    21. WM 134.

    22. WM 135.

    23. Gadamer writes: "To be expressed in language does not mean that a second being is acquired. The way in which a thing presents itself is, rather, part of its own being. Thus everything that is language has a speculative unity: it contains a distinction, that between its being and the way that it presents itself, but this is a distinction that is not really a distinction at all." WM 450.

    24. WM 465.

    25. Friedrich Nietzsche, *Philosophy and Truth,* trans. and ed. Daniel Breazeale (Atlantic Highlands: Humanities Press, 1979), p. 85.

    26. *Ibid.*

    27. "We have arranged for ourselves a world in which we can live—by positing lines, planes, causes and effects, motion and rest, form and content; without these articles of faith no one could endure life. But that does not prove them. Life is no argument. The conditions of life might include error." Friedrich Nietzsche, *The Gay Science,* trans. Walter Kaufmann (New York: Random House, 1974), sec. 121.

    28. See Friedrich Nietzsche, *The Birth of Tragedy,* sec. 1–12.

    29. In *Crossings: Nietzsche and the Space of Tragedy,* Sallis probes the "shining image" of the Apollinian with a series of questions that one could only assume are questions that Sallis intends to take up in a more encompassing project: "What must be the constitution of imagination if it has the capacity to engage images that are disclosive of a higher truth? Does it suffice to term it *phantasy*? How, then, would one need to reformulate the distinction between imagination and phantasy, a distinction that in constantly varying forms runs throughout the entire

history of metaphysics? Furthermore, if in its productive engagement with shining images, imagination effects a disclosure of truth, then what must be the character of disclosure and of truth that they can be so linked to imagination? How extensive is Apollinian imagination? . . . Is there a Dionysian imagination, a form of imagination that comes into play in tragedy?" (p. 29–30) This issue of shining is also taken up in "Monet's Grainstacks: Shades of Time" in *Tema Celeste*, 30 (March–April 1991), 56–67.

NOTES TO CHAPTER THIRTEEN

1. Friedrich Nietzsche, *The Birth of Tragedy*, transl. W. Kaufman (New York: Random House, 1967), p. 69. Hereafter referred to in the notes as BT.

2. BT, *Fragments posthumes*.

3. Immanuel Kant, *Critique of Judgment*, Section 23.

4. Friedrich Nietzsche, *La Vision dionysiaque du monde*, Section 3, in *Ecrits posthumes 1870–1873* (Paris: Gallimard, 1975), p. 1; in German in the *Kritische Studienausgabe*, ed. G. Colli and M. Montinari (Berlin: Walter de Gruyter, 1980), I, 567. This text will be hereafter referred to as VD.

5. *Ibid.; Kritische Studienausgabe*, I. 566.

6. Friedrich Nietzsche, *Werke* (Leipzig: Alfred Kröner Verlag, 1912), I, 186. Hereafter this edition will be referred to as Kröner.

7. Cf. BT, Chapter 18.

8. This is no longer the same in Euripides (*Medea*) or, later yet, in Shakespeare (*Macbeth*).

9. Arthur Schopenhauer, *The World as Will and Representation*, Section 51.

10. Kröner, I, 186: "The hero is calm—this has until now escaped the authors of tragedies."

11. BT, Chapter 9, p. 67.

12. *Ibid.*, p. 68.

13. *Ibid.*, p. 72.

14. *Ibid.*, Chapter 5, p. 50.

15. *Ibid.*, Chapter 16, pp. 103–104.

16. Both of these projects—rethinking the sublime and thinking *Geist der Musik* as the *Grundstimmung* at the root of the "musical"—belong centrally to this thinking of "tragic joy." Unfortunately there is no space here for taking up these two issues in detail. See, however, my essay "The Joyous Struggle of the Sublime and the Musical Essence of Joy" in *Research in Phenomenology*, forthcoming.

17. *Ibid.*, p. 59. [Kaufman translation modified by trans.]

18. *Ibid.*, p. 130. (My emphasis: *finally*.)

19. BT, Fr. 7 (123): "Dionysos possesses the dual nature of a cruel and savage demon and of a benevolent sovereign, insofar as he is ἀγριόνιος and μειλίχιος."

20. *Ibid.,* Fr. 1 (1).

21. *Ibid.,* p. 43.

22. *Ibid.,* Fr. 7 (128).

23. *Ibid.,* preceding fragment. (My emphasis: *his proper state.*)

24. BT, p. 36.

25. BT, Fr. 7 (123). This duplicity is found in the fragments in his last years—cf. *Wille zur Macht* (Kröner), Section 1049: "Dionysos: sensuality and cruelty."

26. The complexities of these rites and these myths has been admirably analyzed by Marcel Detienne, *Dionysos mis a mort* (Paris: Gallimard, 1975), p. 54.

27. VD, p. 54.

28. BT, *Posthumes.*

29. BT, p. 40.

30. *Wille zur Macht,* Section 798 (1888).

31. *Ibid.,* Section 799 (1888).

32. *Ibid.,* Section 1050 (1888).

33. *Ibid.*

34. Cf. my *Le Chant de la Terre,* pp. 280–281.

35. Friedrich Nietzsche, *Unschuld des Werdens,* ed. A. Bäumler in *Nachlaß* (Stuttgart: Kröner Taschenausgabe, 1956), I, 391. Hereafter this two-volume text will be referred to as K I or K II.

36. K I, 391–2; K I, 390.

37. Notably B. Pautrat, in *Versions du Soleil* (Paris: Seuil).

38. BT, p. 130.

39. R. Otto, *Le Sacré* (Paris: Payot).

40. Cf. citation below.

41. BT, Chapter 22, p. 131. (Except for *Dionysian* and *tragic myth*—words emphasized by Nietzsche—all other words are emphasized by me.)

42. *Ibid.,* p.132.

43. *Ibid.,* p. 131.

44. BT, Fr. 3 (54).

45. BT, Fr. 3 (37).

46. K I, 387 (emphasized in the text).

47. Schopenhauer, *The World as Will and Representation,* Section 39.

48. F. W. J. Schelling, *Philosophy of Art,* Section 66.

49. Rainer Maria Rilke, first *Duino Elegy.*

50. Cf. *Thus Spoke Zarathustra,* "On the Sublime."

51. In effect, Sallis translates both *Überfluß* and *Übermaß* with the English word *excess,* whereby he contracts into one both immoderation and the ability to

"make an echo" (echoing), both the disruptive flux of every boundary and pre-artistic musicality, the irrepresentable rhythmic matrix.
52. Pautrat, *op. cit.*, p. 75, note 25.
53. Cf. *ibid.*, p. 57, note 13.
54. *Wille zur Macht,* Section 65.
55. Nietzsche, *The Gay Science,* Section 342.
56. *Ibid.*, Section 109.
57. BT, Chapter 15, p. 97.
58. *Wille zur Macht,* Section 1051.

NOTES FOR CHAPTER FOURTEEN

1. Regarding the "active" character of thinking, see my essay "The Echo of Being in *Beiträge zur Philosophie—Der Anklang:* Directives for Its Interpretation," *Heidegger Studies* 7 (1991), 15–35.

2. Martin Heidegger, *Sein und Zeit,* ed. F.-W. von Herrmann, GA 2 (Frankfurt: Vittorio Klostermann Verlag, 1977), p. 11.

3. The term *Betroffenheit* in Heidegger is one of those seemingly innocuous words that requires careful attention. For a discussion of this term in relation to *Being and Time,* see my paper "The Question of Technology and Will to Power," in W. Biemel and F.-W. von Herrmann (eds.), *Kunst und Technik: Gedächtnisschrift zum 100. Geburtstag von Martin Heidegger* (Frankfurt: Vittorio Klostermann Verlag, 1989), pp. 125–140.

4. At one point Sallis seems to come close to recognizing the "sameness" of "the interrogator and interrogated"—cf. E 50. However, he does not pursue this "sameness" and interprets it, without the slightest consideration given to *"Betroffenheit vom Sein,"* as "the coincidence of questioner and questioned." (See E 50, note 4.)

5. J. J. Kockelmans explains a "Dasein-oriented" versus a "being-oriented" period in Heidegger when he says: "In his later works (1935–1976), i.e., in the period of the 'turn' *(Kehre),* Heidegger continues to think the basic relationship between Being and man, but whereas in *Being and Time* he seems to give the privileged position in this relation to Dasein, the later works grant this to Being itself." See J. J. Kockelmans, *Heidegger on Art and Art Work* (The Hague: Martinus Nijhoff, 1985), p. 76.

6. Martin Heidegger, *Sein und Zeit,* p. 10.

7. *Ibid.*, p.11.

8. F.-W. von Herrmann, *Subjekt und Dasein: Interpretationen zu "Sein und Zeit"* (Frankfurt: Vittorio Klostermann Verlag, 1974), p. 23.

9. H.-G. Gadamer, *Philosophical Hermeneutics,* trans. D. E. Linge (Berkeley: University of California Press, 1976), p. 199.

10. Martin Heidegger, *Der Begriff der Zeit,* ed. H. Tietjen (Tübingen: Max Niemeyer Verlag, 1989), p. 31.

11. See E 45, note 3, and E 46, note 12.

12. It is perhaps useful to point out that what Heidegger meant when he wrote to Gadamer that "everything began to get slippery" (quoted in E 44) has nothing to do with what Sallis calls "slippage" (E 47 and *passim*). In their intention these two words—one from Sallis, one from Heidegger—have nothing to do with each other.

13. Martin Heidegger, *Être et temps,* trans. F. Vezin (Paris: Gallimard, 1986), pp. 45ff.

14. Martin Heidegger, *Der Begriff der Zeit,* p. 21.

15. Martin Heidegger, *Zollikoner Seminare,* ed. M. Boss (Frankfurt: Vittorio Klostermann Verlag, 1987).

16. Martin Heidegger, *Sein und Zeit,* p. vii.

17. Martin Heidegger, *Zollikoner Seminare,* p. 150.

18. *Ibid.*

19. *Ibid.,* p. 157.

20. *Ibid.,* p. 163.

NOTES TO CHAPTER FIFTEEN

1. Max Müller (ed.), *Symposion. Jahrbuch für Philosophie* (Freiburg-Munich, 1952), III, 471–508.

2. This lecture has been published, under the same title, in John Sallis (ed.), *Reading Heidegger: Commemorations* (Bloomington: Indiana University Press, 1993), pp. 29–46. In this essay all numbers appearing in parentheses without any other notation refer to the pages of this text as published.

3. Martin Heidegger, *Beiträge zur Philosophie (Vom Ereignis),* GA 65 (Frankfurt am Main: Vittorio Klostermann, 1989), p. 353. Hereafter: GA 65.

4. GA 65, p. 329.

5. *Ibid.,* p. 351.

6. *Ibid.*

7. *Ibid.,* p. 338.

8. *Ibid.*

9. The sentence from Sallis's text reads: "Yet, almost from the outset a displacement of the common commences, giving way finally to the uncommon declaration of the proposition "The essence of truth is the truth of essence" (31).

10. Martin Heidegger, *Wegmarken,* GA 9 (Frankfurt am Main: Vittorio Klostermann, 1976), p. 201. Hereafter: GA 9.

11. GA 9, pp. 185–186.

12. *Ibid.,* p. 186.

13. *Ibid.*, p. 189.
14. *Ibid.*
15. *Ibid.*
16. *Ibid.*, p. 190.
17. *Ibid.*, p. 189.
18. *Ibid.*, p. 191.
19. *Ibid.*
20. *Ibid.*, p. 193.
21. *Ibid.*
22. *Ibid.*, p. 194.
23. *Symposion,* III,499ff. The quotations from Heidegger's text are from GA 9, p. 194.
24. GA 9, pp. 193ff.
25. *Ibid.*, p. 194.
26. *Symposion,* III, 501f.
27. GA 9, p. 197.
28. *Ibid.*, pp. 195ff.
29. *Ibid.*, p. 194.
30. *Ibid.*, p. 197.
31. *Symposion,* III, 502.
32. GA 9, p. 196.
33. *Symposion,* III. 497f.
34. GA 65, p. 369.
35. *Ibid.*

NOTES ON CHAPTER SIXTEEN

1. In *Metaphysics* V 1 Aristotle enumerates the various senses of ἀρχή and concludes: "It is common to all beginnings [κοινὸν τῶν ἀρχῶν] to be the first [thing] from which something either is or comes to be or becomes known" (1013a18–19). Hereafter referred to in the text as *Mtp.*
2. *Enzyklopädie der philosophischen Wissenschaften.* Dritter Teil: Die Philosophie des Geistes. *Werke* (Frankfurt a.M.: Suhrkamp, 1970), 10:255. The passage cited occurs in the *Zusatz* to §449.
3. *Ästhetik,* ed. Friedrich Bassenge (West Berlin: Das Europäische Buch, 1985), 1:309–310.
4. *Ibid.*, 1:298.
5. See *The Being of the Beautiful: Plato's Theaetetus, Sophist, and States-man,* translated and with commentary by Seth Benardete (Chicago: University of Chicago Press, 1984), I. 184.
6. *Ibid.*, I. 107.

7. I have discussed this passage in detail and in context in *Being and Logos*, pp. 428–431.

8. *Grundfragen der Philosophie: Ausgewählte 'Probleme' der 'Logik'. Gesamtausgabe*, vol. 45 (Frankfurt a.M.: Vittorio Klostermann, 1984), p. 163. Hereafter referred to as GA 45.

9. *Was ist Das—Die Philosophie?* (Pfullingen: Günther Neske, 1956), p. 26.

10. This formuluation comes from Eugen Fink: "What breaks out in wonder . . . is an unfamiliarity of the familiar. . . . In wonder the world is inverted [*verkehrt sich die Welt*]" (*Einleitung in die Philosophie*, ed. Franz-A. Schwartz [Würzburg: Königshausen & Neumann, 1985], 19). Klaus Held has also taken up these discussions and described differently the transformation that the world undergoes in wonder: For the wonderer the world comes forth as though emerging for him for the first time, as though it were completely new and utterly surprising. In its reflective moment, Held adds, wonder lets one experience oneself as though one were a newborn child. (See "Fundamental Moods and Heidegger's Critique of Contemporary Culture," in *Reading Heidegger: Commemorations*, ed. J. Sallis [Bloomington: Indiana University Press, 1993], esp. pp. 298–300.)

11. "Circles," in *The Essays of Ralph Waldo Emerson* (Cambridge: Harvard University Press, 1987), p. 190.

12. *Götzendämmerung*, in *Werke*, VI 3: 74f.

13. Heidegger, *Nietzsche* (Pfullingen: Günther Neske, 1961), 1:242. But in the original lectures of 1936–37 the word *Geist* is not used in this context to characterize the nonsensuous world. Instead, Heidegger writes merely: "The Platonic interpretation and classification [*Einstufung*] of the sensible is abolished, but not the sensible itself, just as little as is the nonsensuous" (*Nietzsche: Der Wille zur Macht als Kunst, Gesamtausgabe*, vol. 43 [Frankfurt a.M.: Vittorio Klostermann, 1985], 260).

14. The need for such caution is what seems to me to prescribe a certain reticence (which is not simply silence) regarding philosophical hermeneutics, at least as long as one has not thoroughly destabilized the classical oppositions in such a way as that indicated by Risser's radical reading of *Truth and Method*.

15. These remarks are limited to the *human* body, though without making of this limit a separation in principle or one immune from questioning. For the question of the limit separating the human from the animal as well as the question of animality as such has been vigorously renewed in Jacques Derrida's *De l'esprit: Heidegger et la question* (Paris: Galilée, 1987) and in David Krell's *Daimon Life: Heidegger and Life-Philosophy* (Bloomington: Indiana University Press, 1992).

16. See "Reason and Ek-sistence," D 152–159.

17. Here I forego undertaking to differentiate this moment in deconstruction from the mimetic moment in Heideggerian nonphilosophy. Such differentiation— and one could hardly exaggerate its complexity—would require, perhaps first of

all, a thorough discussion of Derrida's readings (and they are indeed multiple) of Heidegger. I have attempted some steps toward such a discussion in *Delimitations* (chapter 11) and especially in *Double Truth* (chapter 2).

18. Heidegger, *Nietzsche*, 1:249. "In scintillating transfiguration" is David Krell's rendering of "*im Aufschein der Verklärung*" (*Nietzsche, Volume One: The Will to Power As Art* [New York: Harper & Row, 1979], p. 216).

19. "Monet's Grainstacks: Shades of Time," *Tema Celeste* 30 (1991).

20. Nietzsche, *Die Geburt der Tragödie*, in *Werke*, III 1:31.

21. See *Crossings*, chap. 3.

22. Nietzsche, *Die Geburt der Tragödie*, in *Werke*, III 1:152.

23. Nietzsche, *Also Sprach Zarathustra*, in *Werke*, VI 1:45.

24. This description of comedy is from Nietzsche's lectures "History of Greek Literature" (1874–75). Cited in *Crossings*, p. 110.

25. I have discussed this passage in detail—though in quite a different connection—in "Nature's Song," *Revue Internationale de Philosophie* (1991).

26. Kant, *Kritik der Urteilskraft*, in *Werke: Akademie Textausgabe* (Berlin: Walter de Gruyter, 1968), §42.

27. "Introduction" to *Reading Heidegger: Commemorations* (Bloomington: Indiana University Press, 1993), p. 2.

28. *Holzwege, Gesamtausgabe*, vol. 5 (Frankfurt a.M.: Vittorio Klostermann, 1977), p. 310.

29. See Plato, *Phaedrus* 244a–245c. Also *BL* 132–135.

A BIBLIOGRAPHY OF THE
WORKS OF JOHN SALLIS

1965

"World, Finitude, and Temporality in the Philosophy of Martin Heidegger," *Philosophy Today* 9.

1967

"La différence ontologique et l'unité de la pensée de Heidegger," *Revue Philosophique de Louvain* 65.

"The Problem of Judgment in Husserl's Later Thought," *Tulane Studies in Philosophy* 16.

"Art within the Limits of Finitude," *International Philosophical Quarterly* 7.

"Phenomenology and Language," *The Personalist* 48.

1969

"Nietzsche's Homecoming," *Man and World* 2.

"Nietzsche and the Problem of Knowledge," *Tulane Studies in Philosophy* 18.

1970

Heidegger and the Path of Thinking (edited collection). Pittsburgh: Duquesne University Press. Includes "Introduction" and "Towards the Movement of Reversal: Science, Technology, and the Language of Homecoming."

"Language and Reversal," *The Southern Journal of Philosophy* 8. Reprinted in *Martin Heidegger in Europe and America,* ed. E. G. Ballard and Charles Scott. The Hague: Martinus Nijhoff, 1973; and in *Martin Heidegger: Critical Assessments,* ed. C. Macann. London: Routledge, 1992.

"The Play of Tragedy," *Tulane Studies in Philosophy* 19.

"On the Limitation of Transcendental Reflection—Or Is Intersubjectivity Transcendental?" *The Monist* 55.

1972

"Time, Subjectivity, and the Phenomenology of Perception," *The Modern Schoolman* 48.

"Nietzsche's Underworld of Truth," *Philosophy Today* 16.

"On the Ideal of Phenomenology," in *Life-World and Consciousness: Essays for Aron Gurwitsch,* ed. Lester Embree. Evanston: Northwestern University Press.

"Schelling's System of Freedom," *Research in Phenomenology* 2.

1973

Phenomenology and the Return to Beginnings. Pittsburgh: Duquesne University Press.

"On Logos and Phenomenon in Plato," in *Language and Language Disturbances,* ed. Erwin Strauss. Pittsburgh: Duquesne University Press.

"Toward the Showing of Language," *The Southwestern Journal of Philosophy.*

1975

Being and Logos: The Way of Platonic Dialogue. Pittsburgh: Duquesne University Press.

"Image and Phenomenon," *Research in Phenomenology* 5.

1976

"Fichte and the Problem of System," *Man and World* 9.

"Radical Phenomenology and Fundamental Ontology: Review of *Die Grundprobleme der Phänomenologie* by Martin Heidegger," *Research in Phenomenology* 6.

1977

"The Origins of Heidegger's Thought," *Research in Phenomenology* 7. Reprinted in *Radical Phenomenology.* Atlantic Highlands, NJ: Humanities Press, 1978.
Review of *Imagining: A Phenomenological Study* by Edward S. Casey, *International Philosophical Quarterly* 17.
"Hegel's Concept of Presentation: Its Determination in the Preface to the *Phenomenology of Spirit,*" *Hegel-Studien* 12.

1978

Radical Phenomenology: Essays in Honor of Martin Heidegger (edited collection). Atlantic Highlands, NJ: Humanities Press. Includes "The Origins of Heidegger's Thought."
"Where Does *Being and Time* Begin?" in *Heidegger's Existential Analytic,* ed. Frederick Elliston. The Hague: Mouton. French translation: "Où Commence *Être et Temps?*: in *"Être et Temps" de Martin Heidegger: Questions de méthode et voies de recherche.*
"Immateriality and the Play of Imagination," in *Proceedings of the American Catholic Philosophical Association.* Slightly abridged version appears as "Metaphysical Security and the Play of Imagination: An Archaic Reflection," in *Philosophy and Archaic Experience: Essays in Honor of Edward G. Ballard.* Pittsburgh: Duquesne University Press, 1982.

1979

Studies in Phenomenology and the Human Sciences (edited collection). Atlantic Highlands, NJ: Humanities Press. Includes "Introduction."
Review of *Phenomenology and the Social World* by Laurie Spurling. *Human Studies.*

1980

The Gathering of Reason. Athens: Ohio University Press. German translation: *Die Krisis der Vernunft: Metaphysik und das Spiel der Einbildungskraft.* Hamburg: Felix Meiner Verlag, 1983.
Heraclitean Fragments (collection coedited with Kenneth Maly). University of Alabama Press. Includes co-authored "Introduction" and "Hades: Heraclitus, Fragment B 98."

1981

Merleau-Ponty: Perception, Structure, Language (edited collection). Atlantic Highlands, NJ: Humanities Press.
"Into the Clearing," in *Heidegger, the Man and the Thinker,* ed. Thomas Sheehan. Chicago: Precedent Press. Chinese translation in *Culture: China and the World* 2 (1988).
"Forschung und Dekonstruktion," *Phänomenologische Forschungen* 11.
"The Common Root: A Marginal Question," *Proceedings of the Fifth International Kant Congress.* Mainz.
Review of *Hegel: Phänomenologische Interpretation der "Phänomenologie des Geistes"* by Eugen Fink. *The Owl of Minerva* 12.

1982

Philosophy and Archaic Experience: Essays in Honor of Edward G. Ballard (edited collection). Pittsburgh: Duquesne University Press. Includes "Introduction" and "Metaphysical Security and the Play of Imagination: An Archaic Reflection."
"The Identities of the Things Themselves," *Research in Phenomenology* 12. Reprinted in *Philosophy and Science in Phenomenological Perspective,* ed. K. K. Cho. The Hague: Martinus Nijhoff, 1984. Reprinted in *Husserl and Contemporary Thought.* Atlantic Highlands, NJ: Humanities Press, 1983.

1983

Husserl and Contemporary Thought (edited collection). Atlantic Highlands, NJ: Humanities Press. Includes "The Identities of the Things Themselves."
Continental Philosophy in America (collection coedited with H. Silverman and T. Seebohm). Pittsburgh: Duquesne University Press.
"End(s)," *Research in Phenomenology* 13. Reprinted in *Heideggeriana,* ed. G. Moretti. Pescara, 1986.
"Au Seuil de la métaphysique," in *Heidegger,* ed. Michel Haar. Paris: L'Herne.
Review of *Grundbegriffe* by Martin Heidegger. *Journal of the History of Philosophy* 21.

1984

"Apollo's Mimesis," *British Journal of Phenomenology* 15.

"Heidegger/Derrida—Presence," *Journal of Philosophy* 81.
"Heraclitus and Phenomenology," in *La fortuna di Eraclito nel pensiero moderno,* ed. Livio Rossetti. Rome: Edizioni dell'Ateneo.

1985

"Meaning Adrift," *Heidegger Studies* 1. Reprinted in *Martin Heidegger: Critical Assessments,* ed. C. Macann. London: Routledge, 1992.

1986

Delimitations: Phenomenology and the End of Metaphysics. Bloomington: Indiana University Press. French translation: *Délimitations: La phénoménologie et la fin de la métaphysique.* Paris: Aubier, 1990.
Being and Logos: The Way of Platonic Dialogue. Second edition. Atlantic Highlands, NJ: Humanities Press. Includes slight revisions and a new preface.
"Imagination and Presentation in Hegel's Philosophy of Spirit," in *Hegel's Philosophy of Spirit,* ed. Peter Stillman. Albany: State University of New York Press.
Review of *The Poetry of Keats: Language and Experience* by David Pollard. *Man and World.*

1987

Spacings—of Reason and Imagination. In Texts of Kant, Fichte, Hegel. Chicago: University of Chicago Press.
Deconstruction and Philosophy: The Texts of Jacques Derrida (edited collection). Chicago: University of Chicago Press. Includes "Introduction."
"Twisting Free. Being to an Extent Sensible," *Research in Phenomenology* 17. German translation: "Twisting Free—Das Sein eine Spanne weit sinnlich," in *Twisting Heidegger: Drehversuche parodistischen Denkens,* ed. Michael Eldred. Cuxhaven: Junghans, 1993.
"Echoes: Philosophy and Non-Philosophy after Heidegger," *Continental Philosophy* I.
"Introduction" to *Phenomenology: Descriptive or Hermeneutic.* Pittsburgh: Simon Silverman Phenomenology Center.

1988

The Collegium Phaenomenologicum: The First Ten Years (collection coedited with G. Moneta and J. Taminiaux). Dordrecht: Kluwer. Includes "Time Out. . . ."

"Dionysus—In Excess of Metaphysics," in *Exceedingly Nietzsche: Aspects of Contemporary Nietzsche Interpretation,* ed. D. F. Krell and D. Wood. London: Routledge.

1989

"La Mortalité et l'imagination: Heidegger et le nom propre de l'homme," *Cahiers du Collège International de Philosophie* 8. Chinese translation in *Philosophie und Mensch,* ed. Shi-Ying Zhang, 1993.

"Imagination and the Meaning of Being," in *Heidegger et l'idée de la phénoménologie,* ed. J. Taminiaux. The Hague: Martinus Nijhoff, 1988. Italian translation: "L'immaginazione e il senso dell' essere," *Clinamen* 3.

Review of *Radical Hermeneutics: Repetition, Deconstruction, and the Hermeneutic Project* by John D. Caputo. Published with a response by Caputo and a rejoinder, "Moving On." *Man and World* 22.

"Interruptions," in *Dialogue and Deconstruction: The Gadamer-Derrida Encounter,* ed. Richard Palmer and Diane Michelfelder. Albany: State University of New York Press.

"Heidegger's Poetics: The Question of Mimesis," in *Kunst und Technik. Zum 100. Geburtstag Martin Heideggers,* ed. Walter Biemel and F.-W. von Herrmann. Frankfurt a.M.: Vittorio Klostermann. Reprinted in *Martin Heidegger: Critical Assessments,* ed. C. Macann. London: Routledge, 1992.

"L'espacement de l'imagination: Husserl et la phénoménologie de l'imagination," in *Husserl,* ed. Eliane Escoubas and Marc Richir. Grenoble: Jérome Millon. English version: "Spacing Imagination," in *Eris and Eros: Contributions to a Hermeneutical Phenomenology,* ed. P. van Tongeren. The Hague: Kluwer, 1992.

"John Sallis: An Interview," *Warwick Journal of Philosophy* 2.

1990

Echoes: After Heidegger. Bloomington: Indiana University Press.

"Literatuur en filosofie: een interview met John Sallis," *Beaubourg.*

"Flight of Spirit," *Diacritics*. Abridged version appears as "Heidegger und Dekonstruktion," in *Zur philosophischen Aktualität Heideggers*. Bonn: Alexander von Humboldt-Stiftung. Serbo-Croatian translation: "Heidegger i dekonstrukcija," *Godisnjak Instituta za filozofija* 1989.

"Doublures," *Revue Philosophique*. English version: "Doublings," in *Derrida: A Critical Reader*, ed. David Wood. Oxford: Blackwell, 1992.

1991

Crossings: Nietzsche and the Space of Tragedy. Chicago: University of Chicago Press.

"Recondite Image." Text of Mimmo Paladino, *Amici*. New York: Sperone Westwater.

"Monet's Grainstacks: Shades of Time," *Tema Celeste* 30. French translation: "Ombres de temps: les Meules de Monet," *La Part de l'oeil* 7 (1991). Italian translation (in book form): *Ombre del Tempo: I Covoni di Monet*. Syracusa: Tema Celeste Edizioni, 1992.

"Nature's Song," *Revue Internationale de Philosophie* 45.

"Response," *Philosophy Today* 35.

1992

"Babylonian Captivity," *Research in Phenomenology* 22.

"Thresholds of Abstract Art," *Tema Celeste* 35.

"J. G. Fichte," *Encyclopedia of Ethics*, ed. Lawrence Becker. New York: Garland.

"Hans-Georg Gadamer," *Encyclopedia of Ethics*, ed. Lawrence Becker. New York: Garland.

1993

Reading Heidegger: Commemorations (edited collection). Bloomington: Indiana University Press. Includes "Introduction" and "Deformatives: Essentially Other Than Truth."

"Very Ancient Memories," *Tema Celeste* 40. Italian translation: "Antichissime Memorie," *Tema Celeste* 36 (1992).

"Foreword" to *The Song of the Earth* by Michel Haar. Bloomington: Indiana University Press.

1994

Stone. Bloomington: Indiana University Press.

Double Truth. Albany: State University of New York Press.

Delimitations: Phenomenology and the End of Metaphysics. 2nd, expanded edition. Bloomington: Indiana University Press. Includes a new preface and three additional chapters.

"The Question of Origin," *The Southern Journal of Philosophy,* Supplement to vol. 32.

"De la chora," in *Le Passage des Frontières: Autour du travail de Jacques Derrida,* ed. Marie-Louise Mallet. Paris: Galilée. English version: "Of the Χώρα," *Epoché* 2.

Mimesis and the End of Art," in *Intersections: Nineteenth-Century Philosophy and Contemporary Theory,* ed. David Clark and Tilottama Rajan. Albany: State University of New York Press.

"The Truth That Is Not of Knowledge," in *Reading Heidegger from the Start: Essays in His Earliest Thought,* ed. Theodore Kisiel and John van Buren. Albany: State University of New York Press.

NOTES ON CONTRIBUTORS

WALTER BIEMEL, now Emeritus at the Staatliche Kunstakademie Düsseldorf, served for many years as an editor at the Husserl Archives in Louvain and in Köln. In addition to editing several volumes in the *Husserliana* and the *Phaenomenologica* series, he is editor of two volumes of Heidegger's *Gesamtausgabe: Logik: Die Frage nach der Wahrheit* (GA 21) and *Hölderlins Hymne "Der Ister"* (GA 53). His own writings include *Le concept du monde chez Heidegger, Kants Begründung der Ästhetik und ihre Bedeutung für die Philosophie der Kunst, Philosophische Analysen zur Kunst der Gegenwart,* as well as monographs on Sartre and on Heidegger.

PEG BIRMINGHAM is Professor of Philosophy at DePaul University in Chicago. Specializing in ethics and contemporary continental thought, she focuses her research on embodiment, the question of agency, and an ethics of place.

WALTER BROGAN is Professor of Philosophy at Villanova University in Pennsylvania. He is the author of "Is Aristotle a Metaphysician?" and "Plato's Pharmakon: Between Two Repetitions" and several essays on Heidegger and Nietzsche. He is currently co-translating Heidegger's *Aristotle, Metaphysics Θ 1–3, On the Essence of Actuality of Force* (GA 33). His teaching and research focuses on Greek philosophy and contemporary continental thought.

FRANÇOISE DASTUR is Maître de conferences in philosophy at the Université de Paris-I (Pantheon-Sorbonne). She teaches general philosophy and history of philosophy (German philosophy) and is attached to the Phenomenological Seminar, a research unit of the Centre National de la Recherche Scientifique. She has published several articles in French, English, and German on Husserl, Heidegger, Meleau-Ponty, Ricoeur, and Derrida and is the author of *Heidegger et la question du temps* and *Hölderlin, Tragédie et Modernité.*

JACQUES DERRIDA is Professor at the École des Hautes Etudes en Sciences Sociales in Paris. From 1975 to 1986 he was Visiting Professor of Humanities at Yale University and currently holds visiting professorships at the University of California at Irvine and at Cornell University. Among his many books are *La voix et le phénomène, L'écriture et la différence, De la grammatologie, La dissémination, Marges de la philosophie, Glas, La vérité en peinture, La carte postale,* and most recently *De l'esprit, Psyché,* and *Du droit à la philosophie.*

PARVIS EMAD is Professor of Philosophy at DePaul University in Chicago and is founding co-editor of *Heidegger Studies.* He is the author of *Heidegger and the Phenomenology of Values* and of many essays on Heidegger and on phenomenology. He is also co-editor (with Kenneth Maly) of *Heidegger on Heraclitus: A New Reading.* He has translated (with Kenneth Maly) Heidegger's *Hegel's Phenomenology of Spirit* (GA 32) and *Phenomenological Interpretation of Kant's Critique of Pure Reason* (GA 25) as well as Heinrich Wiegand Petzet's *Encounters and Dialogues with Martin Heidegger 1929–1976.* He is currently translating (with Kenneth Maly) Heidegger's *Beiträge zur Philosophie (Vom Ereignis)* (GA 65).

ELIANE ESCOUBAS is Professor of Philosophy at the Université de Amiens. She is the author of *Imago Mundi: Topologie de l'art* and the editor of several collections on Heidegger, Husserl, and the phenomenology of art. She has translated Husserl's *Ideen 2* into French.

BERNARD FREYDBERG is Professor of Philosophy at Slippery Rock University in Pennsylvania. He is the author of essays on Plato, Kant, Hegel, and Nietzsche and the book *Imagination and Depth in Kant.*

RODOLPHE GASCHÉ is Professor of Comparative Literature at the State University of New York at Buffalo. He is the author of *The Tain of the Mirror: Derrida and the Philosophy of Reflection.* His forthcoming book is entitled: *Inventions of Difference: On Derrida and De Man.*

MICHEL HAAR is Professor of Philosophy at the Université de Paris-XII. He has published two major books: *La chant de la terre. Heidegger et les assises de l'Histoire de l'Être* and *Heidegger et l'essence de l'homme.* He is also the author of numerous articles on Heidegger, Nietzsche, Hölderlin, Derrida, and Levinas. He is editor of the Cahiers de l'Herne volume on Heidegger.

JOHN LLEWELYN was most recently Visiting Professor at Memphis State University in Tennessee and before that the Arthur J. Schmitt Distinguished Visiting Professor of Philosophy at Loyola University of Chicago and before that Reader in Philosophy at the University of Edinburgh. He is the author of *Beyond Metaphysics?, Derrida and the Threshold of Sense,* and *The Middle Voice of Ecological Conscience: A Chiasmic Reading of Responsibility in the Neighbourhood of Levinas, Heidegger and Others.*

KENNETH MALY is Professor of Philosophy at the University of Wisconsin-La Crosse. He is founding co-editor of *Heidegger Studies* and co-editor (with John Sallis) of *Heraclitean Fragments* and (with Parvis Emad) of *Heidegger on Heraclitus: A New Reading*. He has translated into English (with Parvis Emad) Heidegger's *Hegels Phenomenology of Spirit* (GA 32) and *Phenomenological Interpretation of Kant's Critique of Pure Reason* (GA 25) as well as Heinrich Wiegand Petzet's *Encounters and Dialogues with Martin Heidegger 1929–1976*. He is currently translating (with Parvis Emad) Heidegger's *Beiträge zur Philosophie (Vom Ereignis)* (GA 65).

ADRIAAN PEPERZAK is Arthur J. Schmitt Professor of Philosophy at Loyola University of Chicago. Previously he was Professor of Philosophy at the Universities of Nijmegen and Amsterdam and has taught at several other universities in the United States, as well as in Italy, Spain, and Indonesia. Among his publications are *System and History in Philosophy*, three books on Hegel (*Le jeune Hegel et la vision morale du monde, Philosophy and Politics*, and *Hegels praktische Philosophie*), as well as numerous articles on Levinas and on the relations between metaphysics, epistemology, and ethics. In addition he has published on Plato, Aristotle, Heidegger, and Ricoeur.

JAMES RISSER is Professor of Philosophy and holds the Pigott-McCone Chair of Humanities at Seattle University in Washington. In addition to articles on Nietzsche, Gadamer, and hermeneutics, he is currently editing a collection of essays on Heidegger's work in the 1930s.

JOHN SALLIS was born in 1938 in Poplar Grove, Arkansas. After studying mathematics at Columbia University, he graduated with a doctorate in philosophy from Tulane University. For many years he was Professor of Philosophy at Duquesne University in Pittsburgh and then the Arthur J. Schmitt Professor of Philosophy at Loyola University of Chicago. Presently he is the W. Alton Jones Professor of Philosophy at Vanderbilt University in Tennessee. To support his scholarly work he has received, at various times, grants from the Alexander von Humboldt-Stiftung, the Fritz Thyssen-Stiftung, and the American Council of Learned Societies. He is the author of *Double Truth, Stone, Crossings: Nietzche and the Space of Tragedy, Echoes: After Heidegger, Spacings—of Reason and Imagination. In Texts of Kant, Fichte, Hegel* (presently being translated into French), *Delimitations: Phenomenology and the End of Metaphysics* (translated into French), *The Gathering of Reason* (translated into German), *Being and Logos: The Way of Platonic Dialogue* (now in its second edition), and *Phenomenology and the Return to Beginnings*. He has also edited eleven books, whose themes include Heidegger, Derrida, Husserl, Merleau-Ponty, phenomenology, and continental philosophy in America. He is the founding editor of *Research in Phenomenology*.

CHARLES E. SCOTT is Professor of Philosophy at Pennsylvania State University. His books include *Boundaries of the Mind, The Language of Difference,* and *The Question of Ethics: Nietzsche, Foucault, Heidegger.* He has also edited several collections, including (with Edward Ballard) *Heidegger in Europe and America.*

INDEX

311